THE

ACTING- OUT CHILD

CHILD

COPING WITH
CLASSROOM
DISRUPTION
(Second Edition)

by HILL M. WALKER

Special Education
College of Education
University of Oregon

Edited by Jami McCormick
Page design by Sherri Rowe
Text layout by Venture Publishing
Cover design by Londerville Design

ISBN #1-57035-047-7

Published and Distributed by:

Sopris West
1140 Boston Avenue   •   Longmont, CO 80501   •   (303) 651-2829

Dedication

To All the Important People, Places, and Animals
That Have So Enriched My Life

Jan, Seth, Matilda, Sister, the Mexico relatives, John, Elsie, Deward, Candy, John and Alma, Norma and Cathy, Mike and Lucy, Brevious and Mami, Denny and Diane, Dave and Pat, Willie and Priscilla, Nick and Jody, Marty, Mel, Sugar and Spice, Kodi, Rusty, Henry, Eclipse, Blaze, the "Jabba the Hut" squirrels of 7 Olympic Lane, the pig birds of Fillmore Street, the Muscovy Duck of ECC, Stewart's Mountain, Carlyle Lea, John Turner, Mr. Casio, the doubles racquetball gang, the Cal Young Place, Hell's Canyon, Rush River, Pine Valley, Hy, Charlie, Ann, Jerry, John, Herb, the Shenandoah Valley, the Oregon Cascades, Black Butte, Mt. Bachelor, Tokatee, the Australian Special Education Mafia, Bob, Wes, Vic, Gino, Steve, Frank, Mike, Jim, John, Duane, Stu, Ken, Ray, Bill, my colleagues in the field of behavior disorders, and Kokotan (a.k.a. Koke), consummate philosopher of life and golfing guru who taught me so much about both.

Acknowledgments

My family, Jan and Seth, were very supportive, encouraging, and tolerant during the period in which the original manuscript of this book was produced. This book and its revisions will always be positively associated with these memories.

Glen Martz was most generous in making it possible for me to review disciplinary referrals and school responses to them. His assistance is greatly appreciated.

Michael Bullis gave invaluable advice and technical assistance on organizing the book's content. His superb editing comments on the initial chapters were most helpful and are appreciated.

Note to the Reader

The information presented in this book is based upon two types of knowledge: **formal** and **informal**. Formal knowledge refers to that which is supported by empirical, scientific evidence and has stood the tests of time and replication(s). Informal knowledge is experientially derived and has generally not been verified and validated through scientific research. I believe both types of knowledge are extremely valuable in relation to the tasks of understanding and coping with the acting-out child in school.

The body of knowledge we call formal is many times smaller than that which we know informally, or experientially. Whenever possible in this book, I try to document observations and assumptions with empirical evidence. However, much of what I and other experts know about this population is informal in nature and is based upon our direct experience with acting-out children and their teachers, parents, and peers. I have conducted research and worked directly with this population in school settings since 1966. One of my goals in writing this book is to present as much of this informal knowledge as possible for consideration by school personnel who must deal with acting-out children on a daily basis. I believe it is important to provide a record of such knowledge in a book of this type.

The most important lessons I have learned about acting-out children have been provided by the successes and failures I have had in working with them. In this regard, I have learned far more from my failures than from my successes. Perhaps more than with any other school population, it is as important to know **what not to do** with such children as it is to know what to do with them. Often our best instincts and initial reactions to the behavior of acting-out children are wrong, and actually exacerbate the problem. This is particularly true in the context of the daily interactions that occur between teachers and acting-out children. Chapter 7, which focuses on strategies for teacher-student interactions, describes some of these do's and don'ts for the reader.

My experience with this population indicates that it is dominated by males. The ratio of boys to girls approximates 4 or 5:1; however, due to changing role expectations and social conditions in our society, this ratio may show shifts in the future. Nevertheless, the ranks of acting-out students are overwhelmingly occupied by males in the vast majority of school districts in this country. For this reason, I have chosen to refer to the acting-out child throughout this book using the masculine gender. This is not to suggest that girls who manifest this behavior pattern are at any less risk or are any less deserving of services and school attention than boys. I have made no such assumptions about gender imbalances in textual references to either the peers or teachers of acting-out children.

The material in this book focuses primarily on children in the elementary age range (i.e., kindergarten, primary, and intermediate grade levels). However, the techniques and strategies described have implications for middle/ junior high and high school level students and, in many instances, are adaptable for use with these populations. However, most of my own intervention research and that reported in the professional literature involves the elementary age population. In addition, the earlier systematic interventions occur in a child's school career, the greater the likelihood of achieving satisfactory outcomes.

Preface

The purpose of this book is to present a set of procedures for effectively managing the behavior of elementary age children who act out in classrooms and other school settings. This material, if mastered, will give teachers and other school support personnel working in regular, special, and resource classrooms, as well as specialized educational environments (e.g., day treatment programs, residential settings) the necessary skills to effectively manage the behavior of acting-out children as well as that of less disruptive children. In many respects, *The Acting-Out Child* is designed as a desk reference resource for the teacher or other professional who is charged with the daily management and instruction of groups of students that include one or more acting-out, disruptive youth. This book may also have value for school administrators and professionals who serve teachers in consultive roles, including counselors, special educators, school psychologists, and social workers. The material herein attempts to: (1) characterize acting-out behavior in the context of schooling, (2) describe what we know about coping effectively with it, and (3) illustrate applications for the reader.

Teachers at every level are well aware of the management problems presented by the child who consistently "acts out" against classroom rules and the management routines that are necessary to operate classrooms effectively. Since the introduction of formal education systems charged with the mass instruction of groups of students, the disruptive behavior of such children has been a persistent challenge to effective teaching. Unless this behavior is controlled and managed effectively, it can disrupt the learning and achievement of an entire classroom, and especially of the acting-out child. Impaired academic achievement and poor social-behavioral adjustment can lead to very serious long-term problems.

For reasons that are not well-understood, some children adjust to the school experience, with its new and unique demands, in very satisfactory ways, while other children experience difficulties with these same demands from the first day of school. There are a number of theories that attempt to explain the origins of disruptive classroom behavior. For example, some professionals suggest that the adequacy of a child's school adjustment is largely a result of the kinds of preschool experiences the child has had that are similar to those encountered in the regular school setting. This explanation has great validity and considerable explanatory power, but it doesn't account for the school adjustment patterns of **all** children.

Others suggest that the educational level of the child's parents and their general attitudes toward learning and achievement have a profound effect upon how a child perceives and reacts to the experience of schooling. The value parents place on the school experience, their skills in motivating their child to learn, and their active support of the child's achievement and school participation are all part of this general explanation. This theory may be partially true, but it is not clear how it specifically operates to account for a child's school adjustment.

A third explanation holds that an acting-out child has not mastered the key "survival skills" necessary for successful school adjustment upon entering first grade. Survival skills are the minimum behavioral requirements necessary for the child to effectively consume instruction. These include such behaviors as paying attention, listening to instructions, following directions, working independently, making assistance needs known appropriately, and complying with teacher demands. It is suggested that failure to master these skills early in the educational process can handicap a child's school adjustment in both academic and social areas, and may lead eventually to the development of severe behavior problems. While this explanation seems highly plausible, it has not been clearly established as yet that acting-out children identified in later school grades are deficient in survival skills upon entering first grade.

Finally, it has become clear that the deteriorating social and economic conditions of our society are having a profound effect upon children's readiness to learn and their ability to meet the minimal behavioral demands associated with the instructional process. The stressful home and societal conditions that place such children at risk include neglect, abuse, violence, poverty, and lack of support, and they can "spill over" onto school performance in a negative, most unfortunate manner. Schools can never solve these massive problems alone nor be held completely accountable for failed solutions to them. However, the nature of schooling and the kinds of support systems schools must provide are likely to change radically in the future because of the highly pressurized needs of children and families.

Until careful longitudinal studies are carried out on the specific processes involved in successful and unsuccessful school adjustment, and comprehensive intervention procedures are documented that successfully impact upon them, the various theories accounting for the origins of acting-out behavior will remain only theories. Although we cannot, at present, determine precisely how and why some children develop disruptive behavior patterns, we do possess the means to effectively reduce acting-out behavior among students who behave in this manner. In the last two decades, an effective and very impressive collection of behavior management techniques has been developed for remediating both behavioral deficits, such as social withdrawal and depression, and behavioral excesses, such as acting-out behavior and aggression. This technology is based upon principles of social learning that determine how human behavior is acquired, maintained, and eliminated.

This body of knowledge consists of a series of proven techniques for changing human behavior that have been validated in literally thousands of empirical studies reported in the professional literature. These techniques have been applied with a great deal of success in such varied settings as regular classrooms, special education classrooms, homes, playgrounds, clinics, and institutions. They have developed to the point where it is feasible for teachers, teacher consultants, and school-wide teacher assistance teams to apply them systematically in order to improve the conditions of learning for all children.

These techniques are especially applicable to remediation of the learning and behavioral problems of the acting-out child. In this regard, we need to find ways to effectively use the information and techniques that are currently available to us rather than continuing to search for the magical, five-minute intervention that works every time and lasts forever! Such an intervention is clearly not in the cards for acting-out behavior problems in the foreseeable future. In Chapter 6, some perspectives on treatment outcomes for acting-out students are presented that address such issues as treatment versus control, how long interventions must be in place to be effective, what we can reasonably expect from our interventions, and so forth.

It is intended that the material in this book will give the classroom teacher the skills necessary to successfully apply these techniques to the acting-out child and to manage the general classroom environment more effectively. Increasing pressures are being placed upon the management skills of classroom teachers with the current emphases upon individualizing instruction, mainstreaming children with disabilities, and accommodating a greater range and diversity of behavior patterns and disabilities in the regular classroom. It is hoped that this book will be responsive to the needs of classroom teachers in designing an optimal learning environment; one that will facilitate the development of both academic and social competencies in acting-out children.

Table of Contents

1

Introduction to the Acting-Out Child

The Acting-Out Child in the Classroom

The scene in Mrs. Moore's second grade classroom is typical of those found in thousands of classrooms each day. Following a teacher-led discussion of that day's reading assignment, Mrs. Moore instructs her class to complete a series of reading worksheets during the remaining 20 minutes of the reading period. The children begin organizing themselves to work on the assignment; all, that is, except Tracy, who leaves his seat and begins moving in the direction of the pencil sharpener.

Mrs. Moore . . . . . . Tracy, what are you doing?

Tracy . . . . . . I'm going to the pencil sharpener.

Mrs. Moore . . . . . . You know what the class rule is. You're supposed to sharpen all the pencils you need before class starts—not after. Besides, you're supposed to raise your hand before getting out of your seat.

Tracy . . . . . . I only have two pencils. I broke the tips off both of them working on my math assignment.

Mrs. Moore . . . . . . All right! Then hurry up and sharpen them and get to work.

(Tracy continues moving toward the pencil sharpener. Mrs. Moore turns to answer a question about the assignment from another student. Tracy engages several peers in conversation about nonacademic matters. Mrs. Moore notices this, and begins to get visibly angry.)

Mrs. Moore . . . . . . Tracy, I told you to sharpen your pencil and get to work! I wasn't kidding. You'd better do what I tell you, now!

Tracy . . . . . . Okay, okay. I'm going.

(Tracy has the attention of nearly the entire class, which he seems to be enjoying. He also appears to enjoy Mrs. Moore's obvious irritation with his behavior. He approaches the pencil sharpener and slowly begins to sharpen his pencils, making a production of it and continuing to exchange glances and gestures with the peers to whom he was talking. Mrs. Moore observes this and "does a slow burn.")

Mrs. Moore . . . . . . Tracy, I'm telling you for the last time to sharpen your pencils and get to work. You're getting behind in your work and you're keeping others from doing theirs.

Tracy . . . . . . I'll be through in just a minute. I'm going as fast as I can.

Mrs. Moore . . . . . . I'm going to stand right here beside you until you finish and escort you back to your seat.

(Mrs. Moore takes Tracy by the arm and leads him to his seat. She waits beside him while he takes out his assignment and begins to work.)

Unfortunately, the exchanges between Tracy and Mrs. Moore are too often typical of the classroom interactions between acting-out children and their teachers (Colvin & Sugai, 1989). Teachers invest enormous amounts of energy and time in encouraging acting-out children to comply with the minimal tasks and demands that are a part of the daily routines of schooling. Whatever the reasons, the acting-out child has not learned, or been taught, to pay attention, to listen to instructions, to follow simple directions, and to comply with teacher requests and directives promptly. To make matters worse, the acting-out child often engages in social behaviors (such as disturbing others, tantrumming, defying the teacher, sulking, and so forth) that have a disruptive effect on the classroom and that are extremely unpleasant for the child's teacher and classmates.

Children like Tracy are very difficult for teachers to manage and teach effectively. They tend to dominate the teacher's valuable time that could be spent in instructing other children. Teachers are pulled into endless confrontations with acting-out children in vain attempts to control their behavior. However, teachers are generally not successful in this process and often resent the time wasted on these children's continuing resistance to their efforts.

The confrontation between Tracy and Mrs. Moore illustrates some important points about the behavior of acting-out children and their relationships with teachers, parents, and peers. For example, it is the acting-out child who is usually in control of the behavioral episodes occurring with the teacher. It is the acting-out child, and not the teacher, who normally decides when the confrontation will end. As long as the teacher is willing to respond to the acting-out child's questions, comments, and "yes but" counter arguments during these exchanges, the child remains in control of the situation.

Second, the acting-out child's maladaptive behavioral repertoire is well-developed and is usually **very** resistant to change. As a rule, the further along acting-out children have progressed in their school careers, the more resistant is their behavior pattern to change and remediation due to the massive amounts of teacher, parental, and peer attention they have typically received for their disruptive behavior.

Third, the amount of emotional intensity and the level of direct control exerted by the teacher in confrontations with the acting-out child are usually related to how long the child decides to prolong the confrontation. In some cases, the teacher must resort to ever higher levels of emotional intensity and direct control in order to prompt the acting-out child to terminate the aversive interaction. In such cases, the emotional and psychological costs of managing such children can be extremely high.

The story of the acting-out child in school is one of resistance to the tactics of adult influence that are typically applied to all children as part of the schooling process. Thus, noncompliance with rule governed behavioral standards is a highly salient characteristic of acting-out children. Such children violate at a high rate the social-behavioral norms that define appropriate behavior in a range of school settings that are controlled by adults. They also violate the social-behavioral norms of free play settings in which peer dynamics are dominant. Some children have conflicts only with teachers; some have conflicts only with peers; and some have conflicts with both. It is not clear in what proportions acting-out children are divided into these three groups. However, it is likely that those who engage in conflicts with both teachers and peers are more severely at risk (Loeber & Dishion, 1984).

Peers usually find the acting-out child's social behavior to be extremely aversive; this fact can, and often does, lead to the acting-out child's social isolation and active rejection by peers. The scene following depicts a typical social exchange between an acting-out child and a peer, and illustrates the process of coercion (Patterson, 1983; Patterson, Reid, & Dishion, 1992) that is so often an unfortunate component of the acting-out child's behavioral repertoire.

The Acting-Out Child on the Playground

Ritchie, an acting-out child in the third grade, approaches Bryan at recess. Bryan is playing a game of catch with a friend. Although in the same classroom, Bryan is smaller than Ritchie, who seems to tower over him.

Ritchie . . . . . . I'm gonna play a game of catch with Tommy and Jason. So I need the ball.

Bryan . . . . . . Sorry. I'm using the ball. It's my turn to play with it.

Ritchie . . . . . . I asked the teacher for the ball first. You got it by mistake. **Hand** it over!

Bryan . . . . . . I don't care! You're wrong. It's my turn to have the ball. So you'll just have to wait like everybody else.

(Ritchie moves toward Bryan while displaying menacing body language. He "gets in Bryan's face" and shoves him in the chest.)

Ritchie . . . . . . Are you calling me a liar?

Bryan . . . . . . (now beginning to become frightened) No, I said you're wrong; I didn't call you a liar.

Ritchie . . . . . . Okay. You choose. Give me the ball, **now**, or I'll pound you into the ground!

(Visibly upset and beginning to cry, Bryan hands Ritchie the ball.)

Bryan . . . . . . It's not fair! I'm telling the teacher on you!

Ritchie . . . . . . You do and I'll see you after school. You'll wish you'd never seen this ball.

(Bryan leaves the playground in tears.)

This scenario shows the process many acting-out children use to successfully bully their peers. It's called **coercion**, and has been studied extensively by Patterson (1983) and his associates as it operates among groups of very aggressive, antisocial boys and their peers.

The process of coercion begins with a desire (i.e., for power, control, dominance, revenge, etc.) by the acting-out child which is then expressed as a forceful demand for something (e.g., "Stop that or else!"; "Hand it over, now!"). The coercive demand is usually applied to a weaker peer who can be dominated, and in a situation adults do not normally control. If the weaker peer resists the demand, the acting-out child usually escalates the pressure to encourage submission. Tactics of intimidation are used to achieve this goal. Humiliation of the victim, in the presence of other peers, is often a result of this pressure.

If the peer gives in and submits to the acting-out child's demand(s), he/she is generally rewarded by the acting-out child's termination of the coercive pressure because he has now gotten his way. Simultaneously, the acting-out child has been rewarded for using coercive pressures and tactics of intimidation to achieve his demands. Thus, the coercive process simultaneously rewards the acting-out child **and** his victims for the respective roles they play in such social exchanges. This cycle is repeated numerous times and is highly reinforcing of the behavior of both parties. This result explains why the maladaptive, aggressive behavior patterns of acting-out children are so resistant to change and why peers tend to both reject and avoid contact with acting-out children whenever possible. In fact, sociometric measures of the social status, or popularity, of acting-out children show that substantial numbers of them are actively rejected by their classmates (McConnell & Odom, 1986).

Unfortunately, through many repetitions of this process, the acting-out child learns a destructive behavior pattern that is socially unacceptable, but which has very powerful, instrumental value for him. As the child grows and develops, the use of coercion often generalizes to many other situations and settings and can become a permanent feature of his behavioral repertoire. The array of intimidating tactics and coercive pressures used becomes more diverse and the child's skills in applying them are elaborated. The early acquisition of this behavior pattern can lead to very serious long-term consequences for the acting-out child **and** for the key social agents in his environment (e.g., parents, teachers, and peers).

The previous scenarios are characteristic of acting-out children's interactions with peers and adults, and provide a "snapshot" of their typical behavioral styles. It is little wonder that they do not do well, either socially or academically, in school and that they experience widespread social rejection by teachers and peers in that setting.

Analysis of School Discipline Referrals

The author recently reviewed the referral and discipline records of a suburban high school over a four-month period in order to gain a perspective on the magnitude and complexity of the behavior problems with which school personnel must cope in dealing with acting-out students who are developmentally mature. Although this book focuses on the problem(s) of acting-out behavioral patterns in the elementary age range, the results of this review show what can happen when such problems are not addressed effectively at earlier developmental levels. The types of procedures used to consequate teacher disciplinary referrals, along with their effectiveness, were examined as well. Results of this review are described following.

School disciplinary records for the fall semester of the 1992-93 school year were used in this review. The high school had approximately 1,000 students enrolled in grades 9-12. During this same four-month period, teachers in the school made 1,159 referrals for disciplinary reasons that were seen by the vice principal or other front office personnel, for a per student average of 1.15. A total of 868 of these referrals involved males, and 291 involved female students. The distribution of the referrals by grade level was as follows: 9th grade = 689; 10th grade = 254; 11th grade = 144; and 12th grade = 72.

Table 1.1 provides a frequency breakdown of these referrals by disciplinary reason, and indicates that the six most frequent reasons for referral were: (1) being off campus during school hours; (2) Saturday school violations; (3) unexcused absences; (4) tardy violations; (5) tobacco use/possession; and (6) unsatisfactory behavior. Other categories of offenses with relatively high frequencies were insubordination, fighting/assault, hall pass violations, leaving class without permission, and use of profanity/obscene gestures. Consequences that the school had developed to apply to these disciplinary infractions were as follows: detention; grounding or loss of privileges; student contracts; warnings; removal from class; Saturday school; suspensions for one, two, three, four, or five days; denial of academic credit; and other responses.

These statistics provide an interesting profile of the student actions that require disciplinary sanctions as a part of the ordinary process of schooling. The high school involved in this review is probably representative

Table 1.1
Student Actions Resulting in Disciplinary Referrals for the Period 9/9/92-1/29/93

Disciplinary Reason	Grade Breakdown				Male	Female	Total
	9	10	11	12			
Alcohol possession	1	0	0	0	1	0	1
Automobile/permit violation	0	1	2	1	3	1	4
Burglary of school building	2	0	0	0	2	0	2
Drug possession	2	3	1	0	6	0	6
Fighting/assault	23	11	8	0	28	14	42
Forgery	1	0	0	0	0	1	1
Hall pass violation	34	8	7	4	40	13	53
Hazing/harrassment	7	5	2	0	12	2	14
Insubordination	30	8	2	1	33	8	41
Leaving class without permission	10	8	1	4	21	2	23
Lying to staff	6	2	0	0	4	4	8
Poss./use of inappropriate object	8	0	0	0	7	1	8
Off campus during school hours	134	70	35	33	205	67	272
Other action	3	1	2	2	6	2	8
Profanity/obscene gesture	12	9	3	1	16	9	25
Profanity toward staff	17	1	0	1	16	3	19
Safety violation	6	1	0	0	7	0	7
Saturday school violation	111	33	26	11	137	44	181
Skateboarding on campus	1	0	0	0	1	0	1
Unexcused absences	90	34	29	5	111	47	158
Tardy violation	72	22	3	?	48	51	00
Theft	2	0	0	0	2	0	2
Tobacco use/possession	50	14	18	5	81	6	87
Unsatisfactory behavior	48	14	5	2	60	9	69
Vandalism	5	2	0	0	7	0	7
Weapon possession	3	1	0	0	4	0	4
Walkman®/radio on campus	11	6	0	0	10	7	17
TOTAL	689	254	144	72	868	291	1159

of many suburban high schools that are well administered and have competent teaching and support staffs. It is not atypical that there were more disciplinary infractions in the first semester than there were students in the school! Increasingly, teachers are confronted with classes of students in which many are angry, poorly motivated, and disrespectful of school rules and adult authority. Explosive interactions between teachers and students are an inevitable result of these conditions; when they happen, teachers have few options other than to refer for disciplinary reasons. Unfortunately, these referrals and school responses to them are generally not effective in adequately solving the problem; yet, they continue to be applied repeatedly without noticeable effect. In all fairness, schools are limited in the options they can legitimately bring to bear in consequating such problems effectively.

Table 1.2 provides a record of the frequency with which the available school response options were used to consequate the 1,159 disciplinary referrals for the fall semester. Saturday school assignment, a one-day suspension, and warnings were far and away the most frequently used sanctions. A total of 1,131 of the 1,159 disciplinary referrals received a sanction of some type.

Table 1.2
School Action and Response Summary for Disciplinary Referrals for the Period 9/9/92-1/29/93

School Response	Grade Breakdown				Male	Female	Total
	9	10	11	12			
Grounding/loss of privileges	0	1	0	0	1	0	1
Detention	5	1	0	0	6	0	6
Other response	17	9	4	6	34	2	36
Removal from class	10	3	0	0	10	3	13
Saturday school assignment	334	99	66	23	397	125	522
Suspension: 1 day	136	35	34	13	169	49	218
Suspension: 2 days	23	10	0	0	22	11	33
Suspension: 3 days	51	19	4	0	62	12	74
Suspension: 4 days	1	3	0	0	3	1	4
Suspension: 5 days	8	1	1	0	10	0	10
Warning	93	60	32	29	136	78	214
TOTAL	678	241	141	71	850	281	1131

There appeared to be little relationship between effectiveness of the sanctions used and the occurrence of student actions resulting in disciplinary referrals. Although lower in frequency, the same pattern of sanctions seemed to be applied to disciplinary infractions by girls as to those by boys.

Some school staff indicated that a broader array of sanctions and a more preventative approach were required to cope with the situation. Development of a school-wide discipline plan and a careful analysis of school rules resulting in disciplinary infractions would be useful exercises in this context. Sometimes school staffs inadvertently become overly invested in defining rule infractions that might be better handled in other ways, including the use of selective ignoring in some situations. Excessive school demands for student conformity can contribute to a less positive school climate and a sense of alienation among students.

In order to gain a clearer picture of the referral-consequation process (i.e., student action followed by school response[s]) and its relative effectiveness, the author examined the records of the first 100 ninth grade referrals of the 1992-93 school year. When a referral occurred, the referring teacher completed a standard referral form that provided information about conditions associated with it, the specific student behavior(s) that prompted the referral, and the actions or responses used to consequate the referral.

Appendix A contains a record of these referrals and the school actions taken to consequate them. The 100 referrals were accounted for by 36 ninth graders, and involved 23 males and 13 females. Twenty-one of the referrals involved girls and 79 involved boys.

Several patterns emerge from inspection of these disciplinary school records. First, the school responses applied to the students' problem behaviors were generally ineffective in controlling these behaviors or reducing their occurrence. Second, certain students recycle through the "behavioral episode-referral-school consequation loop" over and over. One student had 12 referrals within the first semester. Third, across loops or recycles of this process, both the severity/intensity of student behavior and the magnitude of the consequences applied tended to escalate. Fourth, students often appeared to be in an agitated state when these behavioral infractions and referrals occurred, which may partially explain their continued escalation over time. Finally, the number of referrals for insubordination suggested that some students and their referring teachers were engaging in ongoing power struggles that probably intensified across episodes and time.

These referrals provide a picture of the types of acting-out behavior that high schools, and substantial numbers of middle/junior high and elementary schools, must contend with on a daily basis. As children grow and develop, the problems they present to school officials become more complex and difficult to solve. This is particularly true if the problems are severe and of a long-term nature. A fact of life concerns the growing working relationship between school personnel and police officers, who are necessary to deal with such issues as weapons, assault, and rape. Teacher safety is an issue of vital concern to teachers' unions and school administrators; the safety of students has emerged as an issue of excruciating national concern. On the face of it, the notion that schools should be able to accommodate and effectively educate **all** students under such conditions seems ludicrous. It seems clear that educators must intervene systematically much earlier in the school careers of such children, and that parents/guardians must assume greater responsibility for their children's actions in the school setting. Otherwise, the conditions of schooling are likely to continue to deteriorate for everyone.

Behavioral Characteristics of the Acting-Out Child

The specific behavioral characteristics of acting-out children, and how they clash with typical demands of the school setting, are described following. Children who display disruptive behavior patterns are easy to place within existing psychiatric and psychological classification systems. Such children are often diagnosed and described by clinical experts as having either a **conduct disorder** or as being **oppositional-defiant**. Children with oppositional-defiant disorder are negative and resistant in their social interactions, especially with adults. Conduct disorder involves serious violations of behavioral norms and is often a precursor of delinquency. Kazdin (1987) defines conduct disorder as excessive amounts of aggressive and noncompliant behavior that involves the persistent violation of social norms and standards of rule-governed behavior.

Aggression, which often accompanies acting-out behavior patterns, includes such acts as verbal abuse, teasing, humiliation, threats, arguing, fighting, lying, stealing, and property destruction (Bullis & Walker, in press). A child's early investment in aggressive behavior which leads to peer rejection is strongly associated with a host of long-term, negative developmental outcomes, including delinquency and adult criminality (Parker & Asher, 1987).

The author conducted an observational study of six aggressive and six acting-out/disruptive students within an instructional setting to see if these two behavior patterns could be distinguished from each other within the regular classroom context. The students were enrolled in the primary grades and had been previously referred by their schools for inclusion in an experimental program for elementary students exhibiting serious behavior problems. All 12 students were male. The observations were conducted by professionally trained observers who demonstrated acceptable levels of inter-observer agreement and were recorded under identical seatwork conditions for all the target students. Six categories each of appropriate and inappropriate classroom behaviors were contained in the coding procedure. This study was a subcomponent of a larger investigation designed to develop consultant-based intervention programs for acting-out and aggressive children in the K-3 grade range (Walker, Hops, & Greenwood, 1981).

Results indicated that, across the six categories of appropriate behavior, the behavioral rate for aggressive students was .88 versus .46 for the acting-out/disruptive students. In contrast, the rate of inappropriate behavior for the acting-out/disruptive students was 1.25 versus .84 for the aggressive students. Overall, the two groups had very similar behavioral rates (i.e., 1.72 versus 1.71 per minute); however, the percentage of total appropriate behavior was 51% for the aggressive students versus 27% for the acting-out/disruptive students. Unfortunately, it was not possible to observe these two groups in playground settings where it is likely that the aggressive students would have had higher rates of negative, aggressive social behavior directed toward their peers.

Acting-out students, as described in this book, fit the profile of the conduct disordered child with and without an accompanying pattern of aggressive behavior. The behavioral problems they present in school settings usually involve interactions with adults. However, as noted, a significant number of acting-out children are also aggressive with their peers. In such cases, their behavioral adjustment problems are multiplied in both severity and intensity, and the students involved are at substantially greater risk of school failure and of encountering long-term negative outcomes.

A bi-polar classification system, involving **externalizing** and **internalizing** behavioral dimensions, accounts for most of the behavioral adjustment problems students encounter in school settings (see Achenbach, 1985; Ross, 1980). **Externalizing** problems consist of excessive amounts of a behavior, and the behavioral surplus is considered maladaptive and aversive to others. Examples include aggression, disruptive behavior, antisocial personality, noncompliance, hyperactivity, and so forth. In contrast, **internalizing** problems involve insufficient amounts of a behavior, and are usually associated with skill deficits. Examples include social withdrawal and isolation, anxiety, depression, affective disorders, phobias, and so forth. Thus, acting-out children exemplify **externalizing** behavior problems and disorders.

Characteristically, the acting-out child in the classroom setting is one who defies teacher-imposed rules, structures, and/or procedures. He is a consistent rule breaker and spends a great deal of time in nonacademic pursuits. Because the acting-out child spends so much time on nonacademic matters, he is often deficient in key academic skills and falls below grade level in achievement (Kauffman, 1993; Walker, Block-Pedego, Todis, & Severson, 1991).

As a rule, the acting-out child's disruptive behavior pattern either develops early in his school career (Zax, Cowen, Izzo, & Trost, 1964) or he brings an established, acting-out behavioral repertoire to the schooling experience. The acting-out child quickly becomes identified as a difficult-to-manage student and develops a reputation that can follow him from teacher to teacher, from year to year, and from school to school. Sometimes this reputation becomes a self-fulfilling prophecy; that is, teachers and peers expect the child to misbehave, so it actually happens. Hollinger (1987) cites evidence that neutral behavior displayed by acting-out, aggressive children is interpreted as negative by peers while the same behavior from nonaggressive and popular children is interpreted positively by peers.

The acting-out child, with his accompanying academic deficits, often finds academic tasks to be generally unrewarding. Because of deficient skills and an often negative attitude toward learning, the acting-out child generally finds it difficult to obtain teacher praise and recognition for his academic efforts. The low probability of success or praise being associated with academic performance decreases the frequency of appropriate academic responding in a downward spiraling process (e.g., the less praise, the less academic work attempted, and the less work attempted, the less praise). In addition, the aversive nature of the acting-out child's behavior further reduces the chances of his receiving positive attention and approval from his teacher and classmates.

It should be mentioned that not all acting-out children are deficient in academic skills; some achieve at or above grade level expectations in spite of the relatively large amounts of time they spend in nonacademic pursuits. In such cases, the acting-out child's disruptive social behavior is probably not a direct function of his diminished academic skill level; whereas, for acting-out children with severe academic deficits, there probably is a relationship between their disruptive behavior and deficient academic skills. To date, however, the exact nature of this relationship has not been precisely documented. It is safe to say that academic skill deficits can exacerbate an acting-out behavioral pattern through the frustration(s) they induce.

The acting-out child's relationships with peers are frequently characterized by angry, hostile social exchanges of a verbal or physical nature. As noted previously, if the acting-out child is sufficiently powerful, he may be able to intimidate peers and force them to submit, which often causes them to avoid direct social or personal contact with him whenever possible. If such is not the case, the acting-out child's relationship with peers may be simply antagonistic and characterized by mutual hostility and avoidance. Walker and his associates (Walker, Shinn, O'Neill, & Ramsey, 1987) found that peers collectively match exactly the total amount of negative social behavior which the acting-out child displays toward them in free play settings. Thus, acting-out children are socially punished as much by peers as they punish them. Interestingly, children who are acting-out and aggressive see themselves as victims even though they themselves victimize others at a high rate. Often they set peers, and adults, up to punish them but do not see the relationship between their own behavior and such punishment.

Table 1.3 contains a listing of classroom and nonclassroom behavioral characteristics that are very descriptive of the way acting-out children typically behave in school.

Table 1.3
Characteristic Behaviors Displayed by Acting-Out Children in School
1. Out of seat
2. Yell or talk out
3. Disturb peers
4. Hit or fight
5. Ignore the teacher
6. Complain
7. Argue excessively
8. Steal
9. Lie
10. Destroy property
11. Do not comply with adult commands or directions
12. Have temper tantrums
13. Excluded from peer-controlled activities
14. Don't respond to teacher corrections
15. Don't complete assignments

Acting-out children are different from their peers not so much in the quality of their behavior but in its **quantity**. For example, most children at one time or another fail to comply with teacher commands, hit or shove a peer, disrupt the classroom, talk out, and so forth. However, "normal" children are clearly differentiated from acting-out children in terms of the frequency with which they engage in such behavior(s). Consequently, in managing acting-out children in the classroom setting, the key task is to reduce the level of the acting-out child's inappropriate behavior to manageable proportions and to move his appropriate behavior level to within the normal range, as defined by the behavior of peers.

Gerber and Semmel (1984) have published a now-classic article in which they argue that teachers subscribe to a "teachability standard" against which all students in their classes are informally compared. Students who deviate too far from this teachability standard, in either academic or social-behavioral domains, are viewed as not teachable given the teacher's skills and demands on his/her time. As a result, such students become candidates for referrals for evaluation, specialized placements, and/or consultation from teacher support personnel.

As part of a long-term study on mainstreaming and social integration, the author and his colleagues investigated regular and special education teachers' behavioral standards and expectations regarding student behavior in the classroom (Hersh & Walker, 1983; Walker & Rankin, 1983; Walker, 1986). To assess the behavioral ecology of mainstream classroom settings, they developed the *SBS (Social Behavior Survival) Inventory of Teacher Social Behavior Standards and Expectations* which measures forms of adaptive child behavior necessary for a successful classroom adjustment and forms of maladaptive behavior that disrupt or impair classroom adjustment. Over 1,100 regular and special education teachers across the country responded to this instrument as part of a national norming process. This study identified the most highly valued adaptive student behaviors and the least tolerated maladaptive behaviors by a national sample of classroom teachers in the K-12 grade range.

Table 1.4 contains the ten most highly rated adaptive student behaviors and the ten least tolerated maladaptive behaviors for this sample. The adaptive behavior list in Table 1.4 defines the ten most highly preferred forms of adaptive student behavior, out of a pool of 56 rated behaviors, as indicated by regular and special education teachers. The maladaptive list contains the ten least tolerated behaviors, out of a pool of 51 rated behaviors, as indicated by these same teachers. There was a very high level of agreement on this list between regular and special education teachers, and between elementary and secondary teachers.

The adaptive list provides a profile of the ideal student who is self-motivated, achievement oriented, cooperative, possessed of self-control, and who is highly teachable. In stark contrast, the maladaptive list profiles a student who is every teacher's nightmare. Unfortunately, severely acting-

Table 1.4 Highest Rated Adaptive and Maladaptive Items on the *SBS Inventory of Teacher Social Behavior Standards and Expectations*	
Ten Highest Rated Adaptive Items (Section I)	**Ten Highest Rated Maladaptive Items (Section II)**
1. Complies with teacher commands	1. Steals
2. Follows established classroom rules	2. Is self-abusive (e.g., biting, cutting, or bruising self; head banging; etc.)
3. Produces work of acceptable quality given his/her skill level	3. Behaves inappropriately in class (e.g., shouts back, defies the teacher, etc.) when corrected
4. Listens carefully to teacher instructions and directions for assignments	4. Is physically aggressive with others (e.g., hits, bites, chokes, holds)
5. Expresses anger appropriately (e.g., reacts to situations without being violent or destructive)	5. Makes lewd or obscene gestures
6. Can have conversations with peers without becoming hostile or angry	6. Engages in inappropriate sexual behavior (e.g., masturbates, exposes self, etc.)
7. Behaves appropriately in nonclassroom settings (i.e., bathroom, hallways, lunchroom, playground, etc.); e.g., walks quietly, follows playground rules, etc.	7. Refuses to obey teacher-imposed classroom rules
8. Avoids breaking classroom rule(s) even when encouraged by a peer	8. Damages others' property (e.g., academic materials, personal possessions, etc.)
9. Does seatwork assignments as directed	9. Has tantrums
10. Makes his/her assistance needs known in an appropriate manner (e.g., asks to go to the bathroom, raises hand when finished with work, asks for help with work, lets teacher know when sick or hurt)	10. Ignores teacher warnings or reprimands

out students are characteristically well-below acceptable teacher standards on the adaptive list and outside the normal range on the maladaptive list. These outcomes have ominous implications for the acting-out child's future both within and outside school. Given the potentially explosive mix of these teacher standards and the acting-out child's behavioral characteristics, it is easy to understand why such children are often referred, excluded, contained, and punished as part of their schooling process.

Additionally, the acting-out child's inappropriate behavior is not limited to the classroom. Teachers often complain most vigorously about the behavior of acting-out children in such nonclassroom areas of the school as the playground, hallways, and lunchroom. The misbehavior of children in general is usually more intense and at a much higher frequency in these areas of the school due to such factors as reduced supervision, less structure, and less clearly defined standards governing appropriate and inappropriate behavior.

The behavior of acting-out children is frequently out of control in these areas and is usually more difficult to manage than in the classroom. Due to the acting-out child's traditional lack of self-control and to the reduced behavioral constraints operating in these areas, there is a high probability that he will engage in disruptive and rule breaking behavior. Further, qualitative aspects of acting-out children's behavior may also differ in that physical aggression and hostile verbal exchanges with peers are more likely due to the nature of the activities children engage in within these areas (e.g., active games, running, shouting, jumping, yelling, etc.). As a rule, the more severely deviant the child, the more likely he/she is to engage in inappropriate behavior across all school settings. Acting-out children who have relatively severe levels of involvement characteristically "act out" in both classroom and nonclassroom areas of the school setting and are likely to experience problems at both home and school (Spira, 1989).

The Origins and Development of Disruptive Behavior Patterns Among Acting-Out Children

The origins of disruptive patterns of behavior among children in general, and among acting-out children in particular, is a subject of continuing debate and controversy. There is little agreement on this issue and numerous theories exist as to why some children develop normally while others become deviant. To complicate matters even further, some children develop normally within family conditions that are very problematic and that negatively influence the development of siblings. Such children are referred to as **resilient**, and they have generated considerable research interest over the past decade (Werner, 1987).

Understanding why some children have an apparent immunity to the negative impact of high risk family and social-economic conditions would provide important keys to prevention. The quality of mother-child interactions, the availability of social support networks, and school-related academic competence appear to be three important factors in buffering the effects of stressful conditions that put children at risk (Werner, 1987). The complexities involved in understanding this overall problem are substantial and the specific reasons as to why some children become deviant and others do not, within identical environments versus different environments, are obscure at best.

Three of the most prominently mentioned causal theories involve respectively **temperamental factors**, **environmental factors**, and **neurological factors**. The theory of problems with temperament as a precursor of a host of social-behavioral adjustment problems has strong advocates among both education professionals and lay persons. Restlessness among infants and young children, for example, has been consistently identified as an antecedent for later behavior problems, including depression (Morgan & Jenson, 1988). Children who are born with difficult temperaments are a challenge to parents, and may negatively condition parents to avoid, neglect, suppress, and/or punish them during parent-child interactions. Anything that disrupts normal parenting practices is likely to put the child at some degree of risk for later adjustment problems. If severe enough, these disruptive influences could lay the foundation for the development of a disruptive, acting-out behavioral pattern.

There is a broad consensus in our society that social and economic conditions that put children and families at risk are potent breeding grounds for the development of troubled children. These "at risk" conditions commonly include poverty; neglect; psychological, physical, and sexual forms of abuse; family dysfunction; criminal behavior on the part of family members; and the absence of a stable home environment. This list is by no means fully inclusive or exhaustive; however, it includes the most common indicators of risk as described in the literature and the media.

Patterson (1983) argues that these conditions place great stress upon a family and can severely disrupt normal parenting practices. Disrupted parenting practices can result in harsh discipline; weak monitoring of children's activities, their whereabouts, and who they affiliate with; limited parent involvement with the child; a failure to use positive family management techniques, and fragile to incompetent problem-solving and conflict resolution skills. Empirical evidence indicates that these parenting practices often lead to the development of acting-out, antisocial behavioral patterns which children bring to the schooling process.

Lisbeth Schorr, in her seminal work entitled *Within Our Reach* (1988), has conducted a thorough investigative study of the societal factors that put children at risk. She describes a series of **rotten outcomes** (RO's) that result from the risk conditions cited previously. The most serious of these outcomes are: (1) school failure and dropout, (2) too early parenthood, and (3) delinquency. When these three outcomes come together in the same child, they have an explosive effect and set in motion a life course of criminality, severe adjustment problems, and the absence of economic self-reliance.

Neurological factors are frequently cited as structural antecedents to social-behavioral adjustment problems. Attention Deficit Hyperactivity Disorder (ADHD) is an example of a condition that has powerful social, behavioral, and learning manifestations and is considered to have a neurological basis, (Barkley, 1990; Schaywitz & Schaywitz, 1987). Approximately 40% of ADHD children have conduct disorders, and approximately 20% have a learning disability (Forness, 1993). Drug effected babies present a huge, looming problem in our society because of the long-term negative impact of prenatal drug and alcohol exposure. Such exposed children suffer from severe attentional problems, agitated states, and hyperactivity; they are very difficult for schools to teach and manage.

At present, we do not have the ability to precisely identify and differentially weight the causal factors that influence the development of acting-out behavioral patterns. The role of these factors probably varies significantly from case to case. In addition, we do not have the means to substantially impact or attenuate the causal roles of temperament and neurological factors. However, in a preventive sense, we can do a great deal about the impact of environmental factors. Our greatest hope for reducing the incidence of acting-out behavioral patterns is to increase parental awareness of the factors that contribute to their development and to identify acting-out children as early as possible in the schooling process so interventions can be designed and implemented for them.

In spite of our inability to identify the specific causes of disruptive behavior in children, it is imperative that we improve our ability to prevent and remediate this behavior. Disruptive behavior in the school setting is a dramatically increasing concern of both educators and parents. Gallup polls of the public's concerns about schooling consistently identify discipline and acting-out behavior problems as major concerns. Unfortunately, children's school behavior has become substantially more complex and difficult to manage in the past two decades. Increasingly, school resources are being devoted to managing the behavior of problem children. Teachers' unions are beginning to negotiate for special services for difficult to manage children in order to make their behavior more controllable and less aversive within the classroom setting. Further, school systems are being forced to invest millions of dollars each year in order to maintain the security of school grounds, buildings, and teaching staffs. In some large urban school districts, police are required to patrol school grounds in order to insure the physical safety of children and teachers, and metal detectors are needed to screen for weapons that students bring to school.

Recently, an elementary school was identified in Durham, North Carolina in which 35% of fifth graders brought weapons to school—many bringing them for their self-protection. The Seattle public schools experienced a 300% increase in weapons at school over a two-year period. Each school day, 100,000 students in this country bring weapons to school, and 40 are killed or seriously wounded by these weapons daily. In 1991, there were three million acts of violence and theft in U.S. schools. All of these developments suggest that the concerns of parents and educators are well-founded and that school behavior problems seem to be approaching new levels of severity and danger. As a society, Americans should elevate this escalating pattern of behavior to the level of a national emergency! If left untreated, it will likely only get worse, and **much** worse at that!

What accounts for the dramatic rise in children's disruptiveness and deviance levels within the school setting? There appear to be no easy answers. For example, the changed social conditions that exist in the larger society are no doubt reflected in the school behavior of children who are exposed to these conditions on a daily basis. Many children are so stressed by these conditions that they are unfit to learn and consume instruction. Unfortunately, there is a massive spillover of society's problems with criminality, drug abuse, family breakdown, and poverty into the school systems. Schools are not equipped to offset the impact of these conditions except in a piecemeal fashion. And while there is no doubt that these social conditions are contributing to increased levels of child deviance and disruption in schools, educators' understanding of the manner in which they operate to **specifically** account for such increases is relatively obscure at present.

A perennial viewpoint in accounting for deviant child behavior in school settings is to blame the schools, and classroom teachers specifically, for failing to educate children effectively. There is no doubt that children can learn maladaptive behavior patterns in school and that schools sometimes inadvertently build in and strengthen disruptive child behavior through their attempts at controlling this very behavior. Some professionals and educational critics have suggested, however, that inappropriate child behavior is a direct function of ineffective teaching and the teacher's lack of skill in managing child behavior. According to this position, maladaptive child behavior can be accounted for by simply examining the instructional and management competence of the teacher. In one sense, it would be ideal if the problem were really this simple.

It is difficult to accept unconditionally such a view of why children display disruptive behavior in schools. For example, it is obvious that some children display highly disruptive patterns of behavior from the very first day of school. Such children could not have learned these behavior patterns in school, and teachers cannot be held accountable for causing or prompting the disruptive behavior of these students. It is apparent that children who fit this profile have learned very maladaptive patterns of behavior outside the school setting and continue to engage in them upon entering school. Unfortunately, as previously noted, empirical studies have shown that schools can maintain and actually strengthen such behavior patterns, even though they were learned and acquired outside the school setting (Patterson, 1983; Patterson, Reid, & Dishion, 1992).

It is apparent that a child's behavior pattern at school is the result of a complex interaction of: (1) the behavior pattern the child has been taught at home, including attitudes toward school; (2) the experiences the child has had with different teachers in the school setting; and (3) the relationship between the child and his/her current teacher(s). Trying to determine in what proportion the child's behavior pattern is attributable to each of these learning sources is an impossible **and** quite unnecessary task. Disruptive child behavior can be changed very effectively without knowing the specific, original causes for its acquisition and development. Further, these causes may no longer play a role in its maintenance. A major purpose of this book is to present a set of practical strategies for use by school personnel in effectively remediating acting-out behavioral patterns.

The Situational Specificity of the Behavior of Acting-Out Children

Much of personality theory rests upon the assumption that human behavior is characterized by relatively stable traits (Allport, 1966, 1974). Trait labels are frequently used in the description of human behavior. For example, it is common for individuals to describe the behavior of others using such labels as sensitive, conscientious, aggressive, hostile, loving, independent, capricious, dependent, warm, and so forth. The list of trait labels goes on and on.

These labels **do** communicate information about human behavior albeit at a relatively gross level. However, they are based upon the assumption that the behavioral dimensions being described are stable and relatively unchanging over time. That is, if we describe someone as conscientious, dependent, or sensitive, it is assumed that he/she displays manifestations of these behavioral dimensions consistently over time and across settings. There is clear empirical evidence in support of the existence of both traits **and** situational specificity in the analysis of human behavior. In dealing with the behavioral challenges presented by acting-out students in school, it is important to understand how these attributes or characteristic patterns operate.

Mischel (1969) argues that while cognitive and intellectual dimensions of human functioning are highly stable, personality and interpersonal behavioral patterns are less likely to be so. Mischel (1968), in a now-classic review of the research evidence on this issue, concluded that the available evidence was persuasive as to the situational specificity of human behavior. That is, human behavior tends to be a function of the specific situation(s) in which it occurs. Another way of saying this is that human behavior is highly reactive and sensitive to the conditions that exist in the situation in which it occurs. This is a most desirable attribute because of its survival value as well as the implications it holds for human adaptability and change in relation to differing environmental conditions.

In practical terms, the concept of situational specificity means that not everyone is aggressive, sensitive, dependent, or conscientious **all** of the time. It is more likely that most people are, as a rule, aggressive, sensitive, dependent, or conscientious **some** of the time or in some situations and not in others. For example, individuals may be aggressive in some situations and not in others. However, an individual who is generally regarded as "aggressive" probably engages in aggressive behavior at a much higher frequency and in more situations than normal (Olweus, 1979; Patterson, 1983; Patterson et al., 1992). Although it is extremely unlikely that any individual is aggressive **all** of the time and across **all** situations, individuals who have learned aggressive behavioral patterns as a lifestyle are highly predictable in terms of their aggressive behavior. For example, I.Q. is highly stable over a ten-year period showing test-retest stability quotients of approximately .70; aggressive behavioral patterns among antisocial populations show similar stability quotients in the range of .60-.80 (Patterson, Reid, & Dishion, 1992; Quay, 1986).

Mischel's arguments have generated considerable controversy in the years following their publication. It should be noted that some scientists believe that Mischel has overstated the case for the situational specificity of personality and interpersonal domains of behavior (Patterson, 1983; Patterson et al., 1992). It appears that as one moves closer to the extreme ends of such behavioral dimensions as aggression, individuals representing these behavioral extremes behave in a very predictable, trait-like fashion and show substantial behavioral consistency across time, situations, and settings. Very aggressive behavior is **highly** predictable and such predictability is one of the defining characteristics of a trait.

This view of human behavior bears directly upon strategies for explaining and changing behavior. For example, if one's behavior is markedly different in two different situations, a major portion of this difference **may** be accounted for by whatever differences exist in the stimulus conditions and setting demands in those situations. By way of illustration, some children are deviant at school and not at home, while others are deviant at home and not at school. Studies by Johnson, Bolstad, and Lobitz (1976) and Patterson (1974) show that approximately half of the children who are deviant in either the home or school setting are also deviant in the other setting. When a child is deviant in one setting and not in another, it is obvious that at least part of the explanation of this difference can be attributed to differing conditions in the two settings in which the child's behavior is a function. However, it is important to note that human behavior is very complex and that one's behavioral history is also an important factor in explaining how one behaves in any given situation.

Mischel (1969) argues that cross-situational consistency of human behavior should only be expected if the conditions within situations are similar. To the extent that they are different, one can expect cross-situational differences in behavior or lack of behavioral consistency. This observation, however, would not necessarily hold true for extremely deviant or aggressive individuals as per the previous discussion.

Another salient characteristic of acting-out children is their ability to "read" contingencies within a given situation and to respond to them specifically. Contingencies refer to the relationships that exist between the stated rules or behavioral expectations in a situation (e.g., classroom, home, playground) and the consequences that back them up. Thus, an acting-out child's behavior may be quite different in two situations or settings where the contingencies differ radically. If, for example, the relationship between rules and back-up consequences is not clear or the rules are not consistently backed up by consequences, the acting-out child may follow the rules only infrequently. If, however, the rules are clearly stated and consistently followed by positive consequences (i.e., praise, approval, privileges) the acting-out child, as well as other children, are much more likely to behave appropriately.

Sensitivity to the presence and absence of such contingencies has enormous survival value to children in general and to acting-out children in particular. It is a skill that can be used to adapt to a given environmental setting and the social agents within that setting.

Conclusion

This chapter has attempted to characterize the acting-out child and to profile the behavioral attributes and academic skill deficits that so often accompany this unfortunate, difficult behavioral pattern. Causal factors that seem to be associated with its origins and the course of its developmental progression were identified and reviewed. Typical school responses (and their effects) that are used to cope with the disciplinary infractions of this school sub-population indicate that: (1) they are repeated over and over, and (2) they have little appreciable effect in reducing the acting-out child's behavior problems or in improving overall school adjustment. Often, our best attempts to cope with this behavior disorder actually strengthen it and serve to make it more resistant to intervention. The more severe the behavior disorder, the more trait-like and difficult to change it becomes.

2

Common School and Teacher Attempts to Cope With the Acting-Out Child

Acting-out children and youth are among the least liked and most difficult students that schools are charged with educating. They consume an inordinate amount of the school's most precious resource—teacher time and attention. Acting-out students are among the first of those most teachers would choose to refer out of their classrooms. This chapter describes school and teacher attempts to cope with and manage the myriad behavioral challenges presented by these students.

Characteristic School Approaches Used to Manage the Acting-Out Child's Behavior

Intense pressures have developed both within and outside schools for the application of more effective methods of addressing child deviance in the school setting. Much of this pressure comes from the public and from policy makers at both federal and state levels who are alarmed at the manner in which schools provide a mirror of the larger social and economic problems plaguing our society. Accountability pressures of the type now being experienced by our public schools are somewhat unfair in that: (1) schools can only do so much to educate children who come to school in no condition to learn because of abusive and stressful home conditions, and (2) schools are being asked to solve very complex problems that children bring with them to the schooling experience. In the past decade, public schools have expanded their roles in response to these pressures, but they are severely limited in being able to adequately address problems that are really the responsibility of the larger society and that require much broader solutions.

How do schools generally respond when they are pressured to remediate, or at least accommodate, the problem behavior of acting-out students?

Characteristically, the first response usually has been to try to fix blame for children's maladaptive behavior. This is not an unexpected response given the pressurized vortex in which schools find themselves on this issue. School personnel have tended to blame parents exclusively for their children's disruptive or aggressive behavior in school. The clear implication is that family pathology and/or parenting incompetence is the root cause of children's problems. In the past, schools have often referred parents to mental health clinics because of their children's behavior problems in school, with the implication that the parents are to blame and it is the parents' responsibility to ensure that their children's behavior problems are reduced to acceptable limits at school.

As would be expected, parents are not always receptive to this view of their children's behavior problems. Instead, they often blame the schools for their inability to control their children's school behavior. The criticism is voiced frequently by parents that schools are not teaching their children adequately, nor are they assisting them in developing socially and emotionally (Epstein, Nelson, Polsgrove, Coutinho, Cumblad, & Quinn, 1993).

Students, even at relatively young ages, become sensitized to these parental views. If they are internalized, such children are likely to develop negative attitudes toward teachers and schooling. Further, when teacher-student conflicts occur that spill over into the family/school relationship, the involved teacher often feels unsupported by school administrators who must accommodate the interests of all parties to the dispute.

The task of fixing blame and defining responsibility for children's behavior problems at school is largely a fruitless one. Parents are not usually convinced of the school's point of view and vice versa. For example, mental health agency records indicate that the highest frequency of self-cancellations of family therapy sessions are by families who are referred by school systems because of their child's behavior problems at school. Clearly, these types of interactions between parents and schools concerning school behavior problems have not resulted in adaptive, positive responses to them nor have they advanced the quality of family/school relationships.

Another popular response to child behavior problems at school has been drug therapy. This approach has been especially prevalent for problems of inattention and overactivity (Barkley, 1990). Provided that the dosage is titrated appropriately and proves effective, drug therapy for a given child can have a number of obvious advantages for the teachers and parents who must manage the child's behavior. For example, the overall rate or frequency of child behavior is usually substantially reduced, and it tends to become less disruptive. A typical dose of Ritalin (5-20 Mg per administration, given one to three times daily) produces immediate reductions in disruptive behavior through its effect in lowering activity level **and** increasing compliance (Swanson, Cantwell, Lerner, McBurnett, Pfiffner, & Kotkin, 1992).

Given that drug therapy of this type makes a child's behavior more compliant and less disruptive, it is not surprising that children experiencing behavior problems at school are often referred by schools, individual teachers, and/or parents to physicians for possible placement on drug therapy programs. In fact, some school districts are known to have placed intense pressures upon parents to allow their children to participate in drug therapy programs in order to make their behavior more compliant and acceptable at school.

During the decade of the seventies, considerable public concern over the possible undesirable side effects of drug therapy programs was voiced in the media and the professional literature (Bendix, 1973; Connors, 1973; Ladd, 1970; Novack, 1971; Walker, 1974). These side effects included: (1) the risk of drug dependency in later years, (2) suppression of growth, and (3) increased heart rate or blood pressure problems (Cohen, Douglas, & Morganstern, 1971; Knights & Hinston, 1969; Rapoport, Quinn, Bradbard, Riddle, & Brooks, 1974; Safer & Allen, 1973). The side effects issue, though by no means resolved, has attenuated substantially in the last ten years or so, and the use of stimulant medications to control child behavior in school and nonschool settings increased dramatically during this period. Debates about the precise effectiveness of such drug therapy continues unabated in the professional literature (Kavale, 1982).

It is estimated that approximately 5% of the school age population qualifies as Attention Deficit Hyperactivity Disordered (ADHD) (Barkley, 1990). Further, experts suggest that 3% of the school age population is receiving drug therapy medications for this problem (Safer, 1988). Swanson, Shea, McBurnett, Potkin, Fiore, and Crinella (1990) have argued that stimulant medications in this country are overused, particularly when compared with usage rates in other countries such as England. This is especially true, in the author's view, when these medications are used in lieu of other, nondrug-based interventions, primarily because they serve the convenience needs of adults rather than the actual needs of the child.

Two of the more common stimulant medications used with acting-out and/or hyperactive children are dextroamphetamine and methylphenidate. There is little doubt that such drugs can have a powerful and immediate impact upon child behavior; over two decades of research on this topic provides substantial empirical evidence to support this observation (Barkley, 1990; Comly, 1971; Conrad, Dworkin, Shai, & Tobiessen, 1972; Denhoff, Davids, & Hawkins, 1971; Schaywitz & Schaywitz, 1987; Swanson et al., 1992). However, even when the correct dosage is found, drug therapy of this type is ineffective with approximately 40% of cases to which it is applied. Further, when treatment effects **are** achieved, they are short-term in nature and vanish when the medication is no longer in the child's system (Fish, 1971; Swanson et al., 1992).

The goal of drug therapy with children is generally not to "cure" a given child's behavior problem(s) and/or disorder(s). Drug therapy does not produce enduring changes in child behavior, nor does it have an impact upon a child's personality. Studies have shown that a child's behavior quickly reverts to pre-drug levels of intensity and frequency when the drug therapy program is terminated (Ayllon, Layman, & Kandel, 1975). Drug therapy essentially suppresses the more undesirable features of child behavior but does not teach the child strategies for achieving behavioral self-control and/or self-management.

It has been argued that while drug therapies do not cure behavior disorders they may make children more receptive to instructional and/or counseling efforts. That is, they are designed to increase children's ability to focus and sustain attention on meaningful stimuli and to organize their body movements more purposefully. Additional research in the context of school environments is required to determine the degree to which this actually occurs in a manner that has meaningful instructional implications. Further, the extent to which drug therapy facilitates academic performance and/or achievement is also not clear, in spite of the claims by drug therapy proponents to the effect that stimulants make children more receptive to instruction.

Swanson and his colleagues (Swanson et al., 1992) have reviewed extensively the empirical studies and evidence on this question conducted over the past 15 years. They conclude that " ... the short-term effects of stimulants on academic performance are minimal compared to the effects on behavior, and that there is no evidence of beneficial effects on learning or academic achievement" (p. 20). In fact, these authors cite evidence that suggests the short-term effects of stimulant medications on child behavior (i.e., behavioral suppression, isolation, overfocusing of attention) may actually impair performance on some cognitive learning tests and academic tasks. Thus, improvements in behavioral manageability may be achieved at the expense of academic achievement for substantial numbers of children.

It is apparent that stimulant drug therapy is relatively easy to administer, low cost, convenient, and is often an effective treatment procedure for children. Its major disadvantages are that: (1) it teaches children nothing about methods or techniques for managing their own behavior; (2) it does not produce enduring changes in child behavior—that is, the child's behavior is changed only so long as the drug therapy program is in effect; and (3) it appears to have no direct effect whatsoever on academic performance and achievement. The possible undesirable physical side effects of stimulant drugs are also an important consideration in their use, particularly over the long term. Whenever feasible, nondrug alternatives should be pursued vigorously in the treatment of child behavior problems, especially at school.

Currently, the National Institute of Mental Health and the U.S. Office of Special Education Programs are jointly funding a six-site, national study of interventions for ADHD. This study will compare psychosocial, drug-based, and combined treatments against no-treatment control groups in order to determine their relative effectiveness. The results of this study will have important implications for school policy in developing interventions for ADHD children with and without acting-out behavioral patterns.

Another response of school systems to the problem of disruptive, inappropriate child behavior in the classroom has been removal from mainstream educational settings. Although students with behavior disorders represent only 9% of the total disabled population certified and served in this country, they account for 40% of the students who receive home tutoring and instruction.

The behavior of acting-out children often places intense pressures upon the management and instructional skills of classroom teachers. Such children are extremely difficult to manage and teach effectively. Consequently, the treatment of choice for them traditionally has been placement in settings external to the regular classroom (e.g., in resource rooms, special classrooms, or institutional settings). The principal effect of such placement decisions has been to relieve the teacher and peers of the burdens imposed by the acting-out child's disruptive behavior. However, removal from the regular classroom also deprives the child of the opportunity to develop a behavioral repertoire that would ensure entry into and maintenance within the educational mainstream. Further, research has shown that treatment gains achieved in such restrictive settings tend not to be maintained after reintegration into the regular classroom (Morgan & Jenson, 1988; Walker & Buckley, 1972).

It is entirely understandable why regular classroom teachers would like to have acting-out children assigned to special settings, particularly since teachers have historically been encouraged to refer students with behavior problems for possible placement in such settings. However, passage of Public Law 94-142 in 1975, the recent mainstreaming movement, and increasing pressures for the full inclusion of individuals with disabilities in regular schooling contexts have created a powerful press for all children with disabilities, including those with behavior problems, to be educated in the least restrictive educational setting possible (Kauffman, 1993). The regular classroom setting is viewed by the courts, child advocates, and Congress as the least restrictive of available educational placements.

The implications of these developments for regular classroom teachers are direct and far reaching. For example, placement of larger numbers of students with atypical patterns of development in regular classrooms will severely test the management and instructional skills of regular classroom teachers. Extensive consultant and support services from expert educational and psychological personnel should accompany assignment of such children to regular classrooms; however, teachers, in the final analysis, will be responsible for educating these children effectively. In order to do so, many regular classroom teachers will need to acquire some relatively complex skills in the areas of behavior management and instructional programming, and will also need to be supported by school-wide teacher-student support teams.

Counseling and psychotherapy have also been used frequently as vehicles for coping with the disruptive classroom behavior of acting-out children. Surveys of teachers often indicate that counseling is the most preferred intervention for the problems presented by such children. The appeal of counseling is understandable, in that the child is expected to change through the counseling process and become more accommodating and responsive. With counseling, teachers do not have to assume responsibility for or play a role in achieving behavior change.

Unfortunately, counseling is among the least effective options we have available to us if the goal is to produce reliable, meaningful changes in student behavior. The focus of this intervention approach is generally upon: (1) helping the acting-out child to identify and understand the reasons for his disruptive, aggressive, and/or rule breaking behavior; and (2) to change his behavior accordingly. Usually, acting-out children are quite aware of the appropriateness or inappropriateness of their behavior and are sensitive, in many cases, to the effects it has upon others. Unfortunately, there is no evidence to indicate that an acting-out child's awareness of the probable causes of his behavior has **any** effect upon improving his actual classroom behavior (Dryfoos, 1990).

Providing the acting-out child with feedback about the extent to which he is following classroom rules also appears to have little effect in reducing disruptive behavior. In fact, studies have consistently shown that classroom rules alone have little effect in changing the behavior of **any** children (Greenwood, Hops, Delquadri, & Guild, 1974). This would be especially true of acting-out children.

However, school counselors are in an excellent position to serve teachers as consultants and support personnel in dealing with difficult children. Counselors can also play crucial roles in delivering social skills training and serving as members of school-wide assistance teams (Phillips & McCullough, 1993).

Developing intervention procedures for changing the acting-out child's behavior in the regular classroom setting has been one of the least frequently selected treatment alternatives. The reasons for this development are not clear at present. Possible reasons might include the following: (1) it may be that the teacher's intolerance of the child's inappropriate behavior and the teacher's relative inability to cope with it causes the teacher to reject the child and become less than receptive to in-class procedures for changing the child's behavior; (2) teachers may be perceived as either too busy or not sufficiently skilled to implement such procedures effectively in the classroom; (3) given that the child can be referred to a resource/special classroom, a home tutoring regimen, or a special facility wherein the child is "taken off the teacher's hands" for a period of time, teachers may be relatively unmotivated to develop and implement in-class intervention procedures designed to change the inappropriate behavior; and (4) it may be that the necessary intervention procedures and/or sufficiently skilled teacher consultants (i.e., psychologists, counselors, resource teachers, etc.) have been perceived as not available in a form necessary to make this alternative an effective reality. Whatever the actual reasons, it is apparent that, given the advent of Public Law 94-142 and the continuing pressures for full inclusion and equal access to the educational mainstream, this alternative will be pursued increasingly by school personnel in the future.

It is apparent also that relatively few school systems have dealt systematically or successfully with the problems presented by disruptive, acting-out children. Excluding children from the educational mainstream or the school building, and suppressing their behavior through the use of drugs do not appear to be fair or just responses to child deviance. Systematic behavior management procedures represent a constructive alternative to such methods of managing the behavior of acting-out children. A well-developed technology (i.e., effective intervention procedures) for changing student behavior in school settings does exist (Kauffman, 1993; Morgan & Jenson, 1988; Stoner, Shinn, & Walker, 1991), and these procedures have been adapted for effective use in a range of school and nonschool settings (i.e., regular, resource, and self-contained classrooms, playgrounds, day treatment and residential programs, vocational settings, and so forth). To date, however, we have not been entirely successful in adapting these procedures for use by teachers in a maximally cost effective manner. One of the major goals of this book is to address this goal.

Teacher Attempts to Cope With the Acting-Out Child

Teachers have tried a variety of techniques for controlling and/or managing the behavior of acting-out children. Unfortunately, most of the practical techniques used by teachers to respond to acting-out children are only of limited effectiveness and some, such as reprimands, arguing, and escalated hostile interactions, can actually strengthen the target behavior(s) they are designed to suppress or terminate.

No two teachers respond to acting-out children in exactly the same way. However, there is considerable similarity among teachers in their general attempts to manage the acting-out child's behavior. Most often, the teacher responds in a way that is designed to persuade or encourage the acting-out child to stop his disruptive behavior and to behave more appropriately. In these situations, peers usually provide support for the child's inappropriate behavior. The teacher's negative attention in these situations and the support provided by peers strengthen the acting-out child's behavior, and make it more likely that he will act out again in the future in order to gain attention and approval or to obtain social control over a situation. It is indeed ironic that the teacher's direct efforts to prompt the acting-out child to stop misbehaving are very often instrumental in maintaining the inappropriate behavior of concern.

Teachers are usually quick to respond to the acting-out child's inappropriate behavior because of its disruptive and aversive properties. In such cases, the child's behavior problems are said to be "teacher owned"; that is, the teacher owns these problems and assumes responsibility for doing something about them. As noted, teachers' management efforts are almost always directed at making the acting-out child terminate the inappropriate behavior as soon as possible. The success of teachers in this task has been highly variable.

Thus the acting-out child learns that it is easier to receive attention from peers and the teacher by engaging in disruptive, noncompliant behavior than by following classroom rules, completing assignments, and developing positive social relationships with peers. He learns a set of behaviors and adopts a strategy that forces his teachers and peers to respond to these highly aversive initiations, often in a negative way. Even though the attention received from peers and the teacher is usually negative, critical, and disapproving, it is attention just the same and serves to maintain the behavior on which it is focused. In fact, many acting-out children seem to thrive on the hostile confrontations they have with their teachers. Their ability to irritate the teacher and keep him/her upset is rewarding for acting-out children and is often subtly approved of by peers (Colvin & Sugai, 1989).

Some teachers attempt to ignore the acting-out child's inappropriate behavior in the hope that if it doesn't receive attention, it won't continue. This would be a sound strategy if the behavior were maintained **only** by teacher attention; however, peers often provide massive support for the acting-out child's misbehavior. Further, teachers usually find acting-out children's disruptive behavior very difficult to ignore for any length of time since such children have learned to escalate their demands for teacher attention in the face of a limited teacher response.

Teachers are more likely to respond in an active rather than passive fashion in dealing with acting-out children. This frequently involves the use of negative reprimands, disapproval, and criticism(s). As noted previously, the effectiveness of these techniques in controlling the acting-out child's inappropriate behavior is highly variable. Sometimes these techniques will produce a temporary reduction in the inappropriate behavior; at other times, they seem to have no discernible effect. Unfortunately, the attention the acting-out child receives during this process is probably instrumental in maintaining his inappropriate behavior over the long term. In addition, the teacher's obvious irritation with the content of the behavior, the child's ability to make the teacher upset, and the child's control of the situation can all combine to strengthen the acting-out child's inappropriate behavior and make it very difficult to change.

Studies of the classroom interactions between teachers and disruptive children have shown that: (1) such interactions are more likely to be negative than positive; (2) the teacher is much more likely to critically reprimand inappropriate behavior than to praise appropriate behavior during these interactions; and (3) disruptive children tend to monopolize the teacher's time (Colvin & Sugai, 1989; Walker & Buckley, 1973, 1974). While these findings do not apply to all teachers, they are descriptive of the interactions that occur between many, perhaps most, teachers and the acting-out, disruptive children in their classes.

Walker, Hops, and Fiegenbaum (1976) carried out a study illustrating these points. In this study, five regular classroom teachers, from five different elementary schools, each referred an acting-out child to a demonstration classroom for a two to three month intervention due to their disruptive classroom behavior. The interactions between these five teachers and the referred children were observed and recorded over a two-week period in the regular classroom prior to assignment to the demonstration class. Results showed that the five teachers praised and approved of the acting-out children's appropriate behavior an average of .6 times per hour (about once every two hours), or approximately 2.4 times within a normal school day. However, in contrast, the same teachers showed **active disapproval** of the children's inappropriate behavior an average of 9.1 times per hour, or approximately 36 times per day! This is a ratio of 17:1 negative to positive interactions daily!

Further, as a group, the five children consumed a total of 14% of their teachers' available time. With an average teacher/child ratio of 1:24 in these five classrooms, each child could expect to receive approximately 4% of the teacher's allottable time. These acting-out children consumed considerably more of the teachers' time than did their peers, and the majority of this time was spent in negative interactions with the teacher. It is ironic that this huge investment of teacher time was largely ineffectual in reducing the children's inappropriate behavior and, in fact, was probably instrumental in maintaining the behavior!

Walker and Buckley (1973) carried out a study in which they examined the way in which a regular elementary teacher responded to deviant and nondeviant children enrolled in her fifth grade classroom. The results were quite revealing. A combination of teacher ratings and observation data was used to select the three most deviant and the three least deviant children in her classroom. All the interactions occurring between these six children and the teacher were then systematically recorded over a two-week period. There were 144 separate interactions between the teacher and the six children during the two-week observation period. Seventy of the 144 interactions were the result of a child initiating to the teacher, and 74 were the result of the teacher initiating to one of the six children.

Of the 74 interactions resulting from the teacher initiating to the children, 57, or 77%, involved the three deviant children, and 17, or 23%, involved the three nondeviant children. For the deviant children, 51 of the 57 interactions (89%) were a result of the teacher attending to their inappropriate behavior. In contrast, 14 of the 17 teacher interactions (82%) with the nondeviant children were a result of the teacher attending to their appropriate behavior.

These results revealed that the teacher responded in a clearly different fashion to deviant and nondeviant children enrolled in her classroom. In her interactions with the three deviant children, there were nine times as many interactions involving her attention to their inappropriate behavior as there were interactions in which she attended to their appropriate behavior. For the three nondeviant children, the ratio was 5:1 in favor of interactions in which she attended to their appropriate behavior.

As in the Walker et al. (1976) study, the deviant children in this study consumed a large and relatively disproportionate amount of the teacher's total available time. The three deviant children in this study were involved in approximately 3.3 times as many interactions with the teacher as were the three nondeviant children within the same time period.

The dynamics of these interactions were also quite different for the deviant and nondeviant children. For example, when the teacher directed her attention to the inappropriate behavior of the nondeviant children, they would usually stop the behavior in question on the first or second consequation attempt. However, the deviant children sometimes would not terminate their inappropriate behavior until the fourth, fifth, or even sixth attempt by the teacher to make them do so. At other times, they would terminate their inappropriate behavior on the first or second consequation attempt. Thus, it seemed that the teacher's consequating behavior was partially under the control of an intermittent schedule of compliance furnished by the deviant children. This was clearly not the case for the nondeviant children, who consistently complied with the teacher's instructions to terminate the inappropriate behavior on either the first or second attempt.

These studies illustrate how frustrating it is for teachers to deal with acting-out children. It often appears that the harder a teacher tries to control an acting-out child's behavior, the less effective he/she is. This process can be physically draining and emotionally exhausting. In situations such as this, the acting-out child's behavior is a constant reminder that the classroom atmosphere is not what the teacher would like it to be.

In nonclassroom settings (e.g., playground, hallways, lunchroom), the most commonly used techniques for controlling disruptive behavior include warnings, reprimands, threats, removal from ongoing activities, and systematic exclusion. These techniques also have highly variable effects upon children's behavior. Children who generally do not "act out" are more likely to respond to warnings and reprimands, while acting-out children often require temporary removal from the area, the use of a "response cost" (i.e., loss of earned points), or systematic exclusion in order for their behavior to be controlled effectively. Note however that even though loss of previously earned points (which are exchangeable for privileges) and removal or exclusion from the classroom are often effective in terminating an acting-out child's inappropriate behavior and in teaching him to control the grosser forms of his behavior, they do not teach prosocial skills that would lead to the development of positive behavior patterns and self-control. These skills must be developed through direct teaching and the use of positive behavior management techniques.

To change this situation, very powerful intervention procedures must be applied to the acting-out child's behavior. The application of these procedures (to be discussed in later chapters) requires a fairly substantial investment of teacher time initially; however, as the child's behavior changes from inappropriate to appropriate, the teacher will be required to devote less and less time to management of the acting-out child's behavior. Further, the time that is invested will be much more effective in producing the desired results and is more likely to be positive instead of negative in nature. If these procedures are implemented properly and consistently, the teacher should not be required to invest any more time with the acting-out child over the long term than is the case with other children.

Conclusion

One's understanding and perspectives on child behavior, especially deviant child behavior, can have a powerful impact upon one's receptivity to methods for explaining and changing that behavior. Parents, teachers, and schools undergo enormous pressures and stress in coping with the behavior problems of acting-out children. This book presents a highly effective technology for managing and changing the behavior of such children. Professionals' expectations concerning this technology, like their views of child behavior, are an important factor in determining how and whether they will use the procedures. Their skillful and measured application will more than justify the costs to the implementor in terms of the positive child outcomes achieved.

3

General Rules Governing Classroom and School Behavior

This chapter presents 11 key rules that govern the behavior of both acting-out children and their peers. The social learning foundations for each rule are described and practical examples are given to illustrate how the rule operates. Classroom and/or playground applications of each rule are also discussed.

A knowledge of these rules and how they operate in the general school setting will give the teacher a greater understanding of why children behave as they do. An understanding of causal factors governing adaptive as well as maladaptive behavior can be of invaluable assistance to a classroom teacher in improving her/his behavior management skills. Later chapters discuss how to use specific classroom management techniques that are based upon the following rules.

Rule One . . . . *"Human behavior is learned through a series of interactions with one's environment."*

SOCIAL LEARNING FOUNDATIONS

John Locke, the English philosopher, regarded the newborn child as a "Tabula Rasa," or as a blank tablet to be written upon. He believed that the child's unique life experiences determined what was written upon this tablet. The person the child eventually developed into, and his/her personality characteristics, were the sum total of these life experiences.

Locke's view of human development saw the child as highly malleable and as being greatly influenced by life experiences. If John Locke were alive today, he would probably subscribe strongly to the nurture side of the "nature-nurture" controversy in explaining the human development of intelligence and personality. Locke felt that environmental influences played a powerful role in determining how children develop and learn and that all knowledge was acquired empirically—through experience.

Children are born with almost limitless capacities for learning. In the early stages of development, what the child learns is, to a large extent, acquired through contact with environments such as the home or school. Environmental influences upon the child's development are transmitted primarily through interactions the child has with key social agents in these settings including parents, siblings, teachers, and peers. The quality of these interactions and the kinds of feedback children receive regarding their behavior are instrumental in shaping what is learned.

Specific behavior patterns, as well as values and attitudes, are taught through this process. This gradual training process is known as **socialization**, and is the primary vehicle through which children absorb their culture, acquire the skills they need to cope effectively with life's demands, and develop important friendships and social support networks.

In this training process, children become highly sensitive to the feedback they receive regarding their own behavior. If a particular behavior produces a positive result from the environment, it is likely to be strengthened and become a part of the child's ongoing social-behavioral repertoire. If the behavior is punished or consistently ignored, it will not be strengthened and will eventually cease. In the course of development, the child "tries out" literally hundreds of such behavioral responses in the home and school environments and judges their resulting effects. Whether the behavioral responses are acquired depends upon the effect(s) they have upon the environment. If the effect is positive, they will probably be acquired; if the effect is negative, they probably will not be acquired.

It is clear that learning is, to a large extent, an interactive process. Much of a child's learning is social in nature and involves exchanges with key social agents in the environment (i.e., parents, teachers, peers, and siblings). However, the child also learns and acquires skills through interactions of a nonsocial nature. For example, children learn to discriminate relevant features of the physical environment through contact with materials that teach size, shape, color, and so forth. After basic reading skills are developed, much learning of a nonsocial nature occurs through direct contact with a wide variety of educational print materials.

Adults (usually parents and teachers) are responsible for guiding this interactive process along lines that ensure healthy and normal development. However parents, and sometimes teachers, are not always aware of the remarkable extent to which they can influence the developmental learning processes of children.

CLASSROOM APPLICATIONS

Since no two home environments are exactly the same, children's learning histories and specific life experiences differ and the behavioral repertoires they bring to school reflect these differences. When they begin school, children are expected to behave in certain carefully prescribed ways in order to participate in the learning process. That is, they must learn to listen to teacher instructions, follow directions, sit quietly for relatively long periods of time, attend to tasks, raise their hand before asking questions, cooperate with other children, and respond when called upon. That is, they must learn to be socially responsive to adults and classmates and to abide by an explicit set of rules and behavioral expectations.

Some children experience great difficulty in adjusting to these behavioral demands due to a mixture of negative environmental and/or neurological factors. If these difficulties are not resolved, the result can be a seriously impaired school adjustment process and the development of conflicts between the child and teacher.

The kinds of interactions a child has with her/his teachers and classmates can have a dramatic impact upon the learning process, upon academic achievement, and ultimately upon the child's acceptance within the school environment. Some children enter school with well-developed social skills, are responsive to instructions or commands from adults, and are motivated to learn. Such children are easy to teach in that they generally learn quickly, require only limited amounts of teacher time, and interact constructively with the teacher and their peers. They are referred to as "teachable pupils." Their interactions with teachers are generally also positive and of a cooperative nature. They tend to receive high likability ratings from teachers and peers, and are among those students the teacher would be least likely to refer out of the classroom.

Acting-out children, on the other hand, are another story. Their interactions with the teacher and peers are very often negative, confrontational, and characterized by mutual hostility (Colvin & Sugai, 1989; Walker & Buckley, 1973). The disruptive effects of these interactions upon the learning and achievement of the acting-out child and, in many cases, that of his classmates are well-documented in the literature (Morgan & Jenson, 1988; Rhode, Jenson, & Reavis, 1992). It is nearly impossible for efficient instruction to occur under such conditions since teachers naturally require a certain level of appropriate student behavior before dispensing instruction. Further, the emotional reactions of adults to child behaviors that they find highly irritating or aversive are slow to subside and can condition teachers' instructional and management behavior toward acting-out children long after the specific behaviors in question have terminated.

As mentioned previously, because of the aversive nature of his behavior, the acting-out child systematically trains classmates and peers to either: (1) avoid social interactions with him; or (2) respond to his social initiations in a negative, controlling, or hostile fashion. Consequently, the acting-out child loses valuable opportunities to learn prosocial patterns of behavior from peers through mutually positive and reciprocal social exchanges with them. Acting-out students typically receive very low likability ratings from their teachers. They are also among the first to be referred out of the classroom and among the last to be reintegrated back into this setting (Hersh & Walker, 1983; Sarason & Doris, 1978).

In the classroom setting, positive teacher-student interactions can facilitate constructive learning processes. On the other hand, if such interactions are aversive and characterized by mutual hostility, little in the way of **constructive** learning may occur. Consequently, acting-out children face much higher risks of teacher rejection, school failure, and ultimately school dropout because of these factors. A national transition study found that children of this type, who are identified by schools as behavior disordered and socially maladjusted, have a 19% arrest rate while still in school. Within two years of leaving high school, this figure rises to 43% (Wagner, 1989).

· ***Rule Two*** .... *"Deviant as well as nondeviant behavior is learned."*

SOCIAL LEARNING FOUNDATIONS

Probably no parent or teacher would deliberately teach a child to act out, be disruptive, or engage in deviant behavior. Yet it is ironic that many parents and teachers inadvertently but systematically teach children to be aggressive, noncompliant, and generally irritating. This happens because the same principles that govern the learning and acquisition of appropriate behavior also control the acquisition of inappropriate behavior. Whether a child learns appropriate or inappropriate behavior depends largely upon the antecedent (or preexisting) conditions, setting events, and consequences that are associated with these two types of behavior.

The manner in which children are systematically taught to misbehave can be illustrated in a number of ways. For example, most parents and teachers communicate a general expectation to children that they should behave appropriately, follow rules, obey instructions, be responsive to adult influence and so forth. However, children very often receive no (or only limited) adult attention and approval for doing so. The number of positive consequences (e.g., spontaneous compliments, encouragement, social praise, privileges) that are received for behaving appropriately are even fewer. In such situations, if a child wants attention and feedback, he/she learns that it is more likely to be received for such things as **not** following rules, **not** obeying instructions, and **not** paying attention to the task at hand. Even though it is negative, the attention received for those behaviors is far superior to none at all, and is a very powerful motivating force in shaping and maintaining child behavior.

It would be desirable, and certainly much more convenient for adults, if children would learn to behave appropriately in the absence of positive attention and support for doing so. It is true that some children seem to receive only very small amounts of positive attention and feedback for their appropriate behavior and still manage to develop very constructive behavior patterns at home and school. However, such children are probably relatively rare.

Unfortunately, praising, debriefing, and providing positive feedback to children (and each other) do not seem to be "natural" activities for most adults. Plus as the pressures of daily living increase, the burdens upon adults and families have increased exponentially with even less time allocated for these very important parenting practices. The result is that adults are much more likely to ignore long periods of constructive, prosocial child behavior and to respond only to those child behaviors that we find irritating, disruptive, or inappropriate. Consequently, one can see how the adage "the squeaky wheel gets the oil" applies directly to the development of deviant behavior in children.

Whining is an example of a behavior that is systematically, although inadvertently, taught to children by parents and sometimes teachers. If a child has difficulty obtaining parental or teacher attention, he/she often learns that whining will produce an immediate response to his/her demand(s). Most adults find whining extremely irritating and generally respond quickly so as to terminate this behavior. Through this process, whining becomes established and mutually supported since the child is rewarded by adult attention and acquiescence to his/her demand(s), whereas the adult is rewarded by termination of the whining (Patterson, 1983).

Children are also taught to misbehave through a general lack of consistency by adults in their efforts at shaping and developing child behavior. This occurs when sometimes a child receives negative feedback and unpleasant consequences for engaging in a particular inappropriate behavior. Then at other times, the same child receives no consequences or feedback at all when engaging in the identical behavior. Consequently, he/she is taught that sometimes one "gets caught" for engaging in a certain deviant behavior and at other times no negative or unpleasant consequences are forthcoming. Thus, the child learns that occasionally and, sometimes frequently, it is possible to engage in deviant behavior and suffer no unpleasant consequences for this behavior. If the child finds the deviant behavior rewarding, this can be a very serious problem; one which causes the child to view parental discipline as a "lottery" and "play the odds."

Adults are inconsistent in their efforts at managing child behavior for different reasons. For example, sometimes adults have not completely made up their minds about whether a particular behavior is appropriate or inappropriate. Children are usually quick to sense such ambivalence and respond accordingly. At other times, adults may be too tired to consequate the child's behavior consistently, or it may be inconvenient to do so. Sometimes adults also have difficulty remembering how they have responded to a particular behavior in the past. Whatever the reason(s) for such lack of adult consistency in the management of child behavior, the resulting effects are uniformly the same and very often undesirable.

Children can also learn to misbehave because of differing behavioral standards held by the numerous social agents charged with managing their behavior. For example, one parent may be very strict and highly consistent in requiring a child to follow established rules, whereas the other parent may be much less strict and inconsistent in this respect. Thus, the child would learn that one parent maintains consistent behavioral standards while the other does not. The child's behavior in the presence of the two parents is likely to be markedly different with appropriate behavior displayed in the presence of the strict parent and inappropriate behavior displayed in the presence of the less strict and less consistent parent. This kind of child-rearing experience can teach a child to discriminate among social agents in terms of the types of behavior that will be tolerated, and to respond accordingly.

Doubtless, these situations are not the only ways in which children are inadvertently taught to misbehave and to break rules. However, they do illustrate how easy it is for children to learn patterns of misbehavior.

CLASSROOM APPLICATIONS

Children are systematically taught patterns of misbehavior by teachers in the same way they are taught by parents. In some respects, the problem is more acute with teachers than with parents because teachers are charged with the effective management and instruction of 20-30 children at any one time. Great demands are placed upon the teacher's time in this process with little attention available for individual children. Consequently, most teachers develop a set of classroom rules governing appropriate social and academic behavior and then communicate an expectation that all the students in the class should follow these rules. Unfortunately, because of the obvious time constraints involved, children who follow the rules, do their work, and don't create problems for the teacher are generally ignored, while those who act out and disrupt the classroom atmosphere receive a great deal of teacher attention which is usually negative and directed toward the child's inappropriate behavior. Such children put great pressure upon the management and instructional skills of classroom teachers.

Lack of teacher consistency in the management of child behavior is also a very serious problem in the school setting. Because of the sheer numbers involved, teachers find it extremely difficult to be consistent in the consequences they apply to children's appropriate and inappropriate classroom behaviors.

The problem of differing behavioral standards held by social agents who manage children's behavior is a relatively greater problem at school than at home. An elementary student may encounter up to seven or eight different teachers in an ordinary school day, all of whom probably have different behavioral standards and expectations in relation to the child's overall behavior. These standards and expectations can vary from teacher to teacher not only in their specific behavioral content but in their intensity or restrictiveness as well (Hersh & Walker, 1983; Walker & Rankin, 1983). Children in general, and acting-out children in particular, become very discriminating when it is apparent that their teachers hold different behavioral standards and enforce those standards differentially. Instead of learning a consistent, prosocial behavior pattern that is maintained across settings, some children learn to try to "get away with" whatever behaviors they believe the situation will bear (i.e., they engage in the discipline lottery game and playing the odds). The unfortunate result may be the acquisition of a consistent pattern of misbehavior that can permanently handicap a child's school adjustment.

Rule Three .... *"Observational learning explains the acquisition of much human behavior."*

SOCIAL LEARNING FOUNDATIONS

In the course of their development, children acquire a great deal of information through the simple process of observation. The capacities of children for observation and their sensitivity to what they observe are sometimes truly amazing. Through observation, children develop an understanding of how their environment works as well as an awareness of relationships existing among situations and between individuals within the environment.

Observation and the capacity to imitate what is observed is one vehicle through which children acquire new behavioral responses. For example, a young child will observe a sibling or parent performing a certain behavior and may attempt to reproduce that behavior. This process is called **modeling**, and is an attempt by the child to behaviorally reproduce through imitation what he/she has observed.

Usually a child's first attempts at imitating a new behavior are unskilled, relatively crude, and poorly developed. With practice, however, the child's skill level increases and the behavior in question comes to approximate more closely that of the model. This acquisition process is facilitated if the child receives positive feedback/consequences for attempting to imitate the behavior. If ignored or punished, the child may cease such attempts altogether, thus reducing the chances that the modeled behavior will be acquired.

Parents are well aware of the power of observation and modeling as methods through which children are educated and socialized. A number of behavioral responses and attitudes are purposefully transmitted from parents to children through this process. Unfortunately, the child is just as likely to imitate undesirable attitudes and behavior patterns as desirable ones. When parents give their children advice to the effect, "Do what I say, not what I do!" children are much more likely to imitate their parents' actual behavior than to follow their instructions to the contrary.

Children are also more likely to observe and imitate the behavior of individuals whom they regard as having power and/or high social status. Consequently, children are more likely to be influenced by their parents (at least in their younger years) than any other social agents with whom they have contact. Thus, parents' actual behavior as observed by the child and their expressed attitudes can have a profound effect upon the child's development.

Research has shown that children respond positively to symbolic models (in film) and will acquire new behavioral responses through this process (Bandura, 1969; O'Connor, 1969). Children acquire a great deal of information through viewing television, and often imitate the behavior of televised models. In recent years, substantial controversy has developed around the issue of whether children are influenced adversely by televised violence. There seems to be no clear cut agreement on this question at present; however, a large number of parents, educators, legislators, and policy makers remain concerned about this issue. The entertainment industry is under enormous pressure to attenuate its depiction of violent behavior and to regulate the images it puts forth through television and film.

Research has also shown that children learn by simply observing the behavior of others and by taking note of the **consequences** of that behavior. This is called **vicarious** learning. If a child observes a model receiving a positive consequence for engaging in a certain behavior, that behavior is more likely to be imitated by the child. If the model is observed being punished for engaging in a particular behavior, that behavior is not likely to be imitated by the observing child.

Modeling and vicarious learning operate for people of all ages, and these two processes explain the acquisition of much human behavior. In recent years, there has been an increasing awareness of how teaching methods based upon these processes can be used to develop complex skills and behavior patterns (e.g., acquiring friendships).

CLASSROOM APPLICATIONS

In the school setting, a child learns from the teacher and from other children through observational processes. Teachers make use of modeling techniques to teach certain academic and social skills. Teachers will often use verbal instructions to explain a skill to be learned, model the skill for the children, and then provide positive feedback and encouragement as the children attempt to master the skill. If used correctly, this can be a highly effective teaching strategy.

Children imitate each other's behavior in the classroom and acquire behavior patterns and novel social responses from each other. High status, popular children are more likely to be admired and imitated than low status children. Children who are perceived as having power and influence are also likely to be imitated by their peers (McConnell & Odom,

1986). Acting-out children, about a quarter of whom can be rated as popular by their peers depending upon the situation, frequently model deviant behavior patterns for their peers. Under the right conditions, this situation can contribute to a higher rate of deviant behavior in the classroom than may otherwise be the case.

Vicarious learning processes operate constantly in every classroom. The teacher's interactions with children are constantly being observed and evaluated by peers. The teacher's reaction to and interactions with students can powerfully influence how peers evaluate and regard individual students. The teacher's consistency in managing children's behavior and the consequences applied to both prosocial and inappropriate behaviors are carefully noted by students. The classroom behavior of children is thus powerfully affected by what they have learned through these observational processes.

Children in general, and acting-out children in particular, become very sensitive to the contingencies that exist in different settings through observational learning processes. Where contingencies differ markedly across settings, children's behavior is likely to reflect those differences and vary accordingly.

Children can learn to imitate prosocial, appropriate behavior, especially if positive consequences are provided for doing so. Some teachers will occasionally single out a child who is following classroom rules and praise him/her publicly in order to provide a model for the class. Some teachers will also use modeling procedures to consequate deviant behavior; that is, if a child is acting out or misbehaving, the teacher will select a child nearby and praise him/her aloud for following the rules. Thus, the correct behavior is modeled for the misbehaving child and it is learned that teacher attention will be received for appropriate rather than inappropriate behavior. Both of these techniques have proven effective in changing classroom behavior.

Traditionally, modeling and vicarious learning processes have been used primarily to explain how behavior is acquired. Increasingly, however, productive applications of these processes are being developed for the purpose of changing behavior from inappropriate to appropriate and for teaching complex academic and social skills (Bornstein & Kazdin, 1985; Kauffman, 1993; Kazdin, 1985). Their demonstrated effectiveness will no doubt lead to the development of additional applications in the future.

Rule Four . . . . *"A behavior followed closely in time by a rewarding consequence will tend to occur more often in the future."*

SOCIAL LEARNING FOUNDATIONS

This principle is referred to as **reinforcement**. It means that if a consequence which the child finds rewarding immediately follows a particular behavior, the child is more likely to engage in that behavior in the future in order to obtain the reward. This principle is fundamental to the way all children learn (Engelmann & Carnine, 1982; Skinner, 1953).

From birth onward, children learn to respond in ways that produce rewarding consequences from the environment. For example, an infant quickly learns that crying is usually followed by maternal attention accompanied by efforts to identify the cause of the crying. The mother's efforts to change the condition(s) (e.g., pain, hunger, trauma, fear, etc.) causing the crying gradually teaches the child that crying is an instrumental response which will usually prompt attention from adults, expressions of concern, and changes designed to eliminate the reason for the crying. Such consequences are highly rewarding to most children and increase the chances that crying will occur again in the future under similar circumstances.

There is almost a limitless array of consequences that can be considered rewarding. However, what is rewarding for one child may not necessarily be rewarding for another. Some events that are commonly assumed to be rewarding for most children are hugs, smiles, kisses, expressions of approval, attention, compliments, free time, sympathy, money, toys, games, candy, and food in general. If a child is willing to work hard to earn a given reward, that may be a good indication of whether it is rewarding for him/her.

Activities can be either rewarding or nonrewarding. People sample a very large number of activities over the course of their lives. Some of these activities are found to be rewarding and others are not (i.e., they are boring or actually aversive). As a general rule, people tend to avoid those activities they find unrewarding and to spend time in those activities they enjoy and do find rewarding. How such preferences develop is a complex and not well understood process. Their formation is probably influenced by a host of genetic, biological, psychological, and environmental factors. The reasons why someone finds an activity or event rewarding are not really important in explaining human behavior. The important point to remember is that people usually behave in ways designed to maximize their chances of obtaining, receiving, or engaging in consequences they find rewarding and to avoid situations that may lead to or prompt the occurrence of punishing consequences.

CLASSROOM APPLICATIONS

The principle of reinforcement explains much of the classroom behavior of the acting-out child and his peers. Perhaps the most powerful rewarding consequence available to all the children in most classroom situations is teacher attention; however, attention from peers also represents a very powerful source of reinforcement. At any given time in a typical classroom, 20-30 children are simultaneously competing for the teacher's attention. Some are more successful than others in this process. For example, children with deficient academic skills require larger amounts of the teacher's time and attention than do their more academically skilled classmates. They are highly dependent upon the teacher for encouragement, feedback, and reassurance in the completion of tasks and thereby consume large amounts of teacher attention.

However, the acting-out child far and away consumes the largest amount of the teacher's time and attention. As noted in Chapter 2, huge amounts of the teacher's time are devoted to the task of simply managing the acting-out child's classroom behavior in often vain attempts to keep it within normal limits. Acting-out children learn to dominate the teacher's time and are very skilled in coercing attention, even when the teacher does not have the energy, time, or willingness to give him attention.

Interestingly, acting-out students also tend to have higher than normal rates of **nonaversive** interactions with the teacher around the issue of assignments and instructions for completing them. That is, because they tend to not be fully engaged in the instructional-learning process and often do not pay careful attention when instructions and directions for assignments are given, acting-out children require clarifications and additional elaborations from the teacher in order to complete the assignment. Even though these interactions are nonconfrontational and generally range from neutral to positive in quality, they are an unnecessary and duplicative expenditure of the teacher's time, and create resentment over the long term.

It is apparent that acting-out children have learned a variety of methods for obtaining teacher attention whether the teacher wishes to give such attention or not. Unfortunately, most of the methods such children use are maladaptive and aversive to the teacher and/or peers. The attention received in this process, though usually negative and designed to suppress their behavior, is at least partially instrumental in strengthening it, thus making it more likely that such behaviors will be exhibited by acting-out children again in the future.

Children who do not generally act out, on the other hand, learn to engage in appropriate behavior for long periods of time and receive only minimal amounts of the teacher's attention and time. As mentioned previously, there are a number of theories, none of them validated, to explain why some children learn this behavior pattern and others do not. Two of the attributes that teachers value most in students are **independence** and **self-control/self-management**. The ability to engage in sustained effort and concentration, without teacher assistance and for long periods of time, reflects both of these values.

Even though it is not known why some children are able to develop this behavior pattern and others are not, it is clear that teacher attention is a highly rewarding consequence for both acting-out children and their peers. Because of its potency, teacher attention can be a valuable tool in changing the acting-out child's behavior from inappropriate to appropriate. Through a gradual process, the acting-out child can be taught that his appropriate behavior is more likely to produce positive teacher attention than is inappropriate behavior. This is no easy task, and at least initially it may be necessary to supplement this teaching process with more powerful intervention procedures in order to change the long established behavior pattern. Further, the systematic pairing of teacher attention with powerful rewards (e.g., free time, special privileges, home rewards earned at school) can enhance the effective reward potential of teacher attention. Because of its rewarding qualities and its availability, teacher attention can be one of the most effective tools at the teacher's disposal for changing the acting-out child's behavior in preferred directions.

Rule Five .... *"A previously rewarded behavior that is no longer rewarded will eventually extinguish."*

SOCIAL LEARNING FOUNDATIONS

The process of withholding rewards for a previously rewarded behavior is referred to as "placing the behavior on **extinction**." If rewards are consistently withheld for the behavior for a sufficient period of time, the behavior will decrease in frequency and may cease altogether. When the behavior no longer occurs, extinction is said to have occurred.

A parent withholding attention from a small child's pestering is an example of placing a behavior on the path to extinction.

Laboratory studies have shown extinction to be an effective technique for reducing a variety of behavioral responses. In controlled settings, such as a laboratory, it is a fairly simple task to ensure that a response is no longer rewarded, thus maximizing the effectiveness of extinction. However, in real world settings such as the home and classroom, it's much more difficult to control all the sources of reinforcement for a particular behavior, especially if attention from others is the primary rewarding consequence.

Careful studies of the extinction process have shown that there are characteristic patterns of responding during extinction (Ferster & Skinner, 1957). When the behavior is first placed on extinction, there is usually an **increase** in its frequency, magnitude, or intensity followed by a gradual and sometimes irregular decline prior to eventual cessation. The initial increase in the behavior results from attempts to produce a reward that is no longer forthcoming. Eventually, it is learned that the behavior will not be rewarded and it ceases to occur.

If the pressures that are applied to produce the reward are occasionally successful in the early stages of extinction, then extinction procedures will be unsuccessful in reducing the behavior. In fact, this could result in the behavior in question being maintained at higher levels of intensity, magnitude, or frequency for a period of time. Consequently, if extinction is applied incorrectly, it may produce the **opposite** effect from that intended.

CLASSROOM APPLICATIONS

If applied to the right behaviors and used correctly, extinction can be a practical behavior management tool for the classroom teacher. Extinction can be used to reduce certain "attention getting" behaviors that may be minimally disruptive to the classroom setting. Extinction, in the form of ignoring, can be applied successfully to such "teacher irritant" child behaviors as dawdling, pencil tapping, asking irrelevant and unnecessary questions, and minor rule breaking. If the child engages in these behaviors primarily to irritate the teacher and to get attention, then systematically ignoring these behaviors may be quite effective in reducing their rates of occurrence.

While consulting to the school program of a residential and day treatment center for severely disturbed children and youth, the author followed a group of 12 middle school students as they rotated through five different teachers during the day. Several members of this group had a tendency to challenge and confront their teachers through the use of provocative comments and gestures. The first two teachers of the school day responded to each and every comment or gesture made, attempted to control and/or punish each one, and became quite irritated at the students' continuing high rates of provocative behavior. When the student group entered the classroom of the third teacher, there was no such evidence of provocative comments or gestures and the students immediately began to work on their assigned tasks. Further, they generally raised their hands when they wanted assistance. It turns out that through prior repeated attempts to provoke this teacher, the students had learned they were unable to do so; that is, she had effectively extinguished their provocative comments and gestures through selective ignoring of them and consistent maintenance of a calm, unperturbed demeanor.

It is impossible to determine in advance how long it will take for a given behavior to extinguish for a particular child. If a decision to use extinction is made, the teacher should be prepared to stick with the technique until it has proven successful. The teacher should also be reasonably confident that all sources of reward for the behavior to be extinguished can be controlled effectively and that it is feasible to consistently ignore the behavior. If not, the teacher's use of extinction will be an exercise in futility.

There are certain classroom behaviors for which extinction is **not** appropriate. For example, high magnitude behaviors such as tantrums, fighting, and teacher defiance are not, as would be expected, appreciably affected by extinction procedures applied in the classroom setting. These behaviors usually occur at a relatively low frequency, but at extremely high levels of intensity. They are highly disruptive of the classroom atmosphere, usually cannot be tolerated, and require the application of much more powerful procedures than simple ignoring by the teacher and/or peers. Other classroom behaviors such as talking out, being out of seat, not completing assignments, noncompliance, and off-task behavior also generally require procedures other than simple extinction. As a general rule, extinction should be applied only to those inappropriate behaviors that are minimally disruptive to the classroom atmosphere and that are maintained primarily by teacher attention.

Rule Six .... *"A behavior followed closely in time by a punishing consequence will tend to occur less often in the future, particularly in the presence of the punishing agent."*

SOCIAL LEARNING FOUNDATIONS

Punishment refers to the application of an aversive consequence to a specific child behavior. If the aversive consequence suppresses the behavior to which it is applied, it can be classified as a punishing consequence. Laboratory studies have shown that punishment procedures, if powerful enough, can produce almost a complete suppression of behavioral responses (Azrin & Holz, 1966).

The use of punishment in controlling human behavior has been a highly controversial issue in our society and continues to be. Arguments about punishment have ranged from the use of verbal reprimands and spanking to encourage children to behave to whether capital punishment reduces the incidence of violent crimes. Education professionals and others alike seem to be divided over the issue of punishment and are very passionate in their views on the matter.

A number of moral and ethical arguments have been developed against the use of punishment. Further, it has been suggested that punishment only teaches a child to suppress behavior in the presence of the punishing agent and not at other times (Repp & Singh, 1990). Both rhetorical and empirical resolutions to this fundamental question have proved to be elusive.

If used in isolation as a behavior change technique, punishment is likely to be ineffective, especially if the behavior being punished continues to be reinforced by other social agents in the same setting or by social agents in different settings. If all sources of reinforcement for the punished behavior are controlled, and an incompatible appropriate behavior is reinforced while punishment is applied to the inappropriate behavior, then punishment as a behavior change technique is likely to be much more effective. In managing child behavior, it is sometimes difficult to achieve this goal.

Even though punishment can be effective in changing behavior under certain conditions, a number of difficult questions remain unresolved as to the generality of its effects and whether side effects are associated with its use. Continuing research on the use of mild punishment procedures, in combination with positive behavior management techniques, within applied settings such as classrooms and playgrounds will provide additional information on these questions in the future.

CLASSROOM APPLICATIONS

The role of punishment in the classroom and its use generally has produced enormous controversy in recent years. Americans are regarded as a highly punitive society and are among the world's leaders in the rate of incarcerating our citizens. Rage, aggression, and violence have become rampant in our society within the past two decades, and call for extreme measures to control these social forces. Yet, we see examples daily of how punishment is used inappropriately and leads to unfortunate consequences such as child abuse and trauma.

A number of schools in this country use corporal punishment (i.e., spanking, paddling) as one means of controlling child behavior. Statutes allowing for corporal punishment have been a part of the legal code for a long time. The legal foundation for the use of corporal punishment in schools has been reaffirmed by the United States Supreme Court on several occasions in the face of challenges to its use. However, to date, 24 states have outlawed corporal punishment and another ten states are considering doing so. In the author's view, this is a very positive development and recognizes the inappropriateness of using corporal punishment of any kind on students in school.

Given what is known about the management and control of classroom behavior, it does not appear that the use of corporal punishment can be justified by school personnel as a method for either controlling or reducing child behavior. Further, corporal punishment in the forms of spanking and paddling are easily abused and can result in inadvertent injury and/or psychological trauma, especially to young children. Long-term, traumatic emotional effects are very likely to occur from the consistent use of corporal punishment, and they are **very** difficult to reverse through counseling, psychotherapy, or other means.

Techniques such as timeout, loss of privileges, and temporary suspension are equally as effective as corporal punishment in controlling child behavior. Further, the risks associated with corporal punishment usually do not occur with the use of these techniques. The Council for Children with Behavior Disorders contributed an exemplary set of guidelines governing the use of behavior reduction strategies for children with behavior disorders (*Journal of Behavioral Disorders*, 1990). The reader is urged to consult this position paper for information on best practice standards and guidelines in the use of these procedures.

One of the most heavily used punishing consequences employed by teachers to control child behavior is the verbal reprimand. Unfortunately, reprimands only control the behavior of some children and not others; others argue that public reprimands can damage children's self-esteem and pride in themselves. One study found that the teacher's use of "sit down" commands actually **increased** rather than decreased the number of times children were out of their seats (Madsen, Becker, Thomas, Koser, & Plager, 1968). Occasionally, reprimands will produce a short-term reduction in an inappropriate behavior but the teacher attention received during this process may actually strengthen the behavior over the long term. Thus, the battle may be won but ultimately the war is lost. As a general rule, reprimands should be avoided as a technique for controlling classroom behavior.

There is no substitute for good teaching methods, explicit classroom rules, implementing what we know about good schooling and teaching practices, and a positive behavior management system to reduce the necessity for using punishment procedures in the classroom. From time to time, students will be encountered who cannot accommodate the schooling process or who represent a danger to teachers, peers, and/or themselves. In such cases, school safety and security become very legitimate prerogatives of the school system, and the individual rights of these students may have to be compromised to insure school safety.

In other cases, some very deviant children may require the use of mild punishment procedures for a period of time in order for their behavior to be controlled and managed effectively. However, such procedures should be used only in conjunction with a positive reinforcement system. Two forms of mild punishment that have been used effectively in classroom settings include **timeout** and **cost contingency** (i.e., a **response cost**). These two techniques will be defined and their classroom and playground applications illustrated in later chapters.

Rule Seven . . . . *"Behavior is controlled by antecedent events (conditions that precede it) and by consequent events (conditions that follow it)."*

SOCIAL LEARNING FOUNDATIONS

Human behavior is controlled by events and conditions that precede it as well as by events and conditions that follow it. Controlling events and conditions that precede behavior are called **antecedents**, while those that follow it are called **consequences** (see Figure 3.1).

Figure 3.1
Relationship of Antecedents and Consequences to Behavior

Antecedent ——————— Behavior ——————— Consequent Events
Events and   and Conditions
Conditions   (strengthen or weaken)

Antecedent events and conditions either set the stage for behavior to occur or actually prompt its occurrence. Antecedents are sometimes called "setting events" because they set the occasion for behavior to occur. Consequences follow the behavior and determine whether it is strengthened or weakened.

The controlling relationship that exists between antecedents and subsequent behavior is illustrated in the following examples. A teacher's classroom rules governing appropriate behavior are vaguely defined; consequently, child behavior is unpredictable and often out of control. Two children frequently argue over who gets to play with a favorite toy; the presence of the toy leads to squabbling, bickering, and sometimes fighting. A preschool child falls down and skins his arm at nursery school, but expresses only mild discomfort; however, when his mother picks him up about 30 minutes later, he bursts into tears and gives a long account of how badly he hurt himself on the playground. A mother and father usually have violent arguments around dinner time; their children become upset and begin to show visible signs of anxiety as the dinner hour approaches.

The consequences to child behavior that have been previously supplied by adults in these examples have no doubt contributed to the controlling relationship that exists between the antecedent stimuli and child behavior. This process is known as the stimulus **control** of behavior (Horner, Dunlap, & Koegel, 1988; Patterson, 1974). Examples of how the stimulus control works to determine future behavior are provided following.

If classroom rules are not clearly specified and child behavior is frequently disruptive and out of control, the teacher may spend more time in attempting to manage the class than in instructing the children. Plus the teacher attention dispensed during this process may strengthen the children's inappropriate behavior and make it more likely that such misbehavior will occur in the future. In the case of the two children arguing over a favorite toy, their squabbling, bickering, and fighting will often require parental intervention and again the attention received makes it more likely that another argument will occur in the near future. The preschool child who cries over a minor injury received 30 minutes before has learned that he can obtain sympathy, expressions of concern, and maternal attention by crying and complaining of aches, pains, and injury. Finally, when children are emotionally upset and anxious about their parents' arguing, their behavior may become aberrant or unusual, thus prompting the attention and concern of one or both parents following the argument. The result may be to actually strengthen the children's aberrant or unusual behavior.

Antecedents and consequences are equally powerful in the control they exert over behavior. However, we are often much more concerned with the consequences supplied to behavior than we are with the situations that actually prompt its occurrence and determine its forum. If we were more sensitive to such situations and conditions, it would be possible to **prevent** the occurrence of inappropriate or undesirable behaviors in many instances by the prior manipulation of key setting events.

CLASSROOM APPLICATIONS

The classroom teacher is the most powerful influence in any classroom. One reason for this is that the teacher has such direct control of the antecedents and consequences that precede and follow child behavior occurring during the processes of teaching and managing the classroom.

Teachers generally engage in predictable types of behavior in relation to managing antecedents and consequences. That is, teachers arrange situations and conditions in the classroom that lead to both appropriate and inappropriate child behavior. Similarly, teachers supply positive consequences to appropriate child behavior and negative consequences to inappropriate child behavior.

Unfortunately, many teachers inadvertently arrange classroom conditions that lead to inappropriate child behavior, without recognizing that their own behavior is indirectly responsible for the undesirable behavior of the children. For example, a situation common to all classrooms concerns getting the attention of the class before giving instructions for an assignment or activity. To facilitate the ability of all students to perform the assignment or activity correctly, it is necessary that each student have a clear understanding of the accompanying instructions. Thus it is important that the teacher have the attention of the entire class before giving instructions. In actual practice, however, many teachers give instructions with only a portion of the class attending to them. This can lead to yelling in anger, shouting over the noise level of the class, and general frustration for teachers and students alike. Further, the teacher may find himself/herself repeating instructions over and over to those students who were not attending.

As mentioned previously, teachers spend a great deal of time supplying negative consequences to children's inappropriate behavior. In many cases, teachers have to respond this way in order to cope with deviant child behavior that has been prompted by inappropriate antecedent conditions. However, it would be desirable and more productive if teachers could spend a greater portion of their time supplying consequences to **appropriate** child behavior in the classroom. But in order to do this, it would be necessary to simultaneously rearrange antecedent conditions so that situations leading to inappropriate behavior are reduced to the maximum extent possible.

An analytical process exists, called the *Functional Analysis of Behavior*, for functionally analyzing the roles or influences that antecedents and consequences play in determining the occurrence of child behavior (O'Neill, Horner, Albin, Storey, & Sprague, 1990). An understanding of this approach can be extremely valuable to the teacher in gaining an improved sense of mastery over the process of teaching and managing children in the context of schooling. This process and methods for using it will be reviewed in Chapter 4.

Rule Eight . . . . *"Behavior can be changed either by altering or controlling antecedent events and conditions and/or by manipulating consequences."*

SOCIAL LEARNING FOUNDATIONS

The great majority of studies concerned with changing child behavior have focused on manipulating consequences that follow behavior. Relatively few studies have systematically investigated methods for altering and controlling antecedent conditions so as to permanently change behavior. As a general rule, in the process of changing behavior, one should examine antecedent variables **first** as a means of possibly changing the behavior in question before resorting to the manipulation of consequences.

If it is discovered that inappropriate child behavior is a function of a certain antecedent condition or event, then the teacher may be able to simply rearrange the antecedent(s) in order to change the behavior. There are several advantages to this approach. For example, if altering an antecedent does change child behavior, the behavior change is likely to be **permanent** as long as the changed antecedent condition(s) remain in effect. Further, once the change has been made, the teacher no longer has to worry about it; that is, the personal response cost to the teacher required to change the child's behavior can be extremely low when antecedents are manipulated.

If there are no antecedent condition(s) that can be changed, then one should consider manipulating the consequences in order to change the behavior. There are several types of consequences that can be manipulated. For example, rewarding consequences (e.g., teacher praise, privileges, free time, etc.) can be used to motivate a child and to increase performance. Similarly, extinction procedures (i.e., ignoring) and mild punishment (e.g., timeout, loss of privileges) can be used to decrease inappropriate behavior. Rewarding and punishing consequences can also be applied simultaneously to increase appropriate behavior at the same time that inappropriate behavior is being decreased.

In order for consequences to be effective in changing behavior, they must be applied consistently. It is sometimes difficult for adults to apply such consequences over a long period of time. Therefore, if one has a choice of rearranging antecedent(s) or of manipulating consequences in order to change behavior, a focus on the antecedent(s) should be the preferred method unless special circumstances make it infeasible.

CLASSROOM APPLICATIONS

If a child is not learning and achieving in school, it is up to the school system to determine why and to arrange conditions that will facilitate that child's learning. There are a number of antecedents that could be examined in the task of finding the cause of the child's inability to learn.

For example, one should determine whether the academic performance expectations for the child are consistent with her/his intellectual potential. Examinations should be given to check for sensory deficits that could account for the learning failure (e.g., hearing and/or visual problems). The possibility of a central nervous system injury or neurological problems should also be considered as an explanatory variable, as well as the child's general health status. Increasingly, children and youth are coming to school unable to consume instruction because of the traumatic social conditions they are exposed to at home and outside the school setting. These conditions should be taken into consideration in addition to the child's intellectual potential. Finally, instructional formats and assignment levels should be evaluated carefully in terms of their appropriateness for the child. A number of different instructional formats, sequences, and programs could be tried out to see if they have an effect on reducing the learning deficit.

If all of these antecedent variables prove to be unrelated to the child's inability to learn, then the effect of consequences following the behavior could be investigated. It could be, for example, that the child is not receiving the necessary feedback regarding his/her performance and that the child's attempts at learning are inadvertently being placed on extinction. The problem could be a motivational one. Thus, teacher praise in combination with a formal school or home reinforcement system may be required to motivate the child to achieve.

In some cases, it may be necessary to manipulate both antecedent(s) and consequences in order to effectively remediate a behavioral or learning problem. **Simultaneous manipulation of antecedent(s) and consequences is probably the most powerful and effective method available for changing behavior.** A simple example of the manipulation of both an antecedent and consequences would be in the case where a teacher carefully defines classroom rules and then allows children to accumulate minutes of free time for following them.

Rule Nine . . . . "*A combination of reinforcement for appropriate behavior and mild punishment for inappropriate behavior will produce more rapid and substantial changes in behavior than either one alone.*"

SOCIAL LEARNING FOUNDATIONS

Many intervention programs use either reinforcement alone or punishment alone in order to change and/or control child behavior. It is relatively unusual, but sometimes desirable, for reinforcement and punishment procedures to be used in combination (Morgan & Jenson, 1988; Walker, Hops, & Fiegenbaum, 1976). As noted previously, a combination of rewarding and punishing techniques, applied simultaneously, appears to be much more powerful than either one applied in isolation (Repp & Singh, 1990; Walker & Buckley, 1972; Walker, Hops, & Greenwood, 1981).

If a child's behavior is in the normal range or is only minimally disruptive, a reinforcement system alone can be used successfully to change his/her behavior. When used correctly, this process is called **differential positive reinforcement**. This means that the rewarding consequence is applied differentially; that is, if the child is behaving appropriately and following the rules, he/she is reinforced, while reinforcement is withheld when the child is not behaving appropriately or following the rules. This procedure gradually teaches the child to discriminate between appropriate and inappropriate behavior and motivates him/her to behave appropriately. A number of studies reported in the literature have manipulated positive teacher attention to increase the study habits and appropriate classroom behavior of minimally disruptive children. However, it should be noted that the more severe the child's behavior problems are, the less likely it is that teacher praise or attention alone will be effective in reducing them.

Punishment procedures have been traditionally applied, in isolation, in order to control the more disruptive forms of child behavior (e.g., hitting, yelling, parent or teacher defiance, inappropriate language, fighting, tantrums, and so forth). The most popular punishment technique used to control such behavior is a brief timeout (Patterson & White, 1969; Patterson, 1983). Almost all parents, at one time or another, have sent children to their rooms for misbehaving. This is called timeout, since the child must spend a portion of **time out** from ongoing activities. If the activities from which the child is excluded are rewarding to him/her, then timeout can be a very effective technique, especially in the home setting.

Another popular form of punishment is loss of privileges for misbehaving. Going to bed without dinner and loss of television time are examples of this form of punishment. As mentioned previously, punishment is most effective if used in conjunction with a positive reinforcement system. However, the types of punishment described have proven effective in controlling child behavior when applied in isolation, since they involve either removal from a reinforcing situation or loss of privileges that the child finds rewarding.

One clear finding seems to be emerging from research on the use of positive reinforcement and punishment techniques in applied settings. That is, rewarding and punishing techniques applied in combination generally produce an immediate and dramatic change in behavior that usually exceeds that which would be produced by either one in isolation (Pfiffner & O'Leary, 1987; Walker, Hops, & Fiegenbaum, 1976). Further, the more severe and disruptive a child's behavior, the more likely it is that some combination of reinforcement and punishment strategies will be necessary to effectively change the child's overall behavior (Repp & Singh, 1990).

CLASSROOM APPLICATIONS

The most frequently used combinations of rewarding and punishing techniques in classroom settings are positive social or token reinforcement (i.e., points earned for appropriate behavior and exchanged for back-up rewards) applied in conjunction with either timeout or a cost contingency (i.e., a response cost, or the loss of earned points for engaging in maladaptive behavior). In applications of this type, a number of rules for appropriate behavior are identified for the child and then he/she is told that teacher praise and points will be earned for following them. Conversely, inappropriate and disruptive classroom behaviors are also identified and the child is informed that earned points will be subtracted for engaging in these behaviors. If timeout is being used, the specific behaviors resulting in timeout are labeled for the child.

Walker, Hops, and Fiegenbaum (1976) investigated the effectiveness of different combinations of teacher praise, token reinforcement (points), and cost contingency (loss of earned points) in changing the classroom behavior of acting-out children within an experimental classroom. Teacher praise alone had a minimal effect in increasing the appropriate behavior for four of the five children in the study. One child's behavior was completely unaffected by teacher praise. When a token system was added to teacher praise, there was a moderate increase in the appropriate behavior of all five children (from approximately 47% to 79%). When cost contingency (subtraction of earned points for inappropriate behavior) was added to teacher praise and the token reinforcement, the appropriate behavior level of all five children showed an immediate increase. With cost contingency in effect, the children's appropriate behavior averaged 95%. This study demonstrated that a combination of teacher praise, token reinforcement, and the cost contingency was more effective than either teacher praise alone or teacher praise and token reinforcement in combination.

In a later study, Walker, Hops, Greenwood, Todd, and Garrett (1977) evaluated the effects of the same three intervention techniques upon the interactive behavior of socially aggressive children. Six children with extremely high rates of negative social interactions with their classmates served as subjects in the study, and were referred to an experimental classroom for treatment.

To begin with, the study's authors evaluated the effects of teacher praise alone upon the children's positive social interactions with each other. When the teacher praised the children for interacting positively with each other, there was a **decrease** in their rate of positive interactions! On the first day with teacher praise, the children's percentage of total positive interactions dropped from approximately 80% to 40%! When a token system was later added to teacher praise, there was an initial increase in the children's positive interactive behavior. However, over a five-day period, the children's interactive behavior gradually returned to pre-treatment levels.

Only when a cost contingency was added to teacher praise and the token reinforcement was the children's negative interactive behavior controlled effectively. The children were told that they could earn three points for each positive interaction with peer(s); however, if they engaged in any negative social behavior within an interaction, they would lose six of the points they had already earned. With the cost contingency in effect, the children's negative interactions were reduced to near zero levels. Their percentage of interactions that were positive averaged 95% and above during this period.

These two studies clearly demonstrate that a combination of rewarding and punishing techniques can be extremely effective in changing the behavior of moderately to severely disruptive children. Similar results have been reported by others (see Axelrod, 1990). In the author's opinion, the children in the second study (Walker et al., 1977) were substantially more severely disruptive than those in the first. It is interesting that while teacher praise was minimally effective with the acting-out children in the first study, it caused the socially aggressive children's appropriate interaction levels to actually decrease! This may be, in part, a result of the long history of hostile interactions that such children have had with adults; that is, they are so used to receiving negative reprimands and criticisms from adults that praise from adults is, at least initially, an aversive consequence for them. Other studies reported in the literature have also shown that some disruptive children are unresponsive to adult praise (Thomas, Becker, & Armstrong, 1968).

It would have been impossible to effectively change the behavior of either group of children without a combination of rewarding and punishing consequences. It appears that the more deviant a child is, the more likely it is that such a combination will be necessary to effectively change his/her behavior.

Rule Ten . . . . *"Peer relations illustrate the Golden Rule:*
You reap what you sow!"

SOCIAL LEARNING FOUNDATIONS

The Golden Rule states that you should "do unto others as you would have them do unto you." Fortunately, most children follow this rule in their approach to peer relations. For example, observational studies of the social interactive behavior of normal children within free-play settings (e.g., the playground) indicate that it is overwhelmingly positive. Studies on this question by the author and his colleagues reveal that the social behavior of representative children and their peers during recess is consistently positive over 90% of the time (Walker, 1986; Walker, Hops, & Greenwood, 1981; Walker, Shinn, O'Neill, & Ramsey, 1987). That is to say, all other things being equal, if a child is positive, friendly, helpful, and cooperative with peers, they will reciprocate and respond in kind. Thus, positive behavior invested in peer group relations will generally result in positive behavior received from them (i.e., "you reap what you sow").

Unfortunately, the reverse is true as well. If a child is negative, demanding, aggressive, controlling, or even just simply unskilled in peer relations, the risks of neglect and rejection by peers are extremely high with the resulting consequences of social avoidance and punishment as well as exclusion from peer-controlled activities. As with positive social behavior, peers will respond in kind to behavior they perceive as negative or maladaptive and which they view as socially unacceptable.

In peer relations, social behavior that is seen as aggressive or dishonest is particularly objectionable and is very likely to lead to peer rejection (Horton, Walker, & Rankin, 1986). Aversive social behavior of this type is usually matched blow for blow by the actions of peers toward the child who initiates such behavior. Thus, the ancient Code of Hammurabi, which states, "an eye for an eye and a tooth for a tooth," is perfectly reflected in peer relations.

In an ongoing longitudinal study of antisocial and at-risk middle school boys, the author and his colleagues found that the negative social behavior these students displayed in their peer-related social initiations was matched perfectly by the negative social initiations of their peers directed toward them (Shinn, Ramsey, Walker, Stieber, & O'Neill, 1987). Simply put, if one is positive with others, they will be positive in return; if one is negative with others, they will be negative in return.

This general rule is not limited to social relations among children; it applies to adults as well.

As with every rule, however, there are qualifications and exceptions to consider. For example, it would be well if the story of behavioral reciprocity in peer relations ended here. However, children who display either acting-out or **aggressive** behavior patterns in their peer relations can reap a bitter harvest of punishment, bias, hostility, and victimization (Patterson, 1983; Patterson & Reid, 1970; Strain & Shores, 1977). As reviewed by Hollinger (1987), there is a substantial body of evidence to indicate that: (1) neutral social behavior from such children is viewed negatively by peers while the **same** behavior from their peers is interpreted positively; (2) hostile, manipulative intentions are often attributed to such children by their peers; and (3) the negative reputations they develop can persist among peers for long periods of time and maintain in the face of dramatic, positive changes in the social behavior of such children. Further, peers are often tolerant of bossy or controlling behavior from popular children but react viscerally to such behavior from children they perceive as aggressive and/or disruptive.

These findings are strongly supported by empirical studies of the dynamics of peer relations, and they are very bad news for acting-out children. Both longitudinal and cross-sectional studies strongly target impaired peer relations, evidenced early in children's school career, as an important predictor of a host of long-term adjustment problems (i.e., low self-esteem, school failure and dropout, delinquency, bad conduct discharges from the military, vocational adjustment problems, appearance on community psychiatric registers in adulthood, and even higher hospitalization and mortality rates) (Parker & Asher, 1987).

CLASSROOM (AND PLAYGROUND) APPLICATIONS

The nature and quality of a child's peer relations should be a cause of great concern for educators. Aside from the ominous developmental implications of impaired peer relations, social exchanges with peers and participation in peer-controlled activities are very important vehicles for socialization and for the development of social competence. Mastery of the essential social skills involved in relating to others, in turn, is associated with success in academic, behavioral, and vocational domains (McConnell & Odom, 1986). Although schools are generally held accountable primarily for students' academic performance and achievement, the development of social competence is so important that, in the author's view, it should also be a **major** goal of the schooling process.

In order for peer-related social adjustment to be maximally effective, the social behavior of children with their peers should be positive, cooperative, and reciprocal. Problems arise when children's behavior falls outside the normal range of peer expectations on one or more of these dimensions. Behavioral reciprocity is an especially important quality in peer relations. Eventually, peers become resentful of and avoid contact with children who: (1) use coercive tactics to join ongoing peer group activities rather than waiting their turn; (2) talk more than they listen; (3) initiate more than they are initiated to; and (4) do not respond, or respond inappropriately, when initiated to. Achieving a reasonable balance on these dimensions is extremely important to the quality of one's peer relations.

In the author's work with preschool children in the three to five year age range, he and his colleagues have conducted free-play observations of the social behavior of over 400 children across multiple school years. These observations clearly documented the highly reciprocal nature of social interactions among preschool children (Greenwood, Walker, Todd, & Hops, 1979). The authors created a "sociability" ratio to assess behavioral reciprocity by dividing the number of social initiations to others by the number of social initiations made to the target child by peers. This ratio reflects the equilibrium or balance between "social bids" made and received. Ideally, this ratio would be 1.00 and reflect perfect reciprocity between the two. Across our sample of preschool children (N = 457), this is exactly what we found. The average sociability ratio for the children in our sample was 1.03 with a standard deviation of .28. Individual sociability ratios ranged from a low of .18 to a high of 2.09. Ratios below 1.00 indicate the child's peers initiate to him/her more frequently; ratios above 1.00 indicate the reverse.

Because of their highly aversive behavior, acting-out children find themselves initiating to peers more than peers initiate to them. Often acting-out children have to make a number of social bids in order to get a "taker" from among their peers. Thus, unreciprocated social bids are a major problem in the peer relations of acting-out children.

Correcting this problem involves a relatively easy solution. First, the acting-out child needs to be directly taught, using social skills training and tutoring procedures, the key social skills necessary for initiating and responding to peers (see Figure 3.2). Then he needs to be coached and debriefed on the playground as he uses these new skills. And finally, peers need to be enlisted to assist him in using the skills properly. To make this work, the acting-out child should be given the opportunity to earn praise, feedback, **and** points for using the skills

Figure 3.2
Social Skills and Competencies Required in Successful Peer Relations

- Dispense and receive positive reinforcements to/from others (e.g., praise, affection, compliments)
- Use "low risk" tactics for entering ongoing peer group activities
  - Hover
  - Wait for invitations
  - Avoid disagreements, talking about self, stating feelings, or asking informational questions of those involved in the activity
- Use appropriate social initiations likely to be accepted by peers
  - Initiate during free time as opposed to scheduled work time
  - Be of assistance to others
  - Volunteer
  - Avoid demanding or coercive initiating responses
- Display high rates of positive social behavior toward peers
  - Provide helpful suggestions, give attention and approval, be affectionate to and supportive of peers
- Possess a thorough knowledge of how to make friends
- Possess good communication skills
  - Assume perspective of interacting partner
- Exhibit high levels of academic and/or athletic competence
- Possess specialized or unusual skills/attributes that are valued by peers
  - Make others laugh/have a sense of humor
- Engage in low levels of task-inappropriate behavior
  - Avoid getting in trouble with the teacher

appropriately and for cooperating with peers. If he achieves the daily point total required, he earns a **group activity** reward that is shared with the entire class. The effect of this intervention is usually to dramatically change the nature and quality of peer interactions for the better. As a result, the acting-out child learns new skills, peer relations become more positive, and the attitudes of both parties usually improve.

There are four essentials for improving peer relations in this manner. First, the target child must be directly taught the key skills that support positive peer relations. Second, he must be given opportunities to apply them in natural settings and to receive coaching, cueing, prompting, feedback, and praise for their appropriate use. Third, the target child must be motivated, through rewards, to use the skills. Finally, peers should be involved as therapeutic, supportive agents (i.e., special helpers) in the skills' acquisition, and should share in the free-time rewards that are earned for the skills' use.

If these procedures are implemented correctly, very positive results are likely to be achieved. For example, in addition to the effects obtained for the acting-out child, positive "spillover" effects are likely to occur for the child's peers. That is, they will become more positive in their interactions with each other (Strain, Shores, & Kerr, 1976) as a result of participating in the intervention. In addition, the author and his collegues found that positive spillover effects occur across daily recess periods. That is, by intervening **only** during the morning recess, positive interactions between the acting-out child and peers are increased in noon and afternoon recesses via continuation of the positive social exchanges that began in the morning recess period. Thus these procedures have a great deal to recommend them for improving peer relations and should be considered carefully by school personnel who are interested in doing so.

Rule Eleven . . . . . . *"The timing and nature of teacher commands determine their effectiveness as much as the consequences that follow them."*

SOCIAL LEARNING FOUNDATIONS

Parents, teachers, and even peers and siblings are constantly issuing commands to others. The act of giving commands seems to be an indispensable feature of human relations and of getting along with others.

As a rule, when one gives a specific command to someone else, immediate and full compliance is usually expected. However, it is rare for anyone's commands to be fully complied with all the time. Thus, the gap between expectancy and actual behavior in the realm of compliance sows the seeds of potential conflict between parents and children, teachers and students, and among siblings and peers. Noncompliance of children to adult commands can be a serious problem in adult-child relationships and may lead to a host of other problems including defiance, tantrumming, generalized resistance to adult influence, and so forth (Patterson, 1983). A high frequency of noncompliance can thus have serious developmental implications and may serve as a "gatekey behavior" for more serious problems later on.

The terms **compliance** and **noncompliance** are sometimes used to refer to whether a child follows a general set of rules or complies with behavioral expectations. "Compliant" children are those who are considered to be highly responsive to adult influence and would be generally described as "well-behaved." However, the extensive professional literature that exists on compliance/noncompliance usually involves dyads of adults and children in which a single adult issues a command to a single child (Walker & Walker, 1991).

Studies of adult-child command and compliance ratios indicate that: (1) young children comply with adult commands about 60-80% of the time (Forehand, 1977); and (2) well-adjusted children comply with teacher commands approximately 90% of the time while children who are not well-adjusted do so about 70% of the time or less (Strain, Lambert, Kerr, Stagg, & Lenkner, 1983). Given these findings, it is not realistic for adults to expect that their commands should be complied with most of the time. Such factors as poorly constructed commands, errors in communication and interpretation, situational factors, the child's mood or temperament at the time the command is issued, and child developmental levels all influence the probability of compliance.

On the other hand, some children, and especially acting-out children, learn a pattern of habitual noncompliance to adult instructions and commands. This pattern is usually inadvertently taught through parent-child and/or teacher-child interactions under conditions where: (1) the adults give vaguely worded, nonspecific commands; (2) give commands in a rapid fire series where full compliance is not humanly possible; and (3) communicate an ambivalence about whether full and prompt compliance is actually expected. Under these conditions, many children learn that sometimes commands must be complied with and sometimes simply not responding to them will suffice. Acting-out children, in contrast, often directly refuse to comply with specific commands as a way of defying parental or teacher authority. Whether active or passive in nature, these patterns of compliance and noncompliance accompany the child to school and generalize easily to teachers who rely on giving commands in order to teach effectively and to manage the classroom setting.

CLASSROOM APPLICATIONS

If anything, teachers are guilty of giving too many rather than too few commands in the process of teaching. Strain et al. (1983) had one teacher in their sample who averaged 600 commands daily! Commands should be given judiciously and as sparingly as possible so they do not lose their salience for students.

In the classroom, the two main types of commands teachers give are **initiating** and **terminating**. Initiating commands are necessary to direct the classroom and to set up assignments and organizational patterns. Examples of initiating commands include: "Class, we're going to move into our reading groups now so divide yourselves into five groups of five each."; "Take out your math books and turn to page 321."; or "Johnny, please pair up with Sarah on the flash card drill." In contrast, terminating commands are usually designed to get students to stop doing something. Examples of terminating commands include: "Jimmy, you and Ryan stop talking and get to work."; "Rebecca, if you don't stop daydreaming and do your work, you'll have to finish it after school."; or "Harold, I'm too busy to answer you now, I'll talk to you about it later."

Whenever possible, it is best to avoid or limit the use of terminating commands. A good rule is to try to achieve a ratio of four or five initiating commands to every terminating command used across the entire school day for all students. However, this might be quite difficult to achieve under some classroom conditions and with certain types of student groups. Terminating commands often take the form of warnings, and the persistent use of warnings usually becomes a trap for most teachers. It is better to ensure good classroom discipline with the clear posting of classroom rules and reinforcement of students for following these rules than to rely upon warnings and focusing on students' misbehavior.

Aside from whether the command used is initiating or terminating in nature, the specific form in which it is delivered also has a great deal to do with the child's compliance. For example, the form of a command can usually be described as either **alpha** or **beta**. Alpha commands are precise, carefully worded, communicated directly, and ask the child to do one specific thing. Beta commands, in contrast, are vague, ambiguous, wordy, contain more than one element or directive, and the adult's actual intention is often obscure.

Examples of alpha commands include: "Bill, go to the office and pick up your attendance slip for yesterday."; "Gabriella, I want you to help Sharon find her notebook."; or "Susie, come see me after class." In stark contrast, beta commands include: "Jenny, you and Mary are constantly talking and disturbing others; you can't ever seem to get your work done; if you don't improve, you'll pay the consequences."; or "Jason, I don't care what you and Jeremy are arguing about, it can't be solved here; you're disturbing me and the rest of the class; stop it **now** and get your work done."

Beta commands used in this manner are mini lectures that more often confuse children than direct their behavior. Often, the student who is a target of a beta command can't tell exactly what it is the teacher wants, and furthermore, the command sounds like a lecture. Alpha commands are brief, direct, highly specific, and to the point. The chances are much greater that children will comply more fully and promptly with alpha than beta commands.

The timing of teacher commands can also be an important factor in whether students comply with them. For example, when students are fully engaged in one activity and are given a high pressure command to refocus or change what they are doing without adequate warning or preparation, compliance might not occur or it may be delayed at best. More seriously, if a student is agitated, sulking, or in a bad mood, even an appropriate command from the teacher is likely to meet with non-compliance or passive resistance. If the teacher presses the issue under these circumstances, the situation may escalate into a direct teacher-child confrontation. Such confrontations are to be avoided whenever possible. They can be extremely disruptive of the teacher-student relationship, and also present an unfortunate example for the rest of the class. In these situations, it may be better to time the command, if possible, in such a way that the student is not allowed to avoid an expected task or performance but also isn't pushed into teacher defiance inadvertently.

A knowledge of these 11 rules is very important to achieving a clear understanding about how to teach and manage heterogenous groups of students effectively. Pressures for the full inclusion of all students in mainstream classroom settings means that the makeup of teachers' classes will be more diverse in the future. Highly effective strategies and tactics of behavior management are based directly upon these rules, and are illustrated in later chapters of this book. These rules may be of great value to teachers in coping with the demands of fully inclusive classrooms.

Strategies for Assessing the School Behavior of Acting-Out Children and Their Peers

Introduction

Assessment, within the context of schooling, is one of the most frequently occurring forms of professional behavior. Federal mandates, legal pressures, teacher and parental concerns, and situational contexts all contribute to a press for assessing student characteristics and performance within academic as well as social-behavioral domains. Millions of dollars are invested by schools and districts annually in assessment-related activities. Yet the results of these assessments are often underutilized or used in a less than optimal fashion for purposes of decision making. Far too often, educators collect reams of assessment information that either: (1) has only a limited bearing on the problem(s) of concern, or (2) is far in excess of that which is actually necessary to guide decision making. As a result, many classroom teachers remain unconvinced of the need for some school-related assessment efforts, believing that their importance is oversold. In many instances, they are right if one looks objectively at the actual outcomes of such assessments.

All too often, school-based assessments of student behavior and performance serve "system needs" first and the needs of children, teachers, and parents secondarily. Further, many assessment processes are **reactive** rather than **proactive**, and are driven by protective motivations to avoid potential lawsuits of a civil or legal compliance nature. The interests of the real consumers of such assessments (i.e., students, teachers, and parents) are often lost or ignored in this maelstrom of conflicting motivations. In these cases, the assessment procedures are designed to answer such binary questions as: (1) Is the school district at risk or not? (2) Does the student have a legitimate, verifiable disabling condition or not? (3) Should the student be assigned to a less restrictive, specialized placement or not? and so on. While existing policies and regulations make addressing these questions unavoidable in many instances, assessment efforts are too frequently dominated by these questions and do not yield information that would be valuable in under-standing a student's problems or deficits and that would facilitate the development of interventions.

This chapter describes and illustrates assessment strategies that teachers, and other school professionals, need in order to make good decisions in the context of instructing and managing students—especially acting-out students. Information and recommended strategies are presented in four broad areas:

1. Proactive screening and identification of at-risk students

2. The functional analysis of student behavior

3. Monitoring of student performance and adjustment status over time

4. Evaluation of the outcomes of teacher-directed or assisted interventions

The tools available to school personnel for conducting assessments in these four areas are also described and illustrated. Treatment of this material begins with a brief discussion of the **assumptions that should guide best practices** in the very important area of **school-related assessments**, as follows:

- Whenever possible, assessment procedures and efforts should address the **specific** reason(s) underlying problematic or deficient student behavior and performance.

- School-related assessments should provide a roadmap to guide the design and implementation of effective interventions.

- The vast reservoir of information teachers have about student performance and behavioral characteristics should **always** be given a high priority in student assessments.

- Whenever practicable and feasible, student assessments should be multi-method, multi-setting, and multi-agent in nature. That is, they should involve more than one approach (e.g., rankings, ratings, direct observations), occur in more than one setting (e.g., the classroom, playground, home), and involve more than one social agent (e.g., parents, teachers, and peers).

- Teacher judgment of student performance should be considered one of **the** most valid and valuable sources of decision-making information available in developing alternative solutions to the problem.

- Teacher-supplied information, in the form of ratings and rankings, as well as student self-assessments, ratings by peers, archival school records, academic performance measures, and direct observations should be considered as important information sources in developing a complete picture of the target student's performance.

- When conducting school-related assessments to solve problems posed by students, only the essential information necessary to understand such problems and to design effective intervention procedures for them should be collected.

In the author's view, adherence to these fundamental assumptions will set the stage for best practices in assessment efforts with both acting-out and other students. It is especially important in this regard to take full advantage of what teachers know about the behavioral characteristics and performance of the students with whom they interact on a daily basis. Too often, it is assumed that teachers are biased in their judgments and are overly invested in effecting particular outcomes for students whom they refer. In most instances, nothing could be further from the truth. Research shows that teachers refer students for quite legitimate reasons and independent assessments by other professionals usually bear them out (Gerber & Semmel, 1984). Teachers are often the best and most complete source of information regarding students' performance and behavioral characteristics—irrespective of potential biasing factors. Not taking full advantage of this valuable knowledge base about students is a **huge** waste of available resources. Unfortunately, this practice seems to be the norm in many cases rather than the exception.

This chapter is divided into two main sections. Section One describes the four key best practice domains for conducting student assessments. Section Two describes and illustrates assessment tools that are often used in conducting such assessments (i.e., **ratings, rankings, observations, academic achievement measures, archival school records**, and **self-reports**). The specific tools required for each best practice domain are listed at the beginning of the text addressing that domain.

Section One: Best Practice Domains for Conducting Assessments of Student Behavior and Performance

As noted previously, there are four key domains or areas in which the behavior and performance of acting-out students and their peers should be assessed. Differing goals or purposes are met through assessments conducted in these areas. They are as follows: (1) **proactive screening and identification of at risk students**; (2) **the functional analysis of student behavior**; (3) **monitoring of student performance and adjustment status over time**; and (4) **evaluation of the outcomes of teacher-directed or assisted interventions**. Recommended strategies in each of these assessment domains are described and illustrated following. The assessment tools described in Section Two of this chapter play essential roles in these assessment strategies and activities.

Proactive Screening and Identification of At-Risk Students

Tools needed:	Refer to:
– Rankings	Section Two
– Ratings	
– Direct observations	

In traditional practice, referrals of students by teachers for evaluation, intervention, or specialized placement is a process that has been imbued with both controversy and ambivalence. On the one hand, teachers who refer what is perceived to be "too many" students may be regarded with suspicion by school administrators and other professionals. Referrals in this context can be a negative reflection on the teacher in the sense that it is expected that he/she should be able to handle most of the instructional and behavior management challenges presented by students within the confines of the classroom. However, while there may be a small number of teachers who overuse the referral process, studies of teacher referrals generally indicate that students referred by teachers have serious problems in their academic and/or social-behavioral functioning (Gerber & Semmel, 1984; Lloyd, Kaufman, Landrum, & Roe, 1991).

On the other hand, teachers are to be applauded for their efforts in referring students whose problems need attention and expertise beyond that which can be provided by the classroom teacher. Many acting-out students, along with those who are aggressive, antisocial, depressed, abused, neglected, and generally at-risk fit this profile. That is, they **should** be referred due to the gravity and urgency of their problems.

As the social conditions of our society continue to deteriorate and spill over into the schooling process and as the diversity of most regular classrooms keeps increasing, it is likely that the rate of teacher-initiated referrals will continue to reflect these changes. In the author's view, referrals of this type are a positive development and one to be encouraged rather than discouraged.

Traditionally, a student's only path to referral, evaluation, and access to specialized placements and/or intensive intervention services has been for the teacher to be convinced that external assistance is required to deal with his/her problems. Studies show that teachers are most likely to refer students for severe academic deficits and for behavior problems of an **externalizing** nature (i.e., acting-out behavior) (Brophy & Evertson, 1981; Lloyd et al., 1991). Those students with less severe, but still serious deficits, or those with emotional-behavioral problems of an **internalizing** nature (e.g., social withdrawal, anxiety, depression, phobias) are far less likely to be referred. Yet, many of these students are in urgent need of evaluation and interventions.

The author and his colleagues have developed the *Systematic Screening for Behavior Disorders (SSBD)* procedure (Walker & Severson, 1990) and the *Early Screening Project (ESP)* system (Walker, Severson, & Feil, 1995) for **proactively** screening and identifying students in the 6-11 age range and the three to five year age range, respectively, who may be at risk for either externalizing or internalizing behavior problems and disorders. Both of these systems are highly cost effective and rely upon "**multiple gates**," representing different types of assessment.

In Stage I, the regular teacher nominates a small number of students whose **characteristic** behavior patterns match either the externalizing or internalizing behavioral profiles provided. The teacher then rank orders these nominated students in terms of how closely their behavior matches the respective profile. The highest ranked students then move to the Stage II screening, in which the teacher rates them on a **critical events index** and a **combined frequency index**. Those students who pass this screening assessment, or "gate," move on to screening Stage III, where they are systematically observed in classroom and playground settings. Figure 4.1 illustrates the three screening gates of *SSBD*.

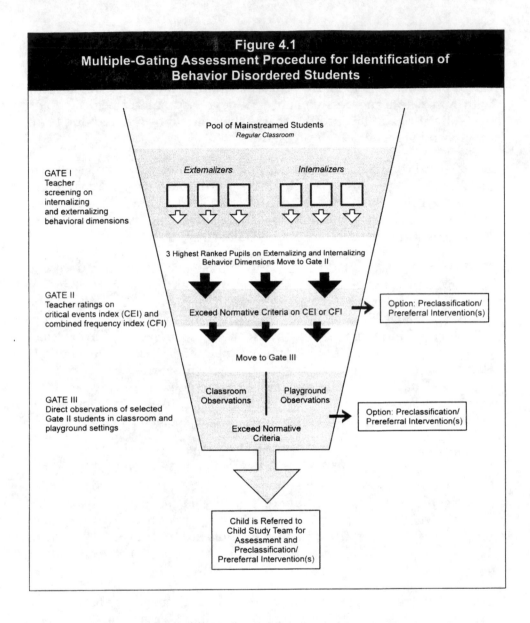

Figure 4.1
Multiple-Gating Assessment Procedure for Identification of Behavior Disordered Students

Students who pass all three screening gates, on either the externalizing or internalizing dimension, are seriously at risk for a host of school-related adjustment problems. This screening-identification approach is highly effective and integrates teacher judgment with direct observations in a structured, aggregated manner that facilitates quality decision making about at-risk students and the severity of their behavioral-adjustment problems.

The Functional Analysis of Student Behavior

Tools needed:	Refer to:
– Direct observations	Section Two
– Archival school records	
– Self-reports Ratings	

In the past five years, the scientific study of behavior has produced an approach that provides for the functional analysis of behavior. Functional analysis refers to a systematic process for: (1) **understanding the nature and causes of problem behavior**, and (2) **developing cost effective interventions for changing or reducing that behavior**. O'Neill, Horner, Albin, Storey, and Sprague (1990) have provided the most complete and useable description of procedures to date for conducting a functional analysis of student behavior, which will be detailed following.

Functional analysis has three main goals: (1) to describe the undesirable or problem behavior in operational terms, (2) to predict the occasions and situations in which the behavior of interest is and is not likely to occur, and (3) to identify and define the purpose(s) the problem behavior serves. Three strategies are used to achieve these goals. First, a functional analysis interview is conducted. Often, in this procedure, the teacher conducts a self-interview using a structured interview form designed for this purpose. This form generally asks questions relating to the nature of the problem behavior(s) of concern, its frequency, duration, intensity, and the times/situations in which it seems most likely to occur. Table 4.1 illustrates a sample description of a problem behavior using the functional analysis procedure.

Table 4.1 Sample Illustration of a Functional Analysis Behavioral Description						
Target Behavior	Form of the Behavior	Frequency	Duration	Occasions	Context	Intensity
Hitting others	Open hand and closed fist	2-3 times daily	5-10 sec. per episode	During recess periods	Arguments about rules during games	High

The functional analysis format provides for obtaining specific information on critical features of the problem behavior and the conditions surrounding the behavior. Parents, peers, and other adults in the school can also be interviewed to allow for comparisons of the perspectives of different social agents on the target behavior and for identifying variations in the occurrence and expression of the problem behavior.

Next, the problem behavior is observed and tracked systematically throughout the school day to identify its situational variations and to search for clues as to what maintains it (i.e., What specific purpose[s] does the behavior serve?). As a general rule, the problem serves one of two purposes: (1) to obtain something or to produce a desired effect, or (2) to escape or avoid something. Two questions should be asked in this regard: (1) **What does the behavior get or produce?** and (2) **What does it allow the student to avoid?** These two purposes are powerful motivaters, and they serve to successfully maintain large amounts of problematic student behavior. In order to successfully change the problem behavior, it is essential to identify its primary purpose or the specific goal it serves.

Finally, an optional component of the functional analysis procedure is to systematically manipulate the conditions surrounding the problem behavior's occurrence in an attempt to certify that the suspected maintaining variables or purposes are actually operating. For example, the first two stages of a functional analysis of a student's oppositional-defiant behavior towards the teacher may suggest that it is associated with academically difficult material. The teacher could confirm this hypothesis by systematically varying the difficulty of the academic material during instructional periods and recording the student's corresponding behavior. If instances of oppositional-defiant student behavior co-occur with difficult material, and not with easy material, then it is likely that difficult academic material is the source of the problem.

It is highly recommended that all teachers consider developing an understanding of the purposes and key features of the functional analysis of student behavior. Knowing how to use this invaluable tool to better understand and cope with the challenging behavior of acting-out students will empower the teacher to manage instances of disruptive and aggressive behavior far more effectively. As classrooms become more diverse and more and more children bring severe behavior problems to the schooling process, it is essential that teachers have the ability to understand, predict, and intervene successfully with those children's behavior problems. Additional information about how to conduct a functional analysis of problem behavior is contained in the O'Neill et al. (1990) book entitled *Functional Analysis of Problem Behavior: A Practical Assessment Guide*.

Monitoring of Student Performance and Adjustment Status Over Time

Tools needed:	Refer to:
– Ratings	Section Two
– Direct observations	
– Academic achievement measures	
– Archival school records	
– Self-reports	

Because of their highly aversive behavior patterns, the behavior and performance of acting-out students are subject to highly irregular monitoring practices. During behavioral outbursts, the behavior of acting-out students is the subject of intense focus and concern from teachers and peers. However, during periods of relative calm and appropriate behavior, their behavior is likely to be ignored. Because of their often severe at-risk status, it is important to monitor the social and academic dimensions of the behavior patterns of acting-out students both carefully and frequently.

For example, the stopwatch method (see Section Two) should be used regularly by the teacher to estimate the percentage of academic engaged time in the classroom and the amount of positive social behavior directed by acting-out students toward peers on the playground. It is much better to monitor such behavior **for shorter periods of time and on more occasions than to use "one shot" monitoring efforts**. For example, if one has an hour total to observe a student's behavior on the playground or in the classroom during a five-day period, it is far better to observe on four, 15-minute occasions than on two, 30-minute sessions, or one 60-minute session. The four occasions should be distributed across four separate days unless circumstances warrant otherwise.

In the area of academic performance, curriculum-based measurement procedures should be used regularly to monitor the student's growth on specific skills and to track error rates. In addition, the results of standardized achievement tests should be carefully analyzed whenever they become available.

Completion of homework is one of **the** most important contributors to academic success and progress. Careful monitoring of homework assignments and working with parents to ensure their correct and timely completion are essential. Acting-out students may pose difficult management problems in this area, but the investment of teacher effort, if successful, will yield high dividends.

Finally, school records should be regularly inspected to monitor the acting-out student's attendance, negative narrative comments by teachers, and discipline contacts with the principal's office. Erratic attendance, negative comments by teachers in student records, and disciplinary referrals by teachers to the front office are powerful risk factors in accounting for later school failure (Block-Pedego, 1990).

At-risk students, particularly acting-out students, fail in school and ultimately drop out because they are often unsuccessful academically and because they view the school setting as a hostile place where no one is concerned about them. Over time, these pressures cause the acting-out student to seek more accepting environments—outside of school. The regular and proactive monitoring of acting-out students not only identifies the problem areas they are experiencing but communicates a caring posture on the part of teachers and the school. Sometimes, this simple best practice can make a huge difference in the path that an acting-out child chooses to follow in school and later in life.

Evaluation of the Outcomes of Teacher-Directed or Assisted Interventions

Tools needed:	Refer to:
– Ratings	Section Two
– Direct observations	
– Academic achievement measures	
– School archival records	
– Self-reports	

Systematic and continuous monitoring of student performance automatically provides for evaluation of school interventions designed to change or improve the academic performance and/or social behavior of acting-out students and their peers. When procedures are changed or new techniques are applied in order to enhance student performance, changes in student achievement and/or behavior should be registered on these ongoing measures if the interventions used are effective in addressing the problem(s).

In the area of academic performance, there are three sources of information that should be considered in evaluating student outcomes expected to result from an ongoing intervention. These are: (1) academic engaged time (AET); (2) academic skills and responses selected from the curriculum; and (3) standardized, norm referenced achievement tests.

Academic engaged time correlates well with measures of academic performance, like achievement tests. It is a **process** measure that provides an estimate of how well the student engages in academic tasks and the teaching-learning process. It also serves as an indirect and highly sensitive measure of classroom behavioral adjustment. Academic production responses, recorded using CBM (curriculum based measurement) measures, are an intermediate monitoring device between AET and summative academic achievement tests. Together, these three information sources provide a complete and sensitive profile of the academic adjustment of most students. They are **critically** important in the monitoring of academic performance for acting-out students.

In monitoring the social-behavioral adjustment of acting-out students for the purpose of evaluating intervention outcomes, it is recommended that three information sources also be considered. These interrelated sources of information are: (1) direct observations recorded in classroom and playground settings, (2) teacher and parent ratings of the student's adjustment status, and (3) discipline contacts and negative comments contained in archival school records. Each of these measures is described briefly following.

Direct observations are highly sensitive to the changing nuances and stimulus conditions of classroom and playground settings. In terms of sensitivity, direct observations are to teacher and parent ratings of child behavior as an electron microscope is to an ordinary magnifying glass. Observations are useful in documenting whether intervention effects are detectable; parent, teacher, and even peer ratings are appropriate for evaluating the more global impact of the behavior change(s) produced by the intervention. Again, both types of evaluation strategies are very important to assessing the presence **and** significance of the behavior changes produced.

There is also a less direct but highly valid set of indices relating to whether an intervention works or not. That is, over the course of the school year, are there fewer **discipline contacts** with the front office involving the student and are there fewer **negative narrative comments** in archival school records contributed by adults in the school? Both of these measures are strongly indicative of the quality of a student's global adjustment to the demands of schooling.

As with academic performance, it is essential to use a multi-measure approach in assessing the social-behavioral status of acting-out students before, during, and following an intervention. The profile that will emerge from the use of this approach allows one to evaluate the intervention's effects through different types of impact. That is, changes can be detected by direct observations, ratings by others, and, finally, through school records. If an intervention registers strong effects on **each** of these measures, it would be considered unusually powerful. As a general rule, classroom and playground interventions will often impact direct observation measures while producing no to only minimal effects on ratings and school record measures.

Evaluating the outcomes of school interventions for acting-out students and their peers also involves the graphing, inspection, and interpretation of data produced by the monitoring/evaluation systems used. Appendix B provides guidelines and illustrations for the reader's use in accomplishing this essential part of the intervention evaluation process.

Section Two: Tools for Conducting Assessments

The primary tools available to teachers and other school personnel for conducting student assessments are as follows: (1) **retrospective ratings by teachers, parents, and peers**; (2) **teacher rankings**; (3) **direct observations**; (4) **academic achievement measures of a norm referenced and continuous monitoring nature**; (5) **analysis of archival school records**; and (6) **direct self-reports by target students**. Each of these forms of assessment, and their purposes, are briefly discussed following. The relative advantages and appropriate uses of each are also described.

Ratings

Ratings of a student's behavior by others allow "judges" (i.e., raters) to focus and express their knowledge of a child in a single, numerical estimate. These ratings are called **retrospective** because judges, or raters, review their past history of information about the target child and then select a numerical rating on a continuous scale (called a **Likert Scale**) that best represents their appraisal.

Adult judges (e.g., teachers) are usually asked to rate the child's behavior or performance along either a **frequency of occurrence** or a **descriptive** or **true** dimension. As a rule, the rater makes a rating ranging from 1-3, 1-5, or 1-7 on some dimension of interest. Examples of typical rating scale items are shown in Figure 4.2.

Teachers and the target child's peers are often asked to make judgmental ratings based upon their knowledge and experience with the child. In making such judgments, teachers and peers have the advantage of being able to base their ratings on a large number of social comparisons they have made involving the target student and other students. That is, teachers and peers are able to judge the **comparative** behavior and performance of the target student and peers within the same classroom or playground contexts. Thus, the manner in which the target child responds to teacher directives, approaches tasks, interacts and plays with others, and so on, is informally

Figure 4.2
Rating Dimensions

	Frequency of Occurence				
	Never		Sometimes		Frequently
1. Student complies with teacher requests.	1	2	3	4	5

	Descriptive or True						
	Not Descriptive or True			Moderately Descriptive or True			Very Descriptive or True
1. Student has a sense of humor.	1	2	3	4	5	6	7

observed and noted over time and across many occasions. These informal comparisons provide a powerful foundation for making informed judgments about the relative competence or appropriateness of the target child's performance. Reliable scales tend to specify the rating standard to be used for comparison (e.g., "Compared to other students you have taught . . . .").

Parents have a much more restricted basis for making such rating judgments about their own children. Generally, they must rely upon their comparative knowledge of the target child's siblings or their experience(s) with the children of acquaintances. In addition, parents are strongly invested in their children's lives and live with them on a daily basis. Thus, they are less than impartial judges of their children's behavior and performance, and are likely to be more susceptible to bias in their ratings than are either teachers or peers.

The most common situation in which peers are asked to make judgments about each other involves sociometric assessments (i.e., peer ratings) in which the goal is to measure each student's perceived social competence and popularity. This is usually accomplished through **peer nomination** or **roster and rating** methods. With peer nominations, each student is asked to nominate the three classmates who he/she would most like to work and play with; these are called positive nominations. Negative nominations are sometimes solicited as well, wherein each student is asked to nominate the three classmates who he/she **would not** like to work and play with.

Peer nominations are always somewhat controversial due to the nature of the judgments they elicit and the possibility that peers will compare nominations after the sociometric procedure has been administered. Negative nominations are especially problematic in this regard, and are avoided by many professionals because of the possible damage to reputations and self-esteem that they pose. Ironically, negative nominations are much more valid and predict better than positive nominations (McConnell & Odom, 1986).

Peer ratings (i.e., the **roster and rating** method), are less controversial than peer nominations and have better psychometric properties (i.e., reliability, or **consistency**; and validity, or **accuracy**). In this procedure, each student is given a class list with all the students' names on it. Beside each name is a five- or seven-point scale that, for younger children, is usually anchored at one end by a smiley face and by a frowny face at the other end. The students are then asked to rate how much they like to play and work with each of the other students on the list. For very young children, a picture sociometric procedure is used in which selections are made from among an array of pictures of the entire class.

Because of the psychological risks involved, peer nominations and ratings should be considered only when there is a compelling reason calling for their use in instructing and managing the classroom setting. As Gresham and Elliott (1984) have wisely noted, sociometrics are a problem indicator measure only; they communicate very little useful information about the design of interventions to improve students' social competence. Thus, they should be used only when there is a specific reason to identify and know those students who are unpopular with their peers. As a general rule, teachers have a good idea about who such students are anyway.

Acting-out children, for example, are likely to be rejected by their peers because of their aversive behavioral characteristics. They, along with other socially at-risk children, are vulnerable to a host of negative, long-term developmental outcomes. These include low self-esteem, academic failure, delinquency, bad conduct discharges from the military, and appearance on community psychiatric registers in adulthood (Parker & Asher, 1987). These children urgently need to learn friendship-making skills and strategies for accessing groups of peers in order to reduce the damaging effects of such risks.

Ratings by teachers, parents, and peers have proven to be useful and valid in: (1) discriminating between at-risk and other students; and (2) predicting long-term outcomes such as future arrests, school failure, and dropout. Ratings by teachers and parents on a series of items describing either adaptive or maladaptive child behavior are extremely valuable in determining the presence of behavioral deficits and/or excesses. Often, ratings of this type can provide the foundation for designing an intervention that pinpoints problems jointly identified by two of the key social agents in the child's life (i.e., parents and teachers).

Such ratings have the additional advantage of being "norm referenced"; that is, standard scores for normative groups of same age and same sex peers are provided to allow comparative judgments regarding the degree of deviation or severity of the target child's perceived problems. Thus, a student whose score(s) are further from the normative average, or mean, is considered much more at-risk than one whose score(s) are closer to the mean.

In traditional practice, the focus of teacher and parent ratings has been weighted toward "problem" child behavior (i.e., descriptors of maladaptive forms of behavior). While the information produced from these assessments is very important, the specific social skills which students may be lacking are often ignored. Recently, there has been a trend toward including teacher and parent ratings of students' social skills as part of the overall assessment process (Gresham & Elliott, 1989; Merrell, Merz, Johnson, & Ring, 1992; Walker & McConnell, 1988). This practice is highly recommended because of the more complete picture it provides of the target child and its value in guiding the design of intervention(s) to enhance social competence.

A large number of norm referenced rating scales for use by teachers and parents in evaluating child behavior have been developed and published over the years. As a general rule, these instruments have good to excellent psychometric (i.e., reliability and validity) characteristics. The annual *Buros Mental Measurements Yearbook*, available in any university library, provides complete descriptions and detailed reviews of all published rating scales. Consulting this yearbook is highly recommended prior to selecting a technically adequate rating scale. Brief descriptions of some of the better known and more commonly used rating scales are provided following.

1. The **Child Behavior Checklist (CBC) Teacher Report Form** (1991), by Thomas Achenbach. The *CBC* is considered the most comprehensive and technically robust of available rating scales for use in measuring child behavior. The instrument has both teacher and parent versions, and consists of 113 items. The *Teacher Report Form* of the *CBC* asks teachers to judge the child on 113 separate items along a dimension of how true the item is of the student's **characteristic** behavior. Judgments are made along a three-point scale where 0 means the item is not true and a rating of 2 means the item is very true. Standard scores and norms are provided for students age 5-18 and for both males and females. The *CBC* makes it possible to distinguish children having primarily externalizing behavior problems from those having primarily internalizing behavior problems. The major disadvantage of the *CBC* is its length and the amount of time required to complete the scale. (Information about the *CBC Teacher Report Form* can be obtained from Thomas Achenbach,

Department of Psychiatry, University of Vermont, Burlington, VT 05401.)

2. The *Revised Behavior Problem Checklist* **(RBPC)** (1987), by Herbert Quay and Donald Peterson. The RBPC is also considered a technically adequate and robust rating scale. The *RBPC* consists of 89 items that describe maladaptive or pathological forms of personal-social behavior exhibited by children and youth. Sample items include: **"expresses beliefs that are clearly untrue (delusions)"**; **"teases others"**; and **"blames others; denies own mistakes."** The *RBPC* consists of six scales: **conduct disorder, socialized aggression, attention problems-immaturity, anxiety/withdrawal, psychotic behavior,** and **motor excess**. The scale items can be rated by teachers and parents. Individual items are rated on a three-point scale where 0 indicates the rater has no knowledge about the item, 1 indicates a mild problem, and 2 indicates a severe problem. The *RBPC* manual contains results of teacher and parent ratings of both "normal" and clinical samples of children and youth ages 5-18. Norms are reported in the "Scale Manual" for students in grades K-12. The primary disadvantage of the *RBPC*, like the *CBC*, is the number of items and the length of time required to complete the scale. (Information about the *RBPC* can be obtained from Herbert Quay, Department of Psychology, University of Miami, Coral Gables, FL 33124.)

3. The *Walker Problem Behavior Identification Checklist* **(WPBIC)** (1983a), by Hill Walker. The *WPBIC* is a 50 item behavior checklist consisting of five scales: **acting-out, social withdrawal, distractibility, disturbed peer relations,** and **immaturity**. The *WPBIC* is designed for use only by teachers in the elementary grade range, and focuses on school-related behavior problems. Items are rated as either **present** (i.e., has occurred one or more times) or **absent** (i.e., has not occurred). Norms are presented for males and females at primary and intermediate grade levels. The small number of items and ease of administration are advantages of the WPBIC; the lack of a national, normative data base is its primary disadvantage. (Information about the WPBIC can be obtained from Western Psychological Services, 12031 Wilshire Boulevard, Los Angeles, CA 90025.)

4. The *Social Skills Rating System* **(SSRS)** (1990), by Frank Gresham and Steve Elliott. The *SSRS* is a comprehensive assessment battery that provides information on three domains of child and youth adjustment: **social skills, problem behaviors,** and **academic competence**. **Social skills** are measured through five scales: **cooperation, assertion, responsibility, empathy,** and **self-control**. Problem

behaviors are assessed through three scales: **externalizing, internalizing,** and **hyperactivity. Academic competence** is assessed by asking the teacher to indicate the student's overall academic performance, comparative reading skills, and motivational level(s). The *SSRS* contains parent, teacher, and student forms. The student self-report form begins in grade three; the teacher and parent report forms span the preschool through high school developmental levels. The *SSRS* is the most comprehensive and thoroughly researched social skills battery on the market today. It is a superb set of instruments that provides multiple perspectives on student competence and adjustment representing different settings. The national normative data base of the *SSRS* is quite extensive and scientifically derived. The *SSRS* sets the standard of excellence for social skills assessment instruments, and has no disadvantages. (Information about the SSRS can be obtained from American Guidance Service, Circle Pines, MN 55014-1796.)

5. The *Walker-McConnell Scale of Social Competence and School Adjustment* **(SSCSA)** (1995), by Hill Walker and Scott McConnell. The *SSCSA* is designed for use by teachers in grades K-12. The elementary version of the scale spans the K-6 grade range, and has 43 items distributed across three scales: **teacher preferred social behavior, peer preferred social behavior,** and **school adjustment**. The secondary, or adolescent, version contains 53 items distributed across four scales: **self-control, peer relations, school adjustment,** and **empathy**. The national standardization sample on the combined scale versions of the *SSCSA* totals approximately 3,600 cases, or 1,800 for each scale version. The *SSCSA* has extensive and excellent psychometric properties; a large number of studies have been conducted in establishing the reliability and validity of each scale version. The major disadvantage of the *SSCSA* is that, unlike the *SSRS*, it does not provide for either parent or student ratings of social skills. (Information about the *SSCSA* can be obtained from Singular Press, 4284 41st Street, San Diego, CA 92105.)

6. The *School Social Behavior Scales* **(SSBS)** (1993), by Kenneth Merrell. The *SSBS* is designed for use by teachers in grades K-12; like the *SSCSA*, it does not provide for ratings by either parents or students. The *SSBS* contains a total of 65 items divided nearly evenly into a **social competence scale** (32 items) and an **antisocial behavior scale** (33 items). The social competence scale is further subdivided into the following subscales: **interpersonal skills, self-management skills,** and **academic skills**; the antisocial behavior scale is subdivided similarly into the following subscales: **hostile-irritable, anti-**

social-aggressive, and **demanding-disruptive**. Like the *SSRS* and the *SSCSA*, the *SSBS* has excellent to superb technical adequacy. Further, the content which the scale measures is highly relevant to school adjustment; the scale items are clearly stated and easy for teachers to rate. Teachers are not asked to make judgments about forms of student behavior they have no chance of observing. Like the *SSRS*, the *SSBS* provides for the assessment of both social skills **and** problematic, antisocial forms of student behavior. The balance achieved by the *SSBS* in this regard is exemplary. Other than not providing for parent and student ratings, there are no disadvantages associated with the *SSBS* and the scale is highly recommended. (Information about the *SSBS* can be obtained from Clinical Psychology Publishing, 4 Conant Square, Brandon, VT 05733.)

Teacher Rankings

Teacher rankings are a convenient and effective means of ordering students along dimensions of interest (e.g., achievement, popularity, social responsiveness, adaptive behavior) for purposes of screening and/or allocating instructional resources. Teacher rankings of this type have proved to be sensitive, valid, and highly reliable (see Greenwood, Walker, Todd, & Hops, 1979; Walker & Severson, 1994). Such rankings are most useful near the extremes of the rank ordering distribution where the most at-risk and most skilled or competent students can be located respectively. That is, the least skilled/competent students will be clustered at one end of the rank ordering distribution and the most skilled/competent will be clustered at the opposite end.

In order to conduct a rank ordering of a class of students, three elements are required: (1) a class list, (2) a rank ordering form, and (3) a definition of the variable or dimension of interest. Appendix C contains a sample rank ordering form for the reader's use. Two example definitions, and accompanying guidelines, that can be used for rank ordering students are provided following:

- **Popularity.** Popularity with peers means the target student is liked by peers, is sought out by them as a work- or playmate, receives a larger number of social bids than average, and numerous students call him/her a friend.

- **Adaptive Behavior.** Adaptive behavior means the target student follows classroom rules, completes assigned work in a timely manner, is self-directed, displays self-control when the situation calls for it, is responsive to teacher corrections, and displays appropriate levels of independence.

The student whose **characteristic** behavior pattern conforms **most** closely to the elements of the definition receives the highest rank (i.e., the rank of 1). The student whose behavior conforms to or reflects the definition the **next** most closely receives the rank of 2, and so on until the entire class has been ranked. With this method, however, it is important to carefully consider all the students in the class with respect to the definition before actually assigning the ranks. All students should receive a numerical ranking in this rank ordering process.

In the area of peer popularity, where gender and cross sex relationships can mediate or affect children's status, it may be advisable to conduct separate rank orderings for girls and boys. Thus, girls would be considered in relation to the definition only in comparison to other girls; similarly, boys would be considered only in comparison to other boys. This concern, however, would not apply to such rank ordering dimensions as academic achievement, social responsibility, risk status for school dropout, or empathy.

Rank ordering procedures are a cost efficient and superior way of ensuring that the individual status of **all** students is carefully considered on dimensions of teacher interest. Typically, teachers reactively nominate individual students for referral or specialized evaluation based on the student's failure to meet some absolute standard of "teachability," "manageability," or "tractability." While such nominations are valid and accurate, they do not provide for the careful consideration of **all** students in the class with respect to the same dimension or issue of concern. Thus, at-risk students with serious needs can be missed if nominations are the only path to specialized assistance and access. Rank ordering procedures, implemented on a regular basis, provide a **proactive** means of identifying students who are potentially in need. A regular teacher can rank order an entire class on most variables of instructional or management interest in about 20 minutes or less.

Direct Observations

Over the past three decades, a powerful methodology for observing and recording the behavior of target individuals within natural situations has been developed. Some of the observation coding systems comprising this methodology are extremely complex. For example, coding systems and recording rules have been developed to capture: (1) teacher-student interactions in the context of teaching; (2) the verbal and nonverbal communications of married partners; and (3) the dynamics of family interactions in the home setting. Coding systems exist that have over 40 separate categories; their use requires individuals with well-developed abilities to handle complex information and to make split second decisions.

Laptop computers are now used in field situations as instruments for observing, recording, and instantaneously storing coded information. This observation methodology has been a valuable research tool and has significantly advanced our understanding of complex forms of human behavior (Dodge, Price, Coie, & Christopoulos, 1990; Patterson, Reid, & Dishion, 1992). The *Mirrors of Behavior* index, available in university libraries, provides a compendium of observation coding systems and information about them. For the reader with more detailed and technical interests in this methodology, inspection of this resource is highly recommended.

The needs of teachers and other school professionals in the area of observing and coding students' behavior are far less demanding than those of behavioral researchers. Even so, the coding systems and approaches that have been traditionally used in assessing the behavior patterns of individual students are far more complex and cumbersome than they need be. As a rule, these systems contain many more codes than necessary and code categories are retained that have extremely low frequencies of occurrence. Low frequency codes and those that are not usable in decision making about the student are "excess baggage" that put undue pressures and burdens on the coder.

The **most** important rule to remember in observing and recording student behavior within school settings is as follows: **code only the information you have access to *and* can fully utilize in decision making about the student**. That is, **keep it as simple as possible and code only what you can see**. For example, it is usually far better to observe and code a student's **actual** behavior than to try to infer the presumed intent of the student's behavior through the coding process.

The author is convinced that many teachers and other school professionals are "turned off" by some observational coding systems because of their complexity and a perception that the effort invested in using them does not justify the outcomes achieved. In many cases, they are right! Coding systems can also be very simple and extremely valuable in furthering our understanding of students' behavior patterns and peer reactions to their behavior. Thus, coding complexity is not necessarily associated with superior outcomes in using observations.

Within school settings there are three ways to code behavior, each described following. These coding methods are:

1. Interval recording

2. Event recording

3. Duration recording

Interval recording (IR) means that the target student's behavior is coded every so many seconds (i.e., in intervals). The length of intervals usually varies between five and 15 seconds, with ten-second intervals perhaps being the most commonly used. Some interval coding systems allow more than one code category to be recorded during each interval. More often, only one of the available code categories is recorded for each interval—the one that **best** represents or captures the target student's behavior for that interval.

An interval coding grid with names or labels for the code categories contained in a sample classroom coding system is provided in Table 4.2.

Table 4.2 Sample Interval Classroom Coding System Code Categories					
Coding Interval	Attending	Complying	Cooperating	Initiating	Responding
1	/				
2	/				
3				/	
4		/			
5			/		
6	—				
7	/				

The sample interval coding system shown in Table 4.2 has five code categories: **attending, complying, cooperating, initiating,** and **responding**. In this system, one of these five code categories that **best reflects or captures the target student's behavior during that interval** is recorded every ten seconds. In the first two ten-second intervals, this was the code category of attending, in the third interval it was initiating, in the fourth it was complying, and in the fifth it was cooperating. In the sixth interval, the student was doing something that couldn't be recorded in any of the five code categories (e.g., sharpening a pencil, disturbing another student, tantrumming, etc.). In the seventh interval, attending again best captured the student's behavior.

In using IR coding systems like this one, the observer systematically moves down the grid entering a slash (/) to mark the appropriate category for each interval and a minus sign (-) to indicate an interval in which the student's behavior fits none of the available categories. Additionally, some code categories can be coded as either a plus (+) or minus (-) to indicate adaptive versus maladaptive behavior. For example, the code categories of **initiating** and **responding** could be coded as either + (adaptive) or - (maladaptive).

In contrast, some interval coding systems list four or five categories to capture adaptive behavior and also list four or five to capture maladaptive behavior. Maladaptive code categories appropriate for a classroom code might include: **noncompliance, pestering others, noisy, being out of seat**, and **nonattending**. On the playground, maladaptive code categories might include: **teasing, arguing, aggressing, rule violations**, and **being alone**.

As a rule, each observation session lasts from 15-20 minutes. Sessions should generally be 15 minutes in length at a minimum in order to adequately sample the target student's behavior. Thus, the coding form should have sufficient intervals to cover at least 15 minutes of observation (i.e., 90 ten-second intervals for a 15 minute observation session). The situation in which the observation occurs (e.g., independent seatwork) should remain the same during the 15- or 20-minute session. As a rule, two or three observation sessions recorded on separate days are necessary to obtain an adequate picture of a student's behavior pattern.

With minimum practice, the teacher or other observer can become skilled at estimating the passage of ten-second intervals using the secondhand of an ordinary watch. Some school professionals use an audio tape with equal intervals delineated with an audible "beep" to keep track of intervals. With interval systems, the slash or other marking symbol should not be entered until the **end** of the interval. Remember, the interval that **best** represents the target student's behavior for that coding interval should be selected; in other words, the one in which he/she spends the most time. The observer can't make this judgment until at or near the end of the ten-second coding interval.

A number of generic interval coding systems have been published in the literature that are appropriate for general classroom use. However, in many instances, teachers or school professionals will want to tailor make the coding system to meet their specific information needs. This means selecting code categories and developing definitions for each one that can be coded **reliably** (that is, two or more independent observers can agree that the code category occurred for a specific interval 80% or more of the time). Often, it takes revising code definitions and coding practice to meet this inter-observer reliability, or agreement, standard. The rule to remember is: **code only what one can see/record reliably, and occurs at a reasonable frequency**.

Interval coding systems are extremely valuable when the goal of observing and recording is to capture the target student's **overall** behavior pattern. In this context, both adaptive and maladaptive code categories can be developed to provide a complete picture of the student's behavior. As noted previously, in certain situations it is possible to use one set of code categories that can be coded as either a plus (+) or minus (-), depending upon whether the student displays the behavior in question adaptively or maladaptively. The extent to which the student's overall behavior pattern is appropriate, or inappropriate, can be determined by computing the percentage of observed intervals in which his/her behavior was coded as a plus or minus. The appropriate behavior level of most students in regular classroom settings ranges between 70 and 90%; this provides a normative standard for evaluating the behavioral adjustment of individual students when using coding systems of this type.

Event recording (ER) refers to the coding or recording of the occurrence of discrete events in real time. **Discrete** means the event to be recorded has a clearly discernible starting and ending points. Yelling, hitting, kicking, jumping, and spitting are maladaptive behavioral events that meet this standard. Real time means that the starting and ending times for the observation are recorded in actual time, and the number of events recorded during the observation session are also noted. These two pieces of information make it possible to calculate the rate of occurrence for the event(s) being observed and recorded. For example, if a target student hits others a total of four times during a 20-minute recess, the rate per minute (rpm) of occurrence would be four divided by 20, or a rpm of .20 (i.e., one hit every five minutes on the average). This rate would be far above the normal frequency of students' hitting each other on the playground.

A sample form for event recording is shown in Figure 4.3. A slash (/) is generally used to mark the occasion of each event's occurrence. It is also possible to record more than one target behavior simultaneously using ER procedures. The great advantage of the ER coding method is that it is ideally suited for recording behavioral events that have high salience (i.e., impact) but relatively low rates of occurrence (e.g., fighting, arguing, bullying, teacher defiance, and so forth).

Duration recording (DR) means that the length, or actual duration, of a target behavior is the focus of recording. Target behaviors appropriate for duration recording include: peer to peer social interactions, the amount of time spent in games and structured activities at recess, the amount of time spent engaged with assigned tasks in the classroom, and the extent to which a target student's social behavior directed toward others is negative or aggressive. DR recording methods are best suited for forms of student behavior that occur in continuous streams (i.e., behavioral streams).

Figure 4.3
Event Recording Form

1. Date __3/15__   Time start __12:10__   Time stop __12:30__

2. Target behavior to be recorded: __arguing about playground rules__

3. Name of student: __Alan__

/ / / / / / / /

A stopwatch having a start, stop, and restart function is generally used in duration recording. The stopwatch is allowed to run when the target behavior is occurring and it is stopped and remains off when behavior that is incompatible with the target behavior is occurring. When the target behavior is again in evidence, the stopwatch is restarted and allowed to run as long as the target behavior continues to occur. For example, when recording **academic engaged time** in the classroom (i.e., the extent to which the student is appropriately engaged with an assigned task), the stopwatch runs as long as the student's behavior meets the definitional requirements of academic engagement (e.g., eyes focused on the assigned material; making appropriate motor responses such as computing, writing, etc.). However, when the student's behavior does not meet the requirements of the definition (e.g., looking around the room, talking loudly with another student), the stopwatch is stopped and only restarted when academic engagement is again in evidence.

At the end of the observation session, the time on the stopwatch is divided by the length of the observation session, and the result is multiplied by 100 to obtain the percentage of academic engagement for the period observed. For example, if the target student was observed to be academically engaged for ten minutes of a 15-minute observation period, the calculation would be as follows: $10 \div 15 = .66 \times 100 = 66\%$. Most students in the elementary grade range are academically engaged within the regular classroom setting 65-80% of the time (Walker & Severson, 1990).

The DR method is ideal for estimating the amount of time students spend engaged in particular activities or types of behavior. It is highly accurate and very easy to use. Its major disadvantage is that only one target behavior can be recorded at a time. Thus, DR is the method of choice when one's interest is in one particular type or form of student behavior and the behavior tends to occur in "stream like" fashion, which is very often the case with students in the school setting.

Observational methods can be a very valuable tool for the teacher and other school professionals **if** they are designed appropriately and match well with the informational requirements of the situation. They are highly recommended and are especially useful in combination with other methods (e.g., rankings, ratings, school records) to form a complete picture of the target student's functioning at school.

Academic Achievement Measures

Low academic achievement, as measured by norm referenced tests, is a major risk factor for school failure and dropout among populations of at-risk students (Block-Pedego, 1990). In a systematic study of the factors contributing to later school dropout, Block-Pedego (1990) found academic achievement, as measured by standardized achievement tests in reading, math, and language, to be the **single most powerful factor** in this regard.

Low achievement relative to grade level expectations is a consistent risk factor identified for acting-out students in the elementary grade range (Hinshaw, 1992). Below grade level achievement should be a red flag indicator of potential school failure for all students, but particularly for acting-out students. It is extremely important that the measured achievement of acting-out children be monitored carefully. Such monitoring should be accomplished at least annually, and preferably twice during the school year, using standardized, norm referenced achievement tests.

Norm referenced achievement measures of a standardized nature are constructed so as to: (1) provide standardized achievement comparisons between and among groups of students [i.e., those in the same grade]; (2) provide a general estimate of the extent to which an individual student possesses academic knowledge and skills expected for students at his/her grade level; and (3) verify that the intervention is producing results that are close to the norm. These measures are summative in nature and provide information only on global indicators of academic achievement and clusters of academic skills (e.g., comprehension, word attack skills, number concepts, and so forth).

Information on specific skills and the fluency or rate with which those skills can be applied within an instructional context must be generated through measures and approaches other than norm referenced achievement measures. Curriculum based measurement (CBM) approaches are process oriented and can be used effectively for this purpose (see Shapiro, 1989; Shinn, 1989). The characteristics and advantages of CBM approaches and procedures are described following.

CBM focuses on direct, repeated measurements of student performance **in the curriculum being taught** using production-type student responses that are timed. This is a huge advantage, relative to norm referenced, standardized tests, because it ensures content validity, instructional relevance, and provides for continuous monitoring of student performance over time. Examples of CBM production responses in reading would be the number of words read correctly from a basal reader during a one-minute timed interval or the number of words spelled correctly during a two-minute interval; in math, an appropriate production response for CBM measurement would be the number of correctly written digits during a two-minute interval from grade level computational problems. CBM measures are extremely sensitive to student performance and skill deficits. They are easy to use and of low cost to the teacher in terms of time and effort expended. Further, they yield rich information to guide instructional planning and they provide for careful monitoring and supervision of the student's academic performance over time.

It is highly recommended that **both** norm referenced achievement tests and CBM monitoring of academic performance be used to track the academic adjustment and progress of all students and especially acting-out students. Norm referenced tests can be used to provide a summative indication of how discrepant the acting-out child's achievement level is from grade level expectations. Results of these tests will also identify global skill areas in which the student is deficient. CBM procedures can then be used to monitor performance rate(s) on weak skills, to design appropriate remedial interventions, and to assess their effects.

Figure 4.4 illustrates the use of CBM procedures in monitoring the performance of a student's oral reading rate during hypothetical baseline and intervention periods. This figure plots the rate of words read correctly and incorrectly per minute across school days. As the intervention (e.g., points and praise earned for words correctly read aloud) begins to have an effect, the correct rate slowly accelerates and the error rate gradually decreases.

A broad range of specific skills or skill deficits can be monitored over time in a very sensitive and useful fashion with CBM procedures. This monitoring not only provides key information about a student's performance status on such skills relative to other students, but is extremely valuable in instructional planning and in the design of remedial interventions for addressing such deficits. Normative rates for CBM performance measures are very useful for comparative purposes and can be generated by selecting several

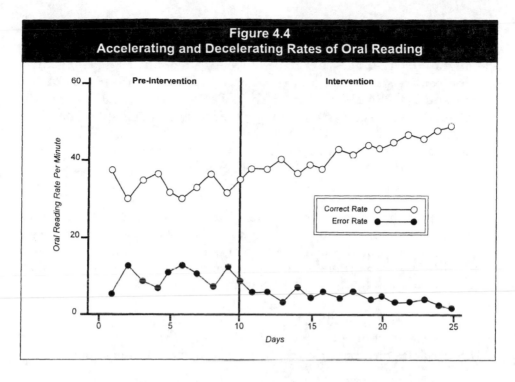

Figure 4.4
Accelerating and Decelerating Rates of Oral Reading

same sex peers who represent the class average, and having them respond to the same timed, academic task(s) as the target acting-out student.

Archival School Records

Archival school records are a treasure trove of valuable information about students—particularly at-risk students who have difficulty in adjusting to the demands of schooling. Archival school records accumulate naturally over time and provide "elephant footprints" that document an individual student's history of adjustment to the schooling process. School records are rarely used systematically in making decisions about students, but they represent some of the most useful information available regarding students' adjustment and achievement.

One of the reasons these records are so underutilized is that they are considered to be largely anecdotal and therefore nonsystematic. Thus, their utility in student decision making is perceived as limited. However, nothing could be further from the truth!

The author and his colleagues (Walker, Block-Pedego, Todis, & Severson, 1991) have developed the *School Archival Records Search (SARS)* procedure to address this situation. Believing that archival school records are a rich and extremely valuable information source about students, the authors developed a coding template to overlay existing school records and extract key information on eleven variables. These variables are as follows: (1) **demographics (i.e., age, sex, grade, etc.)**; (2) **attendance**; (3) **achievement test percentile scores**; (4) **number of grade retentions**; (5) **in-school academic and behavioral referrals**; (6) **special education eligibility**; (7) **placement outside the regular classroom**; (8) **the receiving of Chapter 1 services**; (9) **out of school referrals**; (10) **negative narrative comments**; and (11) **written reports of disciplinary contacts with the principal's office**. *SARS* contains coding instructions and guidelines for inspecting and transcribing each of these variables onto a *SARS* recording form.

Once the information is extracted from the archival records and transcribed onto the *SARS* coding form, the student's profile is scored according to the uniform criteria provided in the *SARS* manual. The *SARS* data can be scored in three different ways depending upon one's purposes. The easiest method is to score each individual *SARS* variable using a plus (+) or a minus (-) scoring system. A plus means that the student is at risk on that *SARS* variable; a minus means that he/she is not. (Students who are not at risk rarely have a + coding on **any** of the *SARS* variables.) Thus, the number of *SARS* variables on which a student is at risk can be counted and added.

The second method is to calculate and profile *SARS* domain scores. Using factor analysis techniques on a sample of 800 *SARS* student profiles, the authors found that the 11 *SARS* variables cluster into three areas, or domains (see Walker et al., 1991). These domains are: (1) **disruption**, (2) **needs assistance**, and (3) **low achievement**. The disruption domain is composed of *SARS* variables that measure poor behavioral adjustment to the demands of schooling (e.g., discipline contacts). The needs assistance domain consists of *SARS* variables that represent specialized school services (e.g., in-school referrals for speech, language, or academic problems). Finally, the low achievement domain indicates lower than average academic performance and access to Chapter 1 services. By counting the number of + individual *SARS* variables, compared to students who are not at risk in each of these domains, the degree of risk or severity for individual students in these key areas of school performance can be estimated.

The third method for scoring *SARS* is fairly complex and is of interest primarily to researchers. This method calculates **factor scores** for each *SARS* domain and requires the conversion of raw scores to standard scores. Instructions for this scoring method are contained in the *SARS* manual, however the calculation of *SARS* factor scores is generally not necessary for the diagnostic, clinical, or prescriptive use of the *SARS* instrument.

The advantages of the *SARS* procedure are as follows: (1) it provides a means for making sense out of the anecdotal "chaos" that characterizes some school records; (2) it makes it possible to quantify and aggregate the school record profiles of individual students; (3) the profiles of individual students can then be compared with "normative" profiles developed for students of the same age and sex; and (4) the severity of a student's school adjustment problems, as indicated by school records, can be reliably assessed.

Perhaps the most powerful uses of *SARS* are in the areas of proactive screening and long-term follow-up. *SARS* profiles student risk status on key variables or dimensions that are associated with later school failure, dropout, and delinquency. The early, regular, and systematic analysis of archival school records for at-risk students provides a means, and a roadmap of sorts, for intervening so as to prevent later problems of a more serious nature. *SARS* is also a means of assessing the school adjustment status of individual students, across school years and diverse school settings, long after they have been exposed to intervention programs or specialized placements. All that is required in this regard is permission, by the students' parents and the school, to conduct a search of school records near the end of the academic year so maximum student information is accessed.

The *SARS* procedure makes it possible to access and use information about students that accumulates naturally over time as a normal part of the schooling process. In this sense, the information is essentially free. Further, it is nonreactive—that is, one does not have to "administer" tests or conduct observations which are not a part of the ongoing regimen of school routines. Thus, the intrusiveness and reactivity associated with unique data collection procedures that are so often a part of behavioral research are avoided.

Analysis of archival school records is highly recommended as a means of evaluating and assisting students whose school status is problematic or at risk. This information can be of great value to school professionals in making good decisions about students that will enhance their school survival and success. For example, in researching the role of *SARS* in predicting school dropout, approximately 80% of high school dropouts in grades 11 and 12 can be predicted from their *SARS* profiles in grades 3-6; this figure goes up to 94% when *SARS* profiles in grades 7-10 are used (Walker et al., 1991). The *SARS* variables that account for this predictive ability across these two grade level blocks are as follows: **low academic achievement, negative narrative comments, number of absences, number of different schools attended,** and **referrals to outside agencies**. A student who fits this profile in the primary and intermediate grades is at **severe** risk for school failure and dropout. By seeing this profile early on in a child's school career, something can be done about it. Too often, educators wait until the profile has played out its negative effects on the child—then it's too late.

Self-Reports

Traditionally, self-report measures used with children and youth have not enjoyed a strong history of application or perceived value in the fields of education and psychology (Ollendick & Hersen, 1984). However, as we have moved toward comprehensive approaches to assessment, it has become increasingly apparent that the self-reports of target students should be included, whenever feasible, in order to acquire a more complete understanding of the problem(s) or areas involved in the assessment. Though subjective in nature, self-reports are very important sources of information when assessing such dimensions as anger, depression, anxiety, and self-concept. Acting-out students, for example, are often angry, depressed, anxious, and possessed of very low self-concepts. The observations and impressions of teachers are often not particularly sensitive to these dimensions because they are affective in nature and play out in subtle forms that are not easily detectable through casual observation.

A variety of self-report instruments have been developed and are reported in the literature (see Finch & Rogers, 1984). The *Buros Mental Measurements Yearbook* provides periodic descriptions and critical reviews of self-report instruments as well. The reader is referred to these sources for access to instruments that can be used with acting-out students in the elementary grade range.

Harter (1982) has developed the *Perceived Social Competence Scale for Children* which contains both a teacher form and a child self-report form. The self-report form measures the student's self-perception of his/her social acceptance/competence in four areas: **scholastic competence**, **social acceptance**, **athletic competence**, and **maternal acceptance**. This is an excellent assessment battery with satisfactory psychometric characteristics. Teacher ratings and student self-report ratings make it possible to compare teacher and student perceptions on the same dimensions. The Harter scale is recommended for use with acting-out students and their peers, as appropriate.

Two distinct disadvantages of most self-report instruments as used with children and youth are: (1) they are dependent upon the student's reading level and comprehension; and (2) situations often have to be represented through words, and student interpretations of verbally represented scenarios can vary significantly. These factors place limitations upon the utility of self-report instruments and reduce their psychometric integrity to some extent. However, recent advances in microcomputer-based video capability allow the development of self-report formats that address these two limitations.

For instance, Walker and his colleagues (Irvin & Walker, 1994; Irvin, Walker, Noell, Singer, Irvine, Marquez, & Britz, 1992; Walker, Irvin, Noell, & Singer,

1992) have researched response formats that provide for the **direct** assessment of young children's **knowledge of strategies, ability to recognize cues**, and **skills in predicting the efficacy of specific strategies** for dealing with three social domains. These domains are: (1) joining ongoing (already formed) play groups; (2) coping with teasing and provocation; and (3) complying with adult commands and directives.

Results of this prototype research indicate that students in the primary and intermediate grades can interact effectively with computer-mediated, video representations of social situations and communicate their responses directly by touching the screen when prompted to supply their answers to narrator queries. Scenes presented in this matter greatly improve the visual reality of key social situations and are not dependent upon high levels of reading skill. Further, the results of these assessments indicate that clear differences in knowledge of strategies, cue recognition, and prediction of outcomes can be detected among groups of students expected to differ on these dimensions (i.e., severely emotionally disturbed [SED], learning disabled [LD], and regular students). This is a promising line of assessment inquiry, but one that is in its relative infancy. Unfortunately, classroom applications of this technology are a long way off.

However, the initial results of this research highlight the importance of attempting to query acting-out children about their views on coping with the social environment. Often, these children have very discrepant views of themselves, compared to their peers, in terms of what is acceptable in seeking to have one's way or to cope with awkward/difficult situations. Behavioral tactics and strategies that acting out students view as acceptable and normative are quite often judged to be unacceptable and **not** normative by their peers and/or teachers. Frequently, acting-out students are not aware of just how discrepant their views and behavioral standards are from those of others. In such instances, their behavior, based upon such standards, is likely to be punished by the social environment. For these reasons, it is important to debrief with acting-out students from time to time regarding their behavior and to suggest alternative approaches for coping with situations they do not handle well. These occasions can be used to teach acting-out students standards of rule governed behavior that have great survival value in both school and nonschool settings.

Conclusion

This chapter has presented information on strategies, guidelines and tactics for assessing the social and academic performance of acting-out students and their peers. Assessment should not occur as a generalized, unfocused activity simply because it is recognized as a best practice. But rather, assessment activities should be initiated only in relation to specific assessment functions that are essential to realizing such priorities as determining eligibility, planning interventions, identifying at-risk students, evaluating the outcomes of interventions, and so on. Having said this, there is no more important activity to ensure the school success of acting-out students than the careful monitoring of their status and response(s) to interventions.

Behavior Management Techniques for the Acting-Out Child

Introduction

This chapter describes and illustrates the use of proven intervention techniques for effectively managing the acting-out child in the classroom setting. Up to this point, the primary behavioral characteristics of the acting-out child; school and teacher attempts to cope with the behavioral challenges presented by these students; the rules that govern their classroom behavior; and principles and procedures for assessing, recording, and interpreting the social behavior and academic performance of acting-out children have been detailed. This chapter outlines how to effectively change the behavior of acting-out children so as to improve their social adjustment and academic achievement, and to generally manage the classroom more effectively.

A series of individual intervention techniques are presented. These include: (1) setting rules, (2) contracting procedures, (3) stimulus change, (4) verbal feedback, (5) teacher praise, (6) reinforcement procedures, (7) modeling plus reinforcement of matching responses, (8) shaping, (9) timeout, (10) response cost, (11) systematic social skills training, and (12) self-monitoring/self-control. Each technique is defined and information and examples are given to illustrate its usage; guidelines for its correct application as well as issues to consider in using each technique are also presented. Finally, the advantages and disadvantages associated with these techniques are discussed.

In Chapter 6, recommended combinations of these and other intervention techniques are described and illustrated along with the conditions appropriate for their use. These illustrations involve behavior problems and deficits commonly displayed by acting-out students. Finally, some perspectives are presented for the reader's consideration on the use of classroom intervention procedures with the acting-out child and with children in general.

The values and attitudes that education professionals hold regarding behavior change procedures can be either an important barrier, or facilitator, of the approaches one is willing to consider implementing.

Individual Intervention Techniques

Setting Rules

— Definition —

Setting rules refers to the process of defining the teacher's expectations concerning classroom behavior in explicit, specific terms.

— Illustrative Examples —

Not all children listen carefully when teachers present the instructions and requirements for assignments. The result can be numerous repetitions of instructions and directions on a student-by-student basis before all are engaged in the assignment and are making progress toward completing it. Much valuable instructional time can be wasted in this process. Acting-out students are particularly vulnerable to this problem because of their generally poor attention spans.

As a first step in solving this problem, the teacher can set up a general rule relating to assignments and how instructions and directions for them will be given. This specific rule might read as follows:

- No instructions or directions for assignments will be given until **all** students are listening and paying close attention.

Another example involves lining up behavior. Children are usually very difficult to manage when they are organizing themselves for a particular activity. This is especially true when they are preparing to go to lunch or recess, which are highly desired activities that make children excitable. In these situations, structure is also greatly reduced, and with it, the teacher's ability to influence child behavior becomes more limited. As would be expected, acting-out children are even more difficult than usual to manage in such situations.

One reason for the greater likelihood of disruptive, out of control behavior in such situations may be a lack of clearly defined rules that communicate the teacher's expectations and behavioral standards. Suggested rule(s) for lining up behavior include:

- Before going to lunch or recess, all assigned work for the preceding period must be completed satisfactorily.

- When you are sitting quietly at your desks and your work has been put away, you can be dismissed.

- Dismissal will be in rows, with one row dismissed at a time.

- Hitting, yelling, pushing, shoving, or fighting while lining up will result in the loss of a recess or the lunch period for the individual(s) involved.

Child behavior in the hallways and on the playground is also difficult to manage for all the reasons mentioned here and in Chapter 1. However, carefully defined rules governing appropriate behavior in these less structured settings can be of assistance in preventing or reducing disruptive child behavior.

Rules for hallway behavior might include:

- Walk at a reasonable pace. **No running** in halls.

- No loud talking or yelling.

- Do not disturb other children in class as you walk by.

- Stop when a teacher tells you to stop.

Playground rules might include:

- Follow the rules of whatever game you are playing.

- Follow the instructions of the playground supervisor.

- No hitting, shoving, or fighting on the playground.

- Cooperate with others and take your turn.

- Use equipment properly.

These rules are presented simply to illustrate the characteristics of such rules in general. They are not intended as the only rules that would be appropriate in such situations or settings, but should serve merely as examples for the reader.

— Guidelines for Correct Application —

There are certain guidelines that should be followed in the development and communication of rules to children. For example, rules should be clearly defined and stated in **behavioral** terms. Vague rules relating to ambiguously defined behavior are probably no more effective than a complete absence of rules. Examples of both clearly defined, behavior specific rules and vague, general rules are presented in Figure 5.1.

Figure 5.1 Examples of Good and Poor Classroom Rules	
Good Rules	**Poor Rules**
1. Raise your hand before asking a question. ⟷	1. Be considerate of others.
2. Listen carefully to teacher instructions. ⟷	2. Behave in class.
3. Pay attention to the assignment and complete your work. ⟷	3. Work hard.
4. Do not talk to others during work time. ⟷	4. Don't disturb others.
5. Take your turn in group activities. ⟷	5. Be cooperative.

A good rule identifies a specific behavior or activity in very precise terms; that is, the target behavior or goal is expressed in **overt** terms. Remember that the correct interpretation of a rule's meaning should require as little inference on the part of the child as possible.

It is usually a good idea to involve all the students, as a group activity, in the process of developing rules for both classroom and nonclassroom areas. However, this is primarily a matter of teacher discretion. Elementary age students in particular may be more committed to the rules if they participate in their development, although this has not been clearly proven.

Rules should be developed at the beginning of the school year so the students have a clear, unambiguous idea of the difference between appropriate and inappropriate behavior from the start of their association with the teacher. This is not to say that rules cannot be developed at any time during the year. However, they are likely to be more effective if developed at the beginning of the school year as a first order of business.

The teacher should be absolutely sure that all the children in the class understand the rules that are developed. Each rule should be thoroughly discussed with the class. Inividual children should be asked to explain what each rule means. It is also helpful to have children role play the behavior or activity identified by the rule with the teacher's assistance, prompting and coaching as appropriate. The rules should also be reviewed on a daily basis until all the class members are thoroughly familiar with them, and then weekly or biweekly thereafter.

Finally, the rules should be posted where all the children can readily view them. Rules are commonly posted on a bulletin board or blackboard. Or, they can be written on construction paper (approximately two feet by three feet) in large letters using a magic marker so that they stand out. The rules should be visible from anywhere in the classroom.

— Issues to Consider in Setting Rules —

It is very important that rules be developed to serve as guidelines for appropriate child behavior. However, a class of children should not be overwhelmed with so many rules that they cannot remember them all, much less follow them. There is no magic figure governing the number of rules that should be developed for any setting. However, each child should be able to at least remember the rules that exist for the setting.

Rules should be fair, reasonable, and within the children's capacity to conform to them. If the rules are perceived as unfair or unreasonable, they will not be effective in positively influencing the behavior of some students, or perhaps even a majority of them.

Finally, the rules should be applied equally and fairly to all members of the class. Rules are really standards that establish behavioral goals for all class members. Even though some children will break the rules much more often than others, it should be understood, on both a cognitive and behavioral level, that the rules apply to everyone. The teacher's application of the rules and consequences supplied for breaking or following them is really the only way to ensure this outcome.

Advantages and Disadvantages of Setting Rules —

The advantages of setting rules are obvious. They communicate the teacher's expectations regarding child conduct in both classroom and non-classroom areas. Rules serve as standards or goals for appropriate child behavior. Consequently, they can prevent the occurrence of maladaptive/disruptive behavior due to a lack of knowledge concerning appropriate versus inappropriate behavior. In this respect, rules can be viewed as antecedent events that actually reduce the probability of inappropriate child behavior. Rules are very easy to construct and their long-term benefits usually far outweigh the effort invested in their development.

However, it should be noted that the effectiveness of rules is dramatically influenced by the consequences backing them up. Rules by themselves usually produce only a minimal effect or no appreciable effect upon child behavior. However, if rules are backed up consistently by appropriate consequences (i.e., rewards for following the rules and no rewards, or loss of privileges, for not following them), then they can be of great assistance to the teacher in managing child behavior (Greenwood, Hops, Delquadri, & Guild, 1974).

Rules alone generally have **no effect** upon the behavior of acting-out children (Madsen, Becker, & Thomas, 1968; Morgan & Jenson, 1988; O'Leary, Becker, Evans, & Saudargas, 1969; Walker, Hops, & Figenbaum, 1976). The behavioral repertoires of acting-out children are usually so strongly developed that rules alone have almost no chance to significantly change their behavior. This is not to suggest that acting-out children should not have a clear understanding of the rules governing appropriate behavior. However, rules alone are more likely to produce a behavioral effect with other children and with the class as a whole than with the acting-out child.

Contracting Procedures

— Definition —

A performance contract is usually a two-party agreement between, for example, a teacher or parent and the child, which specifies the role each will perform in achieving a certain goal. The contract may also specify consequences for one or both parties for meeting (or not meeting) the terms of the contract.

— Illustrative Examples —

Classroom rules designed for the entire class provide only a generalized, albeit very important, form of classroom management. In contrast, a contract is a method for individualizing classroom rules for the acting-out child or other student(s), and for specifying the consequences that back up the rules. An example of a contract is provided in Figure 5.2.

In this contract, the teacher evaluates the child's behavior and/or academic performance at regular intervals throughout the day and makes an overall judgment as to whether the child has complied with the terms of the contract. If the answer is yes, then a point is awarded on a point recording form kept on the child's desk or carried by the teacher. If no, the point is withheld and the child has an opportunity to earn a point during the next available rating period.

Figure 5.2
Contract

_____ **agrees to do the following:**

1. Listen to instructions from the teacher.

2. Complete work neatly, accurately, and on time.

3. Comply with teacher directions.

4. Take part in group discussions.

5. Raise hand before asking a question.

6. Cooperate with others during group activities.

7. Respond to teacher corrections.

The teacher agrees to:

1. Check _____'s behavior/performance at regular intervals during the day.

2. Award a point on a point recording form if _____ has been following the rules.

3. Sign a Good Day Card at the end of each school day indicating that _____'s behavior/performance has been satisfactory, if applicable.

Consequence:

If _____ earns 80% or more of the points available, then the teacher will sign a Good Day Card indicating a satisfactory school day. _____ can exchange the card for a privilege at home. (One Good Day Card can be earned each school day.)

Signed:

_____   _____
     Child   Teacher

A contract can specify a series of behaviors, tasks, or terms a child must comply with, or it can be built around a single behavior or task. For example, the contract shown in Figure 5.3 deals only with a child's academic performance.

Figure 5.3
Academic Contract

_____ **agrees to:**

Complete all assignments with a 90% level of accuracy and make corrections as indicated.

Consequence:

One minute of free time will be earned for each assignment completed with at least a 90% level of accuracy.

Signed:

_____   _____
          Child   Teacher

This is a very simple contract. However, it communicates precisely the teacher's academic expectations for the child and specifies the consequence available for meeting its terms.

Contracts can be as simple or as complex as the teacher chooses to make them. Further, more than one contract can be developed for a given child. The teacher's objective(s), the student's ability and performance level, and the classroom (or nonclassroom) situation to which the contract applies must all be considered in determining the type of contract that is to be developed.

— Guidelines for Correct Application —

As with classroom rules, the terms of the contract should be perceived as fair, equitable, and reasonable. Individual contracts should be negotiated with the child and discussed thoroughly. Both parties should agree to carry out their negotiated responsibilities and to certify this by signing the contract. The consequences to the child for following the terms (and for not following the terms) of the contract should be specified within the contract. It is absolutely essential that these consequences be made available as prescribed.

As with classroom rules, the child should not be overwhelmed with the terms of the contract. It is better to write a series of contracts than to construct one that is so complex it becomes unwieldy and possibly ineffectual.

Finally, the child's ability to meet the requirements of the contract should be carefully monitored. For example, if the terms are not met for two to three days in succession, the teacher should check to see whether the requirements are too difficult. If so, they should be readjusted accordingly. Inappropriate consequences could also be the cause of a failure to meet the terms of the contract. Therefore, the back-up consequences should also be evaluated regularly and varied as necessary.

— Issues to Consider in Using Contracts —

There appear to be no deleterious effects associated with the use of contracts to motivate children to achieve and behave better. The primary caution to be considered with contracts is that they should not be too complex and that an individual student should not be overwhelmed with too many contracts. Parents can be key partners in the development and application of contracts; they are an important resource in this context.

— Advantages and Disadvantages of Contracting Procedures —

Contracting procedures give the teacher a means of individualizing rules for the acting-out child and arranging consequences tailored to the child's preferences. They make it possible for the teacher and child to enter into a meaningful negotiating process concerning teacher expectations and child behavior. After an agreement has been reached, each party is formally committed to the terms of the contract by signing it. All of these factors increase the chances that the child in question will behave more appropriately; however, they by no means guarantee it.

There are few disadvantages associated with contracts. Perhaps their primary disadvantage is the amount of time required to develop an effective contract. It is obvious that individual contracts cannot be developed for all members of the class. It would simply consume too much valuable teacher time to develop 25-30 individual contracts and monitor them effectively. Further, some children would likely require more than one contract.

Consequently, if contracts are to be used, they should be applied to small numbers of children on an individual basis. As a general rule, they should be applied to the performance of those students who are experiencing difficulties in their academic achievement and/or behavioral and social adjustment.

Contracting procedures may or may not be effective in changing the behavior of a given acting-out child, although contracting is likely to be more powerful than rules alone in changing behavior. However, for some acting-out children, performance contracting will have to be supplemented with more powerful procedures.

Stimulus Change

— Definition —

Stimulus change is the alteration of controlling antecedent events or conditions for the purpose of changing child behavior.

— Illustrative Examples —

One of the most common examples of stimulus change is the case where two children who often talk to each other during class are separated (moved to different parts of the room). In this case, it is impossible for them to talk together from across the room. However, it does not mean they cannot talk to other children who are sitting near them. In this specific instance, separating the students may not solve the problem and holds the possibility of actually making the problem worse!

A child who does not always comply with teacher commands and instructions may be deliberately noncompliant. However, it is possible that the child may not hear all the teacher's commands or instructions. Or the teacher's commands may be so vague, complex, and unclear (e.g., beta commands) that the child really can't comprehend what the teacher wants. If this were the case, the teacher would perceive the child as disobedient when in fact the noncompliance is attributable to the hearing problem or to the teacher's giving beta rather than alpha commands.

If an audiological examination revealed a significant hearing loss, then a hearing aid could possibly solve the child's problem. If the noncompliance stopped after the child's hearing capacity was improved to within normal limits, then the changed behavior could be attributed to the hearing aid, (i.e., changed stimulus conditions that made it possible to hear clearly). Similarly, if the teacher shifted from giving beta commands to alpha commands and this shift was accompanied by a substantial increase in the student's rate of compliance, then the child's changed behavior is likely due to the preceding change in the teacher's commands.

A further example of the value of changing stimulus conditions involves reading. A child who is experiencing reading problems will probably be referred to a reading specialist for a diagnostic/prescriptive evaluation. After a thorough evaluation and analysis of the child's performance, the specialist may discover that the child has no knowledge of phonics. If an intensive training program in phonics was developed and applied to improve the child's skills, noticeable improvement in reading performance would occur over time as a result. In this instance, the phonics instruction represents a change in stimulus conditions which improves reading performance.

Yet another example involves a teacher who has a bad habit of giving vague, poorly organized instructions for assignments. Consequently, many children are confused and do the assignments incorrectly. The teacher decides to change this practice and develops very precise, carefully defined instructions for each assignment given. As a result, the rate of confusion about assignments is dramatically reduced; the frequency of follow-up, clarification questions decreases; and the number of children who complete their assignments correctly increases substantially. The changed stimulus conditions in this instance were likely the improved instructions for assignments.

— Guidelines for Correct Application —

To use stimulus change techniques effectively, the teacher must have a good idea about which classroom condition(s) and/or event(s) are influencing or accounting for the child's problem behavior. Second, these condition(s) and event(s) must be changeable. Thus, the teacher must have both keen observing skills and good "engineering" skills to take advantage of stimulus change techniques. As is obvious, the **functional assessment of student behavior**, as reviewed in Chapter 4, is a key tool in making effective use of stimulus change techniques. It takes training or self-study, and practice, to use this approach with maximum effectiveness.

Often the teacher does not know in advance which conditions or events are controlling the child's behavior. Only by carefully noting the circumstances that exist when the behavior occurs is the teacher in a position to identify causal factors that may influence or account for the behavior. After careful observation, the teacher may conclude that there are as many as four or five associated events or conditions that could control the behavior in question. If these events or conditions have the potential for being changed, then the teacher can begin by altering the one that he/she considers to have the greatest influence on the behavior. Then if there is no corresponding change in the behavior, then the next most probable condition or event can be altered until one is identified that actually accounts most powerfully for the behavior.

If altering none of the events or conditions works, then the teacher may conclude that no antecedents under the teacher's control can be identified that will effectively control the behavior. At this point, it would be appropriate to consider consequences that might be manipulated to change the behavior.

Another alternative would be to identify a second set of potentially controlling conditions or events and test them as before. However, the teacher has only a limited amount of time and energy to invest in this process. In changing child behavior, there is always a trade-off between the cost (in terms of time and energy) of a particular technique to the teacher or parent and its effectiveness in producing the desired result. This is usually a judgment that must be made on a case-by-case basis and varies greatly for individuals.

— Issues to Consider When Using Stimulus — Change Techniques

Stimulus change techniques can be used in both a preventive and a remedial sense. Based on his/her previous teaching experience and on a sound knowledge of good teaching techniques, the teacher can arrange classroom conditions or events that will optimally facilitate both academic performance and appropriate classroom behavior. This can result in the actual prevention of much maladaptive, undesirable behavior later on and in a higher rate of academic achievement than would otherwise be the case.

On the other hand, stimulus change techniques can be used to modify inappropriate behavior and to eliminate learning problems after they have developed. This is a remedial use of the technique and can be quite effective if controlling antecedents can be feasibly identified and changed.

As mentioned previously, stimulus change techniques and the manipulation of antecedent events or conditions should be the **very first** approach considered in the task of changing child behavior. However, it is not always possible to identify a controlling antecedent or to identify one within a reasonable amount of time. Further, it is often not feasible to change antecedent(s) even though the teacher suspects they may actually account for the problem behavior or disrupted learning process in question. Much of child behavior and performance is influenced powerfully by positive and negative antecedents occurring outside the school setting. In cases such as these, the teacher should consider other methods for changing the child's behavior.

— Advantages and Disadvantages of — Stimulus Change Techniques

There are two primary advantages associated with stimulus change techniques. These are cost effectiveness and permanence of treatment effects. If a controlling antecedent can be identified fairly easily, and if it can feasibly be changed, then permanent changes in behavior may be achieved with a minimum investment of teacher time and energy. As a rule, once the teacher has identified and changed the controlling antecedent event(s) or condition(s), no further investment of time and effort must be made in order to maintain the changed behavior, provided that it is controlled exclusively by the changed antecedent(s).

As mentioned previously, some child behaviors are not responsive to changed antecedents. Other behaviors are so strongly developed that they require the manipulation of **both** antecedents and consequences in order to be effectively changed.

Stimulus change techniques should be viewed as a valuable tool for facilitating the occurrence of appropriate classroom and playground behavior. However, it is important to remember that while stimulus change can be a highly cost effective behavior management technique, it may not be sufficiently powerful in isolation to change the acting-out child's behavior.

Verbal Feedback

— Definition —

Verbal feedback refers to the process of giving children information about the appropriateness and/or inappropriateness of their academic performance or social behavior.

— Illustrative Examples —

Classroom teachers rely heavily upon verbal feedback in teaching children academic concepts and in managing instructional contexts. Feedback concerning the correctness of academic responding is quite instrumental to effective and efficient learning. Instruction is essentially a process of arranging antecedents, carefully, eliciting child responses in relation to these structured antecedents, and providing feedback as to the correctness or appropriateness of child performance. Precorrections, cueing, prompting, coaching, and debriefing are all forms of verbal feedback that help children learn.

One of the reasons computer-based, programmed instruction is so effective as a teaching device is that the student can supply answers to stimulus items and then check immediately to see whether they are correct. Computer assisted instruction makes use of instantaneous feedback to facilitate the acquisition of new concepts and skills.

Verbal feedback is used constantly by teachers in managing child behavior in the classroom. Feedback in this context can be positive, negative, or neutral. Unfortunately, most teachers are more likely to reprimand inappropriate child behavior than to praise or give neutral feedback regarding appropriate behavior. Studies have shown that reprimands can actually increase rates of the problem target behavior(s) to which they are directed (Madsen, Becker, Thomas, Koser, & Plager, 1968; Morgan & Jenson, 1988).

As mentioned previously, stating rules and giving children feedback when they are not following the rules may have only a minimal effect upon their behavior. Several studies have shown this to be the case (Madsen, Becker, & Thomas, 1968; O'Leary, Becker, Evans, & Saudargas, 1969). These now-classic studies suggest that rules are much more effective when they are backed up occasionally by consequences.

Verbal feedback from classroom consultants has proven to be highly effective in assisting teachers in the process of changing their classroom management practices. For example, Cossairt, Hall, and Hopkins (1973) found that a combination of instructions, feedback, and social praise was highly effective in increasing teacher praise for student attending behavior. Similarly, Hops, Greenwood, and Guild (1975) found that feedback supplied by a teacher consultant in the classroom was instrumental in assisting regular teachers to increase their praise rates to appropriate forms of child behavior. The use of behavioral rehearsals, precorrections, coaching, and debriefing are especially effective in this regard.

A teacher's corrective feedback to a student might sound like the following example: "Jamie, you attempted all the problems you were assigned. You missed only three out of 15. Excellent work! Now can you help me find the mistakes in the three problems you missed?"

— Guidelines for Correct Application —

Feedback during the instructional process should be given immediately following child responses whenever possible. During individual seatwork periods, it is obviously impossible for the teacher to provide students feedback regarding their academic performance except after the assignment or occasionally during its completion. There are simply too many students involved to make continuous or semicontinuous feedback practical.

However, in small group, large group, or one-to-one instructional situations, the teacher does have an opportunity to give immediate feedback following children's oral or written responses. It is extremely important that children receive feedback following both positive and negative responses in these situations. The type and immediacy of feedback given to children in these situations can have a significant bearing upon how well they learn.

If a child's response is correct, or appropriate, the teacher should confirm it verbally and praise the child for giving the correct answer using **behavior-specific** praise. If the response is incorrect or inappropriate, the teacher should communicate in a neutral, **nonpunitive** way that the answer is incorrect. The child should then be given another chance to supply the answer, with the teacher providing prompts when appropriate. If the child

Chapter 5

still cannot produce the answer, it should be given by the teacher or another child should be called upon, depending upon the instructional situation, to supply the answer. However, it is important not to embarrass the child for this inability to respond correctly.

A good rule to remember is that feedback should be delivered in such a way that the child learns something and the chances are increased that a correct response will be given in a similar situation in the future. This is an optimal use of verbal feedback that requires considerable skill, depending upon the nature of the child's problems.

— Issues to Consider in Giving Verbal Feedback —

If used correctly, verbal feedback can be valuable for the teacher in helping children acquire complex academic skills and concepts. However, in the management of child behavior, verbal feedback can be a trap for the teacher which, over the long term, can potentially do more harm than good.

Unfortunately, in the management of child behavior, most teacher feedback is of a negative nature and is expressed in the form of reprimands or criticism. This is almost invariably true with disruptive, acting-out children. Acting-out children, in turn, are often unresponsive to such feedback because: (1) they've heard it so often before from other teachers and their parents, and (2) it allows them to dominate and control their interactions with the teacher (see Chapters 1 and 2).

Although several studies have provided suggestive evidence that teachers' reprimands may have a minimal to moderate effect in reducing disruptive child behavior (Jones & Miller, 1974; O'Leary, Kaufman, Kass, & Drabman, 1970) most experts in the field of behavior management would agree that this is a very inefficient and costly method of controlling child behavior. Further, it could be that the effectiveness of teacher reprimands are only of a short-term nature. It is possible that with some children, particularly children who are only minimally disruptive, teacher reprimands may produce a short-term suppression of the behavior in question but actually strengthen it over the long term. As a general rule, teachers should not rely upon warnings or reprimands to manage child behavior in the classroom.

For instance, the author was observing in a classroom for emotionally disturbed children where the teacher was using a system of warnings, backed up by a brief timeout, for inappropriate behavior. The children were allowed three warnings for each of a series of disruptive classroom behaviors before the consequence of timeout was applied. One of the children came over to the teacher and inquired as to how many warnings he had accumulated for disturbing others. The teacher told him that he already had two warnings and that he had one left. The child then promptly walked over to a classmate who was working on an assignment and engaged him in an argument. This episode illustrates how children, particularly acting-out children, will take advantage of a classroom situation where the teacher relies primarily upon warnings and reprimands to manage child behavior.

If warnings and reprimands are to be used in the classroom, they should be backed up consistently with consequences which are effective in positively influencing child behavior. It may not be possible or even necessary to pair each warning or reprimand with a back-up consequence; however, children should not be taught that warnings and reprimands have no meaning beyond their delivery by the teacher.

— Advantages and Disadvantages of Verbal Feedback —

Verbal feedback can be invaluable in the instructional process. However, its use as a behavior management technique can be very risky for the reasons outlined here (and addressed in Chapters 1 and 2). As long as the teacher is assured that his/her feedback is having a positive, therapeutic effect on child behavior, then its use is justified. However, the teacher should be extremely sensitive to the potentially deleterious consequences of using this technique to manage child behavior.

Teacher Praise

— Definition —

The delivery of a positive verbal, physical, or gestural stimulus for the purpose of increasing the behavior to which it is applied is called teacher praise. The teacher's affective tone and general attitude in delivering praise should be warm, approving, and positive. Praise can be expressed in a variety of forms such as tousling a child's hair, winks, hand and facial gestures, as well as verbal compliments and positive behavioral descriptions.

— Illustrative Examples —

Praise is one of the most positive, most natural, and for many children, one of the most powerful techniques available to the teacher for managing child behavior. Teachers who have mastered the correct application of this technique are often amazed at how effective it is in increasing the appropriate behavior of minimally disruptive and other children. Further, it is a readily available, natural resource in the classroom that requires little effort to use.

Some sample praise statements, commonly used by teachers, include:

- Jim, you and Fred are really playing and talking nicely.

- Susan, I like the way you're working hard on your math assignment.

- Marsha is listening to the directions for the assignment very well.

- Ray, your math problems are 100% correct! Very good work!

- Maureen, you read that passage very well!

A more complete list of sample praise statements is presented in Appendix D.

— Guidelines for Correct Application —

There are a number of rules that should be followed carefully in order to maximize the effectiveness of praise. For example, the timing of praise is of crucial importance. Praise should be delivered immediately after the behavior in question (i.e., the target behavior) has occurred. Through this process, the child learns to discriminate between appropriate and inappropriate behavior or correct and incorrect performance.

Proper timing also ensures that the desired target behavior(s) will be reinforced and strengthened. If the delay between the occurrence of the target behavior and praise delivery is too long, it is possible that an intervening behavior could occur. If this intervening form of child behavior were inappropriate or undesirable, then praise could not be delivered and the appropriate target behavior would go unreinforced.

If certain behaviors are ongoing over time (i.e., as in behavioral or continuous streams), it may be possible to deliver praise unobtrusively while the child is engaging in the behavior. For example, if a child has difficulty attending to tasks and completing assignments on time, the teacher can observe the child's performance carefully during an assignment and covertly deliver praise for attending as this behavior occurs. In certain types of social interactions, particularly on the playground, the teacher can praise children for interacting positively with each other during or immediately following the ongoing social exchange. This procedure should be used for continuous stream type behaviors that extend for relatively long periods of time (e.g., attending to tasks, working on assignments, cooperating with others during group activities, and so forth).

The quality of praise is also extremely important to its overall effectiveness. Praise should be both positive and sincere. Children are very sensitive to the teacher generally, and will quickly sense a lack of sincerity or artificiality in the teacher's praise. The delivery of praise should be accompanied by genuine enthusiasm on the part of the teacher.

Teacher praise should be behavior-specific or descriptive; that is, as part of the praise statement, the child should be told precisely what behavior he/she is being praised for. This descriptive praise helps the child to clearly distinguish between appropriate and inappropriate behaviors.

Finally, teacher praise should be varied whenever possible so that it doesn't become monotonous. (The list of praise statements in Appendix D should help the reader in this regard.) Variety and diversity in the praise statements one uses is very important in offsetting the impression of insincerity or artificiality on the teacher's part.

— Issues to Consider in Using Teacher Praise —

Praise is generally a rewarding and powerful stimulus for most children since adult approval has often been accompanied by the delivery of positive consequences in the past. Teacher praise derives much of its power from this conditioning process.

As mentioned previously, however, teacher praise is not effective for all children. It seems that praise, for largely unknown reasons, is not effective for very deviant children and is not sufficiently powerful to change their behavior. When such children are encountered, it is important to try to make teacher praise more rewarding for them. This can be done by consistently pairing teacher praise with positive consequences. After continued pairings, teacher praise may begin to assume the rewarding characteristics of the accompanying positive consequences. If this occurs, then teacher praise alone may be eventually powerful enough to influence the child's behavior. This pairing procedure will be described in more detail later in this chapter.

Praising does not seem to be a "natural" activity for most adults. As mentioned earlier, adults (e.g., parents and teachers) are likely to communicate their expectations to children, either verbally or nonverbally, and then respond to them only when these expectations are **not** fulfilled. In general, praise for appropriate and desired behavior is a rare event, particularly between adults and children. Studies of natural rates of teacher praise and approval to individual children have shown them to be extremely low in an absolute sense and also in relation to other categories of teacher behavior (Brophy & Evertson, 1981; White, 1975). Therefore, in learning to use praise effectively, the teacher must also ensure that it is applied with a sufficient level of frequency to have an effect on the child's behavior.

When using praise to teach children specific skills or to teach them new patterns of behavior, it is important that praise be given often when the appropriate behavior is exhibited. In the early stages of learning, the child should be praised at least once every ten minutes, with the frequency of praise gradually being reduced as the target behavior(s) or skill(s) are acquired. Keeping track of the number of praises using a golf wrist counter or some other recording method is a good way to monitor one's frequency of praise.

— Advantages and Disadvantages of Teacher Praise —

There really are no disadvantages associated with the use of praise other than it may not be effective with some children and that it does not seem to be a natural activity for most adults. Praise is one of the most convenient, most natural (as opposed to artificial), and potentially effective techniques available to the teacher. The correct use of praise can have a very desirable positive effect upon child behavior in the classroom and other school settings. Considering its potential benefits, the relatively low response cost to the teacher of using praise makes it a highly cost effective technique.

Reinforcement Procedures

— Definition —

Reinforcement refers to the presentation of a rewarding stimulus or event for the purpose of increasing a target behavior or response. A stimulus or event is said to be rewarding when its presentation increases the frequency or magnitude with which the reinforced behavior occurs.

— Illustrative Examples —

There are different types of reinforcement as well as different methods by which it can be delivered. There are also different schedules for the delivery of reinforcing events that control both their frequency and actual distribution or availability over time. As to type of reinforcement, there are both social and nonsocial forms. Teacher praise is a form of social reinforcement. Social rewards include verbal praise, hugs, kisses, pats on the back or head, winks, and so forth. Nonsocial rewards include tangibles (e.g., toys, games), edibles (i.e., food, drink), and activity rewards such as free time, classroom activities, extra television time at home, video and computer games, movies, extra recess, helping the teacher, working on tasks with others, and so forth.

There are a wide variety of rewards available at both school and home that can be used to motivate children and to assist in the teaching of essential skills, concepts, and appropriate patterns of behavior. The classroom teacher is in a unique position to take advantage of these sources of reinforcement in teaching children and in managing the classroom. A list of rewards available at school, outside the classroom, and at home is presented in Appendix E.

The two primary methods of **delivering** reinforcers are **token versus non-token reinforcement** and **group versus individual reinforcement**. Tokens in the form of points, checkmarks, punches on a card, stars, or poker chips, which are exchangeable for back-up rewards, can be a very effective means of reinforcement delivery. There are a number of advantages associated with token reinforcement. For example, children differ greatly in the things or activities they find rewarding. Further, the preferences of individual children change over time. With token reinforcement, a variety of back-up rewards can be provided that may appeal to a broader range of individual preferences.

Additionally, the cost of back-up rewards can be arranged according to their market value (i.e., their cost in dollars and cents) or according to the value assigned to them by the child, parents, and teacher. Thus, an item that costs 50¢ could be assigned a cost of 50 points. Similarly, a less expensive item, with a market value of 20¢, could be assigned a reduced cost of 20 points. By providing a range of back-up rewards, from relatively inexpensive to more expensive, children can be given an option of exchanging their accumulated points early or saving them up for a more expensive item.

Finally, token reinforcement makes it possible to gain considerable "mileage" out of each individual back-up reward. For example, an item that costs 35 points results in 35 separate reinforcements; that is, the child must earn 35 separate points before the points can be exchanged for the back-up reward. Similarly, the teacher can charge one point for each minute of free time consumed (e.g., 15 minutes of free time would cost 15 points). In this way, the reinforcing power of individual back-up rewards is used to maximal effectiveness.

Nontoken reinforcement is used by many teachers and parents on an informal and sometimes unsystematic basis. In this type of reinforcement, there is usually a one-to-one relationship between the reward and the behavior that earns the reinforcement. For example, parents often set up contingencies such as the following: "When you clean up your room, you can watch television."; "You have to finish your homework before going out to play."; or "After you take out the garbage and help with the dishes, we'll discuss your request to use the car." Similarly, classroom teachers frequently set up arrangements in which children are free to talk quietly with each other or engage in free time after completing their assigned work.

A form of nontoken reinforcement that has been especially adapted for classroom use is called **contingency contracting**. This system was originally developed by Homme, de Baca, Devine, Steinhorst, and Rickert (1963) and is based upon a very simple idea. Basically, it says that what a person likes to do can be used as a reward for what they **do not** like to do. In most classroom applications of this system, free time (a preferred activity) has been used to reward academic work (not a preferred activity). In this system, a portion of the classroom can be designated as a free time area and children allowed to spend time in it after completing designated amounts of academic work. As a rule, small amounts of time spent on free time activities can be used to reward larger amounts of time spent on appropriate academic work. This technique seems to work best with younger children, but has been used effectively with many students in the K-12 grade range.

Contingency contracting is a formal, systematic application of what has been referred to as "Grandma's Law" (Homme et al., 1963): "You get to do what you want to do after you do what I want you to do." Children can be motivated to work hard, even in content areas they don't especially like, through the correct use of contingency contracting. It can be used with individual children, with small groups, or with an entire class. However, the complexity of operating a system of this type greatly increases as the number of children it is applied to simultaneously expands. Teachers wishing to learn how to use this system should consult primary sources (see Sprick, 1995) on how to implement these techniques successfully.

The second method of delivering reinforcement concerns group versus individual reinforcement procedures. Individual reinforcement is essentially a private arrangement between the teacher and a student or between a teacher, parent, and student. That is, the teacher defines target behavior(s) a child is expected to engage in or establishes rules for the child to follow and then systematically reinforces him/her on an individual basis for doing so. At the other extreme, the entire class can be handled as a single group; that is, rules or target behaviors are defined for the class as a whole, and the teacher reinforces the class for either following or not following the rules. In this system, the entire class earns (or does not earn) a group reward. Essentially, the whole class is treated as if it were an individual child. This is known as **group reinforcement**, and is commonly used in many educational settings.

There are many variations and possible combinations of group and individual reinforcement that have been demonstrated in the literature. Greenwood, Hops, Delquadri, and Guild (1974) have suggested that reinforcement procedures consist of at least three key components. These are: (1) behavioral criteria for determining when and how reinforcement is to be given, (2) procedures for dispensing or awarding the reinforcement, and (3) back-up consequences. Each of these components can be established for a single individual or for a group of individuals in a particular setting, such as the classroom.

The effectiveness of both group (Bushell, Wrobel, & Michaelis, 1968; Morgan & Jenson, 1988; Packard, 1970; Schmidt & Ulrich, 1969; Sulzbacher & Houser, 1968) and individual reinforcement procedures (Kazdin, 1985; O'Leary & Drabman, 1971; Patterson, Reid, & Dishion, 1992) has been well-documented. However, there have been only a relatively limited number of studies directly comparing the effectiveness of group **versus** individual reinforcement procedures. Walker and Hops (1973), for example, investigated the efficacy of individual, group, and combined individual-group reinforcement contingencies in remediating social withdrawal among elementary age students. They found the combined procedure to be substantially more powerful than either individual or group contingencies alone. Further, the group contingency appeared to be at least as powerful as the individual contingency while being easier to implement and monitor.

There are substantive issues to consider in using both individual and group reinforcement procedures. For example, O'Leary and Drabman (1971) have suggested that group contingencies should be monitored carefully because of: (1) the possibility that a particular child in the group is not able to perform the required target behavior(s); (2) the resulting possibility of undue pressure on a particular individual; and (3) the possibility that one or two individuals may find it rewarding to try to subvert the program or to "beat the system."

There are, however, appropriate ways of responding to each of these issues. Group reinforcement procedures should **never** be applied to the behavior of a group of children unless the teacher is certain that all members of the group can produce the requisite target behavior(s) or can follow the established classroom rules. If one or more group members cannot meet the reinforcement criterion, the teacher should either: (1) lower the reinforcement criterion by making it easier to earn reinforcement; (2) redefine the target behavior(s) or change the classroom rules involved so all group members can produce the required behavior; or (3) consider using other procedures if these first two alternatives are not feasible.

As to undue pressures mounting on a particular child, it is unlikely that this will happen if the teacher ensures beforehand that all the children can perform the requisite behavior(s) or can follow the classroom rules. When group reinforcement procedures are used, they should be monitored carefully to determine that the children are working together in a cooperative way to achieve the reward criterion. As a rule, when children are working together to achieve a common goal that is highly valued, they are most cooperative and will even help or tutor each other in order to achieve the goal more quickly.

However, it is true that peers will subtly punish individual children who deliberately subvert the group contingency in order to frustrate the entire class. If this situation persists, then the child or children involved should be placed on a separate system, of lower value, where they are unable to play this role. This has the effect of preventing the disruption of the group reinforcement procedures for the group as a whole and of teaching the individuals involved that such behavior will result in a reinforcement system of reduced value. Then procedures should be established so these individuals can earn their way back into the higher value, whole class reinforcement system.

With individual reinforcement procedures, the question of fairness and equitable treatment of all children in the classroom inevitably arises. The argument is often raised by teachers and parents alike that a child should not be rewarded on an individual basis for what other children are doing naturally and without rewards. Further, teachers are sometimes concerned that if other children see a child being rewarded on an individual basis for behaving appropriately or for performing academically, they will misbehave or stop working in order to be put on a similar reinforcement system.

These arguments may be valid, and they are real and vital concerns of classroom teachers and parents. However, it is the author's impression that these issues are of much greater concern to adults than they are to the children involved. Children are usually quite accepting of peers who are less skilled or less well-adjusted to the demands of schooling and receiving special assistance, including the use of reinforcement procedures, to help them succeed in school. If other children inquire as to why a particular child is receiving such special assistance or treatment, a fair explanation of the reasons will usually suffice. The teacher can suggest that some children need temporary help and special assistance to help them learn academic skills, to get along with others, and to follow classroom rules.

Some teachers object to providing individual rewards for children **at school**, but do not necessarily oppose reinforcing children on an individual basis to help them succeed. In this situation, an arrangement can be worked out in which the child's parents may provide appropriate rewards at home when the child brings home a note indicating that he/she met the reinforcement criterion at school. This arrangement can work quite satisfactorily for all parties concerned, including the target child.

A combined individual-group reinforcement procedure can be used to respond to concerns raised about individual reinforcement. For example, an acting-out child can earn a reward for himself **and** his classmates by achieving and behaving well in class. That is, the child earns the reward on an individual basis which is then shared equally with the peer group. This contingency has been used successfully in numerous studies reported in the literature (Patterson, 1983) and is quite effective. It has the following advantages: (1) all children share equally in the reward; (2) the target child's peers are usually very supportive of his/her efforts to achieve the reward criterion; and (3) it represents a powerful motivational system and teaching device for instructing children and assisting them in mastering new, more adaptive behavior patterns.

There are three basic **schedules** for dispensing reinforcers (Ferster & Skinner, 1957). These are: (1) continuous, (2) ratio, and (3) interval schedules. A continuous schedule of reinforcement means that a target behavior or response is reinforced continuously; that is, each time it occurs. Continuous schedules are used most frequently in the early stages of learning when a new skill or behavior is being acquired. Thus continuous schedules are used to build new behavior(s) in a rapid fashion.

A ratio schedule means that a certain ratio of responses to reinforcers exists and that reinforcement is dispensed according to this schedule. For example, a ratio schedule of 1:5 means that one reinforcer will be dispensed for each five responses; similarly a ratio of 1:8 means that one reinforcer will be awarded for each eight responses produced. Ratio schedules are commonly used to reinforce academic responses in classrooms. For example, teachers often demand that so many math problems be completed or a certain number of pages be read before a reward such as free time is made available.

An interval schedule refers to an arrangement in which a reinforcer is delivered after an interval or period of time has passed. In classroom settings, interval schedules are often used to reinforce social behavior(s) and/or behavior that facilitates academic performance (e.g., attending to tasks). In its strictest sense, an interval schedule means that the **first** response occurring after the passage of a specified interval of time is reinforced. However, in most classroom applications of interval schedules, reinforcers are usually delivered for a continuously occurring behavior after a predetermined time interval has elapsed. Reinforcing a child occasionally for following classroom rules is an example of an interval schedule (e.g., on the average, once every 15-20 minutes).

Ratio and interval schedules, known as intermittent schedules, can be either fixed or variable. Table 5.1 summarizes properties of each of these four types of intermittent schedules. Intermittent ratio schedules (both fixed and variable) can be arranged so as to produce very high response rates. As a general rule, the higher the ratio of responses to each reinforcer, the higher the response rate. Thus, a 1:15 ratio schedule would produce a higher overall rate of responding than a 1:5 ratio schedule.

Table 5.1 Properties of Four Types of Intermittent Reinforcement Schedules			
		Effects on Behavior	
Name of Schedule	**Definition of Schedule**	**Schedule in Effect**	**Schedule Terminated (Extinction)**
Fixed Ratio (FR)	Reinforcer is given after each X responses	High response rates	Irregular bursts of responding; more responses than in continuous reinforcement, less than in variable ratio
Variable Ratio (VR)	Reinforcer is given after X responses on the average	Very high response rates; the higher the ratio the higher the rate	Very resistant to extinction; maximum number of responses before extinction
Fixed Interval (FI)	Reinforcer is given for first response occuring after each X minutes	Stops working after reinforcement; works hard just prior to time of next reinforcement	Slow gradual decrease in responding
Variable Interval (VI)	Reinforcer is given for first response occurring after each X minutes, on the average	Steady rates of responding	Very resistant to extinction; maximum time to extinction

Intermittent interval schedules (both fixed and variable) produce very predictable patterns of responding and tend to generate lower response rates than ratio schedules. Fixed interval schedules produce what is referred to as **scalloped responding**. That is, following delivery of each reinforcement, the response rate tends to drop off and then it gradually builds up again as the end of the fixed interval approaches and another reinforcer is delivered. The resulting response pattern acquires a configuration that is scalloped.

A variable interval schedule, on the other hand, produces a moderate and steady level of responding. Because of its intermittent nature, it is impossible to predict exactly when reinforcement will occur. Thus, to maximize their chances of being reinforced, it is necessary for children to respond at a moderate, relatively stable rate over time.

Fixed interval schedules have relatively limited applications within class-room settings. Sometimes children are rewarded for spending fixed amounts of time persisting at certain tasks. For example, a negative, unco-operative child could be reinforced with one minute of free time for each five minutes of constructive behavior exhibited during a joint activity with other children. Fixed interval schedules used in this way are essentially a performance contract between the teacher and child where the child is informed, in advance, of the fixed units of responding required to earn each reinforcer.

Fixed ratio schedules are used much more frequently by classroom teachers, particularly in the area of academic performance. It is a common occurrence for the teacher to assign a child 10-15 math problems that must be completed correctly before a reward of some kind becomes available. Again, this is essentially a performance contract between the teacher and child.

Variable ratio and variable interval schedules are both used very frequently in classroom settings. In fact, most teachers, because of heavy time pres-sures, are only able to reinforce children on an occasional or intermittent basis. Occasional reinforcement of this type that is unpredictable and whose exact delivery cannot be anticipated is truly variable. A variable schedule means that a response or behavior is reinforced, on the average, for a predetermined amount of responding. For example, in a variable ratio schedule of 1:5, the child is reinforced on the average once for every five responses. Thus, the child could be reinforced after the second, tenth, fourth, seventh, and third responses. Although the child was not reinforced on the fifth response, reinforcement was delivered on the average following each fifth response.

Precise variable ratio-variable interval schedules can be constructed that would account for the entire range of potential human responding. How-ever, it is usually not necessary to reinforce children in classroom settings according to a strict and preprogrammed variable ratio or variable interval schedule. In using these schedules, it is usually sufficient to reinforce an arbitrarily determined percentage of the child's responses. However, to take advantage of the positive characteristics of these schedules, it is extremely important to make the actual reinforcement delivery unpredictable so the child is not able to anticipate it in advance.

In teaching new behavioral and/or academic skills or in strengthening responses that occur at a relatively low level, it is advisable to begin with a continuous schedule of reinforcement. However, once the target behavior or response has been acquired and occurs at an acceptable level, a shift to a variable schedule should be made in order to maintain the response over the long term. Reference to Table 5.1 shows that both variable ratio and variable interval schedules build in greater resistance to extinction than do fixed (or continuous) schedules.

It should be noted that it is nearly impossible for classroom teachers to reinforce children on a continuous basis for any target behavior given their time constraints and responsibilities. However, when teaching any new skill or response, every effort should be made to reinforce the child as often as possible when acceptable forms of the target behavior are produced (i.e., make the schedule as nearly continuous as possible during the early acquisition stages).

— Guidelines for Correct Application —

There are a number of best practice guidelines that should be followed in using reinforcement procedures. Adherence to these guidelines will make your use of reinforcement both effective and productive.

For example, it is extremely important that the reinforcement system used have incentive value for the child or children to whom it is applied. If it does not, the system, no matter how well-designed, will not be effective in changing the child's behavior or in motivating him/her to achieve. It is important to provide a diverse array of reinforcing activities and/or events for children to earn. The greater the variety of back-up reinforcers available, the more likely it is there will be something to appeal to each child to whom the reinforcement procedures are applied. Both home and school reward options should be considered in this regard (with the agreement of the parents, of course).

There are several ways to go about gathering information about a child's reinforcement preferences. For example, the teacher can simply ask the child to suggest a list of activities or events that he/she would like to work for. It may be advisable to compile two lists; one for reinforcers available at school and one for those available only at home.

Second, the teacher can put together a reinforcement menu and have the child select events or activities from the menu. If this procedure is used, the menu should contain a list of activities/events as inclusive as possible in order to appeal to the varied reinforcement preferences of children in general. Space should be provided for children to add reasonable reinforcement ideas to the menu.

Third, the teacher can observe the activities a child engages in during free-time periods and/or the objects, toys, games, etc. he/she chooses to play with during free time. A careful recording of this information will provide clues to the child's preferences for different back-up reinforcers.

None of these methods are foolproof. For example, what a child says that he/she would like to work for is not always that which is actually chosen. Children will often select a back-up reinforcer in advance to work for and then later change their minds and exchange for something else, thereby indicating that the original back-up reinforcer has lost its incentive value. Similarly, children will sometimes exchange a number of times for a favorite event or activity and then grow tired of this activity/event. Teachers should keep careful records of the back-up reinforcers children choose or exchange points for. In this way, a determination can be made as to which reinforcers are effective in motivating children and which are not. If the reinforcement system suddenly loses its effectiveness, the first thing that should be checked is whether the back-up reinforcers available coincide with the children's preferences.

Back-up reinforcers should also be arranged in sequential order according to: (1) their actual market value; (2) their magnitude (i.e., perceived value to the child); or (3) the degree to which they are valued and preferred by the children. In this way, higher quality performance or greater amounts of work can be demanded for the more preferred/more valuable reinforcers. Consequently, children can be taught to delay exchanging and to accumulate credits toward more expensive items. As a general rule, children should have the option of exchanging for a back-up reinforcer at least once every day, provided their behavior has been appropriate.

Another rule for the correct use of reinforcement concerns who controls and manages the reinforcement system. In the early stages of learning or acquisition, the teacher should maintain control of the system, particularly with highly deviant children. Child-determined reinforcement and self-control are long-term goals that should be considered. However, substantial and durable changes should be achieved in a given child's behavior before the teacher relinquishes control of the reinforcement system and turns management of it over to the target child.

Teachers should not argue with children about how much work should earn the various back-up reinforcers. Clear rules governing the ratio of amount of work required for various back-up reinforcers should be established and communicated to the child or children involved in the reinforcement system. Once developed, these rules should not be altered if at all possible.

Sometimes children will approach the teacher and say, for example, "If I do ten math problems correctly, may I have some free time?" Under no circumstances should the teacher agree to such a request. If he/she does, then the child is, in effect, in control of the reinforcement system by virtue of being able to dictate reinforcement contingencies to the teacher. It is far better to carefully define the reinforcement contingencies in advance and to remind the children about the details of these contingencies if confusion develops.

Whenever a reinforcement system is established, careful attention should be given to what constitutes a reinforceable response or behavior. This is a relatively complex area since the criterion for a reinforceable response is likely to change over time. For example, an initial goal for an extremely disruptive, hyperactive child might be to simply sit still for brief periods and listen carefully to teacher instructions. After this has been mastered satisfactorily, the reinforceable response can be changed (e.g., the child may now be required to sit still for longer periods of time, listen to teacher instructions, and attend to the assigned task). In this fashion, the reinforceable response can be gradually increased until the child is achieving and behaving satisfactorily.

It should be noted that this is a **gradual** process. It is extremely important that the initial reinforceable response be one that the child can reasonably produce. If the initial response is too difficult or beyond the child's capability, then the reinforcement system will not have a chance to work effectively. The rule to remember is to begin with an appropriate reinforceable response and then gradually increase it until the child has progressed to a satisfactory level of performance. The teacher should ensure that the child has mastered each level within the chain of reinforceable responses, from initial to final response, before the criterion for reinforcement in increased.

When a response or behavior is selected for reinforcement that meets the reinforcement criterion, the reinforcer should be delivered **immediately** after the behavior/response occurs. With interval schedules, the reinforcer should be delivered immediately following the occurrence of the designated interval. Immediate reinforcement delivery serves several purposes. For example, it builds in a clear discrimination as to which response or behavior results in reinforcement. Immediate delivery also has a greater effect in strengthening or building the target behavior. If reinforcement delivery is delayed after the target behavior occurs, it is possible that another behavior could occur in the interim resulting in reinforcement of the wrong target behavior!

As noted previously, some target behaviors occur in a continuous stream fashion. Attending to tasks and cooperating with others in joint activities are examples of such behaviors. It is difficult to single out discrete examples of such target behaviors and to deliver reinforcement immediately after they occur. Instead, reinforcement must be delivered as the behavior is occurring. This can be done in an unobtrusive way so that the target behavior is not disrupted. Observing the ongoing behavior carefully and selecting a time in which reinforcement can be delivered unobtrusively is the key to making this approach work.

Consistency is an important part of the teaching-learning process. Similarly, consistent application is an extremely important part of correct reinforcement delivery. If a child is reinforced for engaging in a given behavior in one situation and then either ignored or punished for engaging in that behavior in another situation or at another time within the same situation, the child's learning and behavior will reflect this lack of consistency. It should be mentioned that while a teacher may not be able to reinforce each occurrence of a given target behavior, under no circumstances should it be deliberately ignored or punished.

It is also important that teacher praise be paired with reinforcement delivery whenever possible. Pairing behavior-descriptive praise with reinforcement delivery has a number of advantages. For example, the praise clearly communicates the teacher's approval of the child's behavior and simultaneously informs him/her why the praise and reinforcement are being delivered. Second, by virtue of being consistently paired with reinforcement delivery, praise can assume the reinforcing properties of the actual reinforcer(s) used. This is especially important since teacher praise is not always initially effective with many acting-out children. By systematically increasing the incentive value of praise through pairing it with reinforcement, the teacher is in a position to gradually reduce the frequency of reinforcement and to substitute praise. After systematic pairing, the teacher's praise may be much more effective in maintaining the child's appropriate behavior.

Frequency of reinforcement delivery is a variable that must be carefully attended to in the correct use of reinforcement procedures. In the early stages of teaching a skill or behavior that occurs either continuously or at a relatively high rate, it is desirable to reinforce the behavior at least once every five minutes. After the behavior has been strengthened and is occurring at a higher rate, the reinforcement delivery can be gradually reduced over time. At this stage, once every ten minutes would be a reasonable frequency. It would also be desirable to occasionally fill in with unpaired praises once the reinforcement frequency is reduced. The reinforcement frequency should be gradually reduced over time as the child's behavior indicates that this is possible in order to: (1) set the stage for withdrawing it altogether, and (2) making the reinforcement more manageable for the teacher.

If a behavior occurs at a relatively low rate, then a much larger percentage of the child's target behavior can be reinforced. As the behavior increases in rate, this percentage will decrease unless the reinforcement frequency is concomitantly increased. As a general rule, it is a good idea to concurrently increase the frequency of reinforcement as a low rate behavior increases until it can be assured that the behavior has been acquired and is consistently occurring at an acceptable level.

As to the frequency of exchanging (e.g., credits or points toward a back-up reinforcer), a general rule to follow is that a child should have an opportunity to exchange for a back-up event or activity at least once per day **provided** his/her behavior has been appropriate for most of the day. Some room should be allowed for errors and mistakes. A good criterion for reinforcement is that if the child's behavior has been 80% appropriate or better for the entire day, then he/she would be able to exchange for the least expensive item or activity on the list of back-up reinforcers at the end of the day. If the program is not in effect for the entire day, the 80% criterion can still be used regardless of whether academic performance or appropriate behavior is being reinforced.

When points or credits are used as units of reinforcement, exchangeable for back-up consequences, a problem can develop with hoarding—the accumulation of large amounts of points. Sometimes, children will accumulate points just for the sake of accumulating them. When this happens, the reinforcement system may lose some of its effectiveness for the child or children involved. One way to prevent this problem is to establish a rule where the children must cash in all their points at the end of each week and begin fresh the next. In this way, children usually do not build up enough points to reduce the effectiveness of the reinforcement system.

— Issues to Consider in Using Reinforcement Procedures —

The question of moral and ethical objections to the use of reinforcement procedures in school inevitably arises in connection with the establishment of reinforcement systems. It is argued, for instance, that reinforcement: (1) restricts a child's choices and behavioral diversity by teaching him/her to engage in a very limited response pattern so as to achieve reinforcement; (2) teaches the child to respond appropriately only when reinforcement is available and not at other times; and (3) undermines a child's natural intrinsic interest in activities. Logical arguments can be developed both for and against each of these issues. Unfortunately, it is not currently possible to prove or disprove either side of these issues. Advocates for positions on either side of them have argued these issues endlessly with little in the way of consensual resolution achieved.

However, there is no question that reinforcement works and that it is effective in teaching children to achieve more and behave better. It is a valuable tool available to the teacher for helping children acquire needed academic and social skills. Reinforcement procedures should be viewed as a short-term remedial tool for teaching children new skills and response patterns. After such skills and behaviors are acquired, the formal reinforcement system can be gradually withdrawn, while ensuring durability or persistence of the newly acquired skills/behaviors with appropriate maintenance procedures.

The term reinforcement procedures, as used thusfar, refers to external reinforcement of either a tangible (e.g., points, free time, objects of interest) or intangible (e.g., praise, physical or verbal gestures of approval) nature. It also refers to a system or schedule of reinforcement that is manipulated by someone else, usually an adult, for the purpose of teaching specific skills or for encouraging the child to behave in a different way. It is not feasible to expect that adults can maintain such systems indefinitely in order to ensure that children follow established rules or continue to display specific skills.

At some point, such externally managed systems tailored specifically for a single child must be removed. The challenge is to remove them in a way that preserves as much of the achieved gains as possible. In this context, the hope is that the changed behavior or skills taught will become a permanent part of the child's repertoire and will be maintained by natural reinforcers (e.g., feelings of mastery and achievement; spontaneous expressions of approval from the teacher, peers, or parents for improved performance; and so forth) available in the school and/or home environment. However, the extent to which this goal is actually achieved is a question of intense speculation and disagreement.

Self-control is the ultimate goal of interventions based upon external reinforcement procedures. However, it is not an easy task to get children, especially acting-out children, to the point where they can or will accept responsibility for maintaining changes produced by externally managed reinforcement systems. If the time, expertise, and resources are available, it is recommended that a three-stage behavior change process be considered. That is, an externally managed reinforcement procedure is implemented initially to produce desired changes. Control of the system is then transferred to the target child, who is **directly** taught to manage and control his/her own behavior. When the child is successful in doing so, the system is gradually faded out, with control shifting to naturally occurring reinforcers available in the child's social environment. The effective use of self-management/self-control with an acting-out child is illustrated in a case study provided in Chapter 8.

Acting-out children place such intense pressures upon the management/instructional skills of teachers and upon school personnel in general that these professionals are usually receptive to techniques and procedures that will teach acting-out children appropriate academic and social skills. Reinforcement procedures, if used properly, can be of invaluable assistance to school personnel in managing the acting-out child. However, while reinforcement procedures can be instrumental in producing powerful changes in an acting-out child's behavior, they are by no means magical. The procedures must remain in effect long enough for the changed behavior to become a **permanent** part of the child's repertoire. Building in changes that become permanent is a very complex process, and one that educators are just beginning to understand.

— Advantages and Disadvantages of — Reinforcement Procedures

The advantages of reinforcement procedures are obvious and have been reviewed indirectly in earlier sections of this chapter. The primary disadvantages concern the response cost accruing to the adult implementing the reinforcement system and the general tendency for behavioral changes not to generalize to those settings in which the reinforcement procedures have not been implemented.

The use of reinforcement procedures is essentially a trade-off between their cost to the implementer, usually the teacher or parent, and their effectiveness in producing the desired changes in child behavior. If the procedures are applied correctly, reinforcement is usually a highly cost effective procedure. However, it should be obvious that the correct use of reinforcement requires the investment of time and effort by the teacher (or parent). The majority of the time and effort that must be invested is expended initially in setting up the system. The actual daily operation of a reinforcement system requires a surprisingly small amount of the teacher's time and effort.

The tendency for the positive effects produced by reinforcement procedures not to generalize to nonintervention settings is a more troublesome problem. A number of studies have been conducted on this issue and most show an overall lack of generalization as a rule (see Horner, Dunlap, & Keogel, 1988). This means that if it is expected that a child's behavior will change across a number of settings (e.g., different classrooms, the playground, the lunchroom, home, etc.), then the reinforcement program or a variation of it must be implemented in those settings as well.

In summary, the potential benefits of reinforcement procedures seem to far outweigh their disadvantages. It should be noted that the precision with which such procedures are applied will usually be reflected directly in the behavior of children to whom they are applied.

Modeling Plus Reinforcement of Matching Responses

— Definition —

Modeling plus reinforcement of matching responses refers to a teaching procedure in which a behavior or skill is demonstrated by a model (usually a teacher or parent), and the child is reinforced for producing correct matching responses.

— Illustrative Examples —

Modeling plus reinforcement of matching responses is an extremely powerful teaching device. It combines the instructional precision of modeling with the motivational properties of reinforcement. Bandura (1969), who has done the seminal work to date on this and related topics involving modeling and imitation, has suggested that the combined use of modeling and reinforcement procedures is perhaps **the** most effective method available for teaching new response patterns. The procedure is most often used when the instructor is not sure the child can produce the desired response or skill on demand.

For example, the technique is often used by speech therapists to improve the enunciation skills of children who have articulation problems. Sounds which the child has difficulty pronouncing correctly are identified. The therapist then models the correct pronunciation of each of these sounds and asks the child to produce the sound. Feedback as to correctness is given following each attempt by the child. Child responses which closely approximate those of the therapist are positively reinforced. Usually, after the child has demonstrated a reasonable mastery of the sounds involved, words are identified which contain them and the teaching procedure is repeated.

Modeling plus reinforcement is also very useful in teaching children social skills and appropriate patterns of social behavior. Many children are rejected by their peers because they do not have the necessary social skills to either initiate or maintain positive social relationships with classmates. Further, some children are highly agitated and negative with others; their initiations to others are often characterized by aggression and hostility. Consequently, peers tend to avoid them whenever possible because of their aversive behavioral characteristics.

These children are also generally unresponsive to the social bids of others and thereby do not reinforce peers for initiating to them. Thus, even when peers do make initiations, acting-out children systematically train them not to do so by punishing the initiation. This detrimental cycle of rejection, and the associated confirmation of negative peer expectancies, effectively iso-lates acting-out children and deprives them of the social engagement op-portunities that: (1) establish social support networks, (2) foster the development of friendships, and (3) provide essential peer group socializa-tion experiences.

In cases such as these, the teacher can model appropriate social skills in private rehearsal sessions and then reinforce the child for matching them in social interactions with classmates. Another option would be to involve one or more classmates in the modeling/role playing sessions and have each child take turns matching the demonstrated social skills in their interactions with each other. Reinforcement could be delivered as each child displayed the appropriate social skills during ongoing social exchanges. If necessary, the reinforcement system could be extended to the target child's social interactions with classmates in the classroom, on the playground, in the lunchroom, and so forth.

While consulting at a residential school for children and youth with severe hearing impairments, the author observed a highly effective demonstration of the use of modeling plus reinforcement in teaching a deaf child correct sign language. The child in question was a male adolescent with very limited communication skills and equally deficient social skills. His teachers had been only minimally successful in teaching him sign language so that he could communicate more effectively with others. A psychologist at the institution designed a teaching routine for him that used modeling plus reinforcement of matching responses.

Three individuals were involved in the teaching procedure. These were the boy, one of his peers, and the resident dorm counselor. The teaching procedure was carried out daily in a private area and went as follows. The counselor asked the peer a simple question using sign language like, "What is your name, please?" The peer responded in sign with, "My name is ____." The peer was rewarded with elaborate praise and an M&M® candy **each** time she responded correctly using sign language. The counselor would then turn to the boy and ask the same question in sign language. If the boy responded correctly after watching the prior scene, he was rewarded with praise and an M&M; if not, he received no reward and another question was asked of the peer and the routine repeated. This proved to be a highly effective teaching procedure; however, a number of learning trials were required before the boy would respond appropriately to the counselor. In the absence of a powerful teaching procedure such as this, it is unlikely this boy would have ever developed the requisite signing skills.

In this instance, the target skill was modeled for the boy by one of his peers. Further, he was able to observe her being rewarded for responding appropriately. After each trial, he was given an opportunity to respond in the same fashion and to be rewarded as she was. This teaching routine combined excellent instructional procedures with a powerful incentive system. As a result, dramatic growth in the boy's mastery of sign language was apparent within a short period of time.

— Guidelines for Correct Application —

Although modeling plus reinforcement is perhaps most appropriate in direct instructional situations where the teacher is not sure whether the target response or skill is within the subject's behavioral repertoire, it can be used for a variety of tasks and teaching situations. Because of its power and precision, this can be a highly cost effective technique for teaching children complex social, language, and academic skills.

The first rule to consider in using this technique is that the target skill be modeled **correctly** for the child. It is literally true that the child will learn what is demonstrated and selectively reinforced by the model. Second, the target skill should be modeled **consistently** from trial to trial; that is, there should be a high degree of similarity between correct demonstrations of the skill by the model. Third, the instructor should ensure that the child is attending very carefully to what is being modeled. Focused and sustained attention is a very powerful component of the modeling process. Skill acquisition and mastery will be greatly impaired if the attentional repertoire of the child is not well-developed and demonstrated during the modeling sessions. Fourth, the child should be given precise and descriptive feedback concerning his/her performance following each modeling trial. Fifth, correct matching responses should be selectively rewarded with either praise and/or tangible rewards. It is extremely important that correct, rather than **almost** correct, matching responses be selectively rewarded since the responses that are rewarded will be the ones that are ultimately learned and acquired. If less than correct forms of the responses are rewarded as the final or terminal reward criterion, the goal(s) of the instructional procedure will not be realized. It should be noted that prompts and cues can and should be used to assist the student in correctly discriminating and reproducing the target skill being taught.

— Issues to Consider in Using Modeling — Plus Reinforcement

As mentioned previously, modeling plus reinforcement is a very powerful and potentially cost effective technique for directly teaching children needed skills and behavioral responses. The teaching routine must be carefully designed and usually it must be operated by the teacher or some other adult. As a rule, it is carried out in a private or semi-private area where direct observation, communication, and modeling demonstrations are feasible. In certain situations and with some students, it may be possible to use an older, more sophisticated student as a model and trainer; however, close supervision and monitoring of the teaching routine would be required in such instances.

Whenever possible, it is desirable to involve a peer or peers as models and facilitators in the teaching process, especially same age peers who are already competent in producing the skill or response that is being taught. In this way, the target child can observe the adult modeling the skill or response, can observe a peer correctly reproducing it and receiving positive feedback or consequences for doing so, and finally can then attempt to reproduce it himself/herself with the encouragement and assistance of both the instructor and the peer or peers. This is an ideal teaching situation, particularly for teaching complex social skills.

Involvement of a peer or peers can also facilitate generalization of the learned response from the private teaching situation to the classroom or playground. Too often children are taught complex social, language, or academic skills in intensive tutoring sessions where generalization to other settings is assumed to occur rather than directly facilitated. It is extremely important that such skills be selectively identified, reinforced, and thereby strengthened within the **natural** setting(s) (e.g., classroom, playground) where they are expected to occur. Peer(s) involved in the original teaching situation can be of great assistance to the teacher in this process, especially if they are prompted occasionally by the teacher to actively support the child's use of these newly taught skills. Peers generally like to volunteer as "special helpers" in such situations.

— Advantages and Disadvantages of — Modeling Plus Reinforcement

The power, instructional precision, and potential cost effectiveness of modeling plus reinforcement are its most salient advantages. There really are no disadvantages associated with the technique. It does require the involvement of an adult and must be implemented in a tutorial fashion. Further, skills/responses taught in private sessions must be strengthened within the natural setting(s) where they are expected to occur. This is **the** most important rule to remember in using modeling plus reinforcement and related techniques to teach skills to children and youth. However, these minor limitations and inconveniences are more than offset by the potential benefits of this technique's correct application.

Shaping

— Definition —

Shaping is used to build totally new responses that have not previously been a part of a child's behavioral repertoire. Shaping is an appropriate teaching technique to use when the target response or behavior does not currently exist in the child's repertoire and he/she is not initially capable of producing a reasonable approximation of the response. Shaping uses a combination of positive reinforcement and extinction (e.g., ignoring) procedures to build new behavioral responses or skills that did not previously exist.

In using shaping, one begins by reinforcing a form of the behavior that may bear only a remote resemblance to the final or desired form of the target response. This is called reinforcing an **approximation** to the target response or behavior. Shaping is simply the process of successively reinforcing ever closer approximations to the final desired form(s) of the behavior or target response.

The process of successively reinforcing closer and closer approximations is a delicate one. Initially, a relatively crude approximation to the target response is selected and reinforced. After this form of the behavior is strengthened and occurs reliably, reinforcement is then withheld and the behavior is placed on extinction. When this occurs, the subject's behavior becomes more varied and a number of responses are produced in an attempt to meet the reinforcement criterion and thus produce the previously occurring reinforcer. During this process, a form of the behavior is selected for reinforcement that represents a **closer** approximation to the final target response. This form of the behavior is then strengthened and, once it occurs reliably, is also placed on extinction. New forms of the behavior are then produced and an even closer approximation is selected for reinforcement. In this way, the criterion for reinforcement is gradually increased until the final form of the target response is demonstrated and ultimately mastered. This process is known as shaping; that is, ever closer approximations are gradually "**shaped in**" until the final form is achieved.

— Illustrative Examples —

The acquisition of language is a good example of how shaping techniques are used to build new behaviors by primary caregivers. The language repertoire of infants is largely undifferentiated at birth and consists of randomly produced sounds that bear little resemblance to any spoken language. However, as the child matures and interacts with family members, the repertoire of sounds increases and becomes more varied. Parents listen to the child's verbalizations carefully and begin to pay attention to sounds that approximate spoken language. In this process, the correct sounds or words are repeated for the child and parental approval is given for the child's attempts at producing these. As a result, the child learns to listen carefully to spoken language and to try to reproduce this language. Over the long term, highly complex language patterns are acquired through this basic process.

In viewing a film on the use of behavior management procedures within an institutional setting, the author once observed an ingenious application of shaping to teach a developmentally delayed child to walk. The subject of the demonstration was a four-year old girl who was physically capable of walking, but for some reason had not learned to do so. One of her favorite pastimes was eating ice cream.

Two child care attendants set up an arrangement where they positioned themselves opposite each other, seated in chairs, with the chair backs facing each other. Initially, the chairs were only about two feet apart with the girl stationed in between. Each attendant had an ice cream cone. The girl was taught to walk from one attendant to the other, and each time she did, she was allowed one lick on that attendant's ice cream cone.

As the child's motor skills improved and she gained confidence, the chairs were gradually moved further away from each other until her outstretched arms would barely reach from one chair to the other. To facilitate the child's walking from one chair to the other as the chairs were gradually moved even further apart, a pulley was attached to the ceiling with a rope with a handle on its end. There was tension on the rope, and holding on to the handle, the child quickly learned to walk from chair to chair using the rope as an aid. After the chairs were moved approximately 15-20 feet apart, the tension on the rope was gradually released until the child was, in effect, carrying the rope from chair to chair. The rope was then clipped off into about a ten-foot length, and gradually shortened until the child was carrying only a small piece of rope in her hand. One day she eventually dropped the rope and apparently thought no more about it.

Once the child developed her walking skills through this procedure, they generalized beyond the experimental situation. There were a sufficient number of naturally occurring reinforcers to maintain her walking so that she did not regress to a nonwalking state when the ice cream and shaping procedures were terminated.

This is an example of a very successful and innovative use of shaping techniques to gradually build a new behavior. The attendants gradually increased the criterion for gaining access to the ice cream, but at the same time provided the necessary prosthetic aids (i.e., chairs, rope, pulley) that were necessary in this case to facilitate progress from one approximation to the next.

Child care workers and related service personnel working in school settings often use shaping procedures to gradually teach children with **internalizing** behavior problems (e.g., social avoidance, anxiety, phobias, social behavior deficits, etc.) new patterns of social behavior. Many withdrawn children are extremely limited and suppressed in both their verbal and nonverbal interactions with peers. This may be because of a traumatic fear of social interaction, because they have not developed the necessary social interactive skills, or because they have been punished when initiating to peers. Whatever the reason(s), social skills cannot develop in the absence of opportunities to interact with others. Thus, the first step in remediating social withdrawal is to make it possible for a withdrawn child to interact with others.

This is no simple task. However, shaping techniques which initially reinforce only crude approximations of social interactions with peers can be used in this process. For example, as a first step, the withdrawn child could be reinforced for being in closer and closer proximity to peers on the playground. If the child could manage this, he/she could then be reinforced for participating in group games or activities that require no verbal interaction. Next, the criterion could be raised to the point where the child was required to simply acknowledge a previously arranged and prompted social initiation by a selected classmate. Eventually, the child could be required to socially initiate to a peer. As a next step, the withdrawn child could be assigned to a joint activity or game with one or more peers that requires no or only limited social interaction (e.g., chess or checkers).

As the child's skills develop, minimal verbal interaction could be required as part of the criterion for achieving reinforcement. The child could be gradually required, for example, to interact, both verbally and nonverbally, with more and different peers as his/her social skills develop. In this instance, shaping would be a very appropriate teaching technique for moving a child from a position of noninteractive behavior to positive social engagement with a range of different peers.

— Guidelines for Correct Application —

Given a working knowledge of how to use reinforcement and extinction procedures correctly, shaping is not a difficult technique to master. Shaping is basically the alternate application of reinforcement and extinction procedures in conjunction with a gradually increasing criterion governing what is a reinforceable response. However, there are some cautions that one should consider when using the technique.

For example, one should be certain that the form (approximation) of the target behavior selected for reinforcement at any point in the shaping process is clearly distinguishable by the child from other nonreinforceable forms of the behavior. This discrimination is apparent when the child consistently engages in the desired form of the behavior when reinforcement is available and other competing forms of the behavior extinguish. Only when this form of the behavior occurs consistently and reliably should the reinforcement criterion be raised and a closer approximation demanded before reinforcement is again made available.

When raising the reinforcement criterion to a new approximation, one should be sure that the new form of the behavior is in fact a closer approximation to the final form of the target behavior or response, and that it is sufficiently different from the previously reinforced approximation to be discriminated by the child. In the application of shaping procedures, one should progress in sequential fashion through ever closer approximations to the final desired form of the behavior. If this is not achieved, the shaping process will be disrupted and skill acquisition will be delayed.

Related to this concern, one should also ensure that once a given form of the target behavior has been placed on extinction, it is never again reinforced. If this were to occur, the now undesired form of the behavior would likely reappear and possibly at a higher rate than before!

When reinforcing a given form of the target behavior in a chain of approximations, it is important to reinforce **each** occurrence of the form of the behavior that meets the reinforcement criterion. There are several reasons for this. First, immediate and continuous reinforcement builds in response acquisition at the maximum rate; that is, learning is usually fastest with this type of reinforcement schedule. Second, responses that have been reinforced on a continuous schedule will extinguish more quickly. Thus, a continuous schedule produces rapid acquisition **and** rapid extinction of responses—a most desired feature in the use of shaping procedures. Consequently, this is an ideal schedule to use in shaping since the goal is to teach new forms of a target behavior rapidly and also to extinguish those forms quickly when the reinforcement criterion is changed.

— Issues to Consider When Using Shaping —

Shaping is a highly effective but complex teaching procedure. It is time consuming and generally demands a one-to-one teaching arrangement. Shaping requires an ability to monitor a child's behavior very carefully on a moment-to-moment basis, and also to use reinforcement and extinction procedures in a very precise fashion. One should be certain, therefore, that shaping is actually necessary to teach the target behavior in question before using the procedure. If a less labor intensive procedure can produce the same outcomes, then it should be considered first.

Sometimes a close approximation of the target behavior is within the child's repertoire but this is not apparent from casual observation. If this is the case, the use of a reinforcement alone, or modeling plus reinforcement of matching responses would be more appropriate and more cost effective procedures. As a general rule, shaping should be used as a last resort in teaching new skills and behavioral responses after it has been determined that other methods would be either inappropriate or ineffective. Whenever possible, other, less costly methods should always be considered first.

— Advantages and Disadvantages of Shaping —

There are no disadvantages associated with shaping other than its relatively low cost effectiveness in certain situations.

Timeout

— Definition —

Timeout is a behavior management technique in which the child is temporarily removed from a reinforcing situation immediately following the occurrence of some form of undesirable or inappropriate behavior. It is a form of mild punishment and its purpose is to decrease the occurrence of undesirable and maladaptive types of child behavior. Timeout is based on the assumption that removal from the situation is aversive to the child and will reduce occurrences of the behavior(s) to which it is applied. It differs from extinction in that extinction removes a rewarding stimulus or consequence from a previously reinforced behavior, while timeout removes the child from a reinforcing situation. Both timeout and extinction effectively deny access to reinforcement.

— Illustrative Examples —

Timeout generally involves removal from a reinforcing situation for anywhere from three to 30 minutes. Timeout, in various forms, has traditionally been a very popular behavior management technique through the ages. It is likely that even the earliest humans used some form of timeout to socialize and manage their young children. Sending children to their rooms for a while or grounding them for egregious acts are long standing examples of timeout use by parents.

Parents are probably the most frequent users of timeout procedures. It would be rare to encounter parents who have not isolated their child at one time or another for misbehaving.

Wahler (1969), in a now-classic study, taught two sets of parents the systematic use of differential attention and timeout in managing their children's oppositional behavior. The children involved were age six and five, respectively, and were described as stubborn, negative, destructive, and unwilling to obey parental requests and commands. That is, they were **very** oppositional children. The parents were told to be especially sensitive to and provide approval for instances of cooperative child behavior. However, a five-minute timeout period was also applied immediately after each instance of oppositional child behavior.

For a timeout, the children were sent to their bedrooms for five minutes of isolation following each such instance. If a child threw a tantrum while in timeout, the period of isolation was extended until the tantrumming behavior had subsided. The combination of parental approval for cooperative behavior and a brief timeout period for oppositional behavior proved highly effective with both children. Across the board and as a general rule, it is likely that the combination of differential attention/timeout would be more effective than timeout alone in changing child behavior.

Wasik, Senn, Welch, and Cooper (1969) used timeout from social reinforcement as part of an intervention designed to teach disadvantaged children new patterns of behavior within a primary level classroom setting. The two students in the study were seven-year old girls enrolled in a second grade classroom. The goal of the intervention was to reduce their levels of inappropriate, unacceptable classroom behavior and to teach behavior patterns that would facilitate positive social and academic development.

The intervention procedure consisted of teacher praise for appropriate behavior, withholding teacher attention and praise for inappropriate behavior, and timeout (five minutes in a quiet room) for aggressive and disruptive behavior. This intervention combination proved to be highly effective in reducing the occurrence of inappropriate and unacceptable behaviors and in increasing the occurrence of appropriate classroom behavior.

Numerous and varied examples of the successful use of timeout procedures have been reported in the professional literature during the past two decades. These procedures have been used effectively in home, institutional, and classroom settings.

— Guidelines for Correct Application —

The effectiveness of timeout rests on the assumption that removal from ongoing activities is a form of mild punishment which proves aversive to the target child. Therefore, if timeout is applied to certain inappropriate or undesirable behaviors and their frequency is substantially reduced as a result, then we can assume that timeout is being applied correctly and that the setting from which the child is being removed is actually reinforcing.

Timeout should be reserved for forms of child behavior that are difficult to tolerate and that cannot be effectively reduced by other, more positive means. Among elementary age children, it is recommended that timeout be reserved for such behaviors as **teacher defiance, physical aggression** of any type, **property destruction, tantrumming**, and other **similar forms of unacceptable behavior**.

The first rule to consider in the correct application of timeout is that the setting or activities from which the child is being removed must be, in fact, reinforcing for the child. If not, timeout will have only a limited effect (if it has any effect at all) in reducing the occurrence of the target behavior(s) to which it is applied.

Second, the area to which the child is removed should be relatively isolated. However, it is **very** important that the proper supervision be available for the child at all times during the timeout period. Most states have laws relating to the supervision of children in school settings. One should be sure that timeout does not conflict in any way with such laws.

Third, if a timeout room is used, it should be well-lighted, well-ventilated, and meet fire code regulations. Areas within the classroom or in other parts of the school, such as the health room or office, can be designated as timeout areas. If a within-classroom timeout area is used, a desk can simply be placed behind a portable folding screen that is commonly found in schools. If the child engages in disruptive behavior while in timeout, thereby disturbing the rest of the class, he/she can then be removed to a timeout room or another suitable area of the school.

Fourth, the timeout period should be a relatively dull and uninteresting experience if it is to be effective. In other words, timeout should not represent an escape from an unpleasant situation, nor should it be something children look forward to. Consequently, when a child goes into timeout, he/she should not be allowed to take along reading materials, objects to play with, or work assignments. An exception to this rule would be a situation in which a child **asks** to go to a quiet area where he/she can concentrate and be free of distractions. Ideally, another part of the room or school should be arranged for this purpose if the teacher chooses to accommodate such requests. However, this option should not be confused with timeout.

Finally, it has been the author's experience that children tend to be ignored by teachers for relatively long periods of time **after** emerging from timeout. This is probably due to the fact that teachers still carry some emotional anger because of the child behavior that prompted the timeout, and a general belief that children should not be reinforced closely in time following punishment. Thus, the child's appropriate behavior following timeout may be ignored for too long and could eventually extinguish. The danger in this is that the child may learn that the most reliable and efficient way to gain teacher attention is to behave inappropriately. That is, the teacher's attention, although negative and disapproving, is successfully coerced. It is important, therefore, that the child's behavior be observed closely following timeout and that an instance of appropriate behavior be selected and reinforced, if possible, within 10-15 minutes after the timeout period is over. The importance of being sensitive to this issue in using timeout cannot be overemphasized.

General guidelines for using timeout are provided next, followed by a six-step procedure for applying timeout. These guidelines can be used for timeout applications both in school and at home.

General Guidelines

1. Select a place.

2. Prepare the room.

3. Explain the procedure.

4. Practice timeout beforehand.

5. Be consistent.

6. Label the behavior that earns timeout.

7. Don't talk to children when they are in timeout.

8. Be calm and neutral when applying timeout.

9. Use a timer.

10. When timeout is over, don't make the child apologize.

Generic Timeout Procedure

1. **Label the problem**. A simple statement such as, "You didn't stop arguing; that's a timeout" is sufficient.

2. **Wait ten seconds** for the child to go into timeout.

3. **Set the timer** or check your watch for the passage of the timeout interval.

4. **Remove yourself** from the situation during timeout.

5. **Remain neutral**. When the timeout interval is over, do not revisit the behavior that prompted the timeout.

6. **Carry on with regular activities** when the timeout is over.

It is important to be prepared for a child to refuse to go to timeout. Strategies to consider in this situation are to remain calm, add up to five extra minutes to the timeout, and/or remove a privilege in addition to the timeout.

— Issues to Consider in Using Timeout —

Timeout is an effective technique for reducing maladaptive or inappropriate child behavior. However, it is a technique that can be easily abused if it is applied incorrectly. Because of its potential for abuse, and because "punishment" is such an emotionally laden descriptive term, timeout has been the subject of some controversy in the literature of the past decade or so (Skiba & Deno, 1991). However, if used correctly and sensibly, timeout can be a highly effective and appropriate behavior management tool, particularly when applied in conjunction with **positive** reinforcement procedures for supporting appropriate behavior.

In recent years, several highly controversial cases have come to public attention where timeout has been used incorrectly, even unethically. For example, in one instance, an old wooden crate was stood on end, bars were installed, and a padlock used to lock children inside. Furthermore, the parents of the involved students were not informed that timeout procedures were being used to control and manage their children's behavior.

This nightmarish example raises a number of issues that should be considered carefully in using timeout. For instance, parents should be fully informed in advance if timeout is to be used with their children. If it is a part of normal school policy, then all parents should be so informed. In contrast, if timeout is to be used selectively with certain students, then the rationale for and correct application of timeout should be discussed with those parents as part of a legally correct and best practice process.

It is not necessary to lock children in enclosed areas in order for timeout to be effective. In fact, within school settings, there is **no** defensible reason for locking children within any area. Timeout simply removes a child from an ongoing, reinforcing activity for a brief period of time. As mentioned previously, timeout can be used effectively within the classroom by simply blocking off a small area with a portable screen. If a child becomes disruptive while in timeout, he/she can then be removed to another area for the timeout, such as the front office or the health room.

Finally, the length of time a child spends in timeout should be carefully considered. The relative effectiveness of varying lengths of timeout periods used in suppressing such behaviors as aggression, self-destruction, and tantrums have been investigated and reported in the professional literature. Overall, such studies indicate that relatively brief periods of timeout duration (e.g., five to 15 minutes) are generally effective in reducing inappropriate child behavior. However, there will always be some students (especially severely acting-out students) for whom timeout is marginally effective or not effective at all. Keeping such students in timeout for more than 30 minutes at a time generally replicates **Ricardo's Law of Diminishing Returns** in economics. That is, whatever the gains achieved are not commensurate with the efforts and time invested in achieving them.

Most classroom applications of timeout use five- to 15-minute timeout durations. More typically, a class of disruptive or inappropriate child behaviors are defined (e.g., teacher defiance, swearing, fighting, disturbing others, and so forth) and a standard timeout duration of five to 15 minutes is applied to them. As a general rule, a standard timeout of five to 15 minutes is recommended unless special circumstances indicate otherwise. If a child is not responsive to repeated 20- or 30-minute timeout periods, then other procedures should be considered for addressing the problem behavior. The reader is referred to Repp and Singh (1990) for a thorough and enlightening discussion of issues and best practices in the use of punishment generally, and particularly with vulnerable, at-risk student populations.

It should also be noted that a behavioral technology of nonaversive intervention procedures is being developed in which very challenging forms of behavior are dealt with **without** resorting to the use of aversive procedures of any kind. This technology is still under development, but is highly promising in its potential and demonstrated success thus far. However, its successful application is labor intensive, requires great skill, and demands considerable sensitivity and attention to detail. The procedure involves conducting a functual assessment (see Chapter 4) of the conditions surrounding the target behavior's occurrence, and then designing procedures to alter those conditions. See Horner, Dunlap, Koegel, Carr, Sailor, Anderson, Albin, and O'Neill (1990) for additional details about this approach and procedures.

— Advantages and Disadvantages of Timeout —

There is no question that timeout can be effective in reducing inappropriate child behavior. However, in the author's opinion, it should be used only as a last resort in changing child behavior. There are several reasons for this. First, timeout removes the child from classroom activities and deprives him/her of the opportunity to engage in appropriate or productive behavior while in timeout. Second, timeout is an easily abused technique and its use must be supervised and monitored very carefully. Third, when timeout is applied to nondisruptive and relatively innocuous classroom behaviors, it constitutes overkill. Finally, other methods, such as reinforcement-based procedures and response cost (i.e., fines or penalties) are, as a rule, equally as effective as timeout, but are easier to manage and less subject to abuse.

Response Cost

— Definition —

Response cost refers to the removal of previously awarded or earned reinforcers for the purpose of reducing behavior that is considered inappropriate and undesirable. Research evidence suggests that a response cost can prevent as well as suppress the behavior(s) to which it is applied (Kazdin, 1972, 1985, 1987; Rapport, Murphy, & Bailey, 1982; Walker, 1983; Walker, Colvin, & Ramsey, 1995).

In the application of a response cost, reinforcers are removed whenever instances of undesirable/inappropriate child behavior(s) occur. Consequently, a "cost," or penalty, is incurred **each** time the child engages in the target maladaptive behavior.

— Illustrative Examples —

There are numerous examples of response costs in everyday life. Parking tickets and fines for traffic violations are two very good examples of a response cost. In addition to providing city governments with needed revenues, such fines discourage traffic and parking violations. Football games represent another area in which a response cost is used to discourage undesirable behavior. Yardage fines are assessed against the offending team for such infractions as clipping, unnecessary roughness, offsides, and interference. These penalties are highly effective in controlling behavioral excesses in football games. It would be hard to imagine modern football without such penalties.

In recent years, the response cost procedure has been used in a variety of settings (e.g., laboratory, institutional, clinic, and school) to control undesirable behavior of a deviant or inappropriate nature. As a rule, it has proven highly effective in suppressing the behavioral responses to which it has been applied.

There are two forms of response cost (Weiner, 1962, 1963). In the first, points or tokens are awarded noncontingently at the beginning of a session and the student can lose these points for engaging in the target inappropriate/deviant behavior during the ensuing session. In the second form, points or tokens for appropriate behavior can be earned during the session and these previously earned reinforcers can be lost (i.e., subtracted or marked off) for the occurrence of the inappropriate behavior.

Although there is some suggestive evidence that a combination of positive reinforcement and a response cost is more effective than a response cost alone, a study by Hundert (1976) found no difference in the effectiveness between positive reinforcement procedures, response cost, and a combination of positive reinforcement and response cost upon the attending rates and academic performance of a group of special education children. At this stage, it seems fair to conclude that the evidence as to whether a response cost alone is either more or less effective than a combination of positive reinforcement and a response cost is not clear.

A response cost, either alone or in combination with positive reinforcement procedures, has been applied to a large variety of behaviors in natural settings. Target behavior examples include violence, loud noises, maladaptive classroom behavior, rule violations, aggressive verbal behavior, out of seat behavior, obscene gestures, nonattending/academic errors, cigarette smoking, and speech disfluencies. Both the utility and effectiveness of the response cost procedure have been amply demonstrated in a number of studies reported in the professional literature over the past two decades.

Over the past 30 years, the author has used a response cost extensively in the process of modifying the behavior of elementary age students having disruptive and aggressive behavior problems in a range of classroom, playground, and residential settings (see Walker, 1983b; Walker, Colvin, & Ramsey, 1995). Walker, Hops, and Fiegenbaum (1976), for example, applied a combination of teacher praise, points (exchangeable for back-up reinforcers), and a response cost to the classroom behavior of five acting-out children. The combination of praise, points, and a response cost was extremely effective in changing these children's behavior to within normal limits. Moreover, this combination was substantially more effective than praise alone or the combination of praise and points backed up by powerful rewards. In this study, the children were required to earn their points through appropriate behavior, a portion of which were then subtracted whenever instances of the inappropriate behavior occurred.

In a series of subsequent studies, Walker and his colleagues (Walker, Hops, & Greenwood, 1984, 1993; Walker et al., 1995) used response cost point systems combined with praise, group and individual contingencies, and home and school rewards, to remediate the aggressive and socially negative behavior of acting-out students. A representative study from this series involving the playground behavior of a very aggressive, primary grade level boy is described following.

In preintervention baseline observations, approximately 30-40% of this student's social interactions with peers were of an aggressive or negative nature. (Typically, peers are completely positive with each other approximately 90-95% of the time during recess periods.) At the beginning of each playground period, the student was given one point for each minute of time in the period (e.g., 15 points for a 15-minute recess). His goal was to keep the points. Five points were subtracted for each instance of aggressive or negative social behavior, and two points were subtracted for playground rule violations. If all the student's points were lost, the remainder of that recess period was forfeited and he would have to sit out the rest of the recess. However, he could exchange the number of points remaining at the end of the playground period for special privileges at home. In addition, if no episodes of aggressive/negative social behavior occurred in any of the playground periods across the school day, he could earn a special group activity for himself and his classmates near the end of the day.

This intervention procedure was effective in almost totally eliminating the aggressive/negative behavior from the child's repertoire on the playground. Further, there appeared to be some evidence of spontaneous generalization, or "spillover," of the child's improved behavior to playground periods in which the program was not in effect. This is a highly unusual outcome, but seems to occur from time to time when addressing peer social behavior wherein positive social exchanges are reinforced during recess periods early in the school day. Sometimes, these positive social exchanges appear to continue during subsequent recess periods in the absence of formal reinforcement systems (i.e., spillover).

— Guidelines for Correct Application —

If applied correctly, a response cost can be an extremely effective intervention technique. However, to take maximum advantage of its considerable therapeutic benefits, particular attention must be paid to how the response cost is implemented.

For example, the response cost procedure should be carefully explained in advance before it is applied to the behavior of children. Each specific behavioral response to which the response cost will be applied should be identified, explained, and, if necessary, role played for the child or children involved beforehand. Further, the number of points, tokens, or units to be lost for each type of behavioral response should also be communicated in advance. For example, the author and his colleagues rank ordered inappropriate classroom behaviors by their relative seriousness according to the combined judgments of two classroom teachers, and assigned higher point loss values to the more serious behaviors (e.g., obscene language cost four points while talking out cost two points).

It is extremely important that a delivery / feedback system be developed that tells the child: (1) when the response cost has been applied, (2) which behavior it has been applied to, and (3) how many points have been lost as a result. Unless this information is communicated effectively, the response cost will not have a chance to impact the target behavior. There are a variety of ways to construct an effective delivery / feedback system for a response cost. The author developed one that worked quite well for individual children within an experimental classroom. It was based on a card system and is illustrated in Figure 5.4.

One card was used per child per week. The card was approximately 4 x 6 inches, and was taped to the corner of each child's desk. The behaviors listed on the card were described and explained to the children, as was the operation of the card system. During the week, whenever a given child engaged in one of the inappropriate behaviors, the teacher simply walked over to the child's desk and, using a colored pen, marked a dot in the box corresponding to the day of the week and the inappropriate behavior to which the response cost was applied. As a rule, no verbal interaction occurred between the teacher and child during this transaction. However, the child was immediately informed of the inappropriate behavior to which the cost was applied, as well as the number of points lost.

In the sample card shown in Figure 5.4, the child lost 11 points on Monday and 12 points on Tuesday. On Monday, a cost was applied once each to talk outs and disturbing others, three times to nonattending, and twice to out of seats. On Tuesday, a cost was applied once to nonattending, noncompliance, and obscene language, and twice to talk outs. As is obvious, the card provides a permanent record of the application of the response cost for individual children, and should be retained to monitor the use of the procedure over time and for multiple students.

Figure 5.4
Response Cost Delivery/Feedback System

Behaviors	Point Values	M	T	W	TH	F
Out of Seat	2	• •				
Talk Outs	2	•	• •			
Nonattending	1	• • •	•			
Noncompliance	3		•			
Disturbing Others	2	•				
Obscene Language	4		•			
Fighting	5					

The author used a second point card to deliver points for appropriate academic and social behavior (Walker & Buckley, 1974). However, opposite sides of the same card could be used to implement positive reinforcement and response cost procedures.

Another factor that greatly affects the impact of a response cost on behavior is the ratio of points earned or awarded to points lost. This ratio affects the degree to which cost functions as an effective consequence for maladaptive behavior. For example, if a child has a total of three points and loses one of them, the magnitude of the cost is substantial; however, if the child has 24 points accumulated and loses one, the magnitude of the cost is greatly reduced as is its impact. It may not be as effective in suppressing the undesirable behavior as a result.

Kazdin (1972) reports studies using response costs where the fines ranged from ten to 10,000 tokens in a system where each child could earn 1,000 points per day versus systems in which fines ranged from three to 15 tokens for each violation and a maximum of 65 tokens could be earned each day.

Walker and a colleague (Walker & Buckley, 1974) effectively used a system where point losses ranged from one to five points per violation, and 35 points could be earned per day. The point is that there are no standard rules for determining the ratio of fines per behavior to the total number of points available each day; however, if the child is going to produce the inappropriate behavior, he/she should learn that it will be costly in terms of points lost.

A related issue concerns the relationship of cost magnitude to the severity of the problem behavior. As a rule, the more severe the behavior, the more it should cost in points, tokens, or units lost. A greater magnitude of the response cost (i.e., number of points lost) applied to these more serious behaviors is often required to reduce the probability of their occurrence.

Probably the most important rule to remember in implementing a response cost is that **the child's point total should never be taken below zero**. If the child is allowed to go into debt, the ability to influence his/her behavior via the response cost is effectively lost. This is especially true of a **response cost only** procedure in which the child does not have an opportunity to earn additional points to make up for those lost. Even in a point earning/point loss system, the effectiveness of the response cost will be greatly reduced if the child realizes that he/she must earn "x" amount of points just to get back to zero. If a child should lose all his/her accumulated or awarded points, some other consequence, such as a brief timeout, should be used to consequate further instances of inappropriate behavior until additional points have been earned or the period is over.

Consistency in the application of the response cost is also extremely important to its overall effectiveness. The cost should be applied **every time** an identified inappropriate behavior occurs. If the application of the response cost is inconsistent, the child may not form a clear discrimination between appropriate and inappropriate behaviors, and may be inclined to risk engaging in the undesirable behavior on the presumption that a response cost might not be applied.

Verbal interaction in the delivery of a response cost should be kept to an absolute minimum, particularly since the delivery system tells the child which behavior precipitated the application of the cost and how many points have been lost. Sometimes children are inclined to argue or protest the application of the response cost in a given instance. Under no circumstances should the teacher argue with the child about the justifiability of the response cost, nor should the teacher ever be talked out of the cost or intimidated into not using it in a given situation because of tantrumming behavior on the child's part. If this happened, the child would learn to engage in emotional/argumentative behavior in order to prevent the application of the response cost when it was warranted.

The response cost procedure is one of the most powerful and effective techniques available for reducing inappropriate behavior in classroom and playground settings. However, it is **very** important that the implementation guidelines described be followed carefully in the application of a response cost so that its full potential will be realized and problems in its use avoided.

The preconditions and implementation rules that should be observed and followed carefully in using response costs are summarized following.

Preconditions

1. The system should be carefully explained before its application.

2. The response cost system should be tied to a reinforcement system.

3. An appropriate delivery system should be developed.

Implementation Rules

1. The response cost should be implemented immediately after the target response or behavior occurs.

2. The response cost should be applied **each time** an instance of the target behavior occurs.

3. The child should never be allowed to accumulate negative points.

4. The ratio of points earned to those lost should be controlled.

5. The teacher should never be intimidated out of applying the response cost by the target child.

6. The subtraction of points should **never** be punitive or personalized.

7. The child's positive, appropriate behavior should be praised as frequently as opportunities permit.

— Issues to Consider in Using Response Cost —

Like timeout, response cost is considered to be a mild form of punishment. The question arises, then, as to whether undesirable side effects associated with punishment (e.g., avoidance, escape, emotional effects) are also side effects of the use of a response cost. In his review of the use of a response cost in natural settings, Kazdin (1972) suggests that the available studies on escape/ avoidance in connection with the use of a response cost indicate that the response cost tends not to elicit these behaviors. As to emotional effects, he concludes that the available evidence is too limited to draw a conclusion. The conclusions of Kazdin appear to still have validity at this time.

In the author's use of the technique over the years, he has never observed attempted avoidance or escape from the therapeutic situation as a consequence of the appropriate application of a response cost. Even when the response cost was used to reduce aggressive social behavior in playground situations, it did not affect the frequency with which a target child interacted with other children. That is, even though the child lost points for episodes of aggressive/negative social behavior, he still continued to interact socially and to make social bids to others. Thus, claims that response costs suppress appropriate behavior in order to avoid losing points seems to have very little merit.

If the response cost is not carefully explained and implemented according to the guidelines described previously, its application could elicit emotional behavior. In the author's experience, however, the use of a response cost has very rarely, if ever, generated emotional responses from children when applied correctly.

— Advantages and Disadvantages of Response Cost —

The advantages of response costs are obvious from the material presented herein. It is also a highly cost effective technique, given the minimal amount of effort required in its implementation. It has an added advantage over timeout in that the child does not have to be removed from ongoing classroom or playground activities in order to experience consequation for the inappropriate behavior.

The disadvantages of response cost appear to be minimal. The slim possibility of emotional side effects was described previously. Given what is currently known about response cost, its advantages appear to far outweigh its disadvantages. As a general rule, it is to be preferred to the use of timeout since its application does not require physical removal of the student from the situation.

Systematic Social Skills Training

— Definition —

Social skills are stategies and competencies that increase one's social effectiveness. They allow one to: (1) initiate and maintain positive social interactions with others, (2) develop friendships and social support networks, and (3) cope effectively with the social environment.

— Illustrative Examples —

During the past decade, tremendous interest has developed among a broad range of school and related service professionals in improving the social effectiveness of children and youth. Many now believe that some of the social ills of our society (e.g., violence, school failure and dropout, mental health problems, delinquency, vocational incompetence) can be traced to a failure to socialize our children to the norms of socially effective behavior. Neglect, poverty, family stresses, and abuse are all risk factors for primary caregivers and their children in this regard. Young children growing up in such households come to school unprepared to learn and to meet the demands of schooling. Further, they tend to adopt behavior patterns of a coercive nature that very quickly get them in trouble and lead to teacher and peer rejection.

There are two critically important adjustments that children must make soon after entering school. These are called **teacher related** and **peer related** (Walker, McConnell, & Clarke, 1985). That is, all children must negotiate two important social relationships in school, as follows: (1) they must be able to respond to the behavioral expectations of teachers who control the instructional settings, and (2) they must meet the behavioral requirements of their peers who control the free play settings.

Failure in either one of these adjustment areas carries ominous impediments to school success; failure in both puts the child at severe risk for not only school failure but a host of negative developmental outcomes including low self-esteem, low achievement, delinquency, bad conduct discharges from the military, relationship problems, job failure, and mental health problems in adulthood. Long-term studies show that students who fail to make these adjustments early in their school careers experience a host of problems and a lower quality of life in their development (Parker & Asher, 1987).

To meet the teacher's expectations, students are expected to do such things as:

- Comply promptly with teacher directives and commands

- Make assistance needs known appropriately

- Cooperate with others

- Work independently

- Focus and sustain attention on academic tasks

- Respond to teacher corrections

- Display self-control

- Participate in small and large group instructional arrangements

Table 5.2 provides a listing of the sorts of skills that are essential to successful peer relations and that socially competent, popular children display as a matter of routine.

Acting-out children **very** often do not produce these critically important behavioral profiles; the consequences to them for not doing so can be severe both within and outside the school setting. While most children acquire these competencies through parental and teacher instruction and via observational learning (i.e., paying careful attention to the social norms expected in different settings and responding to them), acting-out children, for reasons that are not completely understood, respond differently. Often, they come from homes where positive attitudes toward schooling and the importance of social responsibility are not valued and taught. They are generally not read to by their parents, and do not learn to focus and sustain their attention as a result. Basic social skills that are important in peer relations such as social reciprocity, sharing, being of assistance, and so on are also often not taught and modeled for acting-out children. Thus, schools are left with the tasks not only of educating acting-out children but also teaching them the values, skills, and strategies that support socially effective behavior.

Social skill deficits can be divided into four basic types, as conceptualized by Gresham (1986):

- **Skill Deficits** refer to a failure to learn an essential social skill or strategy.

- **Performance Deficits** mean that the student knows how to perform the skill or strategy but does not do so.

- **Self-Control Skill Deficits** refer to deficits in the student's ability to control or manage affective states (e.g., anger, depression, anxiety).

- **Self-Control Performance Deficits** mean that an interfering emotional state disrupts the student's ability to perform the skill.

Skill deficits require the direct teaching of strategies for coping with a particular situation (e.g., how to join an ongoing peer group, how to make friends, how to deal with teasing and bullying). In contrast, performance deficits require that behavior management procedures and environmental arrangements be applied so the student is motivated and able to perform the skill called for.

Table 5.2
Social Skills and Competencies Required in Successful Peer Relations

- Dispense and receive positive reinforcements to/from others (e.g., praise, affection, compliments)
- Use "low risk" tactics for entering ongoing peer group activities
  - Hovering, waiting for invitations
  - Avoiding disagreements, talking about self, stating feelings, or asking informational questions of those involved in the activity
- Use of appropriate social initiations likely to be accepted by peers
  - Initiating during free time as opposed to scheduled work time
  - Being of assistance to others
  - Volunteering
  - Avoiding demanding or coercive initiating responses
- Display high rates of positive social behavior toward peers
  - Providing helpful suggestions
  - Giving attention and approval
  - Being affectionate
  - Being supportive of peers
- Possess a thorough knowledge of friendship-making skills
- Use good communication skills
  - Ability to assume perspective of interacting partner
- Demonstrate high levels of academic and/or athletic competence
- Possess specialized or unusual skills/attributes that are valued by peers
  - Sense of humor/ability to make others laugh
- Exhibit low levels of task-inappropriate behavior
  - Avoiding getting in trouble with the teacher

The author and his colleagues have developed a widely used social skills curricular program called *ACCEPTS: A Curriculum for Children's Effective Peer and Teacher Skills* (see Walker, McConnell, Holmes, Todis, Walker, & Golden, 1983). This program teaches 28 social skills distributed across five areas, or domains. These are: (1) **classroom skills**, (2) **getting along skills**, (3) **basic interaction skills**, (4) **making friends skills**, and (5) **coping skills**. *ACCEPTS* was developed primarily for the purpose of facilitating the entry into and maintenance of at-risk, elementary age students (K-6) within regular educational settings. The curriculum and teaching formats are arranged to allow for large group, small group, and one-to-one instruction.

A basic rule is taught for each skill in the *ACCEPTS* program. For example, for the skill of joining others, the rule is, **"Say your name and ask to play**." Children are then taught how to do this using a nine-step instructional procedure that involves the following:

1. Define and discuss the skill/basic rule.

2. Provide a positive example of the skill (video).

3. Provide a negative example of the skill (video).

4. Review and restate the skill definition.

5. Provide a second positive example.

6. Conduct teaching activities.

7. Provide a third positive example.

8. Conduct criterion role plays.

9. Implement informal contracting.

McGinnis (1984) has developed a very effective **structured learning** approach to teaching elementary students social skills. Structured learning is a cognitive-behavioral approach to teaching prosocial skills that involves four steps: **modeling of the skill, role playing the skill, providing feedback**, and **transfer of training** or practice in natural, real life situations. This program addresses eleven main skill areas as listed following:

1. Listening

2. Asking for help

3. Apologizing

4. Sharing

5. Joining in

6. Knowing your own feelings

7. Expressing your feelings

8. Dealing with fear

9. Expressing affection

10. Dealing with your own anger

11. Dealing with the anger of others

This is a comprehensive and carefully selected listing of critical skill domains whose mastery is appropriate for both behavior disordered and well-adjusted elementary students. The structured learning approach task analyzes each skill area into its subcomponent skills. For example, **listening** involves the following skills and steps: look at the person who is talking, remember to sit quietly, think about what is being said, say "yes" or nod your head, and ask a question about the topic to find out more. Students who master this sequence of specific skills will be able to demonstrate listening effectively in a range of school contexts and situations.

Neel (1984) has developed a social skills training program for use with students who have behavior disorders that is geared toward the concept of "**critical effects**." That is, social behavior is analyzed according to the critical effects or impact that it has on the social environment (i.e., the actual **function** of the behavior). Nearly all of one's behavior serves one or more functions (i.e., purposes, goals) such as: (1) to seek an outcome, (2) to escape from or avoid a situation, (3) to protect oneself, and so forth. Recall the strategies for conducting a **functional assessment of behavior** as discussed in Chapter 4. The strategy and approaches one uses to produce these effects are called **form**, which can be either adaptive or maladaptive.

Two operational examples of this conceptual approach are provided following:

1. **Initiate/Gain Entry**. The function of the behavior allows access to social interactions and joining an ongoing game or activity. Examples of adaptive strategies and skills used to achieve this goal (form) would be greeting others, hovering and waiting for an invitation, offering assistance, asking for permission, starting a conversation, making a request, and so on. Maladaptive strategies would include barging in, bragging, instructing those in the activity or game, asking questions, or making requests at the wrong time, etc.

2. **Problem Solving**. The function of this behavior is to generate, evaluate, and implement solutions to impasses or obstructions to achieving goals. Positive examples of problem-solving behavior would be gathering information, generating alternatives to solving the problem, trying out a solution, evaluating the result, and trying

other strategies if the first solution is unsuccessful. Negative examples of problem solving would be generating only one approach or alternative to solving the problem, trying the same failed solution repeatedly, being insensitive to contextual cues and factors that might account for why the attempted solution is not successful, and so forth.

This general approach has much to recommend it. Developing greater sensitivity to the motives, goals, and dynamics of behavior is a desirable outcome and one that may be enhanced by this approach. It may be more effective with middle/junior high and high school students than with elementary age students because of its greater dependence upon cognitive development and social maturity.

— Guidelines for Correct Application —

Alberg, Petry, and Eller (1994) have developed a comprehensive resource guide for teaching social skills. This guide contains three chapters and two appendices that address respectively the following topics: (1) the need for social skills instruction; (2) guidelines and procedures for teaching social skills according to best practice standards; (3) how to select and evaluate social skills programs; (4) profiles of eight social skills programs for use at preschool, elementary, middle school, and high school levels; and (5) an annotated bibliography of social skills programs. The author served as a resource consultant in the development of this guide; over four years of federally funded efforts are invested in this project. It is highly recommended and contains many helpful strategies and hints for educators in teaching social skills to a range of students with varying abilities and backgrounds.

Alberg et al. (1994) have identified and described seven recommended instructional strategies for teaching social skills, as follows:

1. **Modeling**. Exposing target students to live or film/tape models who perform the desired skill.

2. **Practice/Rehearsal**. Practicing a specific skill or sequence of behaviors in a structured setting.

3. **Role Playing**. Assuming various roles in interpersonal situations.

4. **Incidental Teaching**. Making use of "teachable moments" to provide instruction as opportunities arise in natural contexts throughout the school day.

5. **Positive Reinforcement**. Reinforcing the use and correct demonstration of previously taught social skills with approval, special privileges, or points exchangeable for back-up rewards.

6. **Prompting**. Giving a student cues which help stimulate or evoke the target social skill.

7. **Coaching**. Prompting the use of the skill by giving instructions, facilitating practice of the skill, and providing feedback on performance.

Various combinations of these instructional strategies are required in teaching social skills effectively. The more severe the social skill deficits and the more at risk the target population, the more likely it is that all of the strategies would be required in the teaching process.

Alberg et al. have also contributed some useful strategies for facilitating the generalization and maintenance of social skills. Generalization refers to the use of previously taught social skills in settings other than the one in which they were taught. Maintenance refers to the length of time a skill persists or endures after the instructional process has terminated and the skill has been acquired. These strategies are as follows: (1) teach skills that will be supported in a variety of settings; (2) involve the target student; (3) take advantage of teachable moments; (4) teach a variety of responses; (5) teach in different settings with a multitude of social agents; (6) fade the consequences; and (7) teach the student self-management techniques.

A set of cardinal rules for the generic teaching of social skills is shown in Table 5.3. These rules are derived from the author's experiences in developing and researching two social skills curricular programs over a decade. They are highly recommended as general guidelines for teaching social skills to elementary age students.

Social skills are extremely important to the development of both academic and social competence. All children who are deficient in key social skills should be instructed in them. At-risk students and those with disabilities are especially vulnerable in their social skills repertoire; nearly all of these populations can benefit substantially from systematic instruction in these skills.

— Issues to Consider When Conducting Systematic —
Social Skills Training

There are three key issues to consider in teaching social skills. These are: (1) the distinction between teaching values versus social skills; (2) the two main, generic approaches used to teach socially effective behavior; and (3) the expected treatment effects from social skills training.

Table 5.3
Cardinal Rules for Teaching Social Skills

- Social skills should be taught as **academic** subject matter content using instructional procedures identical to those for teaching basic academic skills (e.g., reading, language, mathematics).

- Whenever possible, social skills should be directly taught along with possible variations in their appropriate application.

- The critical test of the efficacy of social skills training is the functional integration of newly-taught skills into the student's behavioral repertoire and their demonstration/application within **natural** settings.

- The social context and situational factors both mediate the use of social skills and must be taken into account systematically in facilitating students' use of them.

- Social skills training procedures are not an effective intervention for complex behavior disorders or problems. They represent only a partial solution and should not be used by themselves to remediate aggressive or disruptive behavior patterns.

- Social skills training can be an important complement to the use of behavioral reduction techniques in that it teaches adaptive alternatives to maladaptive or problematic behavior.

- The instructional acquisition of social skills does not guarantee either their application or topographic proficiency within applied settings.

- There is considerable inertia operating against the behavioral integration of newly-taught social skills into students' ongoing behavioral repertoire, as is the case with any newly-acquired skill.

- To be effective, social skills instruction must be accompanied by the provision of response opportunities, feedback, and incentive systems within natural settings to provide for the actual demonstration and mastery of the skills.

- Social validation of the social skills by target consumer groups is a critical step in both the selection and training of social skills.

- There are two types of deficits in social-behavioral adjustment: skill deficits (can't do) and performance deficits (won't do). These deficits should be assessed and treated differently as they require different forms of intervention for effective remediation.

The teaching of values has emerged as a controversial issue in recent years. Schools are caught in a dilemma between those parents who want values taught to their children and those who object strenuously to such teaching and reserve this right for themselves. Social skills are interpreted by some parents as the teaching of values.

The way most social skills curricula are constructed, it would be difficult to make the case that they teach values. Social skills have to do with specific strategies that are taught to negotiate key social tasks like making friends, developing social support networks, meeting the demands of instructional settings, and so forth. Values, in contrast, deal with attitudes and perspectives (e.g., honesty, charity, positive regard, and so on) that are usually not directly taught as a part of social skills instruction.

The two main approaches that have developed in the literature for improving students' social behavior are referred to as **social skills training** and **cognitive problem solving**. The social skills training approach focuses on the direct teaching of social skills that are presumed to support socially effective behavior. The cognitive problem solving approach is strategy-based and teaches generic approaches to solving problems; skills are regarded as incidental to this approach and are not directly taught. The evidence is ambiguous as to which is the most effective approach; however, both have been found to produce improvements in social behavior (see Hollinger, 1987).

— Advantages and Disadvantages of Systematic — Social Skills Training

There are no disadvantages to the systematic teaching of social skills other than the time and effort involved in relation to the outcome gains realized. This relationship is greatly improved if **both** steps of the social skills training process are carefully implemented. The advantages are obvious in that this procedure is totally positive, directly teaches normative standards of behavior and strategies for realizing them, and makes children more aware of and sensitive to each other's social behavior. Plus, if this instruction occurs early in a student's school career, it may help offset problems later.

Systematic social skills training alone is a relatively weak intervention that tends to produce low magnitude treatment effects. If social skills are simply taught as academic content, and provisions are not made for ensuring their behavioral practice and mastery within **natural** settings, there are likely to be no discernible effects from such efforts. Social skills training is a two-stage process. The skills must first be mastered at a **conceptual level** through the use of regular instructional procedures. In order for them to register in a child's ongoing behavioral repertoire, however, they must then be cued, coached, and reinforced within natural settings (e.g., a classroom, playground). This second stage of the training process is called **behavioral mastery** and is absolutely essential to producing acceptable outcomes.

Self-Monitoring/Self-Control

— Definition—

Self-monitoring refers to the consistent tracking, recording, and evaluation of the features of one's own behavior over time; self-control refers to the actual management of one's own behavior based, in part, upon the information generated through the self-monitoring process.

— Illustrative Examples —

Approaches to self-monitoring/self-control share many common elements but differ along a number of conceptual and procedural dimensions (Nelson & Hayes, 1981). Kanfer (1970), one of the leading researchers in this area, has contributed a three-stage model for describing the key elements of self-monitoring/self-control approaches. Stage one consists of the self-monitoring and self-recording of one's own behavior. Stage two consists of the self-evaluation of the results or products of one's behavior to some standard of performance. Stage three involves a self-management/self-reinforcement procedure in which the target student self-awards points for performance based either upon his/her judgment or according to preestablished criteria.

The impact of this approach upon child behavior/performance is greatest when all three of these elements are in place and are integrated into an overall intervention procedure. However, Lloyd, Landrum, and Hallahan (1991) note that the process of self-observation and recording alone can positively influence target behavior(s) in desired directions by increasing some students' sensitivity to and awareness of their own behavior.

Self-monitoring can involve process measures (e.g., paying attention, being socially engaged with others), counts of discrete events (e.g., number of social bids made to others, number of times a previously taught social skill is used at recess), or products of one's performance (e.g., percentage of math problems completed correctly, number of pages read). The self-observation process is generally continuous throughout the period in which the self-monitoring occurs. However, the actual recording of one's behavior can occur at certain points during the period or retrospectively after the period is over.

It is often difficult for students to remember to observe and self-record their own behavior while engaged; thus, self-recording and evaluation opportunities are often lost—and with them many of the benefits of self-monitoring as well. For example, the author and his colleagues were developing a program for remediating the negative/aggressive behavior of children in grades K-3 (Walker, Hops, & Greenwood, 1984, 1993). A student they encountered, Paegan, was a very aggressive second grader who responded well to an intervention in which he earned praise and points, exchangeable for home and school rewards, for being polite and cooperative with peers. The authors decided to try a self-observation/self-recording procedure near the end of the adult controlled phase of the intervention. The idea was to transfer the control and management of Paegan's improved behavior to him. The procedure was implemented in a free-time activity period held daily within the regular classroom.

This procedure did not work well initially because Paegan would do one of two things: (1) he would become so engaged in activities with his peers that he would forget to self-observe and record whether he was being polite and cooperative; or (2) he would be so consumed by the act of self-observation and the need to record that his social behavior became artificial and constrained. Neither outcome was desirable or acceptable. The authors then instituted a prompting routine where the program consultant or teacher, at regular intervals, would quietly remind Paegan to observe and record his behavior. The prompting solved the two problems, and allowed the self-monitoring procedure to work as intended. It proved to be a useful maintenance option.

Lloyd, Landrum, and Hallahan (1991) have reviewed evidence indicating that self-monitoring procedures generally work best when a cueing system is built in for regularly prompting the student to self-record. They describe a case example in which a student was prompted regularly during a spelling assignment to observe and self-record at the sound of a tape recorded beep. Whenever the beep occurred, the student stopped and asked himself, "Was I paying attention?" He then marked "yes" or "no" on a recording form attached to his desk. Cueing to prompt observation/recording is probably desirable, whenever feasible, across the full elementary age range. However, it is most essential for children in the primary grade range.

Elementary age students can also be trained to count the number of occurrences of target behaviors as they occur, to rate the quality of their performance after it occurs, and to graph the products or results of their performance. Depending upon the situation, target behavior(s) involved, and student characteristics, all of these procedures may be appropriate in a single self-monitoring/self-control intervention.

Simple golf wrist counters have been a popular way for children to record forms of their behavior that involve counts (e.g., number of turns taken, number of social bids initiated/received, and so forth). In this procedure, the student simply counts each occurrence of the target behavior as it occurs throughout the period. For this to work, the target behavior must be discrete in nature and have clear starting and ending points.

In self-monitoring and evaluation, students are often asked to judge their overall performance after it has occurred. For example, at the end of a period, the target student may make a judgment on a Likert 1-5 or 1-7 rating scale regarding the quality or effectiveness of the preceding performance. For example, a rating of 1 is very poor and well below average; a rating of 5 is excellent and well above average. As a way of teaching the student to make accurate judgments, the teacher may provide a rating for the same period and compare notes with the student. Often, students will tend to overestimate their performance in the direction of a positive bias; this procedure can teach the child to adopt more realistic standards of evaluation over time. Another possibility is to award bonus points for matching the teacher's rating.

Teaching and supervising students in graphing their daily performance, particularly in the area of academics, is an excellent way to sensitize and motivate them toward higher performance levels. Words read correctly and incorrectly or math problems solved correctly and incorrectly are excellent examples of academic pinpoints that can be used for this purpose. A simple graph with the number of words read correctly on the vertical axis and consecutive days plotted along the horizontal axis, for example, will allow such graphing. The student should be supervised by the teacher in graphing the daily performance; this is also an excellent opportunity for debriefing with the student about his/her performance (i.e., to discuss corrections, provide feedback, and praise performance).

In an ingenious use of self-recording and self-evaluation procedures, Rhode, Morgan, and Young (1983) successfully promoted the generalization and maintenance of behavioral gains, produced in a resource room, for the same students when they were assigned to a regular classroom. As a first step, these students' appropriate classroom behavior was improved in the resource room using praise, feedback, point systems, and back-up rewards. They were then taught to judge their own behavior and to use recording and self-evaluation tools in doing so. When they were assigned to a regular classroom, they rated their own performance and compared their judgments with those of the teacher. They received points for matching the teacher's rating; the matching component was then gradually faded over time so the students were judging their own behavior and awarding points accordingly. This was a very successful demonstration of the use of self-monitoring procedures in facilitating the generalization and maintenance of treatment gains in a nonintervention setting (i.e., the regular classroom).

Miner (1990) reported a study in which self-monitoring and recording, praise and rewards, and a timing device were used to decrease the amount of time required for three elementary students with behavior disorders to walk from the regular classroom to a special classroom. One student was eight years of age and the other two were nine; all had serious problems both with disruptive/aggressive forms of behavior and with meeting the school's behavioral expectations in general.

Over a five-week period, the amount of time taken to walk between the two classrooms was recorded. The average times varied for subjects 1, 2, and 3 respectively: 2 minutes and 13 seconds; 3 minutes and 8 seconds; and 4 minutes and 19 seconds. It was then decided that 58 seconds was a reasonable amount of time needed to cover the distance.

At the beginning of the intervention, a stopwatch was set up on the wall of the regular classroom and the wall of the resource room; the two watches were wired together so that by pressing a button on the regular classroom stopwatch, the resource room stopwatch was activated. It was turned off when the student entered the resource room and pressed a button that stopped the timing. Thus, an exact measure of the amount of time required was recorded daily. The students were asked to self-record each day whether they had made the journey within the 58-second time span. They received teacher praise and access to back-up rewards for doing so. The accuracy of their self-recordings were checked intermittently by adults. A form, similar to that shown in Figure 5.5, was used by each student to record daily performance.

Overall, this procedure was highly effective in reducing the amount of time taken to cover the distance between the two classes. During the intervention, there were very few days in which the students did not cover the distance within the prescribed 58 seconds. The number of days in which the students took 58 seconds or less during baseline and intervention periods were as follows: Subject 1—4% during baseline and 97% during intervention; Subject 2—13% during baseline and 99% during intervention; Subject 3—4% during baseline and 94% during intervention. Follow-up data recorded several weeks after the end of intervention showed very strong maintenance effects.

This was a highly effective intervention that required a relatively low time investment on the part of both participating teachers. Further, it made the students much more aware of their own behavior and produced rapid and substantial reductions in wasted time between classroom settings. The author reported excellent agreement between the self-recordings of the students and the participating teachers. This was perhaps facilitated by the students' knowledge that there was a permanent record of the times involved provided by the interconnected timing devices used.

Figure 5.5
Am I On Time?

Student: _____

Week Beginning: _____

Regular Teacher: _____ Resource Teacher: _____

Monday	Tuesday	Wednesday	Thursday	Friday
Yes	Yes	No	Yes	Yes

— Guidelines for Correct Application —

Self-monitoring/self-control, as an intervention procedure, is most useful in: (1) making students more aware of their own behavior relative to absolute standards or in relation to the behavior of others (e.g., same age peers); (2) producing changes in relatively mild forms of problem behavior (e.g., low rates of academic engagement, noncompliance with teacher commands, failure to raise their hand, and so on); and (3) as a strategy for facilitating the generalization of treatment gains to non intervention settings and in promoting the durability and persistence of behavioral gains produced within the intervention setting.

The following generic guidelines should be followed in using this approach:

1. Thoroughly explain the procedure and why it is being applied to the target student.

2. Ask for the student's active cooperation and involvement in making it work—consider presenting it as a fun partnership between the student, the teacher, and/or parent(s), if appropriate.

3. After explaining the self-monitoring/self-control procedures, have the student practice observing, recording, evaluating, and/or self-awarding points as the intervention dictates.

4. Ensure that the target student thoroughly understands all the features of the system and how it works.

5. Consider arranging home rewards and, whenever possible, a daily home and school communication system regarding the intervention.

6. Hold a daily debriefing session with the student about his/her behavior/performance. Use these sessions to offer feedback,

prompts, corrections, praise, and fine tuning adjustments as required.

7. Use the student-teacher "matching" component to instruct and reinforce the student in making accurate performance appraisals.

8. Once the student has mastered the procedures and the behavior or performance is within desired limits, begin fading the more obvious features of the system and transfer as much control of the intervention to the student as possible.

— Issues to Consider When Using — Self-Monitoring/Self-Control

This intervention approach is highly reactive because the target student is so involved in the observing, recording, evaluation, and reinforcement components. In a therapeutic sense, this reactivity can be highly beneficial when working with acting-out children. Acting-out students have a negative history of having adults "do things to them" in order to control, change, and contain their behavior. Thus, they develop elaborate repertoires of strategies for resisting adult influence. Rarely are they given positive opportunities to work with adults as partners in jointly implementing an intervention that could have positive benefits for everyone. It is likely that many acting-out children will respond positively to the chance to work proactively with adults in shaping their behavior toward more appropriate goals.

Having stated this, this approach should not be used to address severely disruptive or aggressive behavior displayed by such students. Self-monitoring/self-control interventions are not up to the task of coping with such salient and potentially dangerous forms of behavior. Adult controlled and managed interventions are required in these situations as a general rule. However, once students' behavioral levels have been brought to within normal limits on these dimensions, self-monitoring/self-control interventions can be considered as generalization and maintenance strategies.

Because of their behavioral characteristics and histories, acting-out children should be monitored very carefully in their responses to this intervention approach. In particular, they should be held accountable for making accurate and honest judgments about their behavior or performance. Teaching them high standards of proficiency in this regard is one of the potentially most beneficial strategies educators can implement for acting-out students.

Finally, in evaluating the results of self-monitoring/self-control interventions generally, it is a good idea to maintain a concurrent data recording system to monitor the intervention. Because of the tendency for students to overestimate their performance, reliance upon student supplied data may be risky (Lloyd, Landrum, & Hallahan, 1991).

— Advantages and Disadvantages of — Self-Monitoring/Self-Control

The major disadvantage of self-monitoring/self-control approaches to intervention is their relative lack of power. They are not suitable for addressing severe forms of maladaptive behavior and they require a certain level of cognitive awareness and social maturity for effective application. Their implementation is also more difficult with younger than older children.

On the plus side, they are very positive in their focus and they address the ultimate goal of any intervention—assumption of responsibility by the target student for the behavior change process and its enduring effects. Lloyd, Landrum, and Hallahan (1991) have listed four advantages of self-monitoring/self-control interventions: (1) they increase the effectiveness of an intervention, (2) they decrease the demand for direct intervention by teachers through saving time, (3) they improve the maintenance of treatment effects, and (4) they increase the chances of transfer of treatment effects. These are huge advantages and they make consideration of this approach very worthwhile.

Conclusion

The goal of this chapter has been to present thorough descriptions and illustrations of the applications of intervention techniques that, in the author's view, are very worthwhile for use with acting-out students. Obviously, these same techniques can be used to good effect with other students having less severe behavior problems.

There will be numerous occasions in which these techniques can be applied singly with great success. However, the more severe the behavior problems of target students, the more likely it is that combinations of these techniques will be required to generate the intervention power necessary to address them effectively. Chapter 6 illustrates how these combinations can be applied successfully.

6

Combinations of Intervention Techniques

Introduction

Various combinations of the intervention techniques described in Chapter 5 are presented following, along with a discussion of: (1) the situations appropriate for their use, (2) relevant implementation details, and (3) their probable effects. These combinations of intervention techniques are illustrated in their applications to behavior problems commonly manifested by acting-out students. It should be noted that any of the described intervention techniques can be applied singly and with effectiveness to achieve specific therapeutic or educational goals in situations where their application is appropriate. However, the combined use of some of these techniques can produce extremely powerful treatment effects that are far greater than those that could be achieved with any single technique.

The more powerful the technique(s) involved, and combinations thereof, the more costly and more time consuming they are likely to be. There is a direct relationship between the implementation power of a technique and the complexity of its application. Intervention specialists should, as a matter of course, first attempt to change behavior without resorting to complex interventions that are intrusive and labor intensive; more radical techniques should be considered **only** when their application is clearly called for.

Acting-out children, whose repertoires of maladaptive behavior are strongly developed and have been acquired over a number of years, are more likely to require exposure to complex interventions in order for their behavior problems to be successfully dealt with. Such children almost invariably require massive intervention procedures and major environmental manipulations over a fairly extensive period of time in order for their behavior to be permanently changed. It is unlikely that simple treatment techniques or environmental changes would significantly alter the behavior of most acting-out children.

This is not to suggest that systematic social skills training, stimulus change procedures, rules and instructions, and self-monitoring/self-control interventions should not be used with acting-out children. These strategies **are** important to the overall change process, however, these procedures by themselves are unlikely to alter appreciably the behavior patterns of most acting-out children.

Therefore, it is recommended for the clear majority of acting-out children that a maximally powerful intervention program, consisting of combinations of techniques, be implemented as a first step in changing their overall behavior patterns. As the target behavior(s) change and gradually becomes responsive to the intervention procedures, components of the intervention can be gradually removed as the child's behavior warrants their removal.

The most powerful intervention available for changing the behavior of acting-out children in school settings consists of a combination of positive reinforcement and mild punishment procedures (Repp & Singh, 1990; Walker, Hops, & Fiegenbaum, 1976). Several combinations of positive reinforcement and mild punishment procedures are available. These are: (1) teacher praise for appropriate behavior and a brief timeout for inappropriate behavior, (2) teacher praise and token reinforcement for appropriate behavior and timeout for inappropriate behavior; (3) teacher praise for appropriate behavior and a response cost for inappropriate behavior; and (4) teacher praise and token reinforcement for appropriate behavior and a response cost for inappropriate behavior. These four intervention combinations are ranked from least to most powerful. Although direct comparisons of the effectiveness of these four intervention combinations have not been carried out, the author's own research experience plus studies reported in the literature on these techniques (Patterson, 1983; Patterson, Reid, & Dishion, 1992) provide suggestive evidence that this may be the case.

The choice as to which of these treatments to apply to a given acting-out child's behavior depends upon the severity of the behavior problem(s) involved and the teacher's preference, as well as willingness to implement the procedures involved. Given that the teacher is willing to implement any one of these combinations for a given child, the severity of the problem behavior repertoire and its relative intractability should determine which combination is to be selected.

For example, if an acting-out child spends more than 50% of his time engaged in inappropriate behavior, a combination of teacher praise, positive reinforcement (i.e., a token or point system), and either a response cost or timeout should be implemented in the form of a comprehensive treatment program. Most children in the elementary age range are appropriate in their classroom behavior approximately 80-85% of the time. Unless there are special reasons (e.g., controlling highly disruptive, aggressive, or tantrumming behavior) for using timeout as the primary technique for consequating inappropriate behavior, a response cost, or simple loss of privileges, is recommended because of its equal power and greater ease of implementation. However, timeout, or brief removal from the classroom situation, should be used as a back-up to a response cost whenever the child has zero points and an instance of problem behavior occurs. Timeout should continue being used until sufficient points have been earned for the response cost to again be applied for episodes of problem behavior.

If an acting-out child spends less than 50% of his time on inappropriate behavior, the behavior problem(s) involved are not overly severe, and the child's behavioral repertoire appears reasonably tractable, a combination of teacher praise for appropriate behavior and a brief timeout for inappropriate behavior should be implemented. This treatment combination is relatively easier to implement but it is also less powerful.

Before implementing **any** combination of intervention techniques, it is essential that careful attention be given to antecedent events that might be maintaining the child's inappropriate behavior. For example, the teacher should ensure that academic instruction for the child is at an appropriate level and that his/her inappropriate behavior is not limited to certain academic periods or social situations during the day. If such is the case, it may be possible to isolate a causal event or factor that is common to these situations. One should also be sure that the child can clearly discriminate between appropriate and inappropriate classroom and/or playground behavior. It is possible (but not likely) that an acting-out child is behaving inappropriately because he is not aware of the rules governing appropriate behavior. After these steps have been taken, a comprehensive intervention program should be designed and implemented to change the child's behavior.

Teacher Praise and Timeout

The combination of teacher praise and timeout can be implemented, in nearly the identical fashion, whether acting-out children are assigned to regular or resource/special classroom settings. The first step in implementing this intervention procedure is to decide which inappropriate behaviors to simply ignore and which to consequate with timeout. If a given form of an inappropriate student behavior is minimally disruptive to the academic performance, if the classroom atmosphere is not seriously disrupted, and there is a possibility that the behavior is maintained primarily by teacher attention, ignoring would be an appropriate consequence to consider. On the other hand, if the behavior is serious, is disruptive to the classroom atmosphere and academic performance, and its consequences cannot be tolerated, timeout should be applied instead. It is important to remember that **completely** isolating attention from maladaptive child behavior in the classroom context is a difficult, but not impossible, task.

Once the decision to apply timeout has been made, the child should be informed as to which behaviors will result in timeout **before** the program is implemented. Then a systematic intervention program should be implemented on a daily basis in which the child's appropriate behavior is carefully and frequently praised, minimally disruptive attention getting behaviors are ignored, and more serious disruptive behaviors are consequated with timeout. In an intervention program of this type, the teacher's management of his/her attention to the acting-out child is extremely important. The purpose of the intervention is to teach the child that inappropriate behavior will result in either no response (i.e., ignoring) or a mildly unpleasant consequence (i.e., timeout), while appropriate behavior will result in a pleasant consequence (i.e., positive teacher attention and approval).

Achieving this goal is much easier said than done. It is not easy for a teacher to, in a sense, turn his/her attention around in relation to the acting-out child's behavior, particularly if prior interactions between them have been of a hostile, aversive nature. The teacher must learn to observe the child's behavior very carefully and to withhold and deliver attention as the child's behavior warrants. The overall amount of teacher attention given the child may not change appreciably in this process, but instead becomes redistributed. That is, teacher attention now becomes much more responsive to the quality (either appropriate or inappropriate) of the child's actual behavior.

It is obvious that a teacher cannot observe an acting-out child's behavior continuously and still teach effectively. Thus, some reasonable compromise must be developed that will provide for effective teaching and the careful monitoring of the acting-out child's behavior. A good rule to remember in this regard is that one should try to "**catch the child being good**" and deliver positive attention and descriptive praise to appropriate student behavior, as is practicable. Rather than focusing upon the acting-out child's inappropriate behavior, the teacher should try to find an episode of appropriate behavior, or at least an approximation of it, during each interval (e.g., every 15 minutes or so) in which the child's behavior is monitored and evaluated. This may be difficult to implement at first, but focusing upon the child's appropriate behavior and praising it as often as possible is extremely important in teaching a new pattern of behavior.

Regular classroom teachers can observe, evaluate, and either praise or ignore an acting-out child's behavior quite feasibly during ten-minute intervals while carrying on normal teaching duties. When implementing this intervention program, it is essential that the teacher observe, evaluate, and consequate the acting-out child's behavior at least once every five minutes during the first part of the intervention program—if at all possible. After the child's behavior pattern has been changed effectively, has stabilized, and has adjusted to the program, the frequency of observing, evaluating, and consequating can be reduced to once during each ten- or 15-minute period. By building upon increments of five minutes, this interval can be gradually extended until the acting-out child is receiving a normal amount of teacher attention, that is, approximately the same amount as received by his peers.

Before implementing this intervention program, the reader should review the sections on the correct application of praise and timeout procedures described in Chapter 5. It is also helpful to monitor the frequency of praise and to record each instance of timeout. Recording praise will tell the teacher how well he/she is doing in achieving the frequency goals established for praising the child's behavior. A record of timeouts, including the behaviors to which the timeout was applied, will provide an indication of how well the overall treatment program is working.

There are several ways to record praise. Perhaps the most efficient method is to divide the school day into continuous five-, ten-, or 15-minute intervals and then to make sure that at least one praise statement is delivered per interval. A form similar to the sample shown in Figure 6.1 can be used for this purpose. As each praise statement is delivered, a notation is made in the appropriate interval space. The form can be kept on a clipboard for use when the teacher is standing away from his/her desk.

A less precise recording method makes use of a golf counter worn on the wrist. Most counters will record up to at least 99 incidents, and can be readily used for counting praise statements each time they are delivered. Their disadvantage is that these types of counters do not provide for the delivery of praise within equally measured units of time.

A third method uses a 3 x 5 index card taped to the child's desk. Each time a praise statement is delivered, a notation is marked on the card. A limitation of this method is that it is unsuitable for free play or playground periods.

Figure 6.1 Form for Recording Teacher Praise					
Student			Week of		
Interval	**M**	**T**	**W**	**TH**	**F**
8:30 — 8:40					
8:40 — 8:50					
8:50 — 9:00					
9:00 — 9:10					
9:10 — 9:20					
Etc.					

The form shown in Figure 6.2 was used by the author to record **timeout** episodes within a demonstration classroom setting for acting-out, elementary age students.

Figure 6.2 Form for Recording Timeout Episodes			
Date	**Precipitating Behavior**	**Duration**	**Child**
1/19	Hitting	10 min.	Jeff
1/23	Noncompliance	5 min.	Jesse
1/24	Fighting	10 min.	Frank & Jesse
1/27	Foul Language	10 min.	Elliot

This form provides a daily record of timeout and allows the teacher to track the target behaviors that timeout is being used to reduce and suppress. The entries in the form are a typical example of the types of maladaptive child behavior to which timeout is usually applied.

The advantage of this intervention variation is that it is fairly easy to administer and is not too demanding of teacher time. The downside is that it may not be sufficiently powerful to substantially affect the maladaptive behavior of many acting-out students.

Teacher Praise, Token
Reinforcement, and Timeout

The addition of token reinforcement to the teacher praise/timeout intervention creates a more powerful intervention program. A powerful treatment
combination such as this would be appropriate for severely disruptive
children who engage in appropriate behavior less than 50% of the time.

The type of token reinforcement system selected should be determined in
part by the setting in which the intervention program is to be implemented.
If the system is being implemented in, for example, a resource room or
self-contained classroom for behavior disorders with an enrollment of six to
12 students, then an individual reinforcement system can be established for
each child. In a system of this type, a certain number of points (and teacher
praise) can be earned each day for appropriate social and academic behavior
by each student. The number of points earned depends upon the teacher's
judgment of each student's performance.

In a self-contained setting, it is also possible to set up concurrent **group**
contingencies that operate in tandem with the individual system. For example,
one of the problems children with behavior disorders in general, and acting-out
children in particular, have is in group instructional situations. Such children
often have great difficulty in meeting the behavioral requirements of group
situations which usually demand the following of participants: (1) paying
attention, (2) listening carefully, (3) following instructions, (4) cooperating with
others, and (5) responding when called upon. It would be possible to set up
group situations during the school day and have the children earn group points
toward a group activity for meeting the behavioral requirements of the situation. That is, **all** the children would have to meet the behavioral requirements
simultaneously in order to earn group points that accumulate toward a group
reward activity shared equally by everyone.

The author and a colleague (Walker & Buckley, 1974) used a group reinforcement procedure to teach appropriate group behavior to six acting-out
children enrolled in a demonstration classroom setting. The group system
operated in addition to an individualized point system for each of the six
children. The context for the group contingency was as follows. For 30
minutes each day, the six children were required to listen to a teacher-led
activity and to answer questions on the material presented. For each five-
minute segment of the 30-minute period in which all the children were
engaged in appropriate group behavior, the group of students as a whole
was awarded one point. If one or more of the six children did not follow the
rules during the five-minute period, the point for that interval was not

awarded. When the group had earned 30 points (six were available each day) the points could be exchanged for a preferred group activity such as a field trip, class party, or special film. This procedure proved highly effective in teaching and maintaining the children's appropriate group behavior. It should be mentioned that the children's individual reinforcement systems did not operate during the daily 30-minute periods in which the group contingency was in effect. Exposing acting-out children to this kind of training is extremely important, as they are often unable to participate effectively in group instructional situations.

If a combination of teacher praise, token reinforcement, and timeout is applied to the behavior of an acting-out child in a regular classroom setting, it is strongly recommended that a dual group and individual contingency be implemented. In past classroom applications, the author and his colleagues have found a group contingency, backed up by school rewards, and an individual contingency, backed up by home rewards, to be a highly effective combination (Walker, Hops, & Greenwood, 1984, 1993). For example, a contingency is established wherein the acting-out child has an opportunity to earn a daily group activity reward for himself **and** his classmates if the reward criterion is achieved at school (e.g., classroom behavior was judged to be appropriate 80% or more of the time). Group activities include such things as extra recess time, special films or cartoons, and classroom games. Regardless of whether the group reward was earned at school, the acting-out child could still earn individual points for his behavior and performance that, when accumulated, qualified him for a special individual reward at home, accompanied by parental praise.

Another variation of this combined group and individual contingency was implemented by the author and his colleagues (Walker et al., 1984) in working with acting-out children who were also highly aggressive with their peers. In these applications, the target acting-out student could earn a group activity reward for himself and his peers at school for avoiding peer directed aggression and rule infractions at recess. In order to do so, he had to retain 80% or more of the points awarded **automatically** at the start of each recess period. The number of points retained and earned each day in school could also be accumulated and exchanged at home for a variety of reward options preselected by the child and his parents. These options included such things as extra television time, "undivided" time with one or both parents, movies, snacks, special food treats prepared at home, trips to the park, bowling, and so forth.

Both of these variations proved to be highly effective in motivating and teaching difficult children to behave differently. Further, it was observed that some children tended to respond primarily to the individual reward at home, others primarily to the group reward at school, and still others to both systems approximately equally. Thus, providing a combination of school and home rewards probably increases the effectiveness of most positive reinforcement systems and increases the likelihood that they will have an impact on the behavior of most children.

Providing combined group rewards at school and individual rewards at home also has a number of other potential advantages that make this combination worthy of careful consideration. For example, teachers are usually concerned about the issue of fairness when one child is singled out and treated in a special or unique way because of serious behavioral and/or academic problems. When a given student is allowed to earn rewards for behaving in approximately the same way as do the other children in the class, teachers are concerned (and justifiably so) that the other children might learn to act out or disrupt the class in order to gain access to the reward system as well. There is no clear evidence that this actually occurs, but such an outcome seems well within the realm of possibility.

A contingency wherein the child earns a group activity reward shared equally with classmates has a number of features that reduce the likelihood of this happening. For example, peers do not see the target child as one who is being treated in a special way, but rather, as an individual whose appropriate behavior can earn special privileges for them (i.e., the entire class). It has been the author's experience that the classmates of target children in such situations are highly motivated to help the target students to achieve the reward criterion. Thus, instead of providing attention and support for a child's inappropriate behavior, classmates usually encourage and attempt to facilitate the target child's efforts to display appropriate classroom behavior under such contingency arrangements, since it is in their best interest to do so. Although it has not been documented as yet, this type of contingency may also have an impact upon the appropriate behavioral level of the entire class. Further, the peer popularity of young children increases when one of them is instrumental in achieving a desired outcome for the whole group (e.g., winning a game, earning extra recess time, and so forth).

It is possible to set up group contingencies designed to have an impact upon the behavior of all the children in a regular classroom setting (Greenwood, Hops, Delquadri, & Guild, 1974; Greenwood, Hops, & Walker, 1988; Packard, 1970). However, it is somewhat more difficult to implement such contingencies in regular classrooms than in less restrictive settings because of the much higher number of children involved. Yet such contingencies can be highly effective in regular classrooms if they are implemented according to best practice standards and monitored carefully. It should be noted though that group contingencies of this type are usually not powerful enough to control the behavior of acting-out children effectively. That is, they are a class-wide, **universal** intervention that is applied to everyone in the same manner; however many acting-out children will require more powerful, individualized interventions for their problems to be adequately addressed.

If the teacher wishes to implement a group contingency in which the entire class works together cooperatively to earned some desired outcome, and there is an acting-out child or children in the classroom, the teacher should be prepared to shift the acting-out student(s) to a different system if those student(s)' behavior causes the group to suffer (i.e., lose access to the group reward). Another recommended option is that an intervention program of some type be applied to an acting-out child's behavior **beforehand** to help him reach the point when he can participate in a group contingency situation. If successful, this can be followed by implementation of the group contingency for the whole class, including the acting-out child. If this is not done, the acting-out child may seriously reduce the potential effectiveness of a group contingency applied to the behavior of the entire class and create resentment by both peers and the teacher.

The author and his colleagues (Walker & Hops, 1993; Walker, Hops, & Greenwood, 1984) designed and implemented a treatment combination consisting of teacher praise, positive token reinforcement, and timeout for six disruptive children who were referred by their teachers from six different elementary schools. The students were enrolled in a model demonstration classroom, over a four-month period, which was designed for elementary age children having acting-out, disruptive behavior problems. This classroom setting and program was set up and operated by the author as part of a larger program of research. Table 6.1 provides an overview of this intervention program's content as implemented for those intermediate grade level students.

The six children were enrolled in grades four, five, and six. They were able to earn individual points, on a daily basis, for appropriate social and academic behavior. Points were exchangeable for a variety of back-up rewards ranging from inexpensive school supplies (e.g., pencils, paper, erasers) to the purchasing of free time to build model airplanes which were also purchased with earned points. Group rewards, available on a weekly basis, could be earned for engaging in appropriate group behavior at certain times during the day.

Three types of consequences were applied to the children's inappropriate classroom behavior. These were **ignoring** for such minimally disruptive target behaviors as asking for help without raising one's hand; asking irrelevant questions; pencil tapping; or pouting, sulking, or whining. A **brief timeout** (i.e., ten minutes) was applied to such moderately disruptive

Table 6.1
Overview of Treatment Program Consisting of Teacher Praise, Positive Token Reinforcement, and Timeout

I. Consequences of Deviant Behaviors

  A. Immediate removal from ELP building for the following behaviors:

    1. Disobedience and/or defying teacher

    2. Fighting

    3. Leaving building without permission

    4. Foul language, lewd gestures

    5. Creating a disturbance during Isolation period (timeout)

  (If expelled during the A.M. the student will stay out for the remainder of the day and return the following morning. If expelled during the P.M., the student will remain home the following day.)

  B. Immediate exclusion from the classroom area for ten minutes minimum for the following behaviors:

    1. Talking out of turn

    2. Unauthorized standing or walking

    3. Talking or standing without raising hand and securing permission

    4. Throwing objects

    5. Other nontolerated behaviors falling within this class of behaviors

  (The student returns to the classroom area after the ten minutes.)

II. Reinforcement

  A. Individual Basis

    1. Social:
      – Raising hand
      – Not talking
      – Remaining in seat
      – Beginning work without talking upon entering room

    2. Academic:
      – Task-oriented
      – Completion of tasks
      – Correct answers on assignments

  B. Group Basis

    1. Clock timer will be set at preselected time intervals each day provided all students are present in the classroom area and are engaged in task-oriented behavior.

    2. Clock continues to run and accumulate minutes as long as all students are on task and following the classroom rules.

    3. A group payoff will be instituted when the group accumulates a preselected number of points.

III. Behaviors to be Ignored
    – Asking for help without raising hand
    – Irrelevant questions
    – Tapping pencils (unless disturbing class)
    – Pouting, sulking, whining

behaviors as talking out of turn, being out of seat, yelling, or throwing objects. A one-half to one-day **suspension from the classroom** was applied to more severe forms of child behavior such as teacher defiance, fighting, leaving the building without permission, swearing, and so forth. This overall intervention program, with these combined techniques operating concurrently, proved to be **highly** effective in modifying the classroom behavior of the six children to whom it was applied.

Figure 6.3 provides a record of the behavioral effects of this intervention program upon the target children's appropriate classroom behavior. Daily observations of these students' behavior, using professionally trained observers, were recorded from behind one-way glass. Individual graphs of their task-oriented behavior (i.e., academic engagement), recorded both during preintervention periods in their respective regular classrooms and during intervention while assigned to the demonstration classroom, are also shown in Figure 6.3. These six children averaged 39% of the time engaged in appropriate classroom behavior when observed in their respective regular classrooms. In contrast, while assigned to the demonstration classroom program over a period of approximately four months, the six children averaged approximately 90% of their time spent on appropriate classroom behavior.

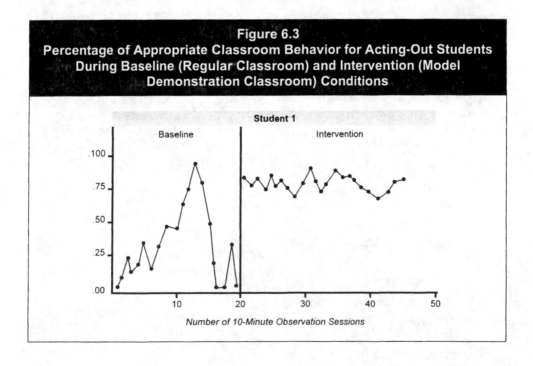

Figure 6.3
Percentage of Appropriate Classroom Behavior for Acting-Out Students During Baseline (Regular Classroom) and Intervention (Model Demonstration Classroom) Conditions

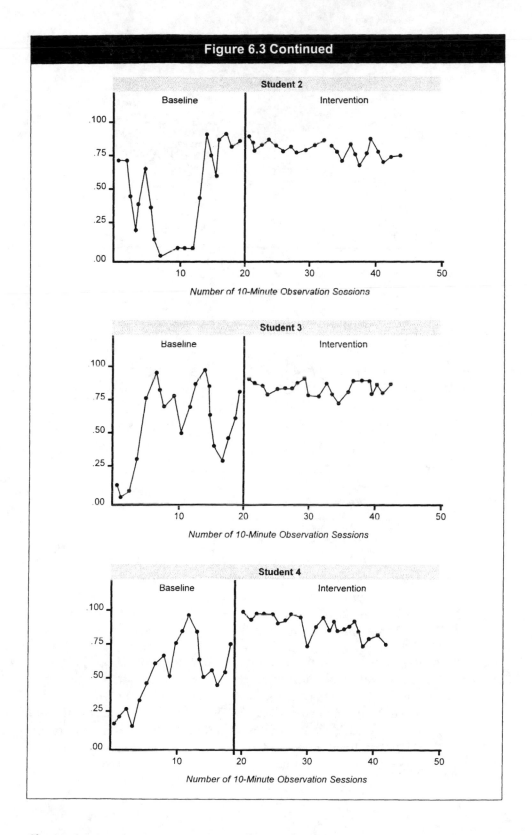

Figure 6.3 Continued

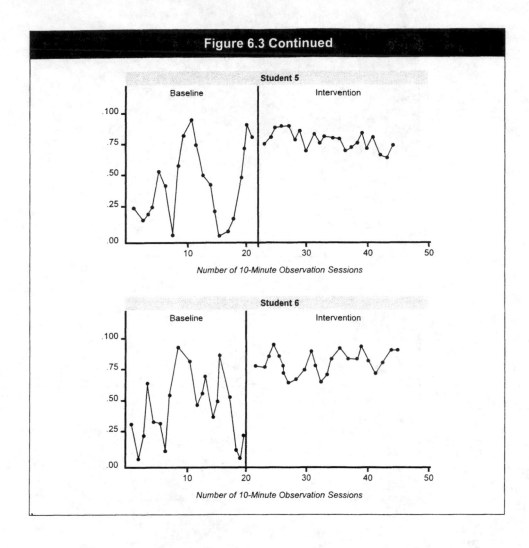

Inspection of Figure 6.3 shows that very powerful behavioral gains were achieved for **each** of the six acting-out children. As a group, they also made some impressive academic gains while assigned to the demonstration classroom. Figure 6.4 presents pre- and post-test results for the six children on the *Wide Range Achievement Test* and on the *Gray's Oral Reading Test*.

All six children showed gains on either one or both of the tests. Thus, the overall impact of this combination of intervention techniques upon both the students' social and academic behavior was substantial. It should be noted, however, that in the absence of a control group of equivalent acting-out children, it is not possible to conclude with certainty that assignment to the model demonstration classroom was the event or factor that accounted for the behavior changes observed. Still, achieving behavioral and academic gains of this magnitude by

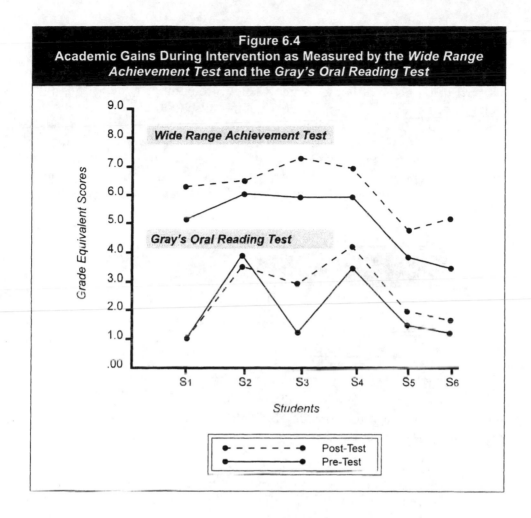

Figure 6.4
Academic Gains During Intervention as Measured by the *Wide Range Achievement Test* and the *Gray's Oral Reading Test*

chance or through some other unknown cause would be highly unlikely. Nevertheless, one must acknowledge the possibility.

This treatment combination can also be applied effectively to the behavior of acting-out children who are enrolled in regular classroom settings. However, it requires some minor adaptations in order to be maximally effective in this setting. For example, it is **highly** recommended that the target child be allowed to earn a group reward at school **and** an individual reward at home, for all the reasons outlined previously. This requires parental cooperation and occasional monitoring to ensure that parents follow through and actually provide the agreed to rewards at home. If not, the effectiveness of the intervention program may be greatly reduced. Daily and then weekly phone calls to parents as needed can be a convenient way of ensuring that this occurs. The child's general school performance can be debriefed during these calls as well.

Good Day Cards, point cards, or tickets may be used to facilitate the delivery of home rewards. Good Day Cards are used whenever an either/or judgment is made at school as to whether or not the child earned an individual reward to be given at home. A good rule to remember is that if a child's behavior has been 80% appropriate or better at school, the acting-out child earns a group reward for himself at school and an individual reward at home. At the end of the day, a Good Day Card indicating this performance and signed by the teacher is sent home with the child if he met the reward criterion at school. If the criterion is not achieved, then no card is sent home, and the parents withhold the home reward for that day. A sample Good Day Card is shown in Figure 6.5.

Figure 6.5
Sample Good Day Card

Good Day Card

_____ earned a home privilege for today.

_____   _____
Teacher Signature   Date

Good Day Cards acquire considerable value for children over time as they signal success at school and are exchangeable for privileges at home.

Point cards can be used in situations in which a child can earn a group reward at school for earning 80% or more of the available points, and then take his/her earned points home at the end of the day to be counted toward an individual reward. In this situation, a reinforcement menu must be established between the teacher, child, and parents wherein the child can purchase privileges or tangibles at home varying from the inexpensive to expensive.

Point cards are very simple to make and use. A sample card is shown in Figure 6.6.

Figure 6.6
Sample Point Card

Point Card

_____ earned _____ points at school today.

_____   _____
Teacher Signature   Date

Tickets can also be used in this situation. Instead of sending points home, the child exchanges his/her points for tickets at school, and then exchanges the tickets for home privileges or tangible rewards of some type. An ordinary roll of theater tickets can be used for this purpose, and any ratio of points to tickets can be considered. As a matter of convenience, a 5:1 ratio of points to tickets is useful. As a rule, children respond positively to tickets, see them as valuable, and seem to enjoy earning them.

The reader is referred to Kelley (1990) for an excellent compendium of resource information, guidelines, and tips on home and school interventions. Using this approach effectively not only leads to improvements in the academic and social behavior of students in school, it can greatly strengthen communication between the school and parents.

The use of timeout sometimes creates special problems in regular classroom settings. Most regular schools and classrooms do not have built-in timeout rooms, so timeout presents something of a logistical problem for the classroom teacher. It is possible to send a child to the office or to an unused room in the school; however there may be problems with both of these alternatives. For example, some children may actually enjoy going to the office, thus making the use of timeout in this situation highly inappropriate. When a child is sent to an unused room, he/she must be properly supervised to ensure his/her safety and to comply with the laws governing supervision of students in school. Even if a special timeout room were available, problems would arise when more than one child was sent to timeout simultaneously.

If timeout is to be used **within** the regular classroom context, it is recommended that a part of the classroom be designated as a timeout area so that children in timeout can be properly supervised and the relative ease with which timeout can be implemented is maximized. The important ingredient in timeout's effectiveness is that the child be temporarily removed from a situation that he/she finds reinforcing. If the activity from which the child is removed is one the child likes and finds relatively pleasant, a brief timeout will serve as an aversive experience and will tend to suppress and discourage the specific target behavior(s) to which it is applied.

If the regular classroom is a pleasant and reinforcing place to be, and even temporary removal from it is unpleasant for the child, a simple screen with a desk behind it in a corner of the classroom can serve as the timeout area. A portable blackboard or ordinary screen can be used for this purpose. It is extremely important that the child not have visual contact with the rest of the class while in timeout. Visual contact with the class would greatly reduce the effectiveness of timeout's use in most classrooms.

If the child creates a disturbance in timeout or refuses to go into the timeout area, it is important to have a back-up alternative. Options for this situation include: (1) referral to the front office with assigned work, (2) a parent-teacher conference, and (3) a half-day or full-day suspension from school if the episode is part of a larger pattern of oppositional-defiant behavior. While suspended, the child cannot earn points or teacher praise and must complete all work missed during the suspension period. This therapeutic use of suspension is quite effective if implemented according to best practice standards.

On the other hand, suspension from schooling, even for a half day, has become increasingly problematic as more and more households have either a working single parent or both parents working. In such cases or where it is not possible for the requirements of suspension to be implemented at home (e.g., adequate supervision, finishing schoolwork), a within-school suspension is recommended. The details of this arrangement would have to carefully established with the principal's office, but it can also be highly effective.

It is extremely important that teacher praise be systematically paired with the delivery of points in regular classroom applications of this intervention combination. In regular classrooms, it is both likely and desirable that the positive token reinforcement system will be eventually faded out. When this occurs, the child's behavior must be maintained by teacher praise or by some other natural means. As noted previously, teacher praise may not be all that effective initially in changing or maintaining the behavior of acting-out children. However, by systematically pairing the delivery of praise and points, praise may assume some of the incentive properties and value of points. If so, the praise will be **much** more effective in maintaining appropriate child behavior over the long term in the absence of a point system.

The combination of teacher praise, points, and timeout is a highly effective treatment combination that is sufficiently powerful to modify the behavior of most acting-out children who engage in appropriate behavior an average of less than 50% of the time. However, its effectiveness depends greatly upon the precision with which it is implemented. In this regard, there are certain guidelines that should be followed to ensure effective application. First, in the early stages of the intervention program (i.e., at least for the first month), the child's behavior should be evaluated for purposes of reinforcement at least once every ten minutes. If the child's behavior is judged appropriate, praise and a point or points should be awarded; if inappropriate, nothing should be awarded.

Second, praise should always be given first, followed immediately by a point or points. This type of pairing increases the chances that praise will assume some of the incentive value of points. Third, daily group and individual rewards should be made available, as earned, for at least the first month of the program. Fourth, the techniques of ignoring, timeout, and/or suspension should be applied **every time** an inappropriate behavior occurs that warrants their application. This is an extremely important point to remember. Finally, after a month or so has elapsed, an evaluation should be made to determine whether fading of the intervention program can be initiated. If the child's behavior is stable and he/she is responding well, then the fading can begin. If not, the program should be maintained in its original form until a reasonable level of stability and responsiveness is achieved.

Teacher Praise and Response Cost

A combination of teacher praise and a response cost can be an easy to manage, effective system for changing child behavior. Its relative ease of implementation makes it especially appropriate for use on playgrounds, in lunchrooms, and in hallways. It is much easier to implement in the classroom than a combination of teacher praise, positive token reinforcement, and a response cost, but it has the disadvantage of being perhaps not as powerful (although, to date, it has not been empirically established that one of these combinations is either more or less powerful than the other). The trade-off between ease of implementation and probable effectiveness is constantly an issue that must be considered by teachers, and other education professionals, in selecting optimal treatment combinations for changing a given child's behavior.

In this intervention, the target child is given x amount of points in advance (e.g., at the start of the period) and is allowed to keep them as long as his/her behavior is appropriate. Praise is delivered intermittently throughout the period for appropriate behavior. Whenever inappropriate behavior occurs, points are subtracted from the child's total. At the end of the reinforcement period or school day, the child is allowed to keep whatever points are left and exchange them for privileges at school and/or home.

The number of points awarded is arbitrary. There is no set rule for determining this in advance. However, several factors should be considered in this decision-making process. For example, the ratio of points available to back-up privileges should be such that a very high proportion of the points available on any given day must be retained in order to exchange for the least expensive privilege. A good rule is that 80% or more of the points must be retained in order to exchange for the least expensive available.

It is usually quite feasible to tie the number of points available to the passage of time. For example, for playground behavior, one could set up a system where a child earns one point for each minute, or each five minutes, of recess in which playground rules are followed and the child's interactive behavior with peers is appropriate. In academic settings (e.g., math or reading), the ratio might be one point for each ten or 15 minutes in which the child is following classroom rules and his/her academic performance is appropriate. The important rule to remember is that the number of points available for the period should be determined and awarded to the child in **advance**, as on a point card of some type.

It is extremely important that the child understand the following: (1) the points are the student's to keep as long as the rules are followed and classroom and/or playground behavior is appropriate, (2) points will be subtracted from the total for inappropriate behavior whenever it occurs, and (3) only the net amount of points retained at the end of the period or day can be counted toward the purchase of back-up rewards and privileges.

A sample point card for delivery of this intervention combination is presented in Figure 6.7. The author has used a point card of this type in numerous instances and found it to be both effective and easy to implement.

Figure 6.7 Sample Point Card for a Praise and Response Cost Only Intervention	
Name	Date
Recess	
Morning	/ / / / / / / / / /
Lunch	/ /
Afternoon	/ / / / / / / / / / / / / / / /

In the classroom, the point card can be placed on the child's desk and points crossed off as the child's behavior indicates. On the playground, the playground supervisor should carry the card, preferably on a clipboard, and mark off points whenever a playground rule is broken or the child engages in inappropriate social behavior. With this system, the supervisor should be within close proximity of the child before points are subtracted for inappropriate behavior. Whenever inappropriate behavior occurs, the supervisor should walk over to the child, describe the inappropriate behavior, indicate the number of points lost, and cross off the points on the point card. If all the the points are lost, the child should sit out the remainder of the recess period.

Variable point loss values can be assigned to inappropriate behaviors occurring on the playground or in the classroom, or they can be assigned identical values. As a rule, variable point loss systems are established according to the severity of the inappropriate child behavior. That is, the more severe the inappropriate behavior the greater the point loss. Thus, fighting would be more severe and cost substantially more than a target behavior such as being out of seat or talking out. Depending upon its severity and the surrounding circumstances, fighting behavior may require additional sanctions as well (e.g., a parent conference, playground restriction[s], suspension). Variable fine systems have the advantage of teaching children about the relative seriousness of differing classroom and playground behaviors.

The author and his colleagues implemented a response cost only intervention procedure in conjunction with adult praise in order to change the playground behavior of a primary grade boy. This study was part of the research and development process for the *Recess Program for Aggressive Children* (see Walker, Hops, & Greenwood, 1993). The target child's classroom behavior was normal, but his playground behavior during all three recess periods was highly inappropriate. A procedure was set up in which the child was awarded one point for each minute of recess at the start of the period. Five points were subtracted for each instance of negative or aggressive playground behavior and two points were subtracted for each instance of rule breaking. A consultant monitored the child's behavior, subtracted points, and praised the child's appropriate playground behavior. Later, the playground supervisor was shown how to operate the program.

Both school and home rewards were made available to the child in this study. If the child had zero negative or aggressive behaviors during the daily recess periods, a group reward was earned at school that was shared equally with the child's classmates. The child could also take home the number of points retained at the end of the school day and exchange them for special privileges. Consequently, even though the group reward may not have been earned, the individual reward system was still available to motivate the child to behave appropriately. This is a very important fail-safe mechanism when using combined group and individual contingency arrangements of this type.

Figure 6.8 illustrates the target child's record of positive interactive behavior with his peers on the playground during morning, noon, and afternoon recesses. This intervention program was introduced first in the morning recess, then in the noon recess, and finally in the afternoon recess. As Figure 6.8 shows, the program produced immediate and very powerful effects in the child's rate of positive social behavior with peers whenever it was introduced. The program was also very easy for the playground supervisor to implement and manage.

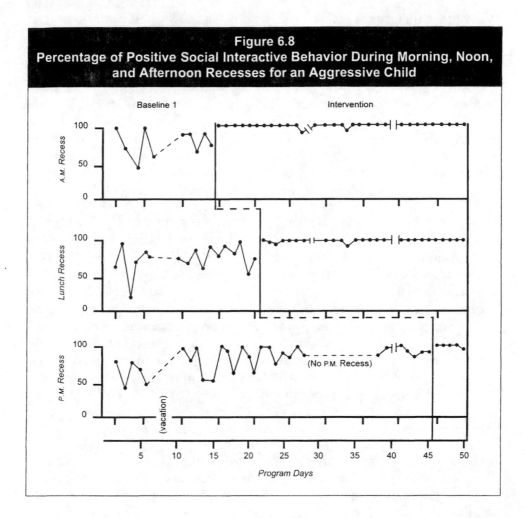

Figure 6.8
Percentage of Positive Social Interactive Behavior During Morning, Noon, and Afternoon Recesses for an Aggressive Child

The most significant advantage of this type of praise and response cost only point system is ease of management. The points are simply awarded non-contingently and taken away only if inappropriate behavior occurs. A child is much less likely to lose all his/her available points in a given period with a system of this type. In contrast, when the child must earn points during the period and can lose them at any time for inappropriate behavior, the risk of losing all available points is much greater.

A disadvantage of this intervention is that it tends to focus attention on negative child behavior. It is extremely important that the child's positive, appropriate behavior be praised frequently when it is exhibited. It is helpful to predetermine a target praise rate in advance (e.g., once every five or ten minutes) and keep a tally during the period to ensure that the praise goal is achieved. Unless the child's appropriate behavior is recognized and approved regularly, the overall effectiveness of this system may be substantially reduced.

Teacher Praise, Token Reinforcement, and Response Cost

In the author's view, this treatment combination represents **the** most powerful and potentially effective intervention available for changing the behavior of acting-out children. It is also much easier to implement in regular and resource/self-contained classrooms than a combination of teacher praise, token reinforcement, and timeout. If applied correctly, this combination of teacher praise, token reinforcement, and a response cost (i.e., a cost contingency) can be extremely effective in changing the classroom behavior of the most disruptive students who are currently accommodated in regular classroom settings.

Walker, Hops, and Fiegenbaum (1976) used this combination in a comprehensive intervention strategy with a group of five acting-out children enrolled in a model demonstration classroom setting. The five children were referred from regular classrooms representing primary grades 1-3, and were selected because of their high rates of disruptive, aggressive classroom behavior (e.g., being noisy and aggressive, yelling, inappropriate peer interactions, noncompliance, teacher defiance, low levels of academic engagement, and being out of seat).

These students were able to earn points for appropriate social behavior and academic performance which could later be exchanged for a variety of backup rewards ranging from free time to the purchase of athletic equipment. Each child could earn a maximum of 35 points per day delivered via two different reinforcement schedules. That is, they could receive points on both a variable interval schedule of reinforcement for appropriate classroom behavior and a fixed ratio schedule for correct academic responses and completion of assignments.

At the end of each day, the points could be exchanged for the available back-up rewards. These ranged in value from 25-200 points, with occasional special items priced at 500 points. The point values were geared to the actual purchase price of the back-up menu items, and were arranged so that a sufficient number of points for the purchase of the least expensive item on the menu could be earned with points received from engaging in appropriate classroom behavior for most of a single school day. The children were free to exchange their points for an inexpensive item or accumulate them for a more expensive one. Teacher praise was delivered as described previously, and was systematically paired with points whenever possible.

A response cost was consistently applied to the children's inappropriate classroom behavior. The target classroom behaviors of talking back to the teacher, talking out, not attending, being out of seat, disturbing others, and playing with objects cost the children one point; teacher defiance cost two points; swearing, three points; and fighting and throwing objects, four points. When one of these behaviors occurred, the teacher placed a mark on a cost contingency record form located on each child's desk. Using this delivery system, the child was immediately aware of the inappropriate behavior to which the response cost was applied, as well as the number of points lost.

When a child had lost or was about to lose more points than he had already earned, a brief timeout was used as a back-up consequence to address episodes of inappropriate behavior until additional points could be earned. Strenuous efforts were made to ensure that no student ever "went in the hole" on the individual point system. The demonstration classroom teacher also discussed in advance the inappropriate classroom behaviors to which the response cost would be applied to be sure that the students understood the system and how it would operate. Reminders were provided from time to time as needed.

Figure 6.9 shows the results of the application of these intervention procedures to the behavior of the acting-out children over a four-month period. This figure displays the results for all five students combined, and for each student individually. Overall, a very powerful treatment effect was achieved for the acting-out students. As a group, these students averaged 38% appropriate behavior during preintervention observations recorded in their respective regular classrooms. In contrast, while exposed to the demonstration classroom intervention, they averaged 96% appropriate behavior.

The effectiveness of this treatment combination was impressive and, at the very least, is as powerful as the combination of teacher praise, token reinforcement, and timeout illustrated previously. Further, it has the added advantage of relying upon the response cost instead of timeout for consequating inappropriate child behavior. Response cost is far easier for most teachers to implement than timeout, and response cost is more adaptive for use in most regular and resource/self-contained classrooms since inappropriate child behavior can be consequated without the necessity of classroom removal.

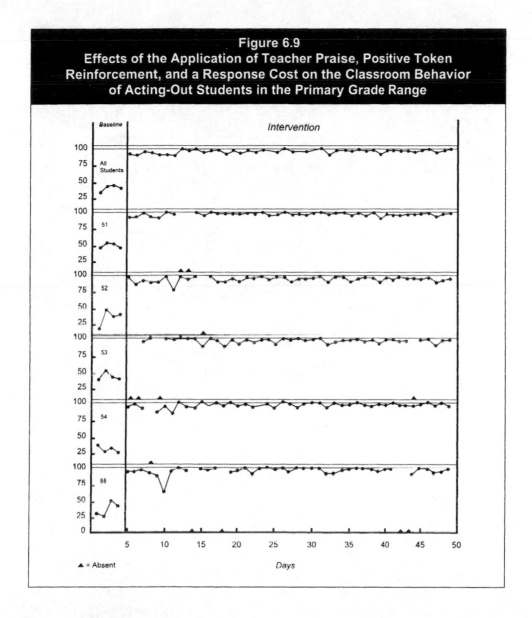

Figure 6.9
Effects of the Application of Teacher Praise, Positive Token Reinforcement, and a Response Cost on the Classroom Behavior of Acting-Out Students in the Primary Grade Range

Figure 6.10 shows the results of a second study conducted by the author and his colleagues (see Walker, Hops, & Fiegenbaum, 1976) in the demonstration classroom setting with a different, but equivalent group, of referred acting-out students. This study systematically evaluated the efficacy of different combinations of the following four intervention techniques: (1) change in setting (i.e., assignment to the demonstration classroom); (2) teacher praise; (3) a point system (i.e., token reinforcement) with back-up rewards; and (4) a response cost.

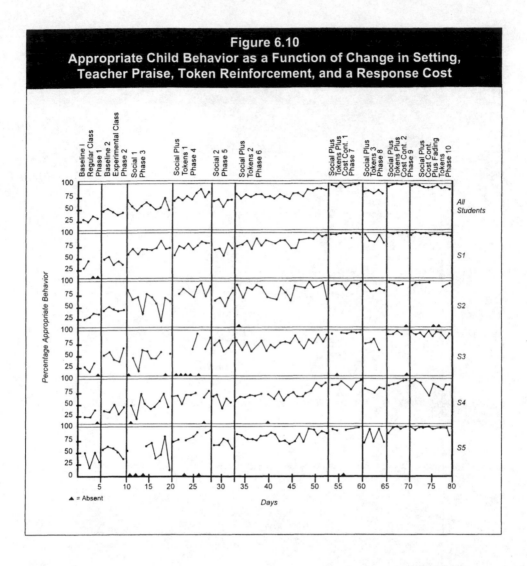

Figure 6.10
Appropriate Child Behavior as a Function of Change in Setting,
Teacher Praise, Token Reinforcement, and a Response Cost

As in Figure 6.9, the results are presented for all five students combined and for each individually. Figure 6.10 indicates that simple assignment to the model demonstration classroom resulted in a slight increase in appropriate behavior for each of the five children. This was probably a result of: (1) a reduced teacher-student ratio, (2) individualized instructional programs for each student, and (3) the use of relatively sophisticated programmed instructional materials. When teacher praise for appropriate child behavior was introduced, there was an increase in appropriate behavior for all of the children except one (i.e., S3) who showed a slight decrease. When a point system was added to the teacher praise, there was an increase in appropriate behavior for all of the children, ranging in magnitude from slight to moderate. With the addition of the response cost for inappropriate behavior, there was an additional increase in the appropriate behavior level of the five children to approximately 96%.

Results of this study showed that a combination of teacher praise, points, and a response cost administered within a self-contained setting produced a more powerful effect upon child behavior than either simple assignment to the setting, with no formal intervention procedures implemented, or the subsequent addition of teacher praise and points. In this instance and with these children, a combination of positive reinforcement for appropriate behavior and mild punishment (i.e., the response cost) for inappropriate behavior was clearly required to produce high levels of appropriate classroom behavior. Without the addition of the response cost, these high levels of appropriate behavior could not have been achieved.

As noted previously, positive reinforcement procedures alone can be successfully applied to increase the appropriate behavior levels of students with minimal to moderately disruptive behavior patterns. However, for acting-out children and for more disruptive children generally, a combination of positive reinforcement and mild punishment procedures is usually required to effectively change their behavior.

In a resource or self-contained classroom setting, an intervention comprised of teacher praise, token reinforcement, and response cost procedures can be implemented quite easily. In such applications, it is highly recommended that a **visible** and **public** delivery system be established for both the positive reinforcement and response cost components of the intervention. If all the children are being exposed to the same overall system, its relative obtrusiveness will not present problems. With students generally, and especially with students having disruptive behavior disorders, it is important that they receive frequent feedback and consequences for their behavior/performance.

A daily point card placed on the target child's desk is recommended for the delivery of positive reinforcement, and a weekly response cost form (taped to the child's desk) is recommended for the delivery of the response cost. Figure 6.11 shows an example of a point card used successfully by the author and his colleagues in the demonstration classroom setting study described.

With this card, it would be possible to deliver 50 points per day: 25 for appropriate classroom behavior and 25 for appropriate academic performance. The size of the card can be easily adjusted to accommodate delivery of either a smaller or larger number of points. Thus, if a teacher were planning to award a child two points during each ten-minute period (i.e., one for classroom behavior and one for academic performance) and the school day was five hours, a total of 60 points could be earned and a larger card would be required.

Figure 6.11 Point Card for Delivery of Positive Reinforcement							
Academic Performance				**Classroom Behavior**			
Net Daily Total:				Net Daily Total:			

A response cost form should be taped securely to a corner of the child's desk and remain there for a week, at which time it should be replaced with a new one. A special colored felt-tip pen should be used to indicate the loss of points on the response cost form.

The number of points on the point card (Figure 6.11) and the number lost (recorded on the response cost form) should be monitored carefully so that the child is not allowed to lose more points than have been earned. If the balance approaches zero, timeout or some other consequence should be applied to any instances of inappropriate behavior until additional points have been earned. At the end of the school day, the number of points on the response cost form is subtracted from the total number earned, and the result is recorded on the point card. The child is allowed to keep the net difference and exchange these points for whatever back-up privileges or rewards are available.

A combined positive reinforcement/response cost system could probably be implemented most effectively in a regular classroom using the delivery system just described. However, the relative obtrusiveness of this system may be a problem for some classroom teachers; that is, they would be most uncomfortable in implementing a special system of this type for a single child using point cards and response cost forms.

There are several alternative procedures which can be considered in such cases. For example, instead of awarding and subtracting points on cards at the child's desk, a less obtrusive system can be implemented using a clipboard. That is, the teacher keeps a tally of points earned and lost throughout the day on forms attached to a clipboard that stays with the teacher. The child's behavior is evaluated every ten minutes, and a point either awarded or withheld. Points are subtracted whenever inappropriate behavior occurs. However, points are not awarded or subtracted at the child's desk, but rather on the clipboard at the teacher's desk or wherever he/she happens to be. If this type of system is used, it is important that the child be informed each time points are subtracted for inappropriate behavior. Further, a progress report on his/her appropriate behavior (i.e., how many points have been earned) should be provided at least once each hour and preferably every 30 minutes. It is also important that children be praised frequently when using a system such as this. It should be noted that while this system will be effective in impacting child behavior, the reduced obtrusiveness obtained may be achieved only at the expense of a slightly less effective system.

A second alternative is to deliver points and the response cost via teacher praises and reprimands. In this variation, the child is taught that each time his/her behavior is praised, one point (or x amounts of points) is earned. Similarly, whenever the teacher reprimands his/her behavior, the inappropriate behavior is verbally described and one point (or x amounts of points) is subtracted from the total earned.

This is a very unobtrusive delivery system, and if implemented correctly will have a positive effect upon child behavior. However, it is important that a covert record of points earned and lost be kept using a golf counter, tally card, or by some other means.

There are several factors to consider in using reprimands as a delivery vehicle for the response cost. For example, the inappropriate behavior should be identified and described for the child and the number of points lost should be indicated. The teacher should not argue with the child about whether he/she did or did not engage in the specific inappropriate behavior; the teacher would simply describe the behavior and indicate the points lost. Likewise, the teacher should not criticize the child for behaving inappropriately. Criticism will have no therapeutic or beneficial effects upon child behavior. Finally, the teacher must attempt to control the expression of active disapproval in delivering the response cost. Teacher disapproval may actually be a reinforcing consequence for some children and would, in such cases, weaken the effectiveness of the response cost.

As noted previously, this intervention combination is potentially **the** most powerful system available for changing child behavior in the classroom setting. It is extremely important that **all** the guidelines for correctly using a response cost be followed in the implementation of this system. It is also highly recommended that the target child be allowed to earn a group consequence only at school where it is shared equally with classmates. If parent cooperation can be achieved, an individual reward system should be set up at home. If this isn't possible, individual rewards can also be made available for the child at school, although this is a less satisfactory alternative than having them provided at home.

As is obvious from the foregoing results and discussion, these four intervention combinations are all highly effective in changing child behavior. The choice as to which combination to use depends upon the following considerations: (1) the severity and nature of the child's behavior, (2) the ease of implementation and available school personnel resources, (3) the relative effectiveness of the different combinations, and (4) the teacher's preferences.

Milder Combinations of Treatment Variables

The four intervention combinations described previously represent combinations of positive reinforcement and mild punishment procedures. They are designed for changing the behavior repertoires of moderately to severely disruptive children in school settings. However, there are other combinations of treatment variables that can be used successfully with less severe children, and for teaching specific social and academic skills. Combinations of this type usually do not involve the use of mild punishment procedures.

During the decades of the late sixties and the seventies, a number of now-classic studies were reported in the literature in which elegant functional analyses of treatment variables were conducted. The implementation procedures and resulting outcomes of these seminal studies continue to have great relevance to the effective teaching and management of diverse classrooms of students. Selected studies are reviewed in the following section that illustrate best practices for use with a range of students.

Rules, Praise, and Ignoring

Madsen, Becker, and Thomas (1968) reported a study in which they taught two regular classroom teachers to apply behavior management procedures systematically to selected students in their classes. Three children, two enrolled in a second grade classroom and one in a kindergarten class, were selected as targets for this study. From the descriptions of their behavior provided by the investigators, these students appeared to be mildly to moderately disruptive. All three were enrolled in regular classrooms. There were 29 children in the second grade classroom, and 20 in the kindergarten class.

The purpose of the study was to evaluate, separately and in combination, the effects of rules, praise, and ignoring in changing child behavior from inappropriate to appropriate. The behavior management procedures were applied to the class as a **whole**. The target children were used simply to document the effects of the intervention. They were not singled out or treated any differently than the other children in their respective classrooms. The teachers were also instructed to use the procedures throughout the entire school day, not just when the investigators and/or observers were present.

The two teachers were first instructed to develop a set of classroom rules that would clearly communicate their expectations governing appropriate student behavior in the classroom. Rules were expressed in overt behavioral terms; they were short and to the point, and they were limited in number to five or six. At the beginning of the study, the teachers reviewed the rules on three or four occasions with their students and asked them to repeat the rules. During the phase in which the rules were evaluated, the teachers were instructed to repeat them at least four to six times per day. They actually repeated them an average of 5.2 times per day during this phase of the study.

The teachers were next instructed to ignore inappropriate classroom behavior. Specific instructions for this phase were given to each teacher and conferences were held to explain and discuss the instructions. Ignoring was defined as not attending to child behaviors that interfered with learning or teaching. Examples of ignoring were given and specific child behaviors to which ignoring was to be applied were identified for the teachers. In Classroom A, the teacher was instructed to continue repeating and emphasizing the rules on a daily basis in addition to ignoring inappropriate child behavior. In Classroom B, the teacher was instructed to discontinue repeating or emphasizing the rules and to use ignoring only.

In the third phase of the study, both teachers were told to praise appropriate child behavior. Both teachers were again given instructions on how to praise. Praise was defined and sample praise statements were provided. The teachers were instructed not only in which child behaviors to praise (e.g., academic performance, prosocial behavior, and following group rules), but also in how to deliver praise correctly. They were given the general instruction to "catch the child being good" in their use of praise. Teacher A was instructed to continue emphasizing the rules, to continue ignoring inappropriate behavior, and now, to also praise appropriate child behavior. Teacher B was given the same instructions for this phase of the study.

At the end of this phase, Teacher A only was given the instructions to discontinue emphasizing the rules, ignoring, and praising. The purpose of this phase was to reestablish preintervention baseline conditions in order to demonstrate the functional role of the intervention program in producing the observed changes in child behavior. Rules, praise, and ignoring were later reinstated and remained in effect for the remainder of the study. No such reversal was implemented for Teacher B.

Figure 6.12 presents the results of the intervention program for the children in Teacher A's classroom. The results show that the introduction of rules had no effect upon the rates of inappropriate classroom behavior. Under the rules and ignoring condition in phase two, the children actually became worse; that is, levels of inappropriate behavior increased for both target children. However, when praising appropriate behavior was added to the rules and ignoring, there was a substantial, immediate, and very clear decrease in inappropriate behavior for both children. When baseline conditions were reinstated, the children's behavior returned to original baseline levels. When rules, ignoring, and praise were put back into effect, there was an immediate return to the behavioral levels occurring in the previous phase (phase three) in which these components were in effect.

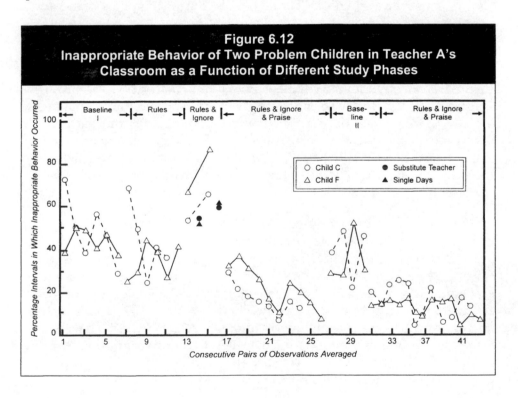

Figure 6.12
Inappropriate Behavior of Two Problem Children in Teacher A's Classroom as a Function of Different Study Phases

Figure 6.13 presents results of the intervention program for the target child in Teacher B's class. Implementation of the rules alone and ignoring alone had no effect whatsoever upon the target child's behavior in Teacher B's class. The combination of rules and ignoring was not evaluated in Teacher B's room. It would have been interesting to see whether this combination would also have made this target child worse, as was observed in Teacher A's room. Rules, ignoring, and praise produced very similar results for this child. (See results for Teacher A's class.) When the combination of rules, ignoring, and praise was introduced, there was an immediate and substantial decrease in inappropriate child behavior as was also observed in Classroom A. The strong replication effects across these children, teachers, and classroom settings establishes this treatment combination as highly effective for use in regular classrooms.

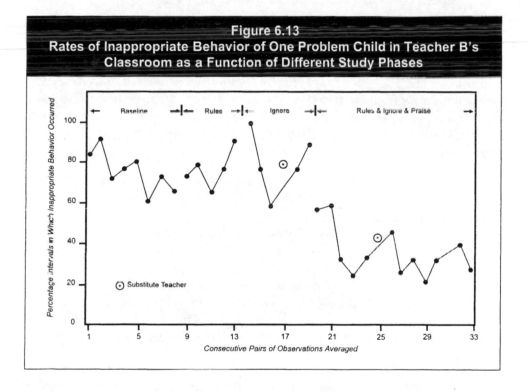

Figure 6.13
Rates of Inappropriate Behavior of One Problem Child in Teacher B's Classroom as a Function of Different Study Phases

The conclusions that can be drawn from this study are as follows: (1) rules alone had essentially no effect upon the children's behavior; (2) ignoring alone also had no effect upon inappropriate child behavior, although this effect could only be observed in Classroom B; (3) the combination of rules and ignoring made the two children in Classroom A worse; and (4) the combination of rules, ignoring, and praise produced almost identical positive results in both classrooms (i.e., a significant and immediate decrease in inappropriate child behavior).

An immediate question that comes to mind with this study is: Would praise for appropriate behavior, by itself, have produced results equivalent to those achieved by the combination of rules, ignoring, and praise? The answer is: probably not. The rationale for this observation is that the contrast effects of praising appropriate behavior and ignoring inappropriate behavior is probably more powerful than the separate effects of either technique used in isolation. Further, the explicit statement and continuing review of classroom rules may have also enhanced the effects of praise once it was introduced. However, it should be noted that these conclusions are speculative only. They are based upon the author's own research experience, and that of others who have done similar work in this area.

A second question concerns the extent to which the target children were representative of the other children in Classrooms A and B. In other words, were the same effects produced for the other children in the class? In addition, were the effects specific only to some children or were they pervasive throughout the two classrooms? Although the investigators did not collect or report data that would answer either of these questions, they noted that both the teachers and classroom observers in the study indicated that there were dramatic changes in the atmosphere of the classrooms as a whole.

If the behavior management procedures had been applied specifically and individually to the three target children involved, the effects for them might have been even more dramatic. Although this is perhaps true, this study provides an important demonstration of the cost effectiveness of **universal**, class-wide interventions. Approaches of this type can have very beneficial effects when the classroom **does not** include highly disruptive or aggressive students. A most impressive magnitude of effect was achieved for the three children with behavior problems when the teacher simply implemented systematic behavior management procedures for the whole class. This demonstration is perhaps the most important contribution of this seminal study.

The study clearly shows that a combination of behavior management techniques is more powerful than the same techniques applied singly and in isolation. The techniques used were effective in changing the children's rates of appropriate behavior to within normal limits. However, the effects of the procedures might have been significantly less dramatic if the children's behavioral and learning problems had been more severe or if there had been a larger number of children with behavior problems in the two classrooms. The commitment of the participating teachers was no doubt also an important factor in the success of this study.

The study also shows that rules by themselves, and ignoring used in isolation, are extremely weak procedures when used to modify inappropriate classroom behavior. In certain situations, these procedures may be effective in altering specific features of child behavior. However, as techniques for producing global behavioral changes in student behavior, their effects will usually be minimal at best.

Rules, Educational Structure, Praise, Ignoring, and Token Reinforcement

O'Leary, Becker, Evans, and Saudargas (1969) evaluated the effects of rules, educational structure, praise, ignoring, and token reinforcement in changing the inappropriate behavior of seven children in a regular, second grade classroom. Combinations of these behavior management techniques evaluated by these investigators were as follows: (1) rules alone, (2) rules plus educational structure, (3) rules plus educational structure plus praising appropriate behavior and ignoring inappropriate behavior, and (4) rules plus educational structure plus praise and ignoring plus token reinforcement.

These techniques were introduced in the sequential order as listed (i.e., rules only first, followed by rules plus educational structure, and so on). According to the study investigators, the four combinations of the techniques were introduced in the order of their expected relative effectiveness. That is, it was thought that rules alone would have less effect on student behavior than a combination including praise and ignoring. Similarly, it was felt that rules, educational structure, praise, and ignoring in combination would have less powerful effects than the addition of a token reinforcement system with back-up rewards.

The classroom teacher had no previous teaching experience other than student teaching. She indicated that there were eight children in the class who displayed unacceptable levels of undesirable behavior. The teacher then selected seven children to be observed. Presumably, the more disruptive of the eight children were nominated by the teacher. Neither the criteria used to select the children nor their behavioral characteristics were described in the study; however, as a group, the seven children averaged approximately 55% **inappropriate** classroom behavior during baseline observations. This is a **significant** deviation from normative levels observed in most regular classrooms (i.e., 15-20% of time spent on inappropriate behavior).

The teacher agreed to cooperate with the investigators in carrying out the study. As in the Madsen et al. (1968) study just reviewed, the behavior management procedures were implemented on a class-wide basis. The seven target children selected were not treated any differently with respect to implementation of the behavior management procedures than were any of the other fourteen children in the class.

Nine **rules**, expressed in overt behavioral terms, were developed and presented to the class. They included such things as, "We sit in our seats," "We raise our hands to talk," "We do not talk out of turn," and so forth. The teacher reviewed the rules twice each day, once in the morning and once in the afternoon.

When token reinforcement programs are implemented in classrooms, they introduce an element of formal structure that may not have existed before. It has been suggested that this structure, rather than the reinforcement contingencies themselves, may account for the program's effectiveness in changing child behavior. To evaluate the effects of this variable, the teacher was asked to reorganize her afternoon instructional program into four 30-minute sessions in which the whole class participated. These were spelling, reading, arithmetic, and science. The purpose of this phase was to assess the importance of **educational structure** per se.

Praise and **ignoring** were introduced in the next phase. The teacher was asked to praise appropriate child behavior and to ignore inappropriate behavior as often as possible. She was also asked to discontinue her use of threats and warnings.

Token reinforcement was introduced in the next phase. The children were told they would receive ratings four times each afternoon based on how well they followed the classroom rules. The points available in each of these rating sessions ranged from one to ten, and were recorded in small booklets placed on each child's desk. The points could be exchanged for a variety of back-up reinforcers that varied in monetary value. Points could be exchanged for back-up rewards only at the end of the school day.

The investigators assisted the teacher in running the intervention program during the first week. After that, the teacher ran the program by herself. In the next phase, the token program (and the back-up rewards) were withdrawn to demonstrate their effect in producing the changes in child behavior. Rules, educational structure, praise, and ignoring remained in effect. In the final phase of the study, the token reinforcement program and back-up rewards were reinstated. They were implemented exactly as before.

Figure 6.14 shows the results of the application of these behavior management techniques. As can be seen, rules and educational structure had no effect whatsoever upon the children's behavior. The praise/ignoring condition actually made the children's behavior slightly worse. The authors noted that the teacher used the praise and ignoring techniques effectively and that, initially, a number of children responded well to them. However, two of the seven children, both boys, had been disruptive all year, and they became increasingly unruly during this phase. This effect also spread to other children in the class. Several children were so disruptive that the academic pursuits of the rest of the class became impossible. The classroom situation became intolerable for the teacher and the praise/ignoring phase had to be terminated much earlier than planned.

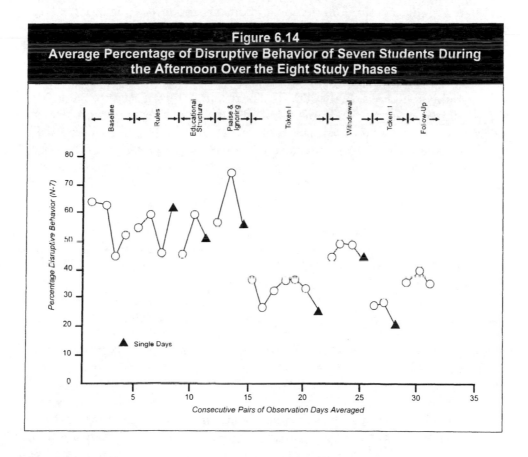

Figure 6.14

Average Percentage of Disruptive Behavior of Seven Students During the Afternoon Over the Eight Study Phases

This result illustrates some important points about applying relatively weak behavior management techniques to the behavior of very disruptive children. It is important to note that praise and ignoring may be sufficient to change the overall behavior patterns of minimally to moderately disruptive children, or to successfully remediate **mild** forms of inappropriate child behavior such as low levels of academic engagement and asking irrelevant questions. However, they are **not** sufficiently powerful to control the behavior of more disruptive children. In this instance, the supervised, correct application of praise and ignoring actually led to **more**, rather than fewer, behavior problems for the teacher. A behavioral contagion effect seemed to occur when other children apparently realized that they could be disruptive with impunity. The result was a classroom situation which quickly got out of control.

This effect might not have been produced had the children been less disruptive or if there had been fewer such children in the classroom. The author has observed a similar effect with a group of six socially aggressive, primary level children assigned to a model demonstration classroom for four months (see Walker, Colvin, & Ramsey, 1995). All six of these students had much higher rates of negative, socially aggressive interactions with their peers than did other children. In one phase of the study, the classroom teacher and aide were instructed to praise positive social behavior occurring among the children during daily free-play activity periods. The results of this procedure were that these children, as a group, became **substantially** worse; the proportion of their positive social interactions with each other was initially reduced by approximately one-half when they were praised for interacting positively! Adult praise of their positive social behavior was, in many instances, an occasion for the children to become very negative or aggressive with each other. This same effect was replicated in a subsequent phase of the study.

The author expected praise either to have no effect or only a minimal positive effect upon these children's behavior. It was totally unexpected that praise would make them so much worse. Given these children's history of interaction with adults (e.g., threats, criticism, warnings, verbal reprimands, and so forth) it may be that **any** attention from adults was initially perceived negatively by them, and would be by other children as well.

Similar adverse effects of adult attention on appropriate child behavior have been reported by Thomas, Becker, and Armstrong (1968) in classroom settings and by Herbert, Pinkston, Hayden, Sajwaj, Pinkston, Cordua, & Jackson (1973) with mothers of disruptive children who were taught, under supervision, to praise their children's appropriate behavior in a one-to-one teaching situation. It appears that the more severely disruptive the child, the more likely it is that adult praise will produce such effects. However, praise seems to work extremely well with generally well-behaved and minimally disruptive children, as evidenced by literally reams of published studies in the professional literature. It may be that a child's deviance level and history of interaction with adults are the primary determinants of their responsiveness to adult social praise.

Taken together, these results have several important implications for changing the behavior of highly disruptive and/or aggressive children. As a general rule, praise alone or praise combined with ignoring **should not** be used, in isolation, as strategies for changing their overall behavior patterns. On the other hand it would be highly advisable to use these procedures in combination with token reinforcement and either a response cost or timeout to manage their disruptive behavior. Praise should always be paired systematically with the delivery of points or tokens so that teacher attention can be developed as a generalized reinforcer for such children. If paired consistently and often enough, teacher praise will likely acquire some of the reinforcing effectiveness of points. Finally, with highly disruptive children, praise or praise and ignoring in combination should only be used to change mild forms of inappropriate behavior (e.g., dawdling or breaking minor classroom rules).

In the O'Leary et al. (1969) study described previously, only **one** of the seven children's appropriate behavior was affected positively by the combination of rules, educational structure, and praise/ignoring. Either there was no effect or there was an adverse effect for the remaining six children. When the token reinforcement program was introduced, the disruptive behavior levels of the remaining six children were reduced. Five of the six showed substantial reductions, while one child showed only a minimal reduction of approximately three percent. For this child, the addition of either a response cost or timeout would probably have been required to impact the disruptive behavior.

In the study phase during which the token reinforcement program was withdrawn, the children's behavior returned to the levels observed in the previous rules and educational structure phase. When the program was reintroduced, there was an immediate return to the "Token I" (see Figure 6.14) program levels.

The results of this study, when compared to the Madsen et al. (1968) study reviewed previously, are instructive in several respects. For example, had the combination of rules, praise, and ignoring that proved successful in the Madsen et al. study been implemented in the O'Leary et al. study, it is **extremely** unlikely that the same results would have been achieved. The teacher in the O'Leary et al. study appeared to have a far more disruptive classroom and a much larger number of disruptive children than either of the teachers in the Madsen et al. study. A token reinforcement program was clearly not required to gain control of the students' behavior in the Madsen et al. study, but it clearly was in the O'Leary et al. study. In addition, the behavior of one of the seven children in the O'Leary et al. study was still not controlled effectively by this more powerful behavior management program. These results indicate that the more severely disruptive the child behavior involved, the more likely it is that a powerful behavior management system will be required to effectively change the target, inappropriate behavior.

Moderately effective gains were maintained in the immediate follow-up phase of the O'Leary et al. study; however, the total intervention program was by no means withdrawn during this phase—only parts of it were changed. That is, the teacher continued to use praise, rules, and educational structure. In addition, a system of "stars" for good behavior was introduced during the follow-up phase that could be redeemed on a weekly basis for a back-up reward if a certain performance criterion had been achieved. In spite of these intervention components remaining in effect, only three of the six children for whom the program had been effective showed satisfactory maintenance of behavioral gains in the follow-up period. It would be interesting to know if these three children were more or less disruptive initially than the three for whom maintenance effects were not achieved. It has been the author's experience that the more severely disruptive the child is initially, the less likely it is that satisfactory maintenance effects will be achieved. Further, relatively greater effort will be required to produce such effects.

No follow-up data were recorded in the Madsen et al. study. Thus, one does not know how the behavior of the children would have maintained in that study following the final rules and praise/ignoring phase. It is likely that, if the teachers involved had continued to use these procedures or some variation of them on a regular basis, satisfactory maintenance effects during follow-up would have been achieved.

The O'Leary et al. study is also valuable in demonstrating that a token reinforcement system, implemented on an **individual** child-by-child basis, can be operated by a regular classroom teacher with a total of 21 students and produce highly satisfactory results. The teacher was not overwhelmed by the recording and point delivery requirements of operating the system because she only had to do so four times in a two-hour period, or once every 30 minutes. Thus, teacher implementation tasks and requirements were held to a minimum, yet powerful effects were still achieved for a very unruly and out-of-control classroom. This demonstration is highly effective in showing how systematic behavior management procedures can be adapted for successful use in a regular classroom without placing unreasonable burdens upon the classroom teacher(s) involved.

Rules, Feedback, and Group and Individual Consequences for Appropriate Behavior

Greenwood, Hops, Delquadri, and Guild (1974) evaluated the effects of rules, rules plus feedback, and rules plus feedback plus reinforcement (social praise and back-up activity rewards) upon appropriate child behavior in three primary level classrooms. The classrooms were all located in one school. There was one participating classroom each at the first, second, and third grade levels. These investigators worked closely with each of the teachers in implementing the study's procedures. Initially, the three teachers were given several inservice training sessions on the procedures to be used, and then they were supervised and given feedback on their implementation of the procedures during the study.

This study is interesting in that the children were given daily feedback on the extent to which they followed the classroom rules. In addition, the behavior management procedures were primarily of a group nature, in that the entire class was treated as a single unit in the rating of performance and the earning and awarding of reinforcements. That is, **all** the children in the classroom had to be following the classroom rules simultaneously in order for the group to earn units toward a back-up reward activity. If one or more children were not following the rules, no units could be earned until those children's behavior again became appropriate.

As a first step in the intervention, each teacher developed a set of explicit classroom rules, reviewed them with the class, and posted them in the classroom on a bulletin board. The rules were reviewed with the class on a daily basis in this rules only phase.

In the rules plus feedback condition, the teacher operated a clock-light instrument which gave the class continuous feedback on whether all the children were or were not following the classroom rules. A standard wall clock was equipped with a light in the center and wired to be operated from a hand-held, radio controlled switch so that when the light was on, the clock ran and when the light was off, the clock stopped. Thus, the teacher would let the clock run when all the children were following the rules and stopped it when one or more children were not.

The program operated in daily reading and math periods. During these periods, the class received continuous feedback as to whether the rules were being followed by everyone. At the end of each period, the teacher calculated and posted a percentage score which indicated the proportion of time during the period the entire class had followed the rules. Thus, two types of feedback were provided, **continuous** during the session and **overall** or **summative** at the end of the session.

In the final phase, group activity rewards and social praise were made available to the children for meeting a criterion based on the extent to which the class rules were followed. As the class improved their performance, the reinforcement criterion was raised accordingly (i.e., a greater proportion of time following the rules was required in order to earn the group reward). Individual children and the entire class were also praised regularly for following the rules during the daily sessions.

Figure 6.15 shows the results of this intervention program. The behavioral level of the entire class, recorded via the clocklight instrument, served as the

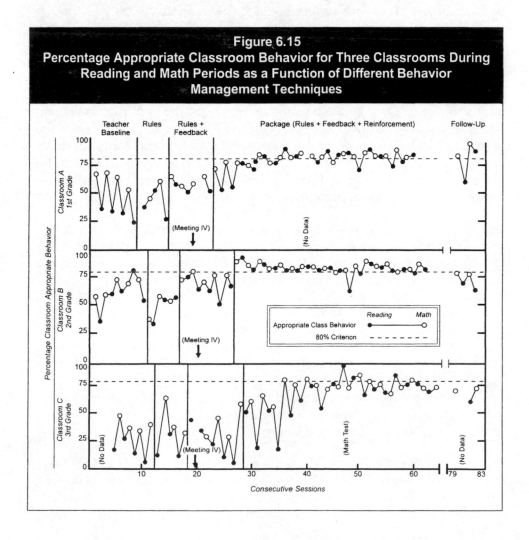

Figure 6.15
Percentage Appropriate Classroom Behavior for Three Classrooms During Reading and Math Periods as a Function of Different Behavior Management Techniques

primary outcome measure in this study. The study results showed that rules produced no change in the overall classroom behavior. The combination of rules plus feedback produced increases in class-wide appropriate behavior in two of the classrooms. However, the increases were only of low to moderate magnitude.

When the full package of rules plus feedback plus reinforcement was introduced, substantial increases in appropriate behavior were achieved for all three classrooms. There was an immediate and very powerful effect for the second grade classroom, and more gradual but equally powerful effects eventually achieved for the first and third grade classrooms.

The program was eventually terminated with all program components removed including the review of the rules, feedback, and the reinforcement procedures. Three weeks after program termination, a series of follow-up observations was recorded in each teacher's classroom. The short-term maintenance effects recorded were quite impressive even though the behavioral levels of the three classes appeared to be slightly lower than those during the full program and slightly more variable as well.

The ultimate question, as always, is how long into the future these gains would have persisted without support by the program or a variation of the program. Data recorded on the teachers' praise rates showed that the praise rates maintained well for two of the three teachers during the follow-up period. The extent to which the teachers continued to praise both the whole class and individual students would in all likelihood have an effect on how long such gains in child behavior would maintain.

This study demonstrates the impact that an easy to operate group behavior management program can have upon an entire classroom. The great majority of students in the three classes were affected positively by the program. A question arises as to the mechanical nature of the recording/reinforcement delivery system (i.e., the clock-light instrument). While such a device makes implementation of a program such as this easier, it is not essential. Similar, perhaps comparable, results can be achieved using a simple rating system of pluses (+) and minuses (-) for the entire class recorded on the chalkboard.

The study results show that the addition of feedback to the development and posting of classroom rules increases their effectiveness. However, it is clear that without an accompanying reinforcement system, this is an extremely weak intervention procedure.

Teacher Attention and Ignoring in the Control of a Preschool Child's Aggressive Behavior

Pinkston, Reese, LeBlanc, and Baer (1973) carried out an intriguing study in which they demonstrated that a preschool child's aggressive behavior toward peers was: (1) being maintained by the attention, in the form of verbal admonitions and reprimands, that it produced from teachers, and that (2) it could be controlled effectively through a combination of simultaneously ignoring the target child and attending to the victim(s) of his aggression.

The target child, Cain, was a three and a half-year old boy from a culturally advantaged background. He had well-developed language skills, but for some reason had acquired an extremely aggressive and destructive style of interacting with his peers. His behavior pattern was clearly unacceptable in the preschool setting and a program was developed to change his behavior.

In the initial baseline phase, the preschool teachers were instructed to respond to the target child's aggressive behavior as they normally would. This consisted mainly of verbal reprimands such as, "Cain, we don't do that here," or, "You can't play here until you are ready to be a good boy."

In the second phase, ignoring (i.e., extinction), the teachers did not attend to his aggressive behavior except to separate him occasionally from the peers he was interacting with (to prevent injury). Instead, the teachers ignored Cain whenever aggressive episodes occurred and they attended, in a sympathetic and caring way, to the peer or peers whom Cain was interacting with. This attention took the form of such statements as, "I'm sorry that happened to you. Why don't you play with this nice truck?"

In the third phase, the ignoring procedures were eliminated and the teachers were instructed to attend to Cain's aggressive behavior by setting limits, reprimanding him, and by attempting to reason with him.

In the fourth phase, the previous ignoring procedures were reinstated. Procedures in this phase were identical to those in the previous ignoring phase (the second phase).

Over the next three phases, spanning approximately 35 school days, reinforcement, extinction, and follow-up conditions were alternated. These phases were implemented to achieve some additional study objectives.

The results of this study are presented in Figure 6.16. The data in Figure 6.16 show that a combination of ignoring the aggressive child and attending to the child's victim(s) was a highly effective procedure for reducing Cain's aggressive social behavior, contrary to what one might expect. These gains were sustained over a 30-day period and maintained into a follow-up phase.

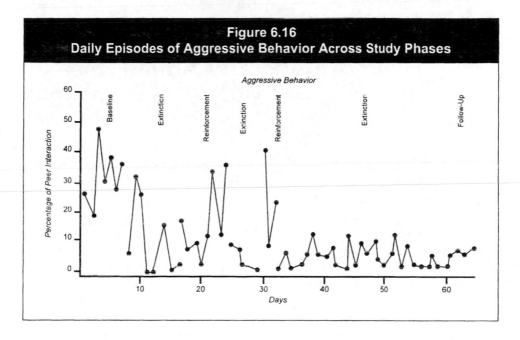

Figure 6.16
Daily Episodes of Aggressive Behavior Across Study Phases

It is interesting to speculate as to why this effect was achieved. It may have been that the teachers' attention was more effective in this study because of the child's age. Preschool children, because of their immature status, are more dependent upon adults. Therefore, adults have greater influence with them, and their attention and approval may be more powerful.

Also, Cain was being deliberately ignored while simultaneously observing the teachers attending, sympathetically, to his victim(s). This particular application could be more powerful than the usual combined use of praise and ignoring because of the built-in contrast and because of the vicarious learning involved (i.e., the teachers were communicating that aggression would be ignored and that nonaggressive behavior would be attended to and positively reinforced).

Finally, whenever an aggressive episode occurred, one of the teachers intervened and terminated it in order to deliver the extinction procedures. This interruptive effect could also have contributed to the overall positive outcomes achieved.

What this study shows is that an ingenious application of praise and ignoring procedures can control the aggressive behavior of a preschool child. However, it is not recommended that these procedures be used to consequate aggressive behavior in older primary or intermediate level children. Much more powerful procedures would be recommended and probably required to achieve this goal with older children.

Prompting and Adult Praise in Modifying Preschool Social Behavior

Strain, Shores, and Kerr (1976) carried out a study in which they evaluated the effects of verbal and physical prompts in combination with verbal praise in facilitating the appropriate social behavior of three preschool children. Strain et al. carried out the study in an early education center for preschool children having behavior disorders. Three boys, all age four years and enrolled in the center, served as target children in the study. The three children had a history of behavior problems including delayed speech, tantrums, and opposition to and withdrawal from peers.

A combination of verbal and physical prompts, plus verbal praise contingent on appropriate social behavior, was used to increase the children's rates of appropriate social behavior. Prompts included such verbal comments as, "Now let's play with the other children."; "Pass the block to Steve."; or "You can play house together." Physical prompts consisted of leading the child into the proximity of other children, modeling play with other children, or moving a child in such a way that he joined in a positive interaction with peers. The teachers timed the prompts so as to facilitate the occurrence of positive social behavior in the target children.

Teacher praise was provided contingent upon a child's positive social behavior. Praise was always preceded by the adult calling the child's name (e.g., "Dan, I like it when you play with friends.").

Figure 6.17 shows the effects of this procedure upon the children's positive and negative social behavior. Whenever the procedure was introduced, there was an immediate increase in the children's positive social behavior. In the case of Dan and Hank, there was a corresponding decrease in their rates of negative social behavior as well. In addition, there were spillover effects of the intervention from Dan to Hank when the procedure was

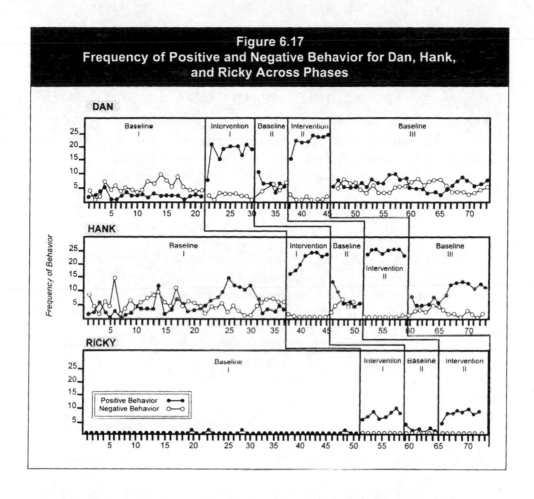

Figure 6.17
Frequency of Positive and Negative Behavior for Dan, Hank, and Ricky Across Phases

introduced for Dan. Similarly, there were spillover effects from Ricky to Hank when the procedure was introduced for Ricky.

This study demonstrates the practical role that verbal and physical prompts can play in facilitating appropriate social behavior among very young children. These prompts served as very powerful antecedent events that set the occasion for appropriate behavior to occur. Once the appropriate behavior occurred, it was immediately consequated with teacher praise. This can be a highly effective teaching strategy with preschool children, especially when used skillfully, as it was in this study. In using a combination of prompts and adult praise to increase any child behavior, the recommended procedure is as follows: (1) wait for an appropriate occasion for a prompt to be used, (2) prompt the response, and (3) reinforce it immediately when it occurs.

When to Use Different Combinations of Behavior Management Techniques

There are no hard and fast rules for using one combination of behavior management techniques over another within an intervention program. Of the twelve techniques illustrated in Chapter 5, it would be possible to apply them either singly or in combination with each other. Following are some general guidelines for determining when to use different combinations of behavior management techniques, and which techniques to use.

As a general rule, a combination of both positive reinforcement and mild punishment techniques will be required to effectively change the behavior of moderately to severely disruptive children. Children who spend more than 50% of their time engaged in inappropriate behavior may fall in this category.

Only positive reinforcement (social and/or nonsocial) is generally required to change the behavior of mildly to moderately disruptive children. Children who engage in inappropriate behavior less than 50% of the time may fall in this category.

Sometimes one doesn't know how a child will respond to an intervention program until it is actually implemented. If a positive reinforcement only system is implemented and the child's behavior does not change effectively, then alternative procedures must be tried, which could include the addition of a mild punishment component such as timeout or a response cost. If the child then responds satisfactorily, nothing else is required.

As a general rule, do not use a combination of praise and ignoring only to change the overall behavior of highly disruptive children. They may actually become worse under a program of this type (see Madsen et al., 1968; O'Leary et al., 1969).

Whenever possible, use prompts to facilitate the occurrence of appropriate child behavior, whether social or academic. Then reinforce the appropriate or correct response immediately as it occurs with either social and/or nonsocial forms of reinforcement. Prompts will greatly improve the effectiveness of reinforcement in changing child behavior.

Rules are a very important component of the process of changing child behavior in the classroom; however, by themselves they are an extremely weak behavior management procedure. Rules should be used in conjunction with a feedback and reinforcement program to motivate students to follow and comply with the rules.

As a general rule, use the simplest and least costly combination of techniques necessary to change child behavior. The fewer the techniques involved, the easier it will be for the teacher to manage the intervention program. If one has a choice of using praise only or a simple stimulus change or prompting procedure to alter behavior, as opposed to a more complex praise and token reinforcement procedure, select the simpler procedure first. A more complex intervention can always be implemented at a later point if the simpler system proves ineffective.

The purpose of the preceding sections has been to illustrate the applications of different combinations of effective intervention variables. Research studies that have achieved success in the application of appropriate combinations of such techniques were selected and described.

Some Perspectives on Changing Child Behavior

Research has clearly shown that teachers' behavioral and academic expectations can affect both academic performance and teacher-student interactions (Brophy & Evertson, 1981). The research literature, for example, shows that students who are perceived by their teachers to be brighter and more competent receive more teacher attention, are given greater opportunities to respond, and receive more praise and verbal cues. Rist (1972) found that children in lower reading groups had more negative interactions with the teacher than other children. Finally, Firestone and Brody (1975) showed that children who experienced the highest percentage of negative interactions with their kindergarten teacher were also those who demonstrated low levels of competence on the Metropolitan Achievement Test at the end of first grade. These studies provide substantial evidence that teacher expectations, as expressed through teacher-student interactions, can have a powerful influence upon child behavior.

If the expectations of teachers relating to child competence and other child characteristics can powerfully influence teachers' interactions with children, then it seems equally plausible that teacher expectations concerning procedures for changing child behavior could affect their own receptivity to these procedures. This is precisely what the author has found in numerous behavior management workshops and inservices he has conducted over the past two decades. Teachers will sometimes reject proven behavior management techniques, such as positive reinforcement, because they perceive these techniques as representing too much work to be practicable, as being forms of bribery, or as involving the special treatment of a single child (which they may believe is unfair to other children in the class). This is indeed unfortunate since both individual children and their teachers are then deprived of access to highly effective procedures that can: (1) improve child learning outcomes, (2) increase appropriate student behavior, and (3) make the classroom a more pleasant place for both teachers and students.

There are some key issues surrounding the use of behavior management techniques that teachers continue to raise in inservice training sessions. These include: (1) the issue of reinforcement as a form of bribery; (2) the special treatment of one child whose behavior is inappropriate versus the fair and equitable treatment of all children in the class; (3) the fear that if one child is singled out and treated in a special way because of behavioral or learning problems, other children will learn to "act out" in order to be treated in the same way; (4) the belief that the amount of work and time required to implement the procedures does not justify whatever changes in child behavior would occur as a result of their application; (5) the perception that behavior management procedures do not produce enduring changes in child behavior that are internalized and displayed throughout all aspects of the child's functioning, regardless of setting(s) or conditions; and (6) the issue of powerful behavior management techniques representing an undesirable form of behavioral control which both restricts a child's freedom and teaches an artificial set of values. A number of teachers have rejected the use of proven behavior management procedures based on one or more of these issues. Thus it is important to address each of these issues and to provide some perspective on them, as follows.

Issue One . . . . *"Reinforcement is a form of bribery."*

Reinforcement is a technique for motivating someone to do something (e.g., to acquire a skill, to learn a task, to behave differently, and so forth). The dictionary definition of reinforcement is: "To strengthen by the addition of something new, as new material . . . . " Reinforcement involves the addition of a stimulus or event to a learning situation which is designed to facilitate the learning or acquisition process. In a sense, it strengthens the response or behavior that is being acquired through a differential conditioning process. A reinforcer is made available if the correct form of the behavior/response is produced and is withheld if it is not.

The dictionary definition of a bribe, on the other hand, is as follows: "A prize, reward, gift, or favor bestowed or promised with a view to pervert the judgment or corrupt the conduct of a person in a position of trust." Given this definition, it is clear that reinforcement is not a form of bribery, but instead is a technique designed to facilitate the learning process. Reinforcement procedures are not used to corrupt individuals or to induce them to do something illegal. Rather they are used in a therapeutic fashion to help individuals become more competent or to change some aspect(s) of their behavior pattern.

It should be noted that bribery does involve the use of rewards dispensed in a contingent fashion (e.g., a building inspector receives an illegal payment for approving a building that is not consistent with the local building code). Reinforcement uses exactly the same principle; that is, the contingent dispensing of rewards, but the similarity ends there. Reinforcement and bribery can perhaps be most clearly distinguished through the purpose for the dispensing of contingent rewards in their respective applications. In the case of bribery, it is designed to corrupt and to induce people to act illegally; in the case of reinforcement, it is used to make people more competent or to induce them to change some feature of their overall behavior pattern in a positive way.

Reinforcement is used in a systematic fashion throughout all levels of our society. The government deliberately sets up incentives to encourage the public to behave in a certain way (e.g., the government frequently uses its vast powers to control the areas in which investors place their money through manipulation of allowable interest rates). This is a systematic use of incentive systems, or reinforcement procedures, designed to control and/or change the way investors behave economically. It is a clear case of behavioral control, of deliberate manipulation, but it is usually accepted without criticism since it is designed to improve the overall economy and to create more economic opportunities for a broad spectrum of the public.

Similarly, parents use reinforcement procedures constantly in the process of socializing children. Most parents apply massive amounts of social, and sometimes nonsocial (e.g., points, privileges), reinforcement in the process of teaching their children language, motor, social, and self-help skills. These procedures are instrumental in helping children achieve essential developmental tasks and in acquiring the behavioral repertoires they need to function effectively in society.

Ironically, many teachers object, sometimes strenuously, to the use of reinforcement procedures in helping children develop educationally and in achieving difficult educational tasks. Our society seems to communicate a generalized expectancy that all children should want to learn, should be motivated to achieve, that they will come to school with a behavioral repertoire which allows them to consume academic instruction easily and efficiently, and that they will be socially responsive to adults. Educators' tasks would be greatly simplified if this were true. As everyone knows, this is often not the case; unfortunately, the negative trends in this regard are discouraging.

It is apparent that many children do not develop the knowledge and acquire the skills expected of them under normal instructional conditions. Such children, especially at-risk children and those with disabilities, will often require **special** instructional and management procedures in order for them to develop at a reasonable rate of progress. The great majority of children do not require such special procedures. However, for those who do, it is incumbent upon the school system to accommodate their needs and to use the most effective methods available for instructing them and for managing their social and academic behavior.

A very powerful knowledge base on instruction and behavior management currently exists and has produced truly remarkable gains in the education of a diverse range of students in school settings. Reinforcement is an integral part of this knowledge base, and it is the author's hope that teachers will counterbalance the moral, esthetic, and philosophical objections they have raised about reinforcement procedures with an active consideration of the therapeutic child benefits that can result from their effective application in classroom settings.

Issue Two . . . . *"The special treatment of a single child through behavior management procedures is unfair to the rest of the class."*

One of the most pervasive objections of teachers to the use of systematic behavior management procedures in the classroom revolves around the fairness issue. Teachers, and people in general, have been taught to be fair and to treat others equitably. Fair treatment is a very powerful value in our society and one that has a broad basis of consensus. Because behavior management procedures are often applied to single children in classrooms and because reinforcement is usually involved in their application, teachers are quite sensitive to interventions that give the appearance of treating children in a special or unique way.

There is nothing wrong with the fair and equitable treatment of all children in a classroom given that they: (1) can meet the behavioral requirements of the situation, and (2) do not have special or unique learning needs. However, many children enrolled in regular classrooms, especially children with disabilities, have learning, behavioral, and/or emotional problems that do require that they be treated in very special ways if they are going to achieve a normal rate of progress. Children with cerebral palsy, hearing impairments, partial sight, learning disabilities, physical disabilities, mental retardation, emotional disturbances, and behavior disorders all require special consideration on the part of their teachers in order to perform to their potential. Plus children without disabilities, but who are not motivated to learn, require special consideration in the sense that efforts should be invested to identify why they are unresponsive to instruction.

Many children with atypical patterns of development require specially designed and/or adapted instructional procedures. Reinforcement procedures, implemented on either a short- or long-term basis, may be necessary in order for them to learn and achieve. In all likelihood, the teacher will have to invest much greater amounts of time, energy, and effort in the process of instructing such children.

Legislation now in effect requires that **all** children be given an equal education. With the advent of Public Law 94-142 and its subsequent reauthorizations, when more and more diverse children are being placed in regular classrooms, educators must reevaluate their traditional position that all students must be treated fairly and equitably. In order to achieve this goal, these children are going to have to be instructed and treated in very special ways, ways that may appear at first glance to be unfair to the other children. However if the school does not recognize their unique learning and behavioral problems and attempt to accommodate them, it will be denying such children access to what is for them an equal education.

There are a number of potential responses to the perceived problem of "unfair" accommodations. One is to simply explain to the other children, when they inquire, that the child involved is going to require some special assistance with schoolwork for awhile. If the child has an obvious disability, the question may not even arise. If the child's disabling condition is more subtle (e.g., a learning disability), inquiries from other children are perhaps more likely.

The extent to which children are cognizant of each other's special problems and their acceptance of unique or different procedures for remediating these problems is truly remarkable. If a reinforcement procedure is being used to teach a given child a specific skill or task, most children will accept this without objection if they are given a logical and rational explanation if they ask about its use.

Another alternative is to have the class share in the rewards earned by the target child. This is a most appropriate procedure when working with a student who has a behavior disorder and who disrupts the class and breaks classroom rules. However, it is not always feasible when working with other types of children (e.g., at-risk students).

A third alternative is to simply treat the target student no differently from any other child in the class. In this alternative, whatever special help the child receives would be delivered outside the regular classroom setting via a resource room or one-to-one instructional situation with a specially trained education professional.

These alternatives are by no means exhaustive of those potentially available. However, of the alternatives currently available to school personnel for responding to this problem, these appear to be the most feasible. The alternative selectedwould likely depend upon such things as the teacher's preferences, the nature of the child's problem(s), and the type of classroom situation involved.

Issue Three . . . . *"If a single child is treated in a special way, other children will 'act out' in order to be treated in the same way."*

There has been a great deal of rhetoric and concern expressed over this issue. In spite of this, however, no one has empirically documented that this effect actually occurs. This is not to say that it could not happen; for logically, it appears to be well within the realm of possibility. However, the fact that it has not been empirically documented suggests that the problem may not be as pervasive as one might expect. Nevertheless, it is a legitimate and real concern of teachers, and it is one that must be addressed.

Teachers are quite concerned that children may be given the expectation that they will be rewarded for breaking classroom rules, disrupting the class, or failing to complete their schoolwork. If a child who displays these behavioral characteristics is placed on a behavior management program where he/she is reinforced for appropriate behavior, many teachers fear that other children would then learn to act out in order to be put on a similar program.

There are a number of ways in which this potential problem can be circumvented, some of which have been discussed previously. For example, an unobtrusive, private program can be developed and implemented so that it is not known to anyone but the child, the teacher, and the target child's parent(s). The teacher can rate the child's behavior covertly during the day, and praise and give feedback where appropriate. However, reinforcers would be awarded only at the end of the day based upon a global assessment of the child's performance. This type of program would not be obvious to the other children in the class, and thus would not produce the undesirable modeling effects described.

Another method, also described previously, is to have the target child earn a group reward at school via his/her appropriate behavior that is shared equally with classmates. The target child is still singled out and treated in a special way, however the rewards earned are shared equally. Thus, other children would not be motivated to act out in order to gain access to the available rewards. However, with this system, children will occasionally ask if they can have a turn at earning rewards for the rest of the class. As a matter of fact, the opportunity to earn a group reward could even be used as a special privilege to motivate children to improve their classroom performance.

A third alternative is to set up a group contingency in which all the children in the class are treated as a single unit. Thus, **all** the children must be following the class rules and behaving appropriately in order to meet the reinforcement criterion. A potential problem with this contingency is that it may be too general to control the behavior of individual children who have aggressive or disruptive behavior patterns. It may be necessary to develop individual programs for such children first to get their behavior under some form of reasonable control before introducing a class-wide group contingency.

A fourth alternative uses a combination of group and individual contingencies to circumvent this problem. With this procedure, the teacher sets a timer for varying intervals of time such as 10, 15, 5, 30, 22 minutes, and so forth. Instructions to the class are that any students who are behaving appropriately, working, and following the class rules when the timer goes off will receive x amounts of points, units, or "stars" that can be exchanged for back-up rewards later. Many teachers have children earn minutes of free time as a back-up reward in this arrangement.

This procedure works extremely well in maintaining a high level of appropriate behavior in the classroom. Its effectiveness is based on the intermittent nature of reward delivery. That is, the children do not know when the timer will go off. Thus to maximize their chances of earning reinforcers, they learn to behave appropriately most of the time.

Every child is treated the same in this procedure. Those who are behaving appropriately earn points toward a reinforcer when the timer goes off, and those who are not earn nothing. There are some potential problems with its use in classroom settings, however. For example, it might be impractical to run the procedure throughout the whole day. Solutions to this problem would include: (1) beginning with small average time intervals, such as ten to 20 minutes, and gradually extending them to an hour or two so that the amount of teacher time involved in implementing the procedure is reduced to manageable proportions; or (2) having the procedure operate only during certain periods throughout the school day, with the class earning the right for it to operate by behaving appropriately during other periods. Either of these alternatives would probably be an effective remedy to this problem.

A second problem concerns the number of children in the class. This procedure would be simple to operate in a special/resource room setting, but not so simple, in terms of the work involved, within a regular classroom. If there are a large number of children involved, say 20-30, then the teacher can simply assume that most of the children will earn a point when the timer goes off and note which children are **not** following the rules when the timer goes off (i.e., the teacher notes which children do not earn a point toward a reinforcer rather than those who do). At the end of the day, a tally is computed for each child. This change would greatly reduce the work involved in managing the program.

A fifth alternative is a procedure called the "Good Behavior Game." The teacher begins by developing a list of classroom rules that govern the more overt forms of inappropriate classroom behavior such as talk outs, being out of seat, being off-task, and disturbing others. The class is then divided into two equal teams with a name for each team written on the chalkboard. When the game operates, the teacher simply writes a mark under the appropriate team listing for any member of the team who breaks a rule. At the end of the period or day, the team with the fewest marks wins, and all the members of that team receive a special privilege. This game has proven highly effective in increasing the appropriate behavior level of the classrooms in which it has been implemented.

There are also some problems with using this game in classrooms. For example, it does not seem practical to run the game the entire day. Second, it may not be powerful enough to control the behavior of highly disruptive or aggressive children. Third, care must be exercised in forming the teams, since it would easily be possible to overload one team with children experiencing learning and behavior problems.

These alternatives give the classroom teacher a great deal of flexibility in responding to the problem of children acting out in order to be placed on a behavior management program. The alternatives involve varying amounts of work and monitoring, and each must be adapted to a given teacher's classroom situation.

Issue Four. . . . . *"The teacher effort involved in implementing behavior management procedures does not justify the changes in child behavior produced."*

It is indeed unfortunate that behavior management procedures have been represented to teachers as all involving considerable effort, time, and energy in order for them to be applied effectively. While such procedures **do** require careful planning and monitoring, they can be implemented effectively without becoming a burden to the teacher. In fact, they can result in the teacher having more rather than less time to devote to instruction.

In the training they have been exposed to vis a vis behavior management procedures, many teachers have been taught that elaborate recording requirements are an integral part of their application. These recording requirements include such things as: (1) observing and recording child behavior, (2) graphing child behavior on a daily basis, (3) completing elaborate forms used for the purpose of delivering points or other units of reinforcement, (4) counting praise rates, (5) keeping track of the reasons a child is sent to timeout, (6) keeping track on a daily basis of the back-up rewards a child selects, and so on. For research purposes, it **is** valuable to have information on such variables, and on others that can help document the effectiveness of different behavior management procedures; however, much of this information is inappropriate when one considers the teacher's usual goals in applying behavior management procedures (i.e., to improve learning outcomes and to increase appropriate patterns of child behavior at the lowest possible cost to themselves in terms of time, effort, and energy).

Cost effectiveness is a major issue of concern to teachers in such applications. That is, given the anticipated outcomes resulting from the application of a given procedure(s), what is the relative cost to the teacher in terms of time, effort, and energy in the implementation process? Many teachers have rejected the use of systematic behavior management procedures because they view them as cost-ineffective. This is often because the recording requirements associated with behavior management procedures are perceived as overwhelming and simply "not worth it." The author has received this feedback literally hundreds of times in behavior management workshops with classroom teachers. It is clearly a legitimate concern of teachers and one that must be addressed if behavior management procedures are going to be adopted for effective use in classroom settings.

The recording requirements associated with behavior management procedures can be **substantially** reduced without affecting their overall effectiveness. The extent to which this goal can be achieved will make such procedures much more palatable to classroom teachers.

The crucial element in the application of behavior management procedures is that a child's performance be rated on a regular basis and that such ratings be tied to a reinforcement system. That is, if the child's behavior is judged to be appropriate, a reinforcer (e.g., a point, "star," token, checkmark, etc.) is delivered; if the child's behavior is not appropriate, then the reinforcer is withheld. In terms of recording, a simple rating and reinforcement delivery system is **all** that is required to implement a system that will be effective.

A simple point card placed either on the child's desk or kept on the teacher's desk or on a clipboard can be used for this purpose. A number of variations of such cards are available. An example of a very simple point card, using pluses (+) both as a rating and as a unit of reinforcement, is shown in Figure 6.18.

Figure 6.18
Sample Point Card

	Classroom Behavior	Academic Work
9:00 – 9:30	+	+
9:30 – 10:00	+	-
10:00 – 10:30	+	+
10:30 – 11:00	+	+
Etc.		

In this variation, each plus counts as a reinforcer (e.g., one minute of free time or as one point toward the cost of some event, activity, or privilege). Minuses (-) mean that the child's behavior was not up to standard, and they do not count toward the earning of an activity.

A second variation, somewhat simpler, is shown in Figure 6.19.

Figure 6.19
Simple Point Card

Classroom Behavior	Academic Work
✓ ✓ ✓	✓ ✓ ✓
✓	

Checkmarks also serve both as ratings and as units of reinforcement for appropriate behavior in this variation. More flexibility is available with this system since it is not tied to time intervals, and a variable number of points can be awarded to differentially reinforce high quality performance.

The important point to remember is that the minimal recording involved in these two systems is all the recording that is necessary to make the systems work effectively. The points, pluses, or checkmarks earned daily become a permanent record of the child's performance. However, it is not necessary to either observe or record child behavior independent of the ratings to determine whether the system is working. If the teacher can see changes in the child's behavior and the child's behavior is meeting the teacher's standards as indicated in the ratings of the child's performance, then that is all the documentation required. It is also not necessary to graph the child's daily point, plus, or checkmark totals unless the teacher is interested in seeing the child's performance visibly displayed over days for inspection.

If a response cost system is used in conjunction with the reinforcement system, then another recording/rating component is added. However, this component can be very simple to administer also. For example, the reverse sides of the point cards presented in Figures 6.18 and 6.19 can be used to deliver a response cost to child behavior. A sample variation is presented in Figure 6.20.

Whenever the teacher must use the response cost, he/she simply turns the point card over and writes a dot, using a felt-tipped pen, in the appropriate column opposite the behavior displayed by the child. Each day, the dots are multiplied times their corresponding point losses, and the appropriate number of points is subtracted from the point total earned for that day. The child is allowed to keep the difference in points.

In the example shown in Figure 6.20, the student had a very bad day. If 35 points were the maximum that could be earned in a single school day, the most points that could be retained at the end of the example day would be 13. That is, a total of 22 points were subtracted for being out of seat, talk outs, teacher defiance, being off task, and for arguing; 22 substracted from 35 equals 13. In reality, this student would have probably been hovering around zero in his/her point totals during most of the day because of the simultaneous earning/losing features of this variation of the response cost.

If the teacher wants the system being used to appear less obtrusive, then the point card can be kept at the teacher's desk and operated from there. It is desirable, but not essential, for the child to be aware each time that a point is earned or lost. The teacher can rate the child's performance and both award and subtract points, as indicated, at the teacher's desk. At certain times during

	Figure 6.20	
	Sample Response Cost	
	Response Cost	
Behavior	**Cost**	**Rating**
1. Being out of seat	-2	• •
2. Talk outs	-2	•
3. Teacher defiance	-5	•
4. Disturbing others	-3	
5. Being off task	-1	• • • • •
6. Arguing	-3	• •
7. Hitting	-5	

the day, depending upon the teacher's preference, the child can be called up to his/her desk and given feedback. A system such as this will work quite well for most children, but there are those who would probably require more immediate feedback and monitoring for the program to impact on their behavior. For such children it may be necessary to leave the card on their desks for a while, and then gradually change the procedure until the teacher keeps exclusive control of the card and the child receives feedback only at certain times during the day.

Another reason teachers have rejected the use of behavior management procedures is that they tend to see them as an add on—that is, as involving extra work for them. If applied correctly, the systematic use of behavior management procedures can significantly **reduce** the amount of time the teacher has to devote to the management and consequation of child behavior. Simultaneously, the classroom would become a much more pleasant environment for both the students and the teacher. It is also possible that if classroom behavior problems were reduced, the rate of learning and achievement per child would show a corresponding increase.

It is sometimes difficult to assist teachers past the point of viewing behavior management procedures as an added burden and to recognize the potential benefits their effective application can yield. However it is truly amazing how much time and energy some teachers invest in the process of managing child behavior via the use of reprimands, warnings, threats, and occasionally yelling. These techniques, at best, produce a temporary suppression in the inappropriate child behavior to which they are applied. Sometimes, they have no effect whatsoever in suppressing this behavior. And, as has already been noted, these techniques are instrumental in actually strengthening inappropriate behavior for some children over the long term. These techniques are not only the weakest and most ineffectual form of behavior management, they are extremely frustrating for the teacher as well. A systematic behavior management program can eliminate the need for such control techniques and allow the teacher to focus upon appropriate child behavior and the process of teaching.

Another reason teachers reject the use of behavior management procedures has to do with their expectations concerning an effective intervention and how much time it should take to produce the desired effects. It appears that many educators are still waiting for the ultimate "miracle intervention" for human behavior. Such an intervention would be extremely easy and simple to implement and would **permanently** change the behavior regardless of the settings or conditions. Unfortunately, such an intervention is not likely to be developed in the foreseeable future.

At present, the closest thing to such an intervention is drug therapy for hyperactive children. Once the correct dosage is found, the treatment is very simple to implement (i.e., the child takes a pill one or more times per day). In those cases where drug therapy is successful, the resulting changes in child behavior can be very reinforcing to adults (i.e., the aversive features of the child's behavior are greatly suppressed or totally eliminated). There is little wonder that drug therapy is such a popular intervention for children who are judged to be hyperactive.

However, as noted in Chapter 2, drug therapy for hyperactivity can have some undesirable side effects. In addition, this approach teaches the child nothing about his/her behavior or how to manage it more effectively. When the drug therapy program is terminated, the child's behavior pattern usually shows an instant reversal to predrug therapy levels. Thus drug therapy does not appear to be a desirable treatment procedure for the great majority of children experiencing behavioral and learning problems in the school setting. Even if it were, it does not appear feasible to keep children on such programs throughout their school careers.

When one considers the problem of changing child behavior in its entirety, it is apparent that there are no easy answers and no shortcuts to producing significant and socially desirable changes in child behavior. Most children with learning and behavior problems in school have developed them over a number of years. Given this length of time and the complex nature of such problems, one should expect that considerable effort will have to be invested in order to reverse this process and to teach a new behavior pattern. This is precisely what is required. Interestingly, educators often accept this perspective for academic failure but strongly resist it concerning social-behavioral adjustment failure.

It should be noted that powerful behavior management procedures can produce dramatic and sometimes immediate changes in child behavior. Unfortunately, their abrupt termination tends to produce equally dramatic and generally immediate reversals of the behavioral gains achieved. What is required are intensive and maximally powerful intervention procedures that are implemented on a short-term basis. These should then be followed by a shift to a low cost variation of the original intervention that maintains the appropriate behavior, but that is significantly easier for the teacher to implement and manage. The low cost maintenance program should be implemented on a permanent basis or until it is clear that it is no longer required to maintain the child's changed behavior. If necessary, such programs should be continued across school years, with each new teacher being taught to operate the program. This may appear to be a great deal of work, but if significant and permanent changes are to be produced in child behavior, this level of effort is usually required.

Systematic behavior management procedures are highly cost effective. The potential benefits to both teachers and children more than offset the effort and energy required in their implementation.

Issue Five . . . . *"Behavior management procedures do not produce enduring changes that are internalized and displayed throughout all aspects of the child's functioning."*

As in the medical treatment of various physical pathologies, the goal of traditional psychotherapies and educational interventions has been to produce comprehensive and enduring changes in human behavior. In fact, the usual standard for judging the efficacy of such treatments has been whether the subject's behavior shows evidence of generalized and enduring changes over time and across settings. Unlike medical practitioners, however, psychologists and educators have been greatly disappointed in their ability to produce such enduring changes with students.

The failure to achieve therapeutic effects of this nature is often attributed to the failure of human behavior to generalize across settings. The research literature in psychology and education provides overwhelming evidence as to the situational specificity of human behavior (Mischel, 1968, 1969). Human behavior, to a great degree, appears to be a function of the situation in which it occurs, and it is highly responsive to the stimuli setting events and contingencies that exist within such situations. To the extent that there is a close "match" of these factors across settings, behavioral consistency within and across them can be expected.

Given that child behavior is highly situation-specific, one would not logically expect behavior changes produced in one setting, through alteration of existing contingencies in that setting via a behavior management program, to generalize to nonintervention settings in which maladaptive behavior had occurred at equivalent or even higher levels. With rare exceptions this is precisely what the research literature on this topic has shown (see Horner, Dunlap, & Keogel, 1988; Stokes & Osnes, 1986).

This is a particular problem in situations in which psychological/educational interventions are administered within artificial or special settings and generalization of the changed behavior to natural settings is expected. Treatments administered within the psychologist's office or clinic and within special or resource classrooms have been very popular within the last two or three decades. However, the effectiveness of such treatments in impacting upon child behavior in natural settings (e.g., the regular classroom, playground), where these treatment procedures are not implemented, is being increasingly questioned by psychologists, educators, and parents.

Given this information, what can teachers expect concerning the long-term durability and generalizability (across settings) of behavior changes produced through the systematic application of behavior management techniques? Teachers should expect that: (1) behavior changes will not endure permanently following the abrupt termination of an intervention program, and (2) behavior changes produced in one setting will not as a rule generalize to other settings where the intervention program has not been implemented. In a sense, these are depressing expectations, since educators tend to think in terms of "cures" that are pervasive in their effects across settings and throughout all facets of a child's life. However, this just does not seem to be the case with human behavior.

Basically, behavior tends to show a change in whichever setting(s) intervention occurs, and it tends to remain unchanged in those settings in which the intervention is not implemented. As a general rule, when effective interventions are introduced, behavior tends to show a change, and when the intervention is withdrawn or terminated, the changed behavior tends to revert back to preintervention levels. There are limited exceptions to each of these assumptions, but they are representative of what teachers can expect, particularly in the school setting.

These effects are not just specific to one type of behavior change procedure or theory. They are characteristic of human behavior in general and apply equally to all procedures capable of producing changes in human behavior.

An intervention procedure has not yet been invented that reliably produces **enduring** changes in behavior or that automatically produces the generalization of changed behavior to nontreatment settings.

What are the implications of these findings for teachers faced with the task of modifying child behavior? To begin with, they suggest that "what you teach is what you get." That is, the teacher should plan to implement the intervention program, or a variation of it, in all settings in which child behavior is problematic and in which a behavior change is expected. Second, the teacher should initially implement an intensive and comprehensive intervention program that is designed to have a powerful impact upon child behavior. After the child has adjusted well to the program and the goals of the intervention have been initially achieved, a fading program should be introduced to gradually reduce the more obvious features of the program and to make it more manageable for the teacher. However, a low cost variation of the intervention should remain in effect for the foreseeable future or until the child's behavior no longer requires this support. Several variations of this procedure are discussed in Chapter 8.

There is considerable reluctance on the part of some teachers to accept such a depressing, but realistic, view of the process of changing child behavior. This is certainly understandable, but given what is known about human behavior and procedures for changing it, this view appears to be the most accurate and valid. The sooner educators accept this reality, the sooner they will be able to respond effectively to the learning and behavior problems presented by the children they are responsible for educating.

Issue Six . . . . *"Powerful behavior management techniques represent an undesirable form of behavioral control."*

Powerful behavior management procedures in general, and behavior modification procedures (i.e., procedures for motivating individuals to change their behavior) in particular, have generated a great deal of controversy in the last two decades. It is unfortunate that behavior modification's controversial status is in part a result of incorrect information concerning what it represents. Behavior modification does represent a powerful form of behavioral control—the power of this technique in changing human behavior has been demonstrated literally thousands of times in studies reported in the professional literature. It is one of the most powerful and effective systems available for changing human behavior.

As such, it is obvious that behavior modification could be easily abused during the behavior change process. Such abuses have been documented over the years, particularly within institutional settings. There have been a number of legal challenges to the use of behavioral procedures with captive, at-risk populations in such settings. The courts have increasingly become involved in the regulation and supervision of behavior management procedures applied in institutional settings.

Behavior modification has also been criticized on the grounds that it restricts the freedom of choice of individuals to whom it is applied by motivating them to behave in carefully prescribed ways. Clearly, this would be theoretically possible, but the author has encountered in the literature no documented instance in which this has occurred. In fact, in classroom applications, it appears that behavior management techniques based upon principles of behavior modification actually broaden a child's freedom of choice by increasing basic competence levels and by teaching a pattern of adaptive behavior. It appears that the **method of application**, rather than the procedures themselves, could potentially restrict the child's freedom.

Concern has also been expressed, particularly by teachers, that the use of systematic behavior management procedures will teach children an artificial set of values. That is, children will learn to expect rewards for everything they do, as a result of being exposed to a program in which reinforcement procedures are used. There is no evidence that this is true. However, it would certainly be possible to give children this expectancy depending upon how the program was represented to them.

It is difficult to abuse the use of behavior management procedures in the educational setting. However, they do represent powerful and highly effective teaching procedures; consequently, teachers should attend very carefully to what is communicated and taught via the implementation of these procedures in the classroom setting. For the most part, teachers tend to be quite sensitive to such issues.

7

Classroom Ecology and Teacher-Student Interactions: Defusing Oppositional, Aggressive Behavior

Introduction

This chapter addresses the social **ecology**, or **context**, in which teachers and students interact daily around the inherent demands of teaching, learning, and schooling. American society organizes the process of schooling so that very heterogenous groups of students are assembled for periods of time each day and instructed by a classroom teacher. In this process, it is essential to have rules and expected routines to guide student behavior as well as clearly specified, quality standards for governing student performance. These rules, routines, and standards provide the organization that makes classroom instruction work.

Public school systems are legally charged with the mass instructing/managing of all students who choose to partake of the schooling process. In the absence of consensual rules, expected routines, and standards that communicate appropriate expectations vis a vis student behavior and performance, schooling would be a chaotic process. Increasingly, schools are populated with students who enter the classroom not prepared or motivated to learn, who have little or no respect for authority, who have not been taught the values and standards governing positive interactions with others, and who do not have a well-developed sense of personal responsibility for their actions. The more of these students there are who populate a given teacher's classroom, the more difficult are the teacher's tasks in effectively instructing and managing that setting. As a result, teaching has become a vastly more challenging process in the past several decades.

Historically, it has been commonly assumed by many education professionals that the degree of effective behavior management and instruction occurring in a given classroom is a **direct** result of the teacher's skills. That is, if the classroom is well-managed and instructed, it is due to the teacher's skills and influence, and vice versa. In other words, it was assumed there was a **direct** relationship between teacher effectiveness and student behavior and achievement. The validity of this observation rests on the assumption that variations in the behavioral characteristics and responsiveness of students to instruction are relatively equally distributed across classrooms.

But it is now clear that educators can no longer blithely assume this to be the case, as has often been done in the past. What goes on in a classroom depends not only upon the teacher's skills, style, and approach but also very much upon the behavioral characteristics, attitudes, beliefs, learning histories, and individual capacities of the students who happen to comprise that classroom at any given time. These factors vary tremendously from classroom to classroom and from year to year. Every teacher knows that the make-up of any classroom of students is never exactly the same. All teachers have "good" years and "bad" years, and the difference is due largely to the random distribution of student attributes comprising each classroom group of students.

Many regular classrooms, for example, are composed of students who are extremely difficult to teach and manage. Further, such students are often confrontive and very oppositional with the teacher. Sometimes, these students even band together and reinforce each other in this behavior pattern. Ironically, some of the more recent educational practices (e.g., cooperative learning groups, use of "houses" in middle school classrooms involving recurring clusters of students [i.e., a school within a school], and so forth) may actually contribute to this outcome, albeit inadvertently.

As noted, the more of these students there are in a given classroom, the more the teacher will be challenged in effectively teaching and managing that classroom. Most teachers are not well prepared, in either their formal or informal training, to cope with such students. Many students now have little respect for adult authority; traditionally effective methods of social influence simply do not work with them. Thus a highly skilled teacher can be made to look very much like an ineffective one depending upon the make-up of the students in his/her class. Similarly, a much less skilled teacher can appear to be an effective instructor and classroom manager if the class is comprised of motivated, well-prepared, academically skilled, and well-behaved students who are easy to teach and manage.

Across the board, teachers must be able to organize their classrooms and instruct and manage the students within them in a way **that works for most students**. However, some students are **so** difficult that they cannot accommodate the minimal demands of regular school settings, or even those of more restrictive school settings (e.g., resource and self-contained classrooms).

Such students are candidates for residential or day treatment placements; thousands of school age children and youth are assigned annually to these very expensive and socially restrictive placements. Still other at-risk students can accommodate the demands of regular school settings only with specialized assistance and strategies provided by the teacher or other school professionals.

The basic goal of this chapter is to empower the teacher to understand and structure an ecology for teaching and managing the classroom that will be generically effective for the **majority of students** encountered in today's schools. A companion goal is to sensitize teachers to their own behavior in dealing with difficult students and to develop an awareness of how their expectations, attitudes, and perceptions of the students can influence the teachers' own behavior and help define the classroom ecology.

This chapter also describes some strategies for: (1) supporting and encouraging difficult students, (2) recognizing the situations in which difficult students have problems with self-control, and (3) responding effectively when their behavior threatens to or actually escalates to out of control levels. The teacher is, by far, the most powerful force in any classroom and his/her style of interacting with students sets the stage for what happens therein. The nature of teacher interactive behavior with acting-out students is of critical importance in this regard.

The material in this chapter is organized into three sections, as follows: (1) the behavioral ecology of the classroom setting; (2) the role of teacher expectations, attitudes, and perceptions as determinants of teacher and student behavior; and (3) specific strategies for preventing and defusing oppositional-aggressive forms of student behavior.

The Behavioral Ecology of the Classroom Setting

The concept of **ecology** grows out of the study of ecological, or environmental, factors and their effects upon human behavior. That is, how does the nature of a given setting influence, shape, facilitate, or impede certain forms of behavior? This is a very important field of study and has enormous implications for schooling and the management and instruction of classroom environments. Every teacher should have some understanding of the concepts and basic principles of behavioral ecology because of its potential for accounting for why the teaching-learning process is either facilitated or impeded. Just as the physical environment determines quality of life in very direct ways, the ecology of the classroom environment plays a strong role in shaping the daily atmosphere and interactions that teachers and students experience. The classroom teacher is the key player in establishing and implementing this ecology.

The generic term, ecology, is defined as the scientific study of organism-environment interactions; in this sense, it is a branch of the biological sciences (Sells, 1966). The term **human ecology** is a sociological concept and has been adapted by Barker and his associates (see Barker, 1968; Barker & Schoggen, 1973) for use in the study of **behavior settings** and their impact on individuals within them. Human ecology consists of **physical** and **behavioral** ecological components, or dimensions. Physical ecology refers to the physical features of environments or settings that influence, constrain, and facilitate human behavior. In classrooms, these components would include such things as room temperature, room size, noise levels, the types of objects present within the classroom, and the number of persons present.

In contrast, **behavioral ecology** refers to the study of the influence of interpersonal factors (e.g., friendship patterns, social support networks, teacher-student interactions, the distribution of positive and negative behavioral characteristics among the students in the class, social contingencies, and so forth) as well as environmental arrangements (e.g., seating charts, classroom organization, rules governing behavioral and academic expectations, etc.) upon student and teacher behavior. To date, far greater use has been made of ecological concepts to **explain** the effects of setting(s) upon behavior than to **design** environments so as to: (1) reduce maladaptive behavior, and (2) to increase adaptive behavior. This is particularly true in the context of schooling.

Behavioral ecology is primarily concerned with the following dimensions: (1) the degree of match, or "goodness of fit," between the individual's behavioral characteristics and the demands and expectations of the environment; (2) the level of disparity between the individual's needs, capacities, and aspirations and the environment's demands, resources, and response opportunities; (3) the manner in which differing environmental conditions and arrangements require accommodations in the behavior of individuals within them; and (4) the mutually reciprocal nature of individual-environmental interactions and influence processes. These dimensions have important implications for teachers and students in **any** classroom. For example, many students enter the schooling process with behavior patterns and attitudes that are **very** discrepant from the social norms that exist in most classrooms.

Acting-out students, in particular, have great difficulty in meeting the minimal behavioral expectations of most teachers, which include such things as working on assigned tasks, cooperating with others, responding to teacher directives and requests, working independently, making assistance needs known appropriately, and so on (Hersh & Walker, 1983; Walker,

　　　　　　　　　　　　　　　　　　　　　　　　Chapter 7

1986). In this context, acting-out students are often outstanding examples of a poor person-environment fit or match. This situation can be addressed by: (1) strengthening the student's adaptive behavior repertoire and reducing or eliminating the maladaptive repertoire; (2) changing the expectations and demands of the setting; or (3) some combination of both. The goal is to reduce the discrepancy between how the student behaves and what the environment demands or expects. When this is achieved, behavioral adjustment improves and a much better person-environment match exists.

The ecological concept of **behavioral demands** produced by the social environment is a very useful concept in the study of school settings. Educational experts have long argued that patterns of social influence in the classroom are two-way in direction and mutually reciprocal; in other words, teachers are influenced as much by students as students are by their teachers (Copeland, 1978; Doyle, 1977). That is, teacher behavior can be as much affected by student behavior as it is a causal influence on student behavior. Copeland (1978) cites evidence that **teachability levels** and **behavioral characteristics** of groups of students can have a profound effect upon the teaching repertoires (i.e., style, management practices, influence techniques) of beginning teachers. In this context, teachers are presented with a powerful set of demands simply by having to manage and instruct x number of students possessing a diverse set of characteristics within an inflexible time frame. The nature and complexity of these demands are largely determined by the behavioral characteristics and teachability levels of the students comprising the classroom unit.

Teachers vary tremendously in their ability to successfully manage these inherent demands of the teaching-learning process. Using direct observational techniques, Kounin and his colleagues (see Kounin, 1970; Kounin & Doyle, 1975; Kounin & Gump, 1974) have studied the group process variables that are consistently associated with high levels of work involvement by students and effective management of the classroom. Effective student work involvement and classroom management are consistently associated with the following teacher variables identified by Kounin et al. in their research: (1) **with-it-ness**; (2) **overlapping**; (3) **smoothness and momentum**; (4) **group alerting**; (5) **accountability**; (6) **valence and challenge arousal**; and (7) **seatwork variety and challenge**. The work of Kounin and his colleagues in this area has great validity and is some of the best research ever conducted on understanding the dynamics of the teaching-learning process. Teachers who are skilled in the techniques of group processes and effective behavior management, who understand the impact of their behavior upon others, and who consistently use best practices in instruction are able to negotiate more successfully the complex demands represented by heterogenous groups of students who vary in their general teachability.

The profile of the effective teacher that emerges through this work describes a person who is highly organized, who can remain calm in the face of challenging circumstances, who can track multiple events and situations in time, who monitors the classroom at differing levels, and who possesses great confidence. The findings of Kounin and his colleagues have consistently withstood the tests of time and replication by independent investigators (see Brophy & Putnam, 1979; Evertson & Anderson, 1979). This body of work stands as one of the most valuable contributions ever to educators' understanding of how to effectively manage groups of students.

The teacher is likely the single most important ecological variable or factor in the classroom since he/she is largely responsible for directing and mediating all aspects of this setting. Just as this situation places inherent demands upon the teacher, the teacher in turn places a variety of behavioral and performance demands on individual students and the class as a whole. Students have varying degrees of behavioral inclination to accept and conform to these demands. The processes governing negotiation of these often conflicting sets of demands and behavioral inclinations define, to a large extent, the nature of the classroom ecology.

The notion of **person-environment fit**, or match, is central to behavioral ecology. It is also a most useful principle in studying the adjustment problems that students experience in the context of schooling. Person-environment fit refers to the individual's level of adaptation or adjustment to a given setting and is a function of the match between the characteristics of the person and the demands of the environment. The ecological term for this process is called **synomorphy**.

This concept assumes that there are environments that more or less match the characteristics of each individual's behavioral profile, attitudes, needs, personality, and skills (Pervin, 1968). Attempts to find the best possible **LRE (least restrictive environment)** mainstreaming placement for a student with disabilities is an example of how this concept is operationalized. A "match" or "best fit" of the individual to the environment is indicated by high performance, satisfaction, and minimal stress levels (i.e., a good adjustment). In contrast, a "mismatch" or "lack of fit" results in decreased performance, dissatisfaction, and high stress levels (i.e., a poor adjustment).

Over the past two decades, the process of mainstreaming and social integration has provided many examples of mismatches between individuals and the requirements of LRE settings, and fewer examples of matches that represent a good fit. The controversial nature of the movement to mainstream students with disabilities on a broad scale is driven in large part by the knowledge that such mismatches do and will continue to occur. The task of educators is to anticipate and plan for such problems so that: (1) they can be prevented, and (2) their deleterious effects can be reduced or minimized.

Failure to effect a match can be attributed to both **person-specific** and **environment-specific** factors. Person-specific factors would include skill deficiencies on the part of the individual, violation of accepted social norms, and poor motivation. Environment-specific factors are represented by inconsistencies in adult expectations across settings and situations, by settings that provide limited choices, or key adults in such settings who establish unreasonably high or inappropriate behavioral demands that the individual cannot meet. In order to facilitate good person-environment matches in the selection of settings and placement processes, it would be necessary to consider carefully three factors: (1) the demands, expectations, support structures, and resources that exist in target, receiving settings; (2) the skill levels and coping abilities of the person to be placed in the selected setting; and (3) the process used to transition the person from one setting to another (i.e., from the sending to the receiving setting).

Acting-out students who move from more to less restrictive educational settings, and those who bring aversive behavior patterns to the beginning of their school careers, are extremely unlikely to achieve good person-environment matches. There is usually a very poor fit between such students' behavioral attributes and the behavioral standards/tolerance levels of most classroom settings.

A concept closely related to the lack of person-environment fit or match is **discordance**. This principle refers to the disparity that may exist between the individual's needs, capacities, and aspirations and the environment's resources and response opportunities. Discordance is often a factor in the inability of individuals to adjust satisfactorily to new environments or settings. That is, they may be motivated to succeed in the new setting, but either: (1) lack the skills and capacity to do so, or (2) the setting is not able to provide the necessary resources or support that they need. The collective history of mainstreaming and social integration also provides numerous examples of this concept wherein adequate support systems are not made available to meet the complex needs of students with disabilities who are placed into LRE settings (Walker & Bullis, 1991).

Behavioral ecology provides an especially useful framework for studying and understanding school adjustment processes. This framework is valuable also in guiding assessments of the individual student in relation to demands of the setting. Chapter 10 presents a model process, based on a behavioral-ecological framework, governing the mainstreaming and social integration of acting-out students, as well as other students, into regular classroom settings. This model process, called *AIMS* (*Assessments for Integration into Mainstream Settings*) (Walker, 1986), pre-assesses the behavioral demands and ecology of potential LRE settings and then evaluates the behavioral capabilities of the target student (the student to be mainstreamed) in relation to those demands. An initial placement is then selected that provides the best match between the student, teacher, and classroom. Next, a transition mainstreaming plan is developed that prepares the target student and the receiving setting (i.e., the regular teacher and students) for the target student's social integration into the setting. The most important step in this process is to achieve the best possible match or fit between the attributes of the target student and the demands of the receiving setting.

The Role of Teacher Expectations, Attitudes, and Perceptions as Determinants of Teacher and Student Behavior

Expectations are defined by Brophy and Good (1974) as predictions about how individuals will behave or perform based upon a set of beliefs that may or may not be supported by actual facts. Another definitional variation views teacher expectations as standards that are communicated to students about how they **should** behave in social and academic domains (Hersh & Walker, 1983). **Attitudes**, in contrast, are affective or emotional responses to social situations and involve such dimensions as likes-dislikes, positive-negative impressions, and acceptance-rejection (see Brophy & Evertson, 1981).

Perceptions refer to awareness processes involved in acquiring information, making evaluative judgments, and identifying attributes (Harvey & Smith, 1977; Kornblau & Keogh, 1980). All three of these constructs have implications for understanding and accounting for teacher behavior in the classroom. The evidence and implications associated with each are reviewed following. A clear understanding of how these constructs work can sensitize teachers to their own behavior and improve their ability to manage the classroom setting. It can also contribute to much more positive and effective teacher-student interactions that are far less likely to escalate into confrontations.

Teacher Expectations

Beginning in the early seventies and continuing through the subsequent two decades, perhaps more research has been done on teacher expectations than on any other variable relating to school and teacher effectiveness. There is considerable doubt that **artificially** induced teacher expectations lead inexorably to a self-fulfilling prophecy of success or failure, as described by Rosenthal and Jacobson (1968). However, the notion of **self-generated** or naturally occurring teacher expectations for student achievement grew out of the controversy surrounding this issue and has stimulated a powerful program of descriptive and correlational research.

Brophy and Good are the principal developers of the conceptual framework and the approach used to investigate this question (Brophy & Good, 1970, 1974; Good & Brophy, 1978). The results of their research are compelling and its implications for teacher-student interactions should be understood by all teachers. Their results are especially relevant for understanding and managing the relationship(s) that teachers have with acting-out students, and other at-risk students, in their classes who consistently challenge the teacher's management and instructional skills as well as his/her tolerance.

The knowledge base on teacher expectations is reviewed and discussed following. Topics addressed are as follows: (1) teacher expectations as a correlate of effective schools, (2) the formation and behavioral expression of differential teacher expectations, (3) replications of the empirical findings on differential teacher expectations, and (4) illustration of the process that explains the effects of differential teacher expectations on student behavior and achievement.

— Teacher Expectations as a Correlate — of Effective Schools

High teacher expectations for student behavior and academic performance has been consistently identified as a key correlate of effective schools in studies reported since the early seventies. Studies by Weber (1971), Edmonds (1979), Rutter, Maughan, Mortimore, Ouston, and Smith (1979), as well as a host of other investigators have all reported high teacher expectations to be a distinguishing characteristic of effective schools. High teacher expectations continue to be cited as a key variable in making schools effective for all students. If high teacher expectations for behavior and academic performance are a central and visible value within the ecology of the school building, it is more likely that the school will be judged as effective (Good, 1981).

— The Formation and Behavioral Expression — of Differential Teacher Expectations

In 1970, Brophy and Good published a now-classic study in which regular classroom teachers were asked to rank order students in their classes along a dimension of academic expectancy. That is, the students the teachers had the highest academic expectations for were ranked highest and vice versa. All the students in each participating classroom were assigned a rank, ranging from high academic expectation to low academic expectation, that reflected the teacher's perception of their ability and motivation to perform academically. Boy and girl pairs drawn from the high and low ranked segments of this dimension were then systematically observed over time as were their interactions with the teacher. The observations captured teacher verbal behavior as well as the nuances and quality of teacher-student interactions.

Results indicated that the behavioral characteristics and academic skills of the high and low ranked students were markedly different. That is, the high expectation students were well-socialized to the student role and were effective in it; in contrast, the low expectation students were clearly not. Further, disadvantaged, at-risk, and low socioeconomic status (SES) students were disproportionately represented in the low expectation student groups.

Of greater interest, however, were the differential teacher responses to the students for whom they held low versus high academic expectations. Teachers tended to maximize the achievement of high expectation students and to minimize the achievement of the low expectation students. That is, high expectation students tended to receive more teacher praise; infrequent criticism; many academic response opportunities; substantial feedback and academic debriefing; second and third chances for correcting errors; and elaborate cues, prompts, and even coaching. The low expectation students tended to be at the opposite end of the spectrum on each of these dimensions. The high expectation students were differentially favored in this regard presumably because their teachers were acting upon their higher academic expectations for these students.

These results appear to reflect a systematic and selective bias on the part of teachers participating in this and subsequent studies by Brophy, Good, and their colleagues. These investigators argue that such **differential** teacher expectations are self-generated and are naturally formed through information gleaned from the following sources: (1) observation and evaluation of the students' performance over time and across situations, (2) test results, and (3) anecdotal records. In the process of managing and teaching groups of students, teachers are constantly making normative comparisons between and among students of varying ability and achievement levels. Thus, they are excellent judges of student performance and adjustment.

Doyle (1977, 1979) suggests that the behavioral communication of differential teacher expectations does not represent so much a bias on the part of teachers per se, but rather is a natural teacher response to groups of students who have markedly different academic abilities and who vary tremendously in their teachability levels. The exact nature and form of differential teacher expectations is probably much less important than recognition of the fact that they do exist and directly affect teacher-student interactions in the classroom.

— Replications of the Empirical Findings on —
Differential Teacher Expectations

Like the work of Kounin et al. (1974, 1975), the findings of Brophy and Good on the formation and behavioral expression of differential teacher expectations has withstood the passage of time and independent replication by other investigators. However, this research has failed to detect the presence of differential expectations for **all** teachers, and has lead to an important caveat. That is, in the early stages of this research, it was assumed that all or most teachers formed these differential expectations and behaviorally expressed them through their interactions with students. However, by 1974, Brophy and Good had acknowledged that strong individual differences exist between and among teachers as to whether they manifested these expectation effects and in the nature of such effects when they were detected.

Based on the results of their research, Brophy and Good classified teachers into three broad categories or types, as follows: **reactive, proactive**, and **over-reactive**. The expectations of reactive teachers are directly shaped by students as opposed to their being independently formed by the teacher. Proactive teachers remain aware of and sensitive to their own expectations and keep them flexible so that they can change accordingly as students change. Over-reactive teachers fit the profile of those that emerged in the early expectation studies. That is, they hold strong and relatively rigid expectations for individual students that are less likely to change as student performance increases or decreases. The differential expectations of over-reactive teachers are most likely to have a negative impact on the behavior of low performing students.

— Process Model for Explaining the Effects of —
Differential Teacher Expectations

The model developed by Brophy and Good (1970, 1974) to explain the behavioral effects of teacher expectations and to guide their research has five basic steps, as follows:

1. The teacher expects specific forms of student behavior and performance from **particular** students in his/her classroom.

2. Because of these expectations, the teacher behaves in a differential fashion toward individual students.

3. Through this process over time, students learn what is expected of them and are affected accordingly in terms of their self-esteem, motivation, and levels of aspiration.

4. If this differential treatment is consistent over the long term and students do not resist it in any way, it will directly influence their achievement and behavior. Students who are exposed to high teacher expectations will be led to achieve at high levels; correspondingly, students who experience low teacher expectations will decline in their performance.

5. Over time, students' achievement and behavior will conform more and more closely to the patterns originally expected of them and behaviorally communicated through their teachers' management practices.

It is likely that teacher expectations play out according to the key features of this model. However, it is important to note that its explanatory power and validity are largely conceptual in nature and have not been thoroughly established through empirical research findings. But this model's face validity is substantial and it has served a very useful purpose in guiding the research on expectancy effects to date.

The work of Brophy and Good has greatly enhanced educators' understanding of the dynamics of teacher-student interactions and their subsequent effects on student achievement and behavior over time. Awareness of the roles that teacher expectations can play at a global, classroom level and at an individual student level is most important to effective teaching and management of the classroom setting. Such expectations are a very powerful feature of the ecology that develops in a given classroom.

As a rule, high teacher expectations for achievement and behavior should be developed and communicated as a valued outcome for **all** students in the classroom. Across the board, students who are clearly expected to behave and perform to their potentials will do better in school and the classroom environment will be more positive and free from conflict. Teacher expectations for individual students can be communicated informally through teacher-student interactions and via debriefing sessions. For the class as a whole, it is best to develop a list of rules governing behavioral and academic expectations in cooperation with all the students in the class. These rules should be posted and reviewed on a regular basis (see Chapter 5 for a discussion of classroom rules).

Acting-out students are especially vulnerable to the negative effects of differential teacher expectations. Because of their aversive behavioral characteristics and generally low achievement, such students are likely to be treated in ways that **do not maximize** their achievement (Kauffman, 1993; Walker, Block-Pedego, Todis, & Severson, 1991). Acting-out students, in turn, will tend to perform in accordance with such low expectations. This is indeed unfortunate since acting-out students generally have ample capacity to achieve academically and, in many cases, to learn how to behave in concert with classroom norms established by the teacher for all students. Teachers of such students need to be especially sensitive to the likelihood that they will unconsciously communicate and behaviorally express very low expectations for these students. This phenomenon then serves as a major barrier to efforts geared toward improving acting-out students' adjustment and ultimate school success.

Teacher Attitudes

The best evidence for the formation and behavioral expression of teacher attitudes and their effects on students was contributed by the early work of Jackson, Silberman, and Wolfson (1969) and Silberman (1969). Their initial findings were further strengthened through replications and extensions of their work by others (see Brophy & Evertson, 1981; Brophy & Good, 1974; Jenkins, 1972; McDonald, 1972). As with teacher expectancy effects, these findings have been established primarily through demonstrations of differential teacher attitudes and their behavioral correlates as reflected in the behavior of teachers directed toward students.

Jackson, Silberman, and Wolfson (1969) demonstrated empirically that teachers hold differential attitudes about the students in their classrooms. In addition, these attitudes were consistently associated with correlated patterns of student behavior. Silberman (1969) further showed that differential teacher attitudes **and** behavior were reflected in students' behavior patterns. For example, Silberman asked a sample of third grade teachers to nominate one student from their classes who represented **each** of the following teacher attitude groups:

- **Attachment**: If you could keep one student for another year for the sheer joy of it, whom would you pick?

- **Concern**: If you could devote all your attention to a student who concerns you a great deal, whom would you pick?

- **Indifference**: If a parent were to drop in unannounced for a conference, which student would you be least prepared to talk about?

- **Rejection**: If your class were to be reduced by one student, whom would you be relieved to have removed?

Silberman used direct behavioral observations in the classroom to examine teacher behavior directed toward students nominated for membership in each of the groups, and also assessed the nature and quality of teacher interactions with them. The divergent behavioral characteristics of students in the four groups and their teachers' behavior toward them are discussed following.

Students in the attachment group were highly socialized to the ideal student role and were viewed as conforming, as fulfilling the personal needs of the teacher (e.g., volunteering, answering questions correctly, and so forth), and as being relatively undemanding. These students were praised more often than other students and were frequently held up to the class as behavioral models to be imitated by their peers.

Students in the concern group tended to be low achievers who tried to complete assignments and follow classroom rules to the best of their ability. However, they were generally unskilled academically and made extensive demands on the teacher for assistance and support. These students required a great deal of supervision and teachers often went out of their way to provide them with needed assistance.

The indifference group students had very low rates of initiating to and interacting with the teacher regarding academic matters. These students had few other distinguishing behavioral or academic characteristics.

Finally, students in the rejection group were demanding, active, aggressive toward others, and very difficult to manage effectively in the classroom. These students were low achievers, exhibited high levels of misbehavior, and had high rates of contact with the teacher—mostly revolving around the issues of control and redirection of these students' behavior.

These four student groups constituted a classroom behavioral ecology that was reflected in very different patterns of teacher behavior directed to the students in each group. Based on the available evidence, Willis and Brophy (1974) argued persuasively that teacher attitudes toward students in their classes are shaped almost exclusively by student behavior and by the manner in which they respond to the teacher. The three key factors involved in this process seem to be: (1) the student's general level of school success, (2) the degree to which the student rewards and responds positively to the teacher, and (3) the extent to which the student conforms to classroom rules.

As a general rule, attachment students are going to be model students who are well-socialized and pleasant for teachers to work with. Concern students will be compliant, dependent, and often personally rewarding to their teachers. Indifference students will be more passive and not especially rewarding to their teachers. Rejection students will present very difficult control and discipline problems, and they will intensely pressure the management and instructional skills of most teachers.

Acting-out students are very likely to be members of this latter group. In addition, there is a very strong possibility that differential teacher expectations will operate among the students in these four groups. A review of the evidence on this question by Brophy and Evertson (1981) suggests the following:

1. Teachers are unusually open to the initiations of attachment students, approve of their behavior, and trust them but tend not to show undue favoritism toward them.

2. Teachers initiate high rates of contact with concern students, are very supportive and nurturing of them, lower their expectations and demand levels for them, and assist them in developing improved skills.

3. Indifference students appear to be seldom noticed by their teachers and are responded to with apathy; teachers often seem unaware of their presence in the classroom.

4. Rejection students produce strong emotional reactions in their teachers, are constantly under surveillance, are criticized frequently, and are subjected to intense, direct control measures including warnings, threats, negative sanctions, and/or dismissal from class.

Although only a minority of teachers exhibit differential expectancy effects for their students, a clear majority form and express differential attitudes in accordance with the respective behavioral profiles of the students in their classes. These differential attitudes, and correlated forms of teacher behavior, seem to be apparent from the early beginnings of the schooling experience (Willis & Brophy, 1974). Like teacher expectations, teacher attitudes are an important part of the behavioral ecology of any classroom. Further, teachers seem inclined to use different management strategies (e.g., direct versus indirect) with students from these four groups. Thus, some very important topics to include in the design of effective schools and classroom environments would be: (1) the role of teacher attitudes; (2) the student types and their corresponding behavior that seem to shape the formation of such attitudes; and (3) the collective impact that they may exert on the classroom atmosphere, school climate, and teacher-student outcomes. Teacher awareness of these factors and how they operate at a school and classroom level can contribute to more effective learner outcomes and better teacher-student relationships.

Teacher Perceptions

Classroom teachers are constantly evaluating students and making judgments about their performance relative to a set of absolute standards.

Teachers are also constantly evaluating students in relation to each other and making comparative judgments about the observed similarities and differences. These processes have important implications for effective teaching and also for the referral of students who need specialized assistance for academic, social, and/or psychological problems. The accumulated empirical evidence on teacher judgment indicates that teachers are: (1) highly accurate in making evaluative judgments about the academic performance of students; (2) moderately accurate in judging the social-behavioral attributes and status of students; and (3) far less accurate in their judgments of psychological dimensions such as depression, anxiety, and other affective disorders (Green & Forehand, 1980; Gresham, 1986; Walker, Severson, Stiller, Williams, Haring, Shinn, & Todis, 1988).

Classroom teachers have a significant advantage in judging student performance and behavior in terms of: (1) the amount of time they spend observing, evaluating, and interacting with their students; and (2) the variety of situations in which they are able to judge the **relative** or **comparative** performance of students in similar situations and contexts. The resulting information is extremely valuable in making informed judgments about the skill levels and behavioral attributes of students in general. Parents, in contrast, do not have this advantage as their information base is generally limited to observational judgments about their own children (or those of others) based on their knowledge of and interactions with them. They do not have access to the rich source of information that is routinely available to teachers as produced through the classroom situational contexts in which a diverse range of students participate (Gerber & Semmel, 1984).

Teacher perceptions of this nature are influenced not only by the observable characteristics of specific, individual students but also by school values associated with student attributes that profile the ideal student role versus the unacceptable student role. For example, Willis and Brophy (1974) investigated the criteria teachers use to make their evaluative judgments of students in a series of attribution studies. They found that positive student attributes associated with the ideal student role included attentiveness, self-confidence, the ability to work independently, compliance, school readiness, high general ability, and healthy social-emotional development. Other early work on this topic by Feshbach (1969) found that, as a general rule, teachers prefer students whose behavior patterns are characterized by conformity, passivity, acquiescence, and being orderly, high achieving, disciplined, and personally rewarding of teachers in their interactions and behavior patterns.

Kornblau and Keogh (1980) argue convincingly that teachers' perceptions of student "teachability" serve as a standard or criterion against which the specific attributes and performance of individual students are compared.

That is, teachers tend to develop an internalized vision of the ideal student against which each individual student is compared, either formally or informally. Those students who deviate too far from this teachability standard, in either academic or social-behavioral domains, become candidates for referral to other school services and tend to be viewed negatively by their teachers. The achievement and adjustment levels of such students tend to be below the norm or the class average (Gerber & Semmel, 1984).

Kornblau and Keogh (1980) suggest that this teachability standard directly influences teacher-student interactions and decision making about individual students. Teachers are more likely to feel uncertain about, uncomfortable with, and even hostile toward those students who deviate too far from their view of the ideally teachable student. Conversely, they are likely to value, feel comfortable with, and have positive interactions with those students who fall within the bounds of acceptabile teachability. Maddox-McGinty (1972) reported a study in which students rated low in teachability by their respective teachers had less social contact and fewer social interactions with both teachers **and** peers than did higher ranked students.

Kornblau (1979) developed a rating scale for assessing teachers' views of the ideal student in which teachers provide ratings of the attributes that define this ideal student profile. The scale consists of 33 descriptors of student attributes in three areas: (1) school-appropriate behavior, (2) cognitive-motivational behavior, and (3) personal-social behavior. The research of Kornblau and Keogh (1980) on this instrument, with samples of regular and special education teachers, indicates that the following student attributes are preferred by teachers across a broad range of grade levels: happy, cheerful, confident, emotionally stable, liked by peers, well-accepted, imaginative, understanding of others' feelings, able to use materials in an original manner, inquisitive, and questioning. Students who are perceived to fit this behavioral profile are much more likely to be accepted and valued by their teachers than those who do not. Their teacher-student interactions are also likely to be substantially more positive as a result of these positive perceptions. Acting-out students, who usually do not match up well with this preferred "teachability standard," often have very negative teacher-student interactions and are frequently rejected by their teachers. These outcomes are certainly understandable given the aversive behavioral characteristics that acting-out students display in the classroom.

The attributions, or causal statements, teachers make to themselves about the reasons that account for students' behavior problems, as well as the specific nature of the problems themselves, affect their perceptions and judgments of student behavior. For example, forms of student behavior that directly challenge the teacher's authority and ability to manage the classroom are considered to be **teacher owned**. That is, the teacher takes owner-ship of the responsibility for dealing with or solving the problem(s). Exam-ples of the teacher owned problems would include student noncompliance, oppositional-defiant behavior, not responding to teacher corrections, dis-turbing others, aggressive behavior, and so forth. Teachers generally as-sume that students engage in these forms of behavior willingly and that they make a deliberate choice to do so.

In contrast, student problems such as peer rejection, social withdrawal and avoidance, anxiety, phobias, and depression are considered to be **student owned**. In other words, they are the student's responsibility to solve. Such problems do not usually engage the teacher and they do not challenge his/ her authority and instruction/management of the classroom. Students with problems of this nature are considered: (1) to be victims of them, and (2) as not being able to control them on their own.

Teacher responses to teacher owned problems that challenge their control and authority are primarily negative and involve criticism, punishment, and sanctions of various types designed to control, suppress, or eliminate the problems. In contrast, teacher responses to student-owned problems in-volve expressions of teacher concern, sympathy, and encouragement. Some-times, students with these problems are referred by their teachers for school-based counseling services.

Teachers generally base their perceptions of students in their classes on repeated observations of their behavioral characteristics and performance across many situations. They are usually accurate in such perceptions— which are unlikely to change much over time. Students in general, and especially acting-out students, must make permanent behavioral changes of a **substantial** nature in order for them to be registered in changed teacher perceptions. Thus, it is very important for both acting-out students and their teachers to learn more positive and adaptive ways of interacting with each other in order to prevent this relationship from being poisoned by mutual hostility and animosity. As difficult as it is, teachers should try to give such students the benefit of the doubt **whenever possible**. Such instances will help counter the impression many acting-out students carry that everyone is against them. Unfortunately, such an outlook causes the acting-out child to behave in ways that too often makes this belief a self-fulfilling prophecy.

The remainder of this chapter addresses the dynamics of managing teacher-student interactions in the classroom. The appropriate use of teacher directives and the management of student agitation levels are very important considera-tions in this context. It is important to remember that teachers too often initiate interactions with acting-out students that quickly escalate into hostile, negative exchanges that prove disastrous to the teacher-student relationship.

The key to meeting these daily challenges of teaching is to know what causes them, to recognize their early stages, and to cease them as soon as possible. If the teacher persists and continues the interaction, he/she is put in a no win situation. That is, if the teacher successfully controls the student's escalated behavior through force, intimidation, or the assertion of adult authority, the student is humiliated in front of his/her peers and will try to "get even" in the future. This process of the student "getting even" generally proves very costly to the teacher and may endure for the remainder of the school year. On the other hand, if the student successfully intimidates the teacher and prevails in the interaction, the teacher's ability to teach and manage the classroom may be severely damaged because of the message it communicates to the rest of the class. At the very least, both parties will carry long-term, residual anger resulting from this situation that will ultimately prove destructive to the teacher-student relationship.

Specific Strategies for Preventing and Defusing Oppositional-Aggressive Forms of Student Behavior

This section covers three main topics: (1) a set of general principles for preventing and defusing oppositional-aggressive student behavior; (2) procedures for managing student agitation levels that escalate into teacher-student confrontations; and (3) strategies for the effective delivery and use of teacher directives. Each of these topics has important implications for the task of coping effectively with oppositional-aggressive student behavior.

General Principles for Preventing and Defusing Oppositional-Aggressive Student Behavior

The following principles, if adhered to, will result in a lower frequency of oppositional-aggressive student behavior over time and across situations. The teacher should:

1. Establish an ecology for the classroom setting that is positive, inclusive, and supportive of **all** students, regardless of their behavioral and academic characteristics.

2. Be aware that adults can unconsciously form and behaviorally express negative impressions of low performing, uncooperative

students to which such students are quite sensitive. The teacher should carefully monitor his/her impressions, keep them as neutral as possible, communicate a positive regard for the students, and give them the benefit of the doubt whenever possible.

3. Establish and communicate high expectations in achievement and behavior for **all** students.

4. Create a structured learning environment in which students know what is expected of them and where they can access needed assistance in completing academic tasks.

5. Allow sharp demarcation to occur between academic periods, but hold transition times between periods to a minimum.

6. Consider using cooperative learning strategies that allow diverse groups of students to interact, problem solve, and develop skills in working together.

7. Systematically teach social skills curricula that incorporate instruction in anger management and conflict resolution strategies.

8. Be sure that academic programming and task difficulty are commensurate with the skill levels of low performing students. Acting-out students, in particular, tend to have weak academic skills and may react negatively to academic tasks or demands they feel are too difficult for them. These situations very often lead to hostile teacher-student interactions.

9. Teach students how to be assertive in an appropriate manner (e.g., to disagree or resist the demands of others without being hostile).

10. Use difficult situations as "teaching opportunities" for developing student skills in responding to such situations without being angry, aggressive, or coercive.

11. Be sure to find ways to praise and encourage low performing students at the same or a higher rate than that for higher performing students.

12. Find ways to communicate a genuine interest in the progress of low performing students and support them as they struggle to meet the complex demands of schooling.

13. Maximize the performance of low performing students through the use of individualized instruction, cues, prompting, the breaking

down of academic tasks, debriefing, coaching, and providing positive incentives (e.g., praise, free time, home privileges).

14. Try to avoid criticizing, ridiculing, verbally punishing, or arguing with any student and especially low performing or acting-out students.

The classroom behavioral ecology represented by these general principles will create a more positive climate and will lay the foundation for effective teacher-student interactions. They are values that reflect best practices in teaching and in managing classrooms containing low performing students, some of whom will have acting-out behavior patterns. The actions based upon these principles will clearly communicate to low performing and acting-out students that they have value and that the teacher cares about them.

These principles represent a universal intervention approach in that they are applicable to **all** students and are designed to prevent or precorrect many of the problems precipitated by students' frustration with the necessary demands of schooling. Adherence to them, however, will not be sufficient to handle the problems that some students experience—especially those of many acting-out students. Because of the life circumstances of many acting-out students and because of the way in which they have been parented and socialized, many carry very high levels of generalized anger (i.e., they tend to be highly agitated and carry a perpetual "chip on their shoulders"). These students are perceived as "touchy," and train their social environments to give them a wide berth and to handle them with kid gloves. To the extent that this posturing allows them to escape or avoid the reasonable demands of others (e.g., parents, teachers, peers), it reinforces and strengthens their investment in this type of behavior. Some students are very successful with this negative behavior pattern and use it as a way of coping with the environment and its demands and tasks. These students are very likely to engage the teacher in difficult exchanges that often emerge from relatively innocuous situations such as giving assignments, issuing commands, providing corrective feedback, and so forth. Knowing how to deal with these exchanges as effectively as possible is a critical teacher skill.

Next is an illustration of principles and procedures for use in managing student agitation levels that often lead to hostile teacher-student interactions. This information can have great value to teachers in avoiding, escaping from, and terminating escalated teacher-student interactions that can prove very damaging to this relationship and to the teacher's ability to manage the classroom.

Procedures for Managing Student Agitation Levels

Colvin and Sugai (1989) have contributed a valuable conceptualization of a behavioral process that often begins with teacher-student contact over a teaching-learning task and quickly escalates into a hostile confrontation. This conceptualization has three key elements, as shown in Figure 7.1.

Figure 7.1 Key Elements of the Agitation-Escalation Cycle		
(Precondition) ———▶	**(Behavioral Process)** ———▶	**(Outcome)**
Student Agitation	Opposition-Defiance to Teacher	Damaged Teacher-Student Relationship

Student agitation (e.g., sulking, anger) is the fuel that, once triggered, drives the oppositional-defiant behavioral process of escalation. The outcome of this process, once unleashed, is an explosion that can cause severe damage to the teacher-student relationship and to the classroom atmosphere as a whole. This is called the "**Behavioral Escalation Game**," and it is a game **teachers cannot win** and **should not play**. The trick for the teacher is to avoid getting caught up in these escalations and to get out of them as soon as the teacher realizes that he/she is engaged in one. An example of this escalation process is provided following.

A teacher, Ms. Jones, gives her class an assignment to take out their math books and to work problems 1-19 on pages 114-116, as previously reviewed. The students begin organizing for the task—all that is, except Taylor, who sits sulking at his desk. Ms. Jones approaches Taylor and the following exchange occurs:

> *Ms. Jones* . . . . . . "Taylor, you're not getting ready for the assignment. Is there something the matter?"
>
> (Taylor ignores Ms. Jones' question and avoids eye contact with her.)
>
> *Ms. Jones* . . . . . . "I asked you a question. Now **what's** the problem?"
>
> *Taylor* . . . . . . "I don't have any problem—except you. I don't feel like working. Just leave me alone!"

Ms. Jones . . . . . . (now visibly angry) "If you're going to be in my class, you will have to do your work like everyone else. Also, when I speak to you, I expect an answer. Your attitude is unacceptable and you're bordering on an office referral."

(This is not the first exchange of this type between Taylor and Ms. Jones. Both carry residual anger from these prior episodes.)

Taylor . . . . . . (laughs sarcastically) "I want you off my case! I don't give a s . . . . about this class. You can write me up any time you like."

(Ms. Jones instructs Taylor to leave the room and report to the vice principal. Taylor blows up, calls the teacher a name, and pounds the wall as he strides out of the room. He continues to curse loudly as he exits the classroom. Ms. Jones writes up the incident as insubordination and submits her report to the front office.)

This is a most unfortunate example of an escalated teacher-student interaction that occurs all too often in the teaching-learning process. Episodes like this occur in thousands of classrooms daily between teachers and acting-out students. They disrupt the classroom, damage the classroom atmosphere, and wreak havoc upon the teacher-student relationship. If teachers respond "normally" to these situations (i.e., they escalate along with the student), they are likely to end up on the losing side of the confrontation with serious consequences for their ability to teach and manage the classroom effectively.

As noted previously, the "**Behavioral Escalation Game**" is one that teachers should not play and cannot win. The behavioral process involved in this game plays out as follows:

1. The student is sitting in class in a highly agitated state which may or may not be noticeably visible.

2. The teacher issues a directive or assigns a task to the student, either individually or to a group of which the student is a member.

3. The student refuses to engage in the task.

4. The teacher confronts the student about his/her refusal.

5. The student questions, argues with, and/or defies the teacher.

6. The teacher reprimands the student and demands compliance.

7. The student explodes, confronts the teacher, and the situation escalates out of control.

Unfortunately, this scenario also plays out in front of 25-30 very interested observers—the student's classmates. If the student prevails and forces the teacher to give in or to otherwise acknowledge the student's control of the situation, the teacher's ability to manage the classroom may be severely damaged. Students quickly lose respect for a teacher who "caves in" and allows the escalating student to end up controlling classroom events. On the other hand, if the teacher is successful in establishing his/her authority and forcing the student to submit, the teacher's victory is usually short lived and will prove to be **very** costly. That is, the student will likely feel humiliated in front of his/her peers, will carry long-term resentment as a result, and will usually find a way to "get even" with the teacher. So even if the teacher "wins," he/she ends up losing in the long run. The battle is won but the war is lost. This is a situation to be avoided at all costs.

As noted previously, the key for the teacher is to avoid getting into these situations and to get out of them as quickly as possible when he/she is inadvertently involved in one. It is not always possible to detect student agitation levels that serve as a precursor to behavioral escalations. Thus, teachers can be involved in the early stages of a behavioral escalation before they realize this is the case. An **avoidance** strategy and an **escape** strategy, two means of dealing with this situation, are described following.

— Avoidance Strategy —

It is very important to know when to leave certain students alone. When an assignment is given and a student does not immediately engage academically, it is often best to wait and to give the student the benefit of the doubt. Delaying tactics in relation to adult assigned tasks is one proven way that acting-out students: (1) provoke parents and teachers, (2) engage them in negative interactions, and (3) assert their control and independence within certain situations. Forcing the issue according to a prescribed time frame rarely produces a good result. Waiting for a reasonable period of time, and not attending to the student in the process, can often be a good alternative to confrontation of the student by the teacher. In the interim, many students will proceed to engage in the task if left alone and given sufficient time. The key is not to reinforce the student for using such delaying tactics by either directing your negative attention toward him/her or by showing clear signs of your irritation or disapproval. Both types of teacher behavior will only strengthen and make more likely the student behavior that produced them.

If it is clear that the student does not plan to engage in the task and expects to wait the teacher out, he/she will have to address the situation. Otherwise, other students may form the impression that the student does not have to play by the same rules that everyone else in the class does. In such cases, the teacher should approach the student and **quietly** inquire as to why he/she is not engaging in the task or assignment. The teacher should keep his/her voice low, remain calm, and try to keep the situation as private as possible. If the student attempts to engage the teacher in an interaction by questioning or arguing, the teacher should immediately disengage and indicate the following: "If you need some time to yourself, go ahead and take it. You can sit quietly as long as you do not bother the other students. Let me know if you need assistance with the assignment or have questions." The teacher should also inform the student that he/she must then make up the lost time and complete the assignment

After saying this or something akin to it, the teacher should leave the student alone and allow him/her to deal with the situation without further assistance. It is thus the student's responsibility to now cope with the situation, and the teacher is not part of the problem. **However, it must be clear to the student that the assigned task must be completed, whether now or later, and that the lost time will have to be made up.** Neither the student nor the observing classmates should form the impression that delaying tactics will allow avoidance or escape from assigned work. In using this strategy, the teacher communicates certain messages to the student, as follows:

- The student will not be able to control the situation by arguing with the teacher or by asking questions. (As long as the teacher is willing to answer the student's questions or to argue, the student and not the teacher is in control of the situation. This is a trap that must be avoided **at all costs**. In the great majority of cases, it leads to a worsening situation between the teacher and student).

- When the student is ready to work, the teacher will be there to provide any assistance and support required.

- The student will not be able to avoid or escape the assigned work by showing signs of agitation, by sulking, or by using delaying tactics.

- The student will not be able to provoke or anger the teacher by using either verbal or physical means (e.g., being unresponsive, sulking, arguing, etc).

— Escape Strategy —

Often, teachers will be answering questions for a student, providing assistance, or simply clarifying instructions and find themselves involved in an escalating interaction. As soon as they realize this, they should terminate the interaction and disengage with the student. A typical interaction might proceed as follows:

Teacher . . . . . . "Eric, you had a question about the assignment?"

Eric . . . . . . "I don't understand what you want me to do."

(The teacher then repeats the directions for the assignment just given to the class.)

Teacher . . . . . . "Does that help? Do you know what I want you to do now?"

Eric . . . . . . "Yeah. But I'm not gonna do it, because it's not fair. It's too hard for me and you know it! I hate math!"

Teacher . . . . . . "Eric, you've had the assignment explained to you. You know what to do. Your job is to do it. If you want help, I'll provide it. You have 15 minutes left to finish this work."

(The teacher disengages and walks away from Eric's desk. Eric sulks for awhile and gradually becomes more and more agitated. He raises his hand and the teacher approaches his desk.)

Teacher . . . . . . "Yes, Eric?"

(Eric proceeds to hassle the teacher about her assignments and how his parents think they are unreasonable. The teacher says nothing to Eric in response and simply walks away. Eric blows up, throws his math book across the room, and curses the teacher. The teacher sends Eric to the front office on a disciplinary referral.)

Nothing would be gained by arguing with or attempting to reason with Eric in his current emotional state. In the vast majority of cases, this situation would only get worse. If the teacher had persisted, along with Eric, in escalating this situation, Eric would have likely gotten very aggressive with the teacher. The outcome would be very unpleasant for everyone concerned with the possible exception of Eric. The resulting damage would not be unlike a tornado or earthquake that: (1) comes out of nowhere, (2) does severe damage in a matter of seconds, and (3) requires a long period for recovery. In fact, these escalated behavioral events are often referred to as "behavioral earthquakes" and they literally cycle out of control in a matter of seconds.

Teacher safety is also an issue in this context. It is never a good idea to allow a teacher-student interaction to escalate out of control. But it is particularly dangerous with older, more mature students who have a history of not being able to control their anger. In some cases, this could lead to physical assault or prompt the student to seek retribution in other settings or situations. Today, it is a common practice by the courts to place adjudicated youth in schools without properly informing teachers of their backgrounds. Such students often have histories of assault and have committed other serious crimes. They may be a danger to themselves and others. Engaging in an escalated interaction with such students could carry considerable risk.

Walker and Walker (1991) provided three general rules for adults to consider in order to avoid being ensnared in such escalated interactions. These rules for the teacher are as follows:

1. **The teacher should not make demands on or initiate to students when they appear to be in an agitated state, if at all possible.**

   The teacher should wait until the mood changes or passes before initiating an interaction that involves a direct request, command, or demand. When a student is agitated, a teacher's directive is likely to be perceived as an aversive, provocative event, **especially when it is delivered in the presence of other students**. In certain situations, the teacher can inquire about the student's problem, but **should not** accompany the inquiry with a command at that time if he/she can avoid doing so.

2. **The teacher should not allow himself/herself to become "engaged" through a series of questions and answers initiated by the student.**

   The teacher should not respond to the student's questions or comments regarding the situation and, especially, **should not argue with the student**. If the student asks a question, the teacher should ignore it and/or simply restate what it is the student needs to do, indicating that the teacher will answer the question(s) after the student does as instructed. If the student refuses, the teacher should leave him/her alone until the agitated state passes.

3. **The teacher should not attempt to force the student's hand.**

If the student chooses not to comply or cooperate, the teacher should not try to coerce him/her through such tactics as hovering and waiting, using social punishment (i.e., glaring, verbal reprimands, social intimidation, etc.), or making threats of future sanctions. **The teacher should never touch, grab, or shake a student in any way in this or other situations.** If the situation calls for the use of a brief timeout, the loss of privileges or points, or some other consequence as part of the classroom rules/behavior management plan, the consequence should be applied promptly and with a minimum of verbalization. If the situation does not call for such action, the teacher should then leave the student's presence and terminate the interaction.

The material in Appendix A, from the author's analysis of the first 100 referrals of the 1992-93 school year in a suburban high school (see also Chapter 1), provides some clear examples of how unresolved, escalated interactions between teachers and more mature students have a way of recycling over and over. Inspection of these episodes indicates that the school consequences applied to them have relatively little effect, and that these episodes seem to involve more serious infractions with repeated occurrences. Both teachers and students become more and more angry with each other over time and the resulting behavior problems tend to increase in their intensity. The consequences and sanctions available to schools are rarely effective in resolving such problems and causing the escalations to diminish.

One of the ways in which these angry episodes are precipitated is through the teacher's use of directives (i.e., requests, commands, demands). Acting-out students are often expert at resisting adult directives and see them as provocations rather than as reasonable requests. Thus, the students' history and behavioral inclinations have a great deal to do with how they react to teacher directives. However, the nature and timing of the commands, and the context in which they are given, have as much to do with student compliance as anything that occurs after a command has been issued (e.g., praise, positive consequences). The next section of this chapter reviews some critical issues relating to adult directives and presents guidelines for the delivery and use of this important technique in teaching and managing groups of students.

Strategies for the Effective Delivery and Use of Teacher Directives

The most commonly referenced definition of noncompliance has been contributed by Schoen (1983, 1986). In this definition, noncompliance refers to a failure to comply with a specific directive and is noted if: (1) no response is forthcoming, (2) no response is produced or initiated within a prescribed time period (usually ten seconds), or 3) some alternative, nonrequested behavior (i.e., inappropriate behavior) is performed instead (see Walker & Walker, 1991). Compliance with the request, demand, or command occurs when the child responds appropriately within ten seconds; otherwise, noncompliance is noted.

Noncompliance can assume different forms, including: (1) simple refusal, (2) direct defiance, (3) passive noncompliance, or (4) attempts to renegotiate the form or terms of the directive. Acting-out students are much more likely not to comply with adult directives than other students. Further, they usually express their noncompliance in the most destructive forms possible, which are **passive noncompliance** and **direct defiance** of the adult giving the command.

As presented in Chapter 3, there are two main types of commands: **alpha** and **beta**. Alpha commands are clear, specific, direct, and request the child to do one thing. Further, they allow a reasonable time for compliance to be demonstrated (usually ten seconds). In contrast, beta commands are vague, nonspecific, and usually contain more than one directive. They also frequently involve mini lectures and/or excess verbalizations, and do not allow sufficient time for compliance with them. Too often, the object of beta commands must guess at the nature of the directive (i.e., what it is the adult is asking for or demanding). Examples of alpha commands include: "John, stop pestering April."; Celene, I want you and Marla to do the flashcard drill with each other."; and "Jennie, tell me what time you have to be in band practice today." Beta commands are illustrated by the following examples: "Jered, if I have to ask you one more time to do what I ask, you're going to the office. I'm tired of your insubordination. You know what you're supposed to do. Now do it!"; "Francie, you and Carie have been fooling around long enough. Now stop what you're doing and get to work!"; and "Frank, you again! If I have to warn you one more time about that, you'll have to stay in from recess."

Children in general, and acting-out students in particular, are more likely to respond appropriately to alpha than beta commands. Beta commands are often confusing and so the child really isn't sure what is being asked; thus, compliance is a matter of the correct guess or mere chance. This is no way to manage behavior—in either home or school contexts. The use of beta commands can lead to the development of serious behavior problems and adult-child conflicts which are totally unnecessary and avoidable.

Forehand and McMahon (1981) have contributed the best work to date on noncompliance involving parents and their children. They have conducted an extensive analysis of the nature and causes of child noncompliance in the context of parent-child interactions. Their work, and that of Patterson and his colleagues (see Patterson, Reid, & Dishion, 1992), shows that weak parenting skills (e.g., poor monitoring, inconsistent discipline) actually teach children to noncomply with parental directives, albeit inadvertently. These parents often give beta rather than alpha commands in managing their children. Further, they do not consistently follow through and ensure that their children actually comply with the directives they give. Thus, the children learn that the requirement for compliance can often be avoided simply by waiting or by actively resisting the demand through behavioral escalation. Over time, this process gives the children considerable control over parent-child interactions and implicitly teaches that adult directives can be successfully resisted.

Upon entering school, the children generalize these lessons to the teacher and the classroom situation. These resistance tactics often work quite well in the classroom setting due to the complex demands on teachers involving the management of a classroom of 25 or more students. Unfortunately, the pattern of noncompliance may become elaborated and strengthened in the school setting. If so, this can lead to more serious forms of problem behavior including conduct disorders and antisocial behavior patterns (Patterson, 1983). Morgan and Jenson (1988) refer to noncompliance as a **"gatekey"** behavior; that is, it opens the gate to serious forms of maladaptive behavior.

There have been relatively few studies of compliance/noncompliance in the classroom. Strain and his colleagues (Strain, Lambert, Kerr, Stagg, & Lenkner, 1983) and, more recently, Golly (1994) have conducted direct observational studies of teachers' use of directives (i.e., requests, commands, and demands) in the classroom setting.

Strain et al. (1983) studied 75 well-adjusted and 55 not well-adjusted elementary students and their responsiveness to teachers' directives. Nineteen teachers were involved with these students and were directly observed in the classroom. The well-adjusted students complied with teacher commands about 90% of the time; in contrast, the not well-adjusted students complied about 72% of the time. Further, the well-adjusted students tended to receive teacher attention for their compliance while the not well-adjusted students were more likely to receive teacher attention instead for their noncompliance. Research shows that elementary age children tend to comply with adult commands approximately 60-80% of the time (see Forehand, 1977; Kucynski, Kochanska, Radke-Yarrow, & Girnius-Brown, 1987). Thus, it is not realistic to expect 100% compliance with all adults' directives all the time by even the best behaved students. However, compliance rates for acting-out students are generally well below those for students who do not generally "act out."

Golly (1994) studied 40 elementary teachers equally divided between lower elementary (grades 1 and 2) and upper elementary (grades 4 and 5) levels. Each teacher was observed during two 30-minute academic periods. Golly studied the teachers' rates of giving **alpha** versus **beta** commands, and also observed the frequency with which students complied with each command type. She found the following:

1. There was no relationship between the number and type of teacher commands given and either grade level of student or gender of teacher.

2. There was considerable variation in the total number of commands that individual teachers gave to students in their classes during a one-hour period, ranging from 7-163 commands across 40 teachers. This finding closely replicated that of Strain et al. (1983) who reported a range across 19 teachers of 12-150 commands given.

3. As a group, the 40 teachers observed gave proportionately more alpha than beta commands (i.e., 59% to 41%).

4. There was also considerable individual teacher variation in the rates of both alpha and beta commands used. For example, across the 40 teachers, alpha commands ranged from three to 81 and beta commands from 11-38 within a one-hour observational period.

5. Overall, 83% of all alpha and beta commands combined were followed by student compliance. Eighty-eight percent of alpha commands and 76% of beta commands were followed by student compliance.

Golly (1994) has contributed an important study to the literature on regular elementary teachers' use of commands and student compliance with them. The work of Strain et al. (1983) shows that well-adjusted and not well-adjusted students are clearly differentiated in the frequency with which they comply with teacher commands. Golly's results demonstrate that, across all students, alpha commands are more likely to be complied with than beta commands. This is a key finding and highlights the importance of paying careful attention to the nature, number, and timing of the commands one gives in managing classrooms of students.

There are some important guidelines that teachers should consider in giving commands so as to maximize their effectiveness and to manage the overall classroom more effectively, listed following. The teacher should:

- Use only as many commands as needed in order to teach and manage the classroom effectively. Morgan and Jenson (1988) argue that the percentage of compliance decreases as the number of commands given goes up.

- Try to limit the number of **terminating commands** given in favor of **initiating commands**. Terminating commands direct the student to stop doing something inappropriate; initiating commands direct the student to start doing something positive or productive.

- Give only one command at a time. If a series of separate tasks is involved, separate commands should be given for each task as appropriate.

- Be specific and direct. The teacher should get the child's attention, establish eye contact, and describe what is wanted in a firm voice using alpha command language that is easy to understand.

- Follow the command with a reasonable period of time (at least ten seconds) in which the student is allowed to respond.

- Not repeat the command more than once if the student does not comply. Instead, the teacher should use some other consequence or action to deal with the noncompliance in this situation.

- Give commands within a close proximity to the student instead of from a distance. This is particularly important with acting-out students.

The judicious and thoughtful use of commands is truly a best practice in the teaching and management of classrooms of students. Their use can be highly ineffective, or highly effective, depending upon their form and timing as well as what happens after the command is given. Compliance with teacher commands and directives is generally a serious problem for acting-out students and is a **major** source of conflict between the teacher and acting-out students. The skilled use of teacher directives will prevent numerous behavior management challenges and potential discipline problems. The reader is urged to study the literature on this topic thoroughly.

Conclusion

This chapter has addressed one of the most important topics in coping with acting-out students in the classroom setting. To the extent that this information is used effectively in the teacher's daily management of the classroom, the likelihood is reduced that complex and formal behavior management techniques will be required to address the behavior problems of acting-out and other students. Teacher-student interactions are a major friction point with acting-out students, but they are also a powerful vehicle for teaching and for socializing such students to a different set of behavioral norms or standards.

8

Case Study Applications

Introduction

The purpose of this chapter is to illustrate practical applications of the intervention procedures presented in Chapters 5 and 6. A second, and equally important, goal is to illustrate potential implementation problems that may be encountered in such applications. Adaptive responses to such problems are presented for the reader's consideration.

This chapter is divided into two sections. Section One presents five case studies illustrating best practice applications of intervention procedures to behavior problems commonly encountered in the school setting. The problem focus of these case studies typify the behavior management challenges presented to teachers on a daily basis by acting-out children and other children with less severe problems. These case studies are fictional; however, they are composites of **actual** intervention programs designed and implemented by the author and his colleagues. The case studies presented in this section contain: (1) a set of behavioral characteristics of the fictional target child, (2) the referral problems involved, (3) the intervention procedures used, (4) the problems encountered in the implementation process and responses to them, and (5) a set of outcomes resulting from the application of the procedures. Each case study addresses a different behavior disorder or problem frequently encountered in the school setting.

Section Two presents background information and child behavioral characteristics **only** for an additional three case studies. Based on the information presented, the reader is asked to: (1) develop an appropriate set of behavior change goals that could be achieved given the correct application of appropriate intervention procedures, (2) develop a set of intervention procedures for achieving the identified behavior change goals, and (3) identify potential problem areas in the implementation process. The reader will be able to compare his/her ideas and responses to those furnished by the author. Hopefully, these tasks will provide the reader with some direct experience in developing original responses to behavior management problems.

Section One: Illustrative Case Studies

Five case studies are presented in this section to illustrate the application of behavior management techniques in the remediation of classroom/playground behavior problems. Case studies are presented respectively for: (1) an acting-out child (Jody); (2) a socially aggressive child (Nathan); (3) a minimally disruptive child (Forrest); (4) an oppositional-defiant child (Dillon); and (5) an entire classroom.

Case Study 1: An Acting-Out Child

— Background —

Jody was an acting-out boy enrolled in a regular third grade classroom. Even though he was only in the third grade, he had already acquired a reputation as a "holy terror." Labels used to describe his classroom and playground behavior included "incorrigible," "hyperactive," "unmanageable," "a little monster," "mean," "out of control," "unteachable," "lazy," "a bully," "sneaky," and "just plain ornery!"

Jody had run the full gamut of school psychological services. He experienced difficulty from the first day of school in meeting ordinary classroom demands such as listening to instructions, following directions, working on assigned material(s), and participating in group activities in an acceptable manner. He was constantly in motion, even when in his seat. He had great difficulty concentrating on any task for more than a minute or two. To make matters worse, he was almost constantly disturbing others whenever he was not engrossed in a task or activity—which was infrequently! Jody was usually the center of attention, in a negative sense, in his classroom—a role he seemed to enjoy immensely.

As might be expected, Jody's academic skills and achievement were both well below grade level. He had difficulties with both oral and silent reading tasks and was especially weak in number concepts.

Jody was literally the bane of his teacher's existence. She commented a number of times how pleasant her life would be if it were not for having to deal with Jody each day. The thing that was particularly irritating for her was the disruptive effect he had on the classroom and the influence he seemed to have with his classmates. It was as though Jody and his teacher were in a contest for influence and control of the allegiance of the other class members. Jody ranked number one as the student his teacher would most like to be free from.

Everything the teacher tried, from reprimands to timeout, seemed to have no effect, or a minimal impact at best, upon Jody's overall behavior. Jody's teacher was extremely discouraged about his behavior pattern and felt that he would have behavior problems and be a low achiever for the remainder of his school career. She predicted dire consequences for his long-term future.

Jody's school record, test results, and the opinion of his previous teachers, the school counselor, and his principal all pointed to the same conclusion— that he would be a school failure and constant adjustment problem. Jody had been referred for psychological testing shortly after entering first grade because of numerous and highly visible behavior problems. The testing confirmed that he was of normal intelligence but suggested that he was unhappy and had low self-image problems. Unfortunately, the testing provided little in the way of useful information for coping with Jody's behavior or for designing remedial interventions.

Jody was assigned to a special classroom for behavior disordered children for awhile. Although he received specialized attention and an individualized instructional program in this setting, his overall behavior pattern was little changed from what he displayed in the regular classroom.

By the time he reached the third grade, Jody had been reassigned to the regular classroom as part of a mainstreaming/full inclusion policy adopted by the school district. He was assigned to a teacher who seemed to relate well to children generally and who had experienced considerable success in working with children, like Jody, having serious learning and behavioral difficulties. By her own admission, however, Jody was the **most** difficult and least cooperative child she had ever encountered in her 12 years of teaching.

Jody's behavior became so disruptive, and aversive to his teacher and peers alike, that a parent-school conference was called to consider alternatives for coping with his behavior. Jody's school records and current school performance were reviewed. This was followed by a discussion of his future prospects. His parents were quite defensive about Jody's school behavior, but they felt incompetent to deal with it. They seemed to have their hands full with him at home. Indications were that Jody's behavior was out of control at home much of the time and that he was a neglected child.

Alternatives that were considered included:

1. Referring the family to a mental health clinic for psychological treatment;

2. Placing Jody on a drug program designed to control his school and home behavior;

3. Assigning Jody to a residential mental institution for severely disturbed children and youth;

4. Suspending him from school for a period of time; and

5. Developing a comprehensive intervention program designed to gain control of his school behavior.

After much discussion, it was decided to try the intervention program, and if that didn't work, to consider either a drug program for hyperactive children or assignment to a residential facility for severely disturbed children and youth. The school psychologist was assigned to work with Jody, his classmates, his teacher, and his parents in developing the most effective intervention possible for coping with his behavior at school.

— The Intervention Program —

Before beginning the task of developing an intervention program for Jody, the school psychologist interviewed Jody, his teacher, and his parents. He had Jody's teacher and parents complete several rating scales designed to provide descriptions of Jody's **overt**, **observable** behavior at school and at home. The parents and teacher were questioned in considerable detail about the following topics: (1) What specific behaviors did Jody engage in that they found particularly irritating and aversive? (2) What situations, if any, seemed to prompt the occurrence of such behaviors? In other words, were there situations that seemed to elicit these behaviors from Jody? (3) Which activities did Jody seem to enjoy most at school and at home?

Results of the parent and teacher interviews revealed that Jody had acquired a set of behaviors that were highly irritating to adults. For example, he had a high frequency of noncompliance with requests and directives from adults. If told to do something, he would often ignore the command or comply only under duress after numerous prompts. At home, he was constantly arguing and fighting with his brothers and sister. Parent intervention was often required to stop these episodes. Jody was just as irritating at school. His noncompliance was equally high with his teacher and his general disruptiveness was a constant source of irritation. Jody also had a habit of interrupting his teacher when she was engaged in tasks or talking with other students rather than waiting until she was free and able to respond to him.

When Jody was interviewed, it was apparent that he was aware that much of his school and home behavior was inappropriate and was irritating to his parents and teacher. However, he was unable to verbalize why he continued to behave in this fashion in the face of such massive disapproval from them as well as his peers.

Next, the psychologist observed Jody's behavior in the classroom on several occasions. The purpose of these observations was threefold: (1) to obtain a visual picture of Jody's inappropriate behavior, (2) to observe his interactions with the teacher and peers, and (3) to determine whether there were any antecedents of a situational nature that prompted Jody's episodes of inappropriate behavior.

The psychologist then called a second parent-school conference to review his findings and to describe the details of a comprehensive intervention program designed to change Jody's behavior. The psychologist revealed that there were marked similarities in Jody's behavior at home and at school, and in the responses of his parents and teacher to his behavior. It was apparent that Jody had learned a very controlling and forceful pattern of behavior in which he usually got his way. He received a great deal of attention in this process, although most of it was negative. Jody was very persistent in his efforts to control situations and to get his own way. Usually, his parents would give in rather than expend the energy required to carry through in a given situation. When this occurred, Jody was rewarded by getting his own way and his parents were rewarded by the termination of Jody's highly disruptive and aversive behavior. If either parent refused to give in during these interactions, Jody usually threw a tantrum—which was even more disruptive and irritating. This pattern of interacting with adults spilled over into the school setting.

It was also apparent that the attention Jody received for his inappropriate behavior from his parents, teacher, and classmates was very reinforcing for him and was also instrumental in maintaining his inappropriate behavior. This was true, even though much of this attention was negative, critical, and disapproving. Jody seemed to thrive on this attention and he enjoyed his ability to dominate situations, to control the behavior of others toward him, and to be the center of attention. It was ironic that the best efforts of adults to manage his behavior actually strengthened the inappropriate behaviors they were focused on.

The school psychologist noted that hostile episodes between Jody and his teacher often followed situations in which Jody appeared to engage in "needling" types of behavior. That is, Jody would engage in teacher irritant behaviors such as asking irrelevant questions, dawdling, ignoring the teacher's instructions, and violating minor classroom rules in the teacher's presence. Often, the teacher would become visibly upset and verbally reprimand Jody for such behavior. Jody usually argued back, which made the teacher even more upset. Sometimes these episodes led to escalations that resulted in tantrums, yelling, threats, and very emotional outbursts between Jody and his teacher.

Finally, it was noted that Jody's behavior was much more likely to be inappropriate in reading and math periods than it was during other academic periods. This was due, at least in part, to Jody's very weak skills in these two academic areas.

The psychologist had two suggestions: (1) that a very powerful intervention procedure would be necessary to effectively change Jody's behavior at school, and (2) that the intervention or a variation of it should be in effect for the remainder of the current year and follow Jody into the next school year. He described an intervention plan consisting of three major components. These were: (1) teacher praise for appropriate behavior, (2) a point system implemented on a short-term basis, and (3) a response cost system backed up by timeout. In addition, he recommended that the teacher develop a set of clear, explicit classroom rules governing appropriate classroom behavior and that she review them with all the students in the class, including Jody.

Finally, it was suggested that a formal written contract be developed which would specify: (1) Jody's appropriate and inappropriate classroom behavior; (2) the consequences at school and at home that would be applied to his behavior; and (3) the role Jody, his classmates, his teacher, and his parents would play in the program.

The psychologist met with the teacher and explained the intervention procedures in detail, provided the necessary forms, and answered all the teacher's questions. The teacher had concerns about how much time the program would require. However, the psychologist pointed out the extraordinary amounts of time the teacher had been spending already in attempting to manage Jody's behavior and noted that the intervention program would, in all likelihood, not require any more time than she had been investing already. Further, the attention given would be directed largely toward Jody's appropriate rather than inappropriate behavior. The psychologist also noted that after the program was over, the teacher would probably have to spend less time managing Jody's behavior and that her efforts would likely be more effective than at present. After expressing some initial skepticism about these arguments, the teacher agreed to implement the program.

The plan was presented to Jody jointly by the school psychologist and his teacher. Jody displayed some initial reluctance and lack of enthusiasm, but agreed to participate in the intervention. As a first step, a contract was drawn up and signed by Jody, his parents, his teacher, and the psychologist. The terms and details of the contract were explained carefully to Jody and all efforts were made to ensure that he understood these details. A listing of Jody's appropriate and inappropriate behavior in the classroom was included in the contract and each behavior was discussed with Jody. Efforts were made to ensure that he could clearly discriminate the difference(s) between expected, appropriate behavior and inappropriate forms of behavior that were unacceptable.

Next, the consequences that would be applied respectively to these two forms of behavior were carefully reviewed with Jody. It was explained that Jody could earn teacher praise and points once during each ten-minute period throughout the day if his behavior was appropriate and he was following the classroom rules. The teacher would make an overall evaluation of his behavior for each ten-minute period and either award or withhold praise and points, depending upon Jody's behavior. The form on which points would be awarded was described and shown to Jody.

The inappropriate classroom behaviors that would result in point losses were also explained to Jody. The list of inappropriate behaviors had been ranked by the teacher from least serious to most serious, and point loss values ranging from one to five points, respectively, were assigned. Each behavior and its corresponding point loss was explained. The form on which point losses were to be recorded was also described and shown to Jody. The use of timeout as a back-up consequence whenever point totals approached zero was also described.

Finally, Jody's pattern of interactive behavior with his teacher was discussed. The teacher irritant behaviors that he engaged in were described, explained, and modeled for Jody. As noted previously, these behaviors included asking irrelevant questions, dawdling, ignoring teacher instructions, and violating minor classroom rules. Sometimes he engaged in angry confrontations with the teacher as well. Jody was informed that the teacher would be keeping track of these behaviors and episodes during the day and that if he did well in controlling them, he could earn bonus points at the end of the day.

Before implementing the intervention, the psychologist collected several days of baseline data on both Jody's and his teacher's behavior during daily 30-minute observation periods. A stopwatch was used to record the amount of time Jody was following the classroom rules and behaving appropriately. A simple tally was used to record his teacher's frequency of praising and reprimanding Jody's behavior during the observations.

Figure 8.1 presents these data for a three-day baseline period.

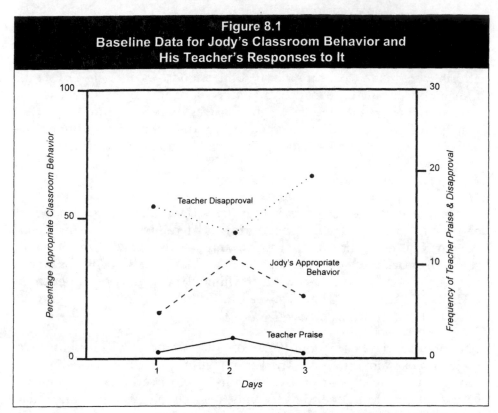

Figure 8.1
Baseline Data for Jody's Classroom Behavior and
His Teacher's Responses to It

The results in Figure 8.1 show that Jody had a very low percentage of appropriate classroom behavior, averaging only 27% for the three days of observation. There appeared to be an inverse relationship between the teacher's frequency of reprimanding Jody and the amount of appropriate classroom behavior Jody subsequently displayed; that is, the higher the frequency of teacher reprimands, the lower the amount of Jody's appropriate classroom behavior, and vice versa. The teacher could manage to praise Jody only once in the three-day period in which the observations were recorded. Aside from having a low praising rate generally, she found it especially difficult to praise Jody for **anything** because of her anger and frustration in dealing with him.

The psychologist and teacher met with Jody the day before the program was to begin and explained in detail how it would work. Jody could earn a school reward for himself and his classmates each day if he earned, and kept, 80% or more of the available points each day. He had an opportunity to earn teacher praise and one point during each ten-minute period. At the end of the ten-minute interval, the teacher would make an overall judgment as to whether or not Jody's behavior had been **reasonably** appropriate and therefore earned praise and one point.

Early in the program, the teacher tended to give Jody the benefit of the doubt and to made it as easy as possible to earn praise and points. Later on, she raised her standards and demanded more of Jody as his behavior improved and he adapted to the program.

Points were subtracted for Jody's inappropriate behavior whenever it occurred. The response cost delivery system described previously was used to implement this component of the program (see Chapters 5 and 6). A prespecified number of points was subtracted from Jody's point total existing at the time the inappropriate behavior occurred. Whenever Jody's total was at zero or near zero, a ten-minute timeout was used to consequate his inappropriate behavior so that he did not "go in the hole" with his points.

Initially, the program operated throughout all the classroom periods during the day, or for a total of approximately four hours each day. Thus six points could be earned each hour for a total of 24 points per day. Point loss values ranged from five points for fighting or physically aggressive behavior to one point for persistent off-task behavior (i.e., nonattending). Thus, the ratio of points available to those that could be lost was rather stringent, thereby making the actual loss of earned points a relatively high magnitude form of mild punishment. If Jody **lost** any points during a given ten-minute interval, teacher praise and the one point possible to earn were withheld for that interval. Thus in a sense, inappropriate behavior resulted in a double cost for Jody—the actual subtraction of previously earned points and the withholding of praise and a point for the ten-minute interval in which it occurred.

It was explained to Jody that he could earn a daily group reward at school that would always be shared equally with his classmates. Most of these rewards were of an activity nature such as extra recess, classroom games, a film, or a class party. A number of such activities were identified, a card was made for each, and the cards placed in a jar with one card to be drawn out (by Jody) each day that he earned a group reward (by earning and keeping 80% [i.e., 20 points] or more of the available points).

It was also explained that Jody could take home the number of points remaining at the end of the day and exchange them for a special privilege there. These points could accumulate toward prearranged home rewards each day even when he did not earn the group reward at school. The psychologist and teacher had met previously with Jody's parents to establish a reinforcement menu to be used at home. Activities and events were included on the menu that his parents felt Jody really liked. A range of options was provided varying from a family picnic in the park, which cost 125 points, to a movie, which cost 100 points, to 15 minutes of extra television time, costing ten points. Jody's parents were very cooperative in setting up the home part of the program; this is not always the case. Had Jody's parents been uncooperative in this respect, an individual reward would have been arranged for Jody at school.

The teacher, with Jody present, explained to his classmates how the program would work, and that they would be included in the group reward each time it was earned. The teacher mentioned that Jody had been having some problems and that he was going to work with her in a new program designed to help him learn and behave better. Jody's classroom problems were no secret to his classmates. As a matter of fact, they were quite supportive of the program and realized that they could assist Jody in achieving the daily reward criterion by encouraging his attempts at appropriate behavior and by withholding their attention and approval from his inappropriate behavior.

— Results —

The first day, Jody had some difficulty with the program. He earned a total of 18 points but lost ten of them because of classroom rule infractions. He ended up with a net total of eight points for the day, thus, he did not earn the group reward because he had only 33% of the available points. The teacher explained to the class that while Jody had made some good progress, he was still having difficulties in some areas, but that she was confident he could do better the next day. Jody agreed.

The next day, Jody proved to be as good as his word, earning 22 points and losing only one. Thus, he earned the group reward and was able to take home a net total of 21 points. With the addition of his total from the previous day (i.e., eight) he was able to purchase 15 minutes of extra television time at home, and to have his favorite dish, hot dogs, for dinner.

Jody was quite enthusiastic about the program at this point, but again encountered difficulties on the third day. He lost a number of points during the math period, a difficult subject area for him, and became emotionally upset several times when points were subtracted. The teacher did an excellent job of ignoring his expressions of anger and did not argue with him about whether he had or had not broken the classroom rules. Jody earned only 17 points and lost five; thus, he did not earn the group reward. His classmates were somewhat disappointed, but did not place undue pressure on him because of his failure to earn the reward.

On program day four, Jody's performance was exceptional. He earned a total of 22 points and lost only one, thereby earning the group reward. Jody's overall status among his classmates had improved dramatically.

For the next seven school days, Jody was a model student. He earned the group reward for seven days in a row. His classmates continued to be extremely supportive of his changed behavior. Both the home and school rewards were meaningful for Jody. Each seemed to represent a powerful source of motivation for him. In checking with his parents, the teacher found that Jody saved his points at home and exchanged them regularly for special privileges that he really seemed to like.

The next week was different, however. Jody would earn the group reward one day and not the next. This inconsistency in his performance concerned the teacher, so she sat down and talked with him about it. By this time, Jody and the class had experienced all of the available group rewards at least once. Jody said he was bored with them and would like to choose from some new back-up activities. Coincidentally, he was losing interest in the available back-up rewards at home as well. This information told the teacher that the change in Jody's behavior was probably due to his losing interest in the available rewards at school and at home. (Burnout of this type is not uncommon with reward systems and is something that should be monitored carefully.) To solve this problem, the teacher met with Jody's parents and planned a new menu at home, and she included Jody in the process of selecting privileges he could earn. She also arranged for Jody and the class to select a new list of group rewards that could be earned at school.

The results were immediately apparent in Jody's behavior at school. Over the next two weeks, he failed to earn the group reward only once and missed on that occasion by only one point. This experience taught Jody's teacher to monitor carefully and frequently the effectiveness of back-up rewards in maintaining appropriate behavior. She learned the importance of varying the available back-up rewards often and checking with the child to detect changing preferences as methods of maintaining the reinforcing effectiveness of back-up rewards.

During the next month, Jody continued to respond well to the program. Jody's teacher, classmates, and other teachers in the school were, frankly, amazed at the dramatic change in his behavior. At this point, Jody's teacher introduced a systematic fading procedure designed to gradually remove the main components of the intervention program. She informed both Jody and his parents of her intent to fade the program (i.e., to teach Jody to maintain his new pattern of behavior with much less reliance upon external rewards). She explained to Jody that instead of being able to earn praise and one point every ten minutes, he would now be able to do so every 20 minutes instead. The exchange ratios for both the school and home rewards were adjusted accordingly, to take into account the reduced number of points that could be earned.

Jody seemed to adjust to the changed routine quite well. His behavior pattern showed no effects of the fading procedure. The teacher was careful, however, to deliver occasional praises in between the 20-minute periods in which teacher praise and points were usually awarded. This was important since, by doubling the interval from ten to 20 minutes, the teacher had reduced her overall attention to Jody by approximately one-half. After having been consistently paired with the delivery of points, the teacher's praise seemed to have more value for Jody. He appeared to be much more socially responsive to the teacher's praise than he had been previously and their interactions improved as well.

The teacher next doubled the interval, to 40 minutes, so that Jody was now earning praise and one point each 40 minute interval. Exchange ratios were again adjusted to take this change into account. The teacher continued to praise Jody's behavior at random times during the 40-minute period. Jody seemed to adjust to the 40-minute interval reasonably well. The reduced teacher attention seemed to be more of a problem for him than was the smaller number of available points that could be earned each day. Overall, his classroom behavior was quite appropriate.

At this point, Jody's teacher introduced a major change in the program by eliminating the point system. Instead of earning points, it was explained to Jody that he could now earn a plus (+) or a minus (-) for each hour of the school day. If he followed the rules and behaved appropriately he would earn a plus each hour; if not, he would earn a minus. A simple 3 x 5 card, with the day divided into five one-hour periods of class time was used to record the results of this new program. The card remained on Jody's desk with an evaluation made each hour as to whether he had earned a plus or a minus. If four out of five hourly ratings were pluses, Jody earned the school reward. If not, the reward was not made available for that day.

Whenever Jody earned the school reward, the teacher filled out and signed a Good Day Card, indicating that he had earned the school reward and that he qualified for a minor, special privilege at home (such as extra television time). Thus, the point system was no longer available at home either. The privileges that Jody could now earn at home were of an activity nature, such as staying up later, watching extra television, or playing special games with his parents. It was no longer possible to earn tangible items such as hamburgers or athletic equipment via the home reward system.

Jody reacted to this change in the system by showing more inconsistency in his day-to-day performance. However, his overall level of appropriate behavior remained quite high—in the neighborhood of 85% on the average.

Next, the teacher changed the reward requirement at school so that Jody had to earn four out of five pluses for **two days** in a row in order to access the school reward and thereby the home privilege. After Jody had adapted satisfactorily to this change, the requirement was shifted to three out of four days, and then subsequently to four out of five days so that he was earning one group and one home reward each week. As the requirement for earning the reward was gradually increased at school, higher magnitude rewards were made available both at home and at school. An attempt was made to make the rewards special and unusual as well. For example, a popcorn party was made available at the end of the week at school instead of five or ten minutes of extra recess time. Similarly, at home, a movie could now be earned instead of just 15 minutes of extra television time.

The higher magnitude rewards were made available at this stage of the program for several reasons. First, the amount of time Jody was required to follow the classroom rules and to behave appropriately in order to earn the reward had increased dramatically. Therefore, it was appropriate to make valuable rewards available to him as he was able to accommodate these increased demands. Secondly, it was important to motivate Jody to work for longer and longer periods of time in order to achieve the reinforcement criterion. Providing higher magnitude/more valuable rewards for doing so is a very effective means of achieving this goal.

The inconsistency in Jody's day-to-day performance increased still more under these conditions. However, he earned the weekly reward approximately two out of every three weeks. His overall level of appropriate behavior hovered around 80%.

At this stage, Jody's teacher met with his parents and reviewed his progress during the program. It was decided to move Jody off the system, except to provide occasional surprise rewards at school and at home for Jody's appropriate school behavior.

The teacher explained that she would give Jody an overall rating each day (i.e., either a plus or minus depending upon the appropriateness of his behavior). She would inform him of the rating and review his school behavior at the end of each day. When he had accumulated a set number of pluses, she would make a surprise class reward available. Whenever this happened, she would send a note home with him and his parents were asked to arrange something special at home on these occasions. The teacher planned the reinforcement schedule so that if Jody's behavior was reasonably appropriate at school, a special surprise reward would be made available every three to four weeks. This system was in effect for the remainder of the school year, a period of approximately four and a half months.

Jody's behavior maintained reasonably well during this period. Compared to his pre-intervention behavior pattern, he was truly a changed child. Both his parents and his teacher were pleased with his progress. In addition to his improved classroom behavior, he made noticeable gains in the basic skill areas of reading, language, and math. His gains in math were especially noteworthy since this was a most difficult subject area for him. Jody was quite aware of his new behavior pattern and verbalized frequently to the teacher how much easier and more fun school seemed to be.

Jody did encounter difficulties from time to time however. If his behavioral episodes were disruptive and out of control, a brief timeout procedure (i.e., ten to 15 minutes) was used. Usually, this worked quite well for Jody. In those cases where it didn't, he was suspended from school for one day and had to make up all his assigned work in order to be readmitted to school the next day. Fortunately it was rare that suspension had to be used to control Jody's behavior.

Jody's teacher tried to maintain a reasonable frequency of praising his appropriate behavior (e.g., once every 20-30 minutes or so). However, she was not always able to reach this goal. It seemed that Jody was more inclined to experience difficulties whenever the teacher ignored his appropriate behavior for long periods of time. After several such episodes, Jody's teacher began keeping a tally, on a 3 x 5 card on her desk, of her praises to Jody. Her goal was ten to 12 praise statements per day, delivered whenever she could "catch Jody being good." Using this system, she was able to maintain a much more consistent and regular praise rate toward Jody's behavior. His appropriate classroom behavior gradually reflected this change.

In reviewing the intervention program, it seemed to Jody's teacher that she had invested a relatively large amount of time, energy, and effort in the process of changing Jody's classroom behavior. The question she mulled over was: Did the change in Jody's behavior justify the effort involved? On balance, she decided that it did.

During pre-intervention baseline observations recorded by the school psychologist, it was found that Jody received approximately 14% of the teacher's total attention. With a teacher-student ratio of 25:1, Jody could expect to receive approximately four percent of the teacher's overall attention. Thus, he was consuming slightly more than three times as much of the teacher's time as the average student in her class. Further, the great majority of this attention was negative in quality and directed toward Jody's inappropriate classroom behavior.

The teacher actually gave less attention to Jody during and after termination of the intervention program than she did before it was implemented. Implementation of the program required far less than 14% of her total time. Further, the attention she did give Jody was almost totally positive—a marked contrast to their interactions prior to the program.

Jody seemed to feel much better about himself and his overall behavior pattern. He was getting along much better with his classmates, and his incidence of rule breaking episodes in the classroom was greatly reduced. His general work rate and the quality of his academic performance were also improved. Jody's teacher saw him as a much more pleasant child and he was far easier to teach than before. For the first time in his school career, Jody's parents had occasion to be pleased with his school performance. As a matter of fact, they asked that the maintenance part of the program be continued into the next school year with Jody's new teacher.

Case Study 2: A Socially Aggressive Child

— Background —

From the earliest recollections of his behavior, Nathan had been perceived as a very active child. He always seemed to be on the go, could rarely sit still for any length of time, and was constantly fidgeting. Nathan was large for his age and he had always been able to physically dominate his playmates. He did so with regularity in his interactions with them.

Nathan was an only child and had been more than a little spoiled by his parents. Nathan was accustomed to getting his own way most of the time. His play behavior was no exception. Almost invariably, he dominated and controlled the play activities that he engaged in with his friends. He controlled the kinds of games and activities that were selected during play times, he decided who assumed which roles in acting out fantasies of popular television heroes, and he determined when play activities would begin and end. Sometimes, he even made up new rules if he did not care for the ones in effect. In short, Nathan was a **very** controlling and dominating child. He was also extremely powerful in terms of the influence he was able to exert on his peers.

Nathan had acquired a generic behavioral strategy that he applied systematically for the purpose of getting his own way. He was very manipulative and quite skilled in the use of social influence tactics designed to ensure that things went his way in his interactions with his peers. If all else failed, he would simply apply intimidating pressures to peers who resisted him until they agreed to do things his way. It was rare that Nathan came out the loser in such confrontations. The early successes he encountered in using such tactics increased the chances that he would behave this way as a matter of course. This is precisely what happened.

Nathan entered preschool at the age of four, whereupon he consistently applied this behavior pattern he had acquired earlier. Generally, he was successful in dominating play situations and controlling events in this setting to his satisfaction. However, he became increasingly negative, aggressive, and forceful in his social interactions with his peers. This was because he faced some stiff competition from several other children in his preschool class who were equally forceful and dominating. In order to maintain his effectiveness in controlling situations, he had to increase both the magnitude and intensity of the coercive pressures he applied to the other children. But because the preschool he attended was largely play-oriented and had only a limited academic focus, Nathan's behavior was not perceived as a serious problem. His teachers felt that while Nathan was definitely assertive and dominating in his social interactions with peers, his overall behavior pattern was well within normal limits and could be tolerated within the preschool setting.

It was a different story when Nathan entered first grade. He was an exceptionally intelligent child, was easy to teach, and had no difficulty with the academic demands placed upon him by his teachers. Although he could not be called a model student, his classroom behavior was clearly acceptable and within normal limits.

However, almost from the first day of school, Nathan was labeled as a behavior problem on the playground. Over the course of his two-year preschool experience, Nathan had become increasingly negative, aggressive, and coercive in his social interactions with peers. The relatively unstructured nature of the elementary school's recess periods seemed to bring out the worst aspects of this socially aggressive pattern of behavior. The severity of his playground behavior was quickly brought to the attention of his classroom teacher and the school counselor.

The playground supervisors blamed Nathan's inappropriate playground behavior on Nathan's classroom teacher, and demanded that she do something to control it or they would deny Nathan access to recess. Nathan's teacher felt helpless to do anything about his playground behavior and was quite surprised at the intense reaction of the playground supervisors, especially since he was a relatively well-behaved and capable student during class times. His teacher felt that Nathan's problems on the playground were probably the result of his basic personality and of his parents' failure to properly socialize him. However, she did agree to talk with Nathan about his playground behavior and to try to persuade him to be less aggressive and more positive and cooperative with his peers.

Nathan and his teacher had quite a lengthy talk about his problems on the playground. Nathan realized that some of his behavior was inappropriate (e.g., fighting and arguing), but he did not see that there was anything wrong or inappropriate with the vast majority of his playground behavior. There was no discernible change in Nathan's overall behavior pattern as a result of his talk with the teacher. The playground supervisors continued to complain loudly and frequently about Nathan's behavior. Further, Nathan's peers began to complain both to the playground supervisors and to their own teachers about his intimidating tactics and generally aggressive behavior.

Nathan was quickly becoming a school-wide problem and it was clear that steps would have to be taken to obtain some control over his playground behavior. This was necessary both from the standpoint of Nathan's social development and from the school's position that certain behavioral standards must be met, even on the playground. So Nathan's teacher and the playground supervisors held a joint conference with the school counselor and principal to discuss Nathan's behavior. It was decided to contact Nathan's parents as a first step to discuss their perspective on Nathan's overall behavior pattern and to see if they could do anything at home to control his school behavior.

Nathan's parents were shocked at the news that he was perceived as a behavior problem at school. They had always seen Nathan as an active, but clearly normal child. They were angry and defensive at the suggestion that they were in any way responsible for Nathan's playground problems. In fact, they insisted that Nathan was no more aggressive than most children. Further, since his behavior was appropriate at home, it must be the school's fault that he was viewed as having difficulties on the playground.

The school, of course, disagreed with this view of Nathan's behavior and insisted that something would have to be done to improve his playground behavior. Nathan's parents were informed that a parent-school conference would be set up in the near future to discuss the nature of Nathan's playground problems and to consider steps that might be taken to address those problems.

The counselor decided to collect some information on Nathan's playground behavior that would help document the exact nature of the problems he was experiencing. The playground supervisors were instructed to keep a running log of the inappropriate behaviors Nathan displayed on the playground over a four-day period. A partial listing of Nathan's inappropriate behavioral episodes is provided in Figure 8.2.

Figure 8.2
Nathan's Playground Tally

10/4

1. Took the kickball away from Pamela.
2. Hit Alonzo for no apparent reason, and knocked him down.
3. Called Jarvis a dirty name.
4. Told Joey he was going to beat him up after school.
5. Insulted the playground supervisor.

10/5

1. Shoved Brad when he refused to play exclusively with him.
2. Told Carol she was stupid.
3. Grabbed the softball and bat and ran away with them (to the gym) so the game could not be played.
4. Threw a rock at Jin-Luen and barely missed his head.

10/6

1. Refused to take his turn on the sliding board—shoved smaller children out of the way.
2. Kicked a child from another class in the shins for no apparent reason.
3. Humiliated a smaller child who refused to play with him.

10/7

1. Continued to play on top of the swing set despite repeated attempts to get him to come down. Suspended from recess for the remainder of the day.
2. Kicked a ball directly at Jessica in an obvious attempt to hurt her.
3. Got into an argument with Stephanie and taunted her until she cried.
4. Teased Megan until she left the playground in tears.

The playground supervisors emphasized that they had not recorded **all** of Nathan's inappropriate social behavior or violations of playground rules— only the more obvious ones. The playground supervisors in all three recesses were quite consistent in their tallies of Nathan's behavior. He seemed to be no better or worse in one recess period than in any other.

The counselor felt she needed some estimate of the actual frequency with which Nathan broke the playground rules and displayed socially aggressive and negative behavior toward his peers. She designed a simple tally sheet for collecting this information, a sample of which is shown in Figure 8.3.

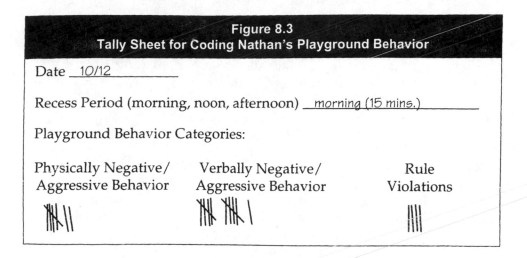

Figure 8.3
Tally Sheet for Coding Nathan's Playground Behavior

Date _10/12_

Recess Period (morning, noon, afternoon) _morning (15 mins.)_

Playground Behavior Categories:

Physically Negative/ Aggressive Behavior	Verbally Negative/ Aggressive Behavior	Rule Violations
卌 ||	卌 卌		||||

The counselor began by coding Nathan's behavior during a 15-minute morning recess on October 12. His rate of physically negative/aggressive behavior in this recess was .47 per minute—a very high rate when compared to that of his peers. His verbal rate of negative/aggressive behavior was .73 per minute, which is also a very high rate. He averaged one playground rule violation about every three and a half minutes of recess.

During the next week, the counselor continued to observe and record Nathan's playground behavior, choosing a different recess period each day. As the playground supervisors had reported, Nathan's behavior was highly consistent and predictable across each of the three recess periods. He displayed a very high rate of both verbally and physically negative/aggressive behavior during each of the periods in which his playground behavior was recorded.

The counselor next met with Nathan's teacher and the three recess supervisors to plan an intervention program designed to gain control of Nathan's inappropriate playground behavior and to teach him a new pattern of prosocial, interactive behavior.

— The Intervention Program —

Because each of the playground supervisors was responsible for approximately 90-100 students during the recess periods they supervised, the counselor tried to design a program that would be as simple as possible to implement, yet would have a significant impact upon Nathan's inappropriate playground behavior. She decided upon an intervention program with the following main components: (1) adult praise, (2) a response cost point system, (3) a group activity reward at school and an individual reward at home, and (4) timeout as an alternative back-up procedure.

The counselor met with the recess supervisors and Nathan's teacher to explain how the program would work. First, the counselor would meet with Nathan to review the playground rules with him. In addition, she would ensure that Nathan clearly understood the difference between positive and negative interactive behavior. As part of this process, the counselor would review with Nathan his playground behavior using the running log kept by the playground supervisors and the frequency data recorded by the counselor.

Nathan would be awarded one point for each five minutes of recess in the three recess periods. The morning and afternoon recesses were 15 minutes in length and the noon recess was 20 minutes in length. Thus a total of ten points were available each day. The points were awarded at the start of each recess period on a simple 3 x 5 index card providing the date and a space for each of the recess period points. A new card was used each day. The cards provided a permanent record of Nathan's performance in each of the three recess periods. An example of the point card is shown in Figure 8.4.

Figure 8.4
Nathan's Point Card

Date ___10/15___

Morning Recess |||

Noon Recess ||||

Afternoon Recess |||

Total Points Retained ___8___

It would be explained to Nathan that it was his task to keep his points awarded him at the beginning of each recess. He could keep his points by not breaking the playground rules and by avoiding negative or aggressive interactions with his peers. If he did not break any playground rules or have any negative and/or aggressive interactions, he would be able to keep all the points awarded to him at the beginning of that recess period. However, he would lose one point for each rule violation and one point for each negative/aggressive behavior that he engaged in. If he lost all his points for any recess period, he would sit out the remainder of that recess.

If Nathan had no negative or aggressive behaviors in two out of the three recess periods and no more than one playground rule violation in each, he would earn a group activity reward for himself and his classmates, arranged by his teacher. He could also take home the total points remaining at the end of the day to be exchanged for a variety of special privileges to be provided by his parents.

The playground supervisors would be expected to scan the playground regularly, to observe and evaluate Nathan's behavior, and to praise him at least once each ten minutes. If he broke a rule or engaged in a negative/ aggressive social behavior, the supervisor would walk over to him, describe the inappropriate behavior or rule violation, and cross out a point on the point card.

Two of the three recess supervisors and Nathan's teacher were enthusiastic about the program. However, the remaining supervisor objected to it, primarily because he felt that Nathan was, in a sense, being rewarded for acting out on the playground. That is, it seemed grossly unfair to make special rewards available to a child like Nathan to help him behave "normally." The supervisor saw the program as a form of bribery.

The counselor argued that Nathan had acquired a very maladaptive pattern of behavior over a number of years, that it was strongly developed, and that a very powerful program would be required to change his behavior. She suggested that a special program, designed to motivate and teach Nathan to behave differently, was necessary to reverse his pattern of deviant behavior. She noted that the total program would be in effect on only a short-term basis, and then gradually withdrawn so that only a low cost variation of the original program would remain in effect over the long term.

After arguing the issues of bribery, fairness, and special treatment of individual children, it became apparent that neither the playground supervisor nor the counselor would be able to change one another's positions. However, the supervisor finally agreed, although reluctantly, to try the program since there did not appear to be any other readily available methods for coping with Nathan's playground behavior.

A parent-school conference was scheduled to present the program to Nathan's parents and to obtain their support, cooperation, and willingness to participate in the program. Nathan's parents were interested in seeing documentation that he was in fact a behavior problem on the playground. The counselor shared the supervisors' logs with them and presented the tally data she had collected on Nathan's playground behavior. Nathan's parents became defensive and said that it was the school's responsibility and not theirs to manage his behavior. They also stated that Nathan had never been a problem at home or in the neighborhood.

The counselor stated that Nathan's playground behavior was a problem and that all efforts by the school to cope with it had proved ineffective. She explained that a program had been developed to teach Nathan a new pattern of appropriate playground behavior, and that she would like to explain how it would operate and what their role in the program would be. Nathan's parents understood the program and agreed to support its use. However, they objected to providing home rewards for Nathan's school behavior and refused to carry through with that part of the program. The counselor asked if they objected to Nathan earning individual activity rewards at school, such as free time. They did not, so it was agreed that an individual reward system would be established for Nathan at school.

Nathan's teacher and the counselor next met with Nathan and explained the program and how it would work. Nathan agreed to participate in the program and to cooperate with the procedures.

The program was then explained to Nathan's classmates with Nathan present, and their role was described. Nathan and the counselor role played various components of the program (e.g., praising, subtracting points) for the class. A discussion was then held focusing on how Nathan's classmates could help him to follow the playground rules and interact more positively with his classmates.

— Results —

Nathan lost all three points during the first recess period. That is, he lost a point on three separate occasions for displaying socially aggressive behavior toward his peers. During the noon recess, he had only one negative interaction with a peer, but violated the playground rules on three separate occasions. Thus, he lost a total of four points and retained none of the points available in the noon recess. During the afternoon recess, he had no negative or aggressive interactions and violated only one playground rule, thereby losing only one of the three available points. Thus, Nathan ended up with a total of two points at the end of the day, out of a possible ten available.

The counselor (who was conducting the program at this point) reviewed Nathan's behavior on the first day and discussed the situations in which he had experienced difficulty. It was as though Nathan was testing the program, its limits, and the counselor to see if things would work as they had been represented to him. Nathan was greatly disappointed that he had not earned the group school reward. The counselor told him that he would have to improve considerably in order to meet the school reward criterion—no negative or aggressive behavior and only one rule violation in two out of the three recess periods. Nathan replied that he felt the counselor was being too strict and was checking his behavior too closely. The counselor told him that her standards were no different for him than for any other children on the playground and that learning a new pattern of behavior was not easy, but that she felt sure he could do so. Nathan promised to try harder the next day.

The next day, Nathan had a perfect morning recess—no negative or aggressive behavior and no rule violations. However, he lapsed into his old behavior pattern during the noon recess, and he became involved in several arguments and a shoving contest with several peers about the rules of a kickball game. He lost three of the four points available in the noon recess, and complained loudly to the counselor that the arguments were not his fault and that he shouldn't have lost the points. She ignored his protests and informed him that she was only following the rules they had previously agreed upon.

During the afternoon recess, Nathan tended to avoid social contact with his peers whenever possible so as not to risk losing his points, and was very careful about following the playground rules. He kept all of his points for the afternoon recess, thereby earning the group reward and ending up with a total of seven points for the day. Both Nathan and his peers were pleased about this outcome and seemed really excited about playing the "Seven-Up" game in class. Nathan exchanged his individual points for some free time. He seemed truly excited about the program, and said that he felt sure he could continue to earn the daily group reward.

However, on the third day of the program, Nathan again experienced difficulties on the playground. He violated several minor, but nevertheless established, playground rules and got into a scuffle with a peer from another class whom he did not like. As a result he did not earn the group reward and was greatly disappointed—as were his peers.

On the fourth program day, Nathan tried really hard and lost only two points during the whole day, thereby easily earning the group reward. He received a great deal of support, encouragement, and appreciation from his peers for doing so. In contrast to day two, he did not avoid social contact with his peers for the purpose of reducing his risk of losing the points. He simply tried harder to get along with his peers. The program seemed to be teaching Nathan to be much more sensitive to and aware of his own behavior and its effects upon others. The playground supervisors had also observed and commented on this change in Nathan.

Nathan earned the group reward for the next three days. There was a marked difference in his overall playground behavior and in the quality of his social behavior. He was a much more pleasant child to be around. The program was having a significant impact upon both his verbal and nonverbal behavior. He was much less verbally punishing with his peers, less inclined to argue as a matter of course, and was also less physically aggressive in his peer interactions.

On the eighth day of the program, the counselor began training the playground supervisors to operate the program. As a first step, she had each supervisor praise Nathan's appropriate playground behavior at least once every five minutes. Next she had the supervisors use the point card and subtract points, whenever necessary, in addition to praising Nathan an average of once every five minutes. Initially, the counselor prompted the supervisors when to praise and when to subtract points. However, as the supervisors' skills in praising and using the card improved, the counselor gradually faded out her prompts. By the eleventh day of the program, the supervisors had assumed complete responsibility for the program, with only occasional support and monitoring provided by the counselor.

Nathan earned the group reward every day except one during this transition period. Because the playground supervisors were responsible for so many students at any one time, they were not able to monitor Nathan's behavior as closely as the counselor, who had remained close to Nathan (within 20-30 feet) throughout the recess period. As a result, Nathan was able to "get away with" subtle instances of negative and/or aggressive behavior and not lose points, since the supervisors often did not see this behavior. However, the program continued to effectively control the more obvious instances of Nathan's socially negative/aggressive playground behavior. The playground supervisors, Nathan's teacher, and other school personnel were most pleased with the overall results of the program.

Nathan's peers, however, began to complain that Nathan was being verbally negative with them and that he was using abusive language on the playground. The playground supervisors had not observed this because, as a rule, they were not able to hear and monitor Nathan's verbal behavior. Nathan had come to realize that he could engage in subtle negative interactions without penalty. The supervisors talked with the counselor about this problem. She suggested that because of the sheer numbers of children involved, it would be impossible for the supervisors to monitor all or even most of Nathan's verbal behavior. She said that it was probably too much to expect that Nathan's subtle verbal negatives could ever be controlled completely in a playground situation. However, she did suggest some procedures that could be tried that might have an impact upon the problem.

As a first step, she agreed to meet with Nathan to discuss the problem with him. By communicating to him that everyone was aware of what was going on, it was possible that he would reduce the frequency of such behavior. Next, the counselor suggested that the supervisors scan the playground more frequently, at least once every three to four minutes, if possible, in an attempt to monitor Nathan's behavior more closely. Finally, the counselor recommended that the supervisors occasionally try to stand within earshot of Nathan so that his verbal behavior could be monitored. In such situations, the supervisors should always subtract the required points if there was any doubt as to whether Nathan's verbal behavior was negative or inappropriate. It was suggested that the quality of Nathan's social behavior could also be judged by watching the reaction of his peers to the behavior.

These changes to the program were introduced, and seemed to have a moderate impact on Nathan's behavior. His peers stopped complaining about his negative/abusive language and the supervisors felt they could see a change in his behavior.

The overall program proceeded without incident for the next several weeks. Nathan missed the group reward three times during this period; however, he was very close to earning it each time. At this point, the counselor suggested that the point system and the individual reward should be discontinued. She met with Nathan and discussed this change with him. He did not object to the change, indicating that the individual reward was not that important to him, but that he really liked the group reward. It seemed that Nathan enjoyed the new status his earning of the school reward had given him with his peers. His interactions with his peers appeared to be much more cordial as well as genuine, and the approval of his peers had taken on a new meaning for him.

It was explained to Nathan that the playground supervisor would award him a plus (+) or a minus (-) for each recess period. If his behavior was appropriate, he would earn a plus; if not, he would earn a minus. He would need two out of three recesses rated plus per day in order to earn the group reward. If his behavior was out of control or grossly negative and/or aggressive, he would have to sit out the remainder of the recess period and also forfeit the chance to earn a plus for that recess.

Nathan responded to this program change reasonably well. However, he tested the program change to see if it would work as described. He had to sit out three recesses within the first two days of the program change. However, he earned the group reward on four out of the next six days.

It was decided to introduce a fading procedure wherein Nathan would be required to work for longer and longer periods of time in order to earn the group reward. The counselor explained this change to Nathan, answered his questions, and told him that as he learned to control his playground behavior for longer and longer periods of time, the group rewards would become more special.

As a first step, Nathan was required to earn a plus for two out of three recess periods per day for two consecutive days in order to earn the group reward. After learning to perform satisfactorily at this level, the criterion was raised to three out of four days, and finally to four out of five days. Nathan had some initial difficulty with each transition, however, he eventually adjusted quite well to a schedule in which a group reward could be earned approximately once each week.

Because Nathan had such a long history of negative and aggressive interactions with other children, it was decided to leave the program in effect for the remainder of the school year, rather than trying to fade it further or eliminate it altogether. Nathan's teacher, the playground supervisors, and the counselor all agreed that Nathan needed the program and that it was relatively easy to manage as it was presently set up.

The counselor cautioned the playground supervisors and Nathan's teacher concerning certain aspects of the maintenance program. She emphasized how important it was to achieve the following goals on a continuing basis: (1) that Nathan's appropriate playground behavior be described, praised, and actively approved of whenever possible—preferably once every ten to 15 minutes at a minimum; (2) that the recess supervisors be consistent (both among themselves and on a daily basis) in the standards they use to judge Nathan's playground behavior was either appropriate or inappropriate; (3) that Nathan be required to sit out the remainder of recess periods whenever his playground behavior is out of control or unusually negative and/or aggressive; and that (4) the array of group rewards that could be earned be varied frequently so that their reinforcing effectiveness could be maintained. The counselor stressed that the extent to which Nathan's changed behavior maintained during the rest of the school year would depend to a great extent upon how well these goals were achieved.

A final parent-school conference was arranged to review Nathan's progress with his parents. They were pleased with the overall outcome, but it was clear that they still saw Nathan's playground behavior problems as the school's responsibility. However, they had no objections to the program remaining in effect for the remainder of the school year.

Case Study 3: A Minimally Disruptive Child

— Background —

Forrest could hardly be called an out of control child; yet, he engaged in a number of classroom behaviors that were of concern to his fifth grade teacher, Ms. Brown. For example, he seemed to be an unmotivated, indifferent student who was not especially interested in school, in spite of ample academic ability. He was easily distractible, was frequently off task, did not listen carefully to instructions, and was somewhat careless about following directions. In addition, he had a habit of asking the teacher irrelevant questions and of interrupting her when she was busily engaged in a task or talking to another student. To make matters worse, Forrest wouldn't pay attention when instructions for assignments were given, and then would ask his teacher for endless clarifications.

Ms. Brown was concerned about Forrest's classroom behavior for several reasons. First, he was performing far below his academic potential. He was approximately one year below grade level in the basic skills areas of reading, language, and math. Second, his classroom behavior, though not disruptive, was a constant source of irritation to his teacher. Forrest required far more of her attention than was necessary; she especially resented the fact that she had to repeat instructions and directions for him constantly. Finally, Forrest was socially powerful and was very popular with his classmates. It appeared that several of his peers were beginning, whether consciously or unconsciously, to imitate his pattern of classroom behavior.

Ms. Brown was sufficiently concerned about Forrest's behavior that she contacted his parents and asked them to come in for a conference. During this conference it was made apparent that Forrest's parents had never perceived him as a behavior problem either at home or school. They were not especially concerned about the problems described to them by Forrest's teacher, but they did agree to work with the teacher in carrying out a program designed to motivate Forrest to do better in school.

— The Intervention Program —

The teacher and Forrest's parents met to compile a list of favorite activities that Forrest enjoyed at home. The activities were ranked from highest to lowest according to Forrest's preference for each. The final list is shown in Figure 8.5.

Forrest's parents agreed to make these activities available to him only when he had earned them by improving his school performance. The teacher said she would develop a contract between herself and Forrest that would

---

Figure 8.5
List of Home Reward Activities for Forrest

1. Going to a favorite matinee movie

2. Having a friend over to spend the night

3. Having a family picnic

4. Shooting pool at a friend's house

5. Not having to carry out the garbage that night

6. Playing chess with Dad

7. Staying up one-half hour later

8. Extra television time

9. Having hot dogs for dinner

10. Playing "Battleship" with the family

---

specify tasks at school he needed to work on and the consequences that would be available to him at home for doing so. The teacher developed several trial versions of a contract and finally settled on the one shown in Figure 8.6.

Ms. Brown met with Forrest and presented the program to him. She reviewed each of the classroom behaviors included in the contract and discussed them with Forrest. She also told him he was capable of doing much better in school and that she expected his academic performance to improve.

Forrest responded well to the discussion with Ms. Brown. However, he seemed upset about the home privileges part of the program. Ms. Brown asked him what was the matter, and he said that many of the privileges on the home reward list were already available to him and that now he would have to earn them. Ms. Brown agreed this was true, but she explained that she was quite concerned about his performance at school and the program was a way of motivating him to do better. She said his parents had agreed to cooperate with the program and that they would also like to see him do better in school. These arguments did not seem to assuage Forrest's objections, but he finally agreed to sign the contract and to give the program a try.

Figure 8.6
Performance Contract for Forrest

Forrest agrees to:

1. Pay attention and concentrate on assignments

2. Listen carefully to teacher instructions

3. Follow directions

4. Work hard on assignments

5. Avoid asking unnecessary questions

6. Not interrupt the teacher when she is busy or talking with someone else

Ms. Brown agrees to:

1. Check Forrest's classroom behavior and schoolwork regularly during the day

2. Review his overall performance at the end of the day and award tickets based on how well he has done on each of the above tasks

Forrest's parents agree to:

Make special privileges available at home for which Forrest can exchange the tickets earned at school

Signatures:

Forrest _____

Ms. Brown _____

Forrest's Parents _____

The intervention program was a private arrangement between Forrest, the teacher, and his parents. His classmates were not informed about either the presence or details of the program. The program operated unobtrusively throughout the school day when Forrest was in Ms. Brown's classroom—a total of three and one-half hours. At regular intervals, usually once each 20 minutes, Ms. Brown would quietly give Forrest feedback on his classroom behavior and, when appropriate, on his academic performance. The feed-back she gave him was realistic. That is, if his behavior or performance had been unacceptable or not up to standard, she would tell him so and why. However, she made a point of finding at least one thing specifically to praise him for as a part of this feedback process. However, if his behavior had been **totally** unacceptable and inappropriate during a given 20-minute period, she did not praise him. Fortunately, these instances were relatively rare.

At the end of the school day, Ms. Brown had a review session with Forrest concerning his classroom behavior and academic performance. She would review the six target behaviors listed on the contract and give Forrest a rating of "good," "fair," "minimally acceptable," or "unsatisfactory" on each behavior, based on his performance for that day. The teacher purchased a role of standard theater tickets and awarded Forrest three tickets for each "good" rating, two tickets for each "fair" rating, one ticket for each "mini-mally acceptable" rating, and no tickets for any "unsatisfactory" rating. Forrest really liked the idea of earning tickets which he could exchange for special privileges at home. He asked Ms. Brown if they would be good for entrance into movies at the local theaters. She answered, only if he had earned enough tickets to exchange for a movie, which was one of the options on his reward list!

The exchange ratios were arranged so that Forrest had to have a nearly perfect day in order to exchange for the least expensive privilege on the reward list. For example, a total of 18 tickets could he earned for a perfect day. The least preferred privilege on the list was playing "Battleship," which cost 15 tickets. The most preferred privilege, going to a favorite movie, cost 80 tickets. The costs for the remaining privileges were spread out between these two extremes.

After answering all of Forrest's questions about the program, the home rewards, and the delivery system, Ms. Brown indicated that the program would begin the next day.

— Results —

There was a dramatic change in Forrest's behavior on the first day of the program. He earned 15 of the 18 available tickets. It appeared that it was quite easy for him to meet the behavioral requirements of the situation. Clearly, he was capable of behaving appropriately and of meeting the teacher's expectations.

During the next five days of the program, Forrest's daily totals ranged from ten to 18 tickets. He made noticeable improvements in each of the six target behaviors included in the contract, but he had the greatest difficulty and slowest rate of progress with his schoolwork. Everyone seemed to be pleased with the way the program was working. Ms. Brown was much more optimistic about Forrest's classroom behavior and felt that he would finally begin to live up to his academic potential. Forrest's parents were very supportive of the program and followed through in implementing the home reward component.

In conversing with Forrest's other teachers about the program she had designed, Ms. Brown discovered that there had been no change in his behavior in other classes. If anything, according to his other teachers, Forrest's behavior was slightly worse in their rooms. It was apparent that his changed behavior was not generalizing to other classrooms in which the program had not been implemented.

Ms. Brown indicated that it was a fairly simple task to extend the program to Forrest's other classrooms. Each of those teachers expressed interest in such a possibility. Ms. Brown explained how the program worked and what would be involved in extending it to their classrooms.

Ms. Brown indicated that she would give Forrest a card each day with their subject areas noted. These subjects were social studies, language, and health. Each day those teachers were to rate Forrest's overall performance in their classes as "good," "fair," "minimally acceptable," or "unsatisfactory." Forrest would then exchange these daily ratings for either three, two, one, or zero tickets, respectively, in Ms. Brown's room. Thus, Forrest would be able to earn a maximum of nine additional tickets each day in classes other than Ms. Brown's. The prices of the home privileges were raised accordingly to take these extra tickets into account.

Ms. Brown explained the program change to Forrest and answered his questions about the new procedures. She indicated that program extension would begin the next day and that she expected him to improve his performance in those classes. Forrest realized he would have to work harder and longer for the home privileges. However, he seemed to accept the change without any difficulty.

There was an immediate change for the better in Forrest's classroom performance in the extension classrooms. None of his teachers had any difficulty in running the program, and all reported seeing significant improvements in Forrest's classroom behavior.

The program ran without incident for the next month. A major change in Forrest's overall behavior pattern was his work output. The amount of work he completed nearly doubled, with a corresponding increase in quality as well. All of his teachers were greatly pleased with the results.

At this point, Ms. Brown began to consider ways of weaning Forrest from the system while maintaining the gains and new behavior patterns he had acquired. The options ranged from terminating the program abruptly and completely, to gradually fading the number of tickets that could be earned each day to zero. Neither of these alternatives appealed to Ms. Brown.

Ms. Brown called a parent-teacher conference to discuss a program for moving Forrest off the system. Forrest's parents and all of his teachers attended. Both his parents and Forrest's teachers were concerned that he not lose the gains he had made. After discussing a number of alternatives, it was decided to implement a system wherein major components of the program would be eliminated a step at a time, while simultaneously reducing the frequency with which home rewards would become available.

As a first step, the ticket system was eliminated. Instead of receiving a point rating on the six target behaviors each day and exchanging the ratings for tickets, a plus (+) or minus (-) system was used to reinforce Forrest's appropriate behavior. During the day, his behavior was rated as either a plus or minus approximately once each hour. Ms. Brown had Forrest in her class for three of the six daily rating periods, and the other teachers had him in their classes for the remaining three. Forrest could now earn home privileges with pluses and minuses instead of tickets. The exchange ratios were adjusted downward to take into account the reduced number of pluses, compared to tickets, that were now available.

Forrest responded well to this program change. He adjusted easily to having his overall performance rated each hour as a plus or a minus. His rate of earning home privileges remained about the same as it had been under the ticket system. Forrest's other teachers had no trouble with the program and reported no change in his classroom performance either.

Next, it was decided to make a single, high magnitude reward available to Forrest once each week. These rewards included such things as a movie, a family outing, a picnic, or a trip to the bowling alley. There were 30 pluses available during a five-day week. In order to earn the weekly reward, Forrest had to receive a plus for 25 of the 30 ratings. If he did not, the reward was withheld.

Forrest also had no difficulty with this program change. His behavior was no different from what it had been in the previous phase.

After approximately three weeks, Forrest was simply given an overall satisfactory or unsatisfactory daily rating by Ms. Brown. If his behavior was satisfactory in all his classes, he earned a satisfactory rating. If it was unsatisfactory in one or more of his classes, he received an unsatisfactory rating. Now, in order to earn the home reward, Forrest's behavior must be rated as satisfactory four out of the five days in the week.

Forrest had some initial difficulty with this program change. He complained that it was more difficult to earn the weekly reward. His behavior reflected this by becoming increasingly variable from day to day. But after approximately three weeks, Forrest's performance began to stabilize as he responded better to this program change.

After approximately a month of satisfactory performance on Forrest's part, it was decided to shift the program to an occasional home reward for good school performance. Forrest was told by Ms. Brown that from that point forward, he would receive an occasional special reward for doing well at school. When his performance warranted it, she would send a Good Day Card home with him. Whenever this happened, he could exchange the card for a special home reward.

Under this system, Forrest's daily performance showed even more inconsistency than before. After approximately a month of such fluctuations, he began to adapt reasonably well to the program change. It was decided to leave this final variation of the program in effect for the remainder of the school year. In this form, the program was no trouble to operate and it continued to have a significant impact upon Forrest's overall behavior pattern for the remainder of the school year.

Case Study 4: An Oppositional-Defiant Child

— Background —

Dillon was a third grader, enrolled in Ms. Watson's class, who had been referred to the school psychologist for testing. Ms. Watson felt Dillon's emotional outbursts and anger were of such unusual intensity that they might signal the presence of an emotional disturbance. Thus, she wanted him evaluated for this possibility in the hope that he could receive treatment or be referred to a more specialized setting designed for children like him.

Dillon had experienced problems in defying his teachers and other school personnel from the time he began his school career in kindergarten. He seemed to be constantly on edge, with a high level of agitation. Although only in the third grade, Dillon's school records were nearly an inch and one-half thick. They provided a litany of complaints from Dillon's teachers about his stubbornness, aggressiveness, temper tantrums, and lack of cooperation. There were also numerous accounts of his academic problems and his refusal to accept corrections of either his academic performance or classroom behavior. Some of the behavioral descriptors that appeared in his records included the following: yells, argues, talks back, won't mind, defies the teacher, screams, teases and bullies his peers, has a negative attitude, is dishonest, is restless and constantly fidgeting, doesn't care about his work, argues constantly, and provokes others. Dillon was easily **the** most disliked student, by his teacher and peers, in the third grade.

Every one of Dillon's teachers from kindergarten on had voiced complaints about him. He had been referred to the principal's office for discipline problems over 20 times already in his young school career. Nothing that had been tried seemed to work for Dillon's problems. As time passed, he seemed to become more and more out of control and to become even more resistant to adults' attempts to influence him in positive ways.

Ms. Watson was at the point of exasperation. She had exhausted her management strategies with Dillon and made the case that his presence in her classroom was no longer tolerable. According to her, the classroom was in chaos because of Dillon—other students couldn't learn because of his disruptions, and she was a nervous wreck.

As a first step, the school psychologist suggested that Dillon's case be reviewed by the school-wide assistance team, which included the school principal, who was very familiar with Dillon and his school history. One of Dillon's previous teachers was also a member of this team. The focus of the team meeting concerning Dillon was on which direction to take with him. One choice was to conduct a comprehensive assessment to determine if Dillon might qualify as severely emotionally disturbed, and thereby become eligible for classification as handicapped under the **Individuals with Disabilities Education Act (IDEA)**. Under this option, he could access specialized psychological services and/or be assigned to a different setting. A second option was to design and implement a systematic intervention plan that would focus on three objectives: (1) to identify and pinpoint the situations in which Dillon's anger escalates out of control; (2) to develop strategies for Ms. Watson, and other school personnel, to use in defusing these problem situations; and (3) to teach Dillon strategies for controlling and managing his own anger.

Dillon's behavior problems and school history were discussed in detail among the teacher assistance team members. Ms. Watson was also interviewed by the team as part of their deliberations. The team was about evenly divided between pursuing an eligibility assessment for Dillon as severely emotionally disturbed under IDEA, and developing a prereferral intervention. Ms. Watson clearly preferred the former course because it might lead to removal of Dillon from her classroom, at least for a time. However, the team decided in favor of the prereferral intervention primarily because: (1) it allowed

Dillon to remain in the educational mainstream, and (2) if it should prove unsuccessful, IDEA eligibility could always be pursued as a follow-up option. Although very disappointed by this decision, Ms. Watson agreed to cooperate in the design and implementation of the prereferral intervention.

The school psychologist, Ms. Maleca, was assigned the lead responsibility in developing the prereferral intervention in cooperation with Ms. Watson and the school-wide assistance team. She indicated that two to three weeks would be required to collect the information needed to design the intervention. Ms. Maleca decided to interview Dillon's parents and his previous teachers as an initial step in the information gathering process.

Ms. Maleca contacted Dillon's parents and asked if she might interview them about Dillon and some of his behavioral escalation problems at school. Dillon's parents were very familiar with these problems since the school had been concerned about Dillon's behavior from the time he began his schooling. The school psychologist arranged to interview Dillon's mother at home after school hours when Dillon was present. The results of the interview were highly revealing and provided clues as to how Dillon had acquired his pattern of oppositional-defiant behavior toward adults.

Dillon's mother expressed considerable frustration about her efforts to socialize and manage Dillon; she saw him as a very difficult child who bordered on being incorrigible. Dillon had had a difficult temperament since his birth. His pediatrician had recommended placing Dillon on a drug regimen to reduce his hyperactivity; Dillon's parents had decided to delay this decision as long as possible, but were now strongly considering this treatment method. When asked to describe Dillon's overall behavior pattern, Dillon's mother said, "He's a strong willed child who hardly ever minds; you have to scream at him before he'll do what you ask." Dillon's mother was close to giving up hope of ever changing Dillon's coercive, difficult behavior. Dillon's father was absent from home frequently due to his work and was not able to discipline and monitor Dillon's behavior on any regular basis. As a result, he did not have much influence over Dillon and what he did.

Ms. Maleca realized that Dillon and his parents had lapsed into a negative, coercive style of interaction where both parties had learned to escalate behaviorally (e.g., yell, scream, argue, threaten, tantrum) in response to the other's demands. By so doing, the demands could be avoided and/or were often withdrawn. This allowed escape, or avoidance of the demands, which was usually accompanied by termination of the escalated behavior from the other party. Whoever yelled and screamed the loudest, and persisted the longest, usually prevailed in these behavioral struggles. This produced a very negative style of interaction in Dillon's home and also affected his relations with his siblings.

It seemed clear to Ms. Maleca that Dillon had been inadvertently taught an oppositional-defiant behavior pattern at home that he then brought to school. Since this behavior pattern comprised Dillon's history of dealing with adults, he displayed this characteristic behavior pattern in responding to the demands of schooling. Subsequent interviews with each of Dillon's teachers in grades K-3 confirmed this hypothesis. All had been exasperated with Dillon's resistance to the simplest demands and requests, and had considerable residual anger from their frustrations in dealing with him. Each of his teachers, and most of his peers, quickly learned to dislike Dillon. He was socially rejected by nearly everyone in his school.

Ms. Maleca asked Dillon's teacher if she might observe Dillon on several occasions in situations where he seemed to have the greatest difficulty. Ms. Watson identified math and language arts seatwork periods and small group instruction in reading as Dillon's most difficult times. After observing Dillon's behavior and his interactions with Ms. Watson in these situations, it became clear that his school behavior was a near perfect replication of his home behavior. Ms. Watson simply substituted for his mother as someone who made demands, gave commands, and was to be resisted. Unfortunately, Ms. Watson responded to Dillon's noncompliance and oppositional behavior in much the same manner as his mother—by escalating. These escalations often became out of control and required the principal's involvement.

Ms. Maleca presented her findings at the next regularly scheduled meeting of the teacher assistance team. All agreed with the accuracy of her findings. Ms. Maleca suggested a three-pronged intervention plan that would: (1) teach Dillon's teacher and parents to give commands and directives in a different way; (2) teach them to avoid engaging in escalated interactions with Dillon; and (3) to work with Dillon to try to teach him how to control and manage his own anger more effectively. Ms. Maleca obtained the team's suggestions and willingness to participate in the intervention, and promised to keep them informed of Dillon's progress during the implementation process.

— The Intervention Program —

Ms. Maleca called a joint meeting between Dillon's mother and his teacher to discuss the intervention for Dillon. The three components of the intervention (i.e., giving commands, defusing oppositional behavior, and anger management) were explained in detail. A rationale for each component of the intervention plan was provided, and the specific roles of Ms. Watson and Dillon's mother were described.

Ms. Maleca began this meeting by explaining her findings and the view that Dillon's school behavior was an extension of his home behavior. All agreed that this was the case. Further, Ms. Maleca noted that: (1) Dillon was given far too many commands and directives at both school and home; (2) that he had learned to successfully resist these commands by escalating his behavior; and (3) that both his teacher and his parents were often entrapped by the ensuing behavioral escalation. It was explained that, through repetitions of these behavioral processes, Dillon had learned that he could control the behavior of adults, could avoid or escape from demands, and could access adult attention almost at will. Ms. Maleca explained that the keys to changing Dillon's behavior were for his teacher and his mother to change the way they interacted with him, and for Ms. Maleca to teach Dillon different strategies for dealing with adult demands and methods for controlling his anger.

Ms. Maleca gave Dillon's mother and Ms. Watson two brief publications to read. One described how to give commands and directives effectively to children (see Walker & Walker, 1991) and the second explained how to cope with escalated adult-child interactions (see Walker, Colvin, & Ramsey, 1995). The publication on noncompliance made the following main points:

- Adults tend to give two types of commands: alpha and beta. Alpha commands are preferred, and beta commands are to be avoided.

- Alpha commands are precise, direct, to the point, and ask the child to do only one thing. Beta commands are mini lectures of disapproval, contain many verbalizations, and do not clearly communicate what the adult is asking of the child.

- Most adults give too many commands—many of which are unnecessary and are better left ungiven.

- Commands are frequently given in anger and expressed in a demanding fashion. Such commands are often accompanied by warnings and threats for consequences of noncompliance.

- Commands are often made that are not followed through with or are withdrawn if the child actively resists them.

A series of brief meetings was held by the school psychologist to review this material with Dillon's teacher and his parent(s). Both his teacher and his mother read the material thoroughly and found it valuable. Clarifications and potential applications of this information were discussed and role played under the guidance of Ms. Maleca.

The school psychologist then assigned reading of the material on escalated adult-child interactions. A similar series of meetings was then scheduled to review, discuss, and role play the key points of this material. These were as follows:

- More and more children like Dillon are engaging in escalated interactions with adults—especially in school. These interactions result from a high level of agitation or anger on the child's part and adult insistence that a command or directive be complied with instantly as prescribed.

- Increasingly these interactions escalate from initial resistance, to hostility, to teacher defiance that carries the threat of a physical confrontation. Teacher safety is an issue of increasing concern, particularly with more mature students, in such interactions.

- It is important to terminate these hostile interactions in their early stages **before** they escalate into emotional, physical confrontations. In this way, their later stages are prevented from occurring.

- The teacher or parent does this by **disengaging** from the interaction but **without** withdrawing or terminating the command that precipitated the escalating interaction. This means not responding to questions from the student or continuing to interact with him/her in any way as long as the student's agitation level is high.

- The child should be given the option of: (1) sitting quietly until he/she can comply with the directive, or (2) going to a quiet area until the emotional agitation subsides and the student can reengage in the task or command.

Details of managing such interactions and guidelines for preventing their escalation were discussed by Ms. Maleca and Dillon's teacher and mother. Potential difficult situations were role played and debriefed. Following the end of these training sessions, Ms. Maleca instructed Dillon's mother and teacher to begin implementing these procedures. Ms. Maleca provided regular monitoring and supervision as needed in their implementation.

Simultaneously, Ms. Maleca began working with Dillon on a social skills training program that focused heavily on anger management. Typically, Dillon had only one strategy for dealing with situations he found not to his liking—to become very angry. He had successfully trained his social environment to the point where this strategy, though unacceptable, worked well and often. The social skills training focused on teaching Dillon to: (1) recognize the interval signs of his approaching anger (i.e., heavy breathing, elevated heart rate, etc.); (2) identify the situations in which he usually got angry; (3) understand the value that anger had for him and the purposes it served; and (4) develop alternative, more adaptive strategies for coping with these situations.

This intervention program was implemented for Dillon over the four months remaining in the school year. Adult praise and individual rewards made available at school and at home were used to motivate Dillon in the early stages of the intervention. These were gradually faded so that by the end of the school year, they had been phased out entirely. This program was implemented with his fourth grade teacher, during the next school year, as well.

— Results —

The success of this intervention program would have to be classified as only partially successful. Dillon, his parents, and Ms. Watson all had great difficulty overcoming their negative history of interacting with each other. Overall, their interactions became less hostile and more cooperative; however, escalated interactions continued to occur from time to time. These interactions tended to occur when one or more parties were so emotionally involved that it was difficult to remember best practice principles of giving effective commands and disengaging from escalating behaviors.

Overall, Ms. Watson found Dillon's behavior to marginally acceptable during the remainder of the school year. She was particularly impressed with his ability to restrain himself in some situations that previously resulted in automatic anger. Dillon become more accepting of and accepted by his peers; as a result, he was able to access many more peer-controlled activities in free-play settings. However, it was clear that Dillon had developed a behavior pattern that was very difficult to change. After all, he had acquired and practiced it over an eight-year period!

Case Study 5: An Entire Classroom

— Background —

Mr. Endicott was a first year teacher in a regular, self-contained second grade classroom. He was assigned a total of 31 children, more than any other teacher in the school. To make matters worse, there were five children in the class who were quite disruptive, underachieving, and very difficult to manage.

Mr. Endicott had the usual adjustment problems common to first year teachers. These problems were further exacerbated by having such a large class, by having a group of disruptive children in the class, and by being overloaded with extracurricular duties such as supervising the production of the school newspaper and coaching.

Mr. Endicott was engaged in a constant struggle to maintain only a minimal level of control in his classroom. The average rate of talk outs, being out of seat, yelling, and class disruptions was quite high when compared to most regular classrooms. The rate of compliance with his commands and directives was below 50%. Mr. Endicott felt the children had little respect for his teaching skills—and he was right!

Mr. Endicott had had no formal or systematic training in behavior management techniques in his undergraduate education and preservice teacher training. He felt unprepared to manage such a difficult group of children. He was extremely frustrated; he began to question his competence and was wondering whether teaching was the profession for him.

Mr. Endicott continued to rely upon verbal reprimands, warnings, and sending children to the office as methods of managing his classroom. These techniques were only minimally effective at best, and, in some cases, seemed to actually prompt the children to act out even more.

The school counselor became aware of the difficulties Mr. Endicott was having with his class. She and the principal were both concerned with the large numbers of children that were being sent to the office each week from Mr. Endicott's class. She met with Mr. Endicott to discuss the situation.

By this time, Mr. Endicott was past the point of being defensive about his inability to control his classroom. The counselor communicated to him that she was aware of the difficulty of his situation (i.e., that he had a large number of students and that many of them had behavior problems that other teachers had also experienced difficulty in managing). She indicated that it was common for first year teachers to have difficulty in the area of behavior management, given their relative lack of experience and lack of preparation in techniques for managing child behavior in the classroom.

The counselor she asked Mr. Endicott if he would be willing to work with her in implementing some behavior management procedures designed to gain some control over his classroom. Mr. Endicott enthusiastically agreed to this proposal.

— The Intervention Program —

As a first step, the counselor said she would like to schedule some times when she could observe in Mr. Endicott's room. He said that any time would be fine with him. She asked if there were times when the children seemed to behave better than others. Mr. Endicott wasn't sure, but said that the class seemed easier for him to manage during individual seatwork times than during activity periods, teacher-led discussions, or instructional activities that involved the whole group. The counselor scheduled class observations for all of these periods.

After completing her observations, the counselor scheduled a meeting with Mr. Endicott to discuss what she had learned. She began by saying that he was not nearly so bad a teacher as he was representing himself to be. However, until he could gain control over his class in a behavioral sense, his teaching would continue to be less effective than he would like. Mr. Endicott couldn't have agreed more.

The counselor noted that in all the periods during which she observed, the children did not seem to have a clear idea of his behavioral expectations for them, nor did they seem to be aware of the rules governing appropriate and inappropriate classroom behavior. She observed further that he had a habit of giving instructions and directions for assignments, especially during group activities, while the class was not paying attention and sometimes were even out of control. This was, in effect, an admission that he could not control the classroom and ensured that only a portion of his students would hear and comprehend the instructions for any given assignment. As a result, Mr. Endicott was spending a great deal of his time repeating instructions for the children who did not hear them the first time. He was becoming increasingly frustrated because of this.

The counselor also observed that the children were giving each other a great deal of attention and approval for "getting under Mr. Endicott's skin." A number of children were very skilled at needling Mr. Endicott and irritating him by doing such things as dawdling, breaking minor classroom rules in his presence, requiring multiple repetitions of the same instructions, and asking unnecessary questions to which they already knew the answers. Mr. Endicott usually responded in a very predictable fashion in such situations—he would become very irritated and reprimand the children involved. Mr. Endicott's reaction only strengthened the children's "needling" behavior and increased the chances that they would behave this way again.

The counselor suggested that it would be impractical to try to solve the behavior management problems in his class on a case-by-case basis (i.e., by designing individual intervention programs for all the children who needed them). She recommended that they design and implement a group behavior management program for the entire class instead. Mr. Endicott agreed to give this a try.

The counselor recommended a program that consisted of the following components: (1) developing a set of explicit classroom rules governing appropriate behavior in Mr. Endicott's classroom; (2) a rating system in which the behavior of the entire class would be rated as either a plus (+) or minus (-) by Mr. Endicott according to whether the children had followed the classroom rules and behaved appropriately; (3) a systematic praising procedure wherein the class as a whole and individual children would be praised intermittently for following the classroom rules; and (4) a daily activity reward made available to the class as a whole when the reinforcement criterion had been achieved. The counselor explained how the program would operate.

First, Mr. Endicott and the counselor would meet with the class to develop a set of classroom rules, couched in overt, observable terms, that would govern appropriate child behavior in the classroom. Mr. Endicott said that he could easily come up with 30 or 40 such rules. The counselor suggested that that would probably defeat the purpose of this part of the program, since children have difficulty keeping track of more than seven to ten rules at a time. She said that it would be much better to develop a list of ten rules that Mr. Endicott felt comfortable with and that clearly communicated his behavioral expectations for the class.

Next Mr. Endicott would mark off a space approximately ten to 12 inches wide on one end of the chalkboard. The school day would then be divided into ten-minute segments and the segments listed vertically from the top to the bottom of the chalkboard within this space. Every ten minutes, Mr. Endicott would award the class either a plus or a minus in the appropriate ten-minute segment. A plus rating meant that the behavior of all the children in the class was reasonably appropriate and consistent with Mr. Endicott's expectations for the class. If a minus was awarded, that meant that the behavior of one or more children in the class had been inappropriate for part or all of the ten-minute period. An example of this rating system is shown in Figure 8.7.

Of the 18 ten-minute intervals between 9:00 A.M. and 12:00 noon, the behavior of the class, in this hypothetical case, was rated as a plus in 11 of the intervals and as a minus in seven of them. Thus, in the morning session, the behavior of the entire class was rated as appropriate in 61% of the intervals.

Mr. Endicott felt that he would have no difficulty in managing this part of the program. However, he was a little concerned that in the process of teaching he might forget to rate the class every ten minutes. The counselor said that this occasionally happened, but that there was no problem with awarding the rating a little later. Besides, she indicated that in operating such systems, teachers become very skilled in estimating time. Further, she

Figure 8.7	
Rating System for Mr. Endicott's Class	
Time	**Rating**
9:00 – 9:10	+
9:10 – 9:20	+
9:20 – 9:30	-
9:30 – 9:40	+
9:40 – 9:50	-
9:50 – 10:00	-
10:00 – 10:10	+
10:10 – 10:20	+
10:20 – 10:30	+
10:30 – 10:40	-
10:40 – 10:50	-
10:50 – 11:00	+
11:00 11:10	-
11:10 – 11:20	+
11:20 – 11:30	+
11:30 – 11:40	+
11:40 – 11:50	-
11:50 – 12:00	+

said she was sure that if he forgot to rate a given interval one of the children would almost certainly remind him to do so.

Next, the counselor discussed the praising component of the program with Mr. Endicott. She emphasized how important it was for him to praise the class and individual children regularly for following the class rules and for behaving appropriately. She gave him a list of sample praise statements (see Appendix D) to help him vary his praises. The counselor and Mr. Endicott then had a role playing session in which they practiced both "call out" praises to the entire class and specific praises to individual children. Mr. Endicott felt some awkwardness initially in praising, but was able to demonstrate behavioral mastery of correct praising skills. The counselor said this feeling of awkwardness would probably disappear as he began to praise his students on a regular basis.

The counselor discussed with Mr. Endicott another use of praise as a behavior management technique. That is, instead of reprimanding an individual student for breaking a classroom rule or for behaving inappropriately, he could praise an adjacent child who was behaving appropriately. In this instance, the adjacent student becomes a behavioral model for the student who is behaving inappropriately. In addition, the procedure communicates that teacher attention will be given for appropriate classroom behavior and will not be given for rule breaking episodes in the form of warnings or verbal reprimands. The counselor indicated that if used appropriately, differential attention could be highly effective in teaching children new patterns of appropriate behavior.

Finally, the counselor and Mr. Endicott discussed the group reward system that would be used to back up the rating system. She said that during the first part of the program, a daily group reward of an activity nature (i.e., games or events the children enjoyed) should be available for meeting the reinforcement criterion. Examples would include such things as five minutes of extra recess, free time in the classroom, and classroom games such as "Seven-Up," "Simon Says," and "Flying Dutchman." The counselor told Mr. Endicott that he was free to make available whatever rewards of this nature that he felt were appropriate.

However, she cautioned that the children should be included in the selection process and should be free to contribute and vote on potential back-up rewards. The counselor recommended that initially, ten to 12 activity reward options should be selected, a card made for each with the cards placed in a jar or box, and that a different student should be selected each day the criterion was met to draw a card from the jar/box. The activity on the card would then be available for that day, and would not be replaced until all the cards had been drawn. At that time, all the cards would be placed back in the jar/box or a new set of cards and back-up rewards would be developed.

Mr. Endicott asked the counselor how he would know whether to give or withhold the daily reward. She said that a good general rule is that the class' behavior should be 80% appropriate in order to earn the daily reward. If less than 80% appropriate, the reward should be withheld. The procedure for calculating the percentage of time during which the class' behavior was appropriate was also explained to Mr. Endicott. That is, the total number of intervals during the day in which pluses were awarded is divided by the total number of intervals in which ratings were given. For example, in a five-hour school day in which the class' behavior was rated every ten minutes, there would be a total of 30 intervals in which a rating would be given. Thus, the class must earn a plus rating for a minimum of 24 of those intervals (80%) in order to earn the group reward. If fewer than 24 intervals were rated as a plus, the reward would be withheld for that day, but the class would begin fresh the next day with the opportunity to earn one of the back-up rewards.

The counselor and Mr. Endicott met once more to plan how the program would be presented to the class and the roles that each would play in explaining the procedures and in developing the classroom rules and list of back-up rewards. It was decided to present the program at the beginning of class time the next day, and to implement it immediately following the presentation—that is, after the class rules had been developed and the back-up rewards had been selected.

The presentation went without incident and a list of classroom rules was prepared in block letters on construction paper and posted on the bulletin board. It took a long time for the class to decide on which ten back-up rewards they would like to work for. They voted on a series of potential rewards, finally selected ten, and a card was made for each. The counselor remained in the classroom for the first hour of the program and came back several times during the remainder of the day to see how things were going.

The counselor told Mr. Endicott that in the early stages of the program it was a good idea to give the class the benefit of the doubt in awarding the plus ratings so as to increase their chances of earning the group reward and experiencing this success. He could then gradually become more strict as the children adjusted to the program and the changed behavioral requirements. However, she cautioned against being too lenient in his ratings, since this would teach the children that only a very minimal effort would be necessary in order to earn the daily group reward. If this were the case, the goals of the program would, in all likelihood, not be achieved.

Mr. Endicott understood the importance of selecting the ratings carefully, but said he would like some feedback from the counselor whenever possible on the appropriateness of his ratings of the class' behavior. The counselor agreed to visit his classroom once each day for the first week of the program to rate the class simultaneously, but independently, with Mr. Endicott, and to compare ratings at the end of the session. Mr. Endicott said that he felt this feedback would be of assistance to him in learning to accurately rate the behavior of the class when using the class rules as a standard for making such judgments.

— Results —

The class did not earn the group reward the first day of the program. There were 33 ten-minute segments rated during the day. The class received a plus ratings in 21 of the 33 intervals, for an overall percentage of appropriate behavior of 63%, well below the 80% level required to earn the reward. The class was greatly disappointed in their failure to earn the reward. At the end of the day, Mr. Endicott reviewed their performance with them and told the children that they had shown some good improvement in their overall performance, but that they would have to work harder to earn the group reward. He said he felt sure they could do it and that they would have a new opportunity to try again tomorrow.

The counselor and Mr. Endicott reviewed the first day of the program and decided that overall it had gone fairly well. The counselor had observed and rated the class for a one-hour period during the day, or for a total of six ten-minute intervals. The counselor and Mr. Endicott had rated the class the same on four of the six intervals. They discussed their differences and the specific reasons for the ratings they had given.

The next day, the class earned the group reward, but just barely. They received a plus rating for 26 of the 33 intervals, the minimum number required to earn the group reward. Mr. Endicott told the class how proud he was that they had earned the group reward. The card drawn out of the jar had "five minutes of extra recess" written on it, which was one of the more desirable reward options. At this point, the class seemed quite excited about the program.

On the third day of the program, the class again earned the group reward— this time by a comfortable margin. The class received 31 plus ratings out of the possible 33 intervals. Mr. Endicott found the change in the class difficult to believe. The class drew a card, which was exchanged for a game of "Seven-Up." Mr. Endicott and the counselor again compared notes and found they agreed on all six of the ten-minute intervals in which they simultaneously rated the overall performance of the class.

The counselor complimented Mr. Endicott on the accuracy of his ratings and on how well he was running the program. However, she indicated that he was not praising either the class as a whole or individual children frequently enough. She suggested that he set a goal of praising the class at least twice each hour when their behavior was appropriate and of praising individual children a total of five to ten times each day. He decided to keep a simple tally sheet on his desk to help him keep track of his praise statements, and said that he would try to do better.

The class earned the group reward for the next three days in a row. Mr. Endicott improved both his praise rate and his praising skills. His accuracy in rating the class' performance continued to be high. Everyone concerned—the counselor, Mr. Endicott, and the children—felt very good about the program.

The class failed to earn the group reward on the seventh and eighth days of the program. The failure to earn the reward was due almost exclusively to the behavior of two children. They were both boys, and were members of the group of five children who had a history of behavior problems prior to their entry into Mr. Endicott's class.

The class as a whole was quite disappointed in this failure to earn the reward. They communicated a fair amount of disapproval to the two boys over this issue. However, this seemed to have little or no impact upon the boys' behavior. Mr. Endicott decided to have a chat with them to see if he could get to the bottom of the matter. The two boys said that they were no longer interested in the program, didn't care about it, and weren't going to cooperate with it any longer.

Mr. Endicott then talked with the counselor about this and she suggested they give the program another try to see if the boys would change their minds. They didn't. The class failed to earn the group reward on the ninth day primarily because of the lack of cooperation from the two boys. Mr. Endicott and the counselor decided that something would have to be done since the two boys were spoiling the program for everyone else.

They decided to place the boys on a separate system from the class wherein they could earn some free time at the end of the day if, in Mr. Endicott's judgment, their behavior had been appropriate 80% of the time during the day. Their system was designed to be (and was perceived as being) of much lower value than the program in place for the class as a whole. The two boys were thus no longer able to deny the rest of the class access to the group reward through their behavior. Plus they were not allowed to participate in the group reward activities earned by the rest of the class.

The class proceeded to earn the group reward for the next five days in a row. But the two boys seemed to be in a power struggle with Mr. Endicott. They earned access to free time only once during the five-day period and had to be sent to the office several times because of their disruptive behavior. Mr. Endicott noted that the other children tended to ignore the two boys, especially when they were behaving inappropriately. This was a marked change compared to the situation existing prior to the program when the children subtly approved of each other's inappropriate behavior.

The class earned the group reward on four out of the next five days, and the two boys earned free time on two of these days; however, the separate system was beginning to have an impact upon them. After approximately two weeks, they asked Mr. Endicott if they could be put back on the program for the whole class. He asked if they were now willing to cooperate, and they said yes. He agreed to place them back on the class program.

The program ran relatively smoothly over the next month. The class earned the group reward for two weeks in a row, and then failed to meet the criterion on two consecutive days. It was apparent that some of the children were beginning to lose interest in the program, especially in terms of the available back-up rewards. This was a cue for Mr. Endicott to work with the class in developing a new list of back-up rewards. In so doing, it was apparent that this was the source of the problem. The class earned the group reward for the next eight days in a row.

The counselor suggested that they should consider a fading program that would both reduce Mr. Endicott's time and effort required to run the program, and would teach the children to be less reliant on extrinsic reinforcement. As a first step, she recommended that the rating interval be expanded. Over the next month, the rating interval was expanded from ten to 20 to 30 to 60 minutes. The criterion for the group reward remained the same (i.e., 80% of the rated intervals must be pluses). There was no change in the behavior of the class as a result of these program changes.

Next, Mr. Endicott changed the rating interval to only once per day. The class was now given a plus or minus rating for the day as a whole. A plus was awarded if, in Mr. Endicott's judgment, the class had been 80% appropriate for the entire day. The class had some difficulty with this change initially, but adjusted to it reasonably well after a short time.

The system was next changed by requiring that two consecutive days be rated as a plus in order for the group reward to be earned. Later, the requirement was raised to three out of four days, and finally to four out of five days so that a reward was available once each week. More valuable rewards were made available at this point in the program in order to motivate the children to behave well for the longer periods of time.

The overall level of appropriate behavior increased in daily variability following this change. However, there was still a marked difference in Mr. Endicott's classroom compared to the pre-intervention situation. Thus Mr. Endicott and the counselor decided to leave the system, in its present form, in effect for the remainder of the school year. Mr. Endicott continued to have difficulty in achieving his daily praising goals, and the counselor reminded him of the importance of frequent praising in maintaining the gains that had been achieved.

The program operated quite well for the remainder of the school year. Both Mr. Endicott and the children were changed by the program. He greatly improved his skills in behavior management, and the behavior of the class as a whole increased and maintained for the remainder of the year.

Section Two: Applying Behavior Management Procedures to Hypothetical Classroom/ Playground Situations

Case Study 1: A Noncompliant Child

Bryan was a fourth grade boy who had established a reputation as being very difficult to manage. He gave his kindergarten teacher a very hard time, right from the first day of school. His primary grade teachers were no exception. Each teacher dreaded teaching Bryan and was greatly relieved when he passed on to the next grade. Mrs. Lumsden, his fourth grade teacher, was extremely frustrated with his behavior, and was considering trying to have him assigned to a special class setting. She felt more specialized techniques could be used to manage him and cope with the more aversive aspects of his behavior in such a setting. In short, she was nearing the end of her rope with Bryan.

Bryan was a highly intelligent child and a good student. His reading skills were well-developed and he achieved at or above grade level in all his subjects. However, he was a very powerful child who had been overindulged by his parents. He managed to "get his way" most of the time. He was often persistent to the point of stubbornness. His most exasperating traits were his noncompliance to adult commands and his tendency to argue about every little point.

Adults were usually no match for him. He could usually dominate his interactions with them by either wearing them down or waiting them out. As a result, Bryan developed a pattern of typically resistive behavior that created severe problems for his teachers, his peers, and ultimately himself.

— Task One: Behavior Change Goals —

Develop a list of appropriate behavior change goals for the teacher to consider in this situation. No set number of goals is required. Compare your list with the list following, provided by the author.

Author's Behavior Change Goals:

1. Ensure that Bryan is **consciously aware** of those specific aspects of his behavior that are considered aversive and/or inappropriate.

2. Teach Bryan to comply promptly with adult commands, directives, and/or instructions.

3. Teach Bryan to suppress his argumentative behavior with adults.

4. Teach Bryan a more cooperative pattern of interaction with adults.

— Task Two: Intervention Procedures —

Describe a specific intervention procedure that would be appropriate for achieving **each** behavior change goal that **you** have listed. Compare your intervention procedures with those presented by the author for the four behavior change goals listed previously.

Author's Intervention Procedures:

Goal #1—Children are sometimes not aware that certain features of their behavior are considered inappropriate. In other cases, adult expectations with respect to classroom/playground rules are not clearly communicated. Thus, as a first step, the teacher should develop a list of specific behavioral pinpoints that are considered inappropriate and review them with the child, being careful to define each one. This could be handled via an individual conference with the child.

Goal #2—There are several options for achieving this goal. The first option would be to praise the child for each compliance on the first trial. A second option would be to award one minute of free time (which accumulates during the day) for each compliance on the first trial. A third option would be to award one point for each compliance on the first trial. If 80% or more of adult commands/directives are complied with, a Good Day Card could be signed and exchanged at home for a special privilege.

Goal #3—As a first step, a series of situations should be identified in which Bryan is likely to argue. Then a private role playing session should be scheduled where these situations are reviewed and Bryan is allowed to rehearse nonargumentative responses to these situations. Bryan could then be awarded a bonus point, which could accumulate toward a special individual reward, for handling such situations in a nonargumentative fashion. Another option would be to subtract one point (previously earned for complying with adult commands) for each episode of argumentative behavior. Or, the teacher could simply ignore instances of argumentativeness and refuse to interact until Bryan can converse without arguing. A back-up consequence such as a brief timeout would probably be necessary to make this third option effective.

Goal #4—The role playing sessions described for Goal #3 would no doubt assist Bryan in acquiring a more cooperative pattern of social behavior. However, they would probably not be sufficient in and of themselves.

It would be important to systematically define for Bryan what constitutes a cooperative pattern of behavior and what does not. The two respective behavior patterns could be contrasted in general terms for Bryan and then specific instances of cooperative and noncooperative behavior discussed and/or role played with him. Bryan should be able to consistently discriminate such instances at a 90% accuracy level or better.

It would be especially helpful to inform Bryan's parents of this procedure and, if at all possible, to involve them at home in supporting Bryan's attempts at acquiring a more cooperative behavior pattern. Bryan should be given positive feedback and praise regularly, both at school and at home, for making progress in this area. He should also be informed when he doesn't handle situations well. An occasional special privilege should be made available either at home or school when Bryan makes significant progress in this area.

— Task Three: Implementation Problems —

List potential implementation problems with the intervention procedures **you** have selected and compare your list with those provided by the author following.

Author's Potential Implementation Problems:

1. Bryan chooses to be uncooperative when the teacher attempts to explain the classroom rules to him and to identify aversive/inappropriate features of his behavior.

2. Bryan deliberately noncomplies, after the intervention program is in effect, to test the program and to see how consistent the teacher can be.

3. Bryan doesn't appear to be especially motivated by the home and other special rewards made available to him as part of the program.

4. The teacher often forgets to reinforce Bryan for handling difficult situations well (i.e., without arguing).

5. Both Bryan's parents and his teacher expect him to become more cooperative with them as a matter of course and are not willing to invest the necessary effort to make this happen.

6. Bryan refuses to cooperate in the role playing sessions.

Any or all of these problems are **possible, not necessarily probable**, in an intervention program of this type. The reader should consider how he/she would respond to them should they be encountered.

Case Study 2: A Socially Withdrawn Child

Maria was an extremely withdrawn child. She was a second grader who had a history of nonresponsiveness to and avoidance of social contact with her peers. She was less withdrawn from adult social contact than peer contact, but interactions with teachers and other school personnel were still quite difficult for her.

Maria's parents indicated that she showed signs of social withdrawal from her earliest contacts with other children. Maria has an older sister who also exhibited social withdrawal tendencies in her first two years of school. At present her social relationships with other children appear to be quite normal. However, both Maria's parents and teachers agreed that Maria's sister had not been nearly as withdrawn as was Maria.

Maria's second grade teacher expressed a growing concern to the school counselor about Maria's social relationships with other children. Basically, her teacher felt that Maria's limited social skills repertoire and her persistent avoidance of social contact with her peers would have a detrimental impact upon Maria's social, and possibly her academic, development. She communicated these concerns to the counselor who decided to observe Maria's playground behavior before proceeding further.

The counselor observed Maria on the playground on three separate occasions and recorded the amount of time Maria was engaged in social contact of any kind with her peers. The results confirmed the extent of Maria's social withdrawal. She engaged in social contact less than ten percent of the time during which she was observed. As a rule, children are involved in social interactions 40-50% of the time on the playground. Thus, Maria was significantly below average in the amount of available time during which she engaged in social interactions with her peers.

Further, it was rare for Maria to initiate social contact with her peers. Most of the social interactions she was engaged in were a result of peers initiating to her. Both the counselor and Maria's teacher felt that a major problem for Maria was her lack of prerequisite social skills, which would allow her to initiate and maintain positive social relationships with others.

Maria's parents were contacted and a conference scheduled to discuss Maria's problems and the counselor's findings. Based on this conference, it was agreed that an intervention program should be developed and implemented to improve Maria's social relationships with her peers.

— Task One: Behavior Change Goals —

Develop a list of appropriate behavior change goals for the teacher to consider in this situation. No set number of goals is required. Compare your list with the list following, provided by the author.

Author's Behavior Change Goals:

1. Provide Maria direct instruction in social skills training for the purpose of ensuring that she develops the competence necessary for participating in social interactions.

2. Give Maria opportunities to rehearse and apply these skills in social interactions with selected peers.

3. Ensure that Maria is not unnecessarily traumatized by social contact with her peers.

4. Motivate both Maria and her peers to engage in social exchanges with each other.

5. Ensure that the interactions between Maria and her peers are of an acceptable quality (e.g., reciprocal, positive, and containing some verbal content).

— Task Two: Intervention Procedures —

Describe a specific intervention procedure that would be appropriate for achieving **each** behavior change goal that **you** have listed. Compare your intervention procedures with those presented by the author for the five behavior change goals listed previously.

Author's Intervention Procedures:

Goal #1—Many withdrawn children appear to have low rates of social contact with their peers due to deficient social skills. That is, such children have not learned to initiate to others, to respond to initiations by others, and to continue social interactions over time.

The author and his colleagues (Hops, Walker, & Greenwood, 1988) have developed a set of social tutoring procedures to teach withdrawn children key components of social interaction. Direct instruction and role playing techniques are used to teach mastery of three key components of the social interaction process. These are: (1) starting interactions, (2) answering social bids, and (3) continuing interactions over time.

Before implementing a program designed to motivate a socially withdrawn child to interact with his/her peers, it is imperative that steps be taken to teach essential social skills. Thus, in Maria's case, it would be important to make sure that she possessed these skills prior to implementing the intervention program.

Goal #2—Maria should be taught key social skills in a one-to-one teaching situation as described in Goal #1. As a next step, she should be given opportunities to practice these skills in limited, carefully supervised social interactions with selected peers. Several socially skilled and responsive peers should be selected to give Maria practice in initiating, responding to, and continuing social interactions over time. These interactive exchanges should be supervised by an adult (e.g., the teacher or counselor), and the children should be given feedback on the quality and appropriateness of their social interactions. These children could then assume the role of "special helpers" on the playground once the intervention program begins (i.e., they would facilitate social interactions between Maria and other peers).

Goal #3—Some withdrawn children actively avoid social contact with their peers because they are fearful of or are traumatized by social exchanges with others. It is difficult to know why such children develop fears of social contact.

However, if this situation should occur, steps should be taken to desensitize the child to social contact in a series of gradual steps. This procedure can be incorporated into the intervention program as a first step. The withdrawn child should be largely desensitized to such fears before he/she is expected to interact with peers for the purpose of earning rewards.

A suggested procedure would be to begin by having Maria practice interacting with a friend in a series of private interactions supervised by an adult. As Maria can increasingly accommodate this type of social contact, more children who are less well-known to her can be scheduled to participate in such sessions. These approximations should continue until Maria can approach social situations without signs of fear or anxiety. If she needs instruction in social skills as well, this training should be scheduled after such desensitization has been achieved (i.e., see Goal #1).

Goal #4—A contingency should be established in which Maria can earn a daily group activity reward for herself and her classmates by achieving a reward criterion based upon her interactive behavior. It is recommended that the program be implemented during recess periods where social interactions are free to occur. Peers should be actively encouraged to facilitate

Maria's interactive behavior. It is in their interest to do so, since they will share equally in whatever activity rewards are earned by her.

Reinforcement can be delivered through two primary methods—by reinforcing Maria with praise and points for **each social interaction** with her peers, or by reinforcing her for interacting for a certain **proportion of the time available** during the recess periods. The amount of time or the number of interactions required to achieve the daily reinforcement criterion can be gradually increased over time as Maria's social skills and competence develop.

Goal #5—It is important that Maria: (1) learn to initiate to peers as well as respond to initiations by others, (2) learn to interact positively, and (3) have a certain proportion of interactions involving verbal exchanges. As Maria engages in greater and greater amounts of social interaction, it is important to inspect her interactive behavior for quality, verbal content, and reciprocity. For example, some withdrawn children will allow their peers to do all the initiating. Others become negative in their social behavior as they interact more frequently. And still others interact nonverbally, but not verbally. When these situations occur, the contingency should be adjusted to produce the desired changes in these parameters.

— Task Three: Implementation Problems —

List potential implementation problems with the intervention procedures **you** have selected and compare your list with those provided by the author following.

Author's Potential Implementation Problems:

1. Maria's parents do not understand why she should be reinforced during recess for her interactive behavior, and do not agree to the intervention program.

2. Maria continues to be fearful about social contact with her peers, even after extensive desensitization training.

3. Maria does not seem to be sufficiently responsive to the intervention program.

4. Maria's "special helpers" appear to lose interest in performing their facilitative roles in the intervention program.

5. Maria's rate of verbal interactions continues to be extremely low, even after the contingency has been adjusted to increase them.

Any or all of these problems are **possible, not necessarily probable**, in an intervention program of this type. The reader should consider how he/she would respond to them should they be encountered.

Case Study 3: A Tantrumming Child

Bobby was a "normal," relatively well-adjusted first grader except in one respect. He would throw screaming tantrums that had the effect of bringing all activities around him to a standstill.

Bobby's parents reported that he began throwing tantrums around the age of two. They were unsure as to how this behavior pattern became established. Bobby's rate of tantrums continued to be high until he began kindergarten. During the first two months of kindergarten he had only one tantrum. However, his tantrum rate then began to gradually increase up to approximately one tantrum per day.

Mr. Unruh, Bobby's first grade teacher, reported that his tantrumming rate was slightly above one tantrum per day. Mr. Unruh, the counselor, the principal, and Bobby's parents all agreed that something must be done to get Bobby's tantrumming under control. Bobby's outbursts had an extremely disruptive effect on the entire class, and it was felt that this behavior pattern would also have a deleterious impact upon both Bobby's social and academic adjustment.

A conference was scheduled to discuss strategy. Both Mr. Unruh and Bobby's parents observed that his tantrums seemed to be prompted by two events: (1) not receiving sufficient attention, and (2) not "getting his way." Bobby's tantrums usually had the effect of providing him with massive amounts of attention, and frequently resulted in his getting his own way.

— Task One: Behavior Change Goals —

Develop a list of appropriate behavior change goals for the teacher to consider in this situation. No set number of goals is required. Compare your list with the list following, provided by the author.

Author's Behavior Change Goals:

1. Interview Bobby to determine whether he is aware of the situations that precipitate his tantrums.

2. Teach Bobby that his tantrums will: (1) no longer have any functional effect in producing desirable consequences as in the past, and (2) that his tantrums will result in a mildly aversive consequence.

3. Teach Bobby more adaptive strategies for producing reinforcing consequences from the environment and for coping with situations which he finds frustrating or is unable to control in a way that he would like.

— Task Two: Intervention Procedures —

Describe a specific intervention procedure that would be appropriate for achieving **each** behavior change goal that **you** have listed. Compare your intervention procedures with those presented by the author for the three behavior change goals listed previously.

Author's Intervention Procedures:

Goal #1—The teacher or counselor should interview Bobby to determine whether he is aware of those situations and events which precipitate his tantrums. In rare cases, a conscious awareness of such factors will make it possible for children to control their own tantrumming.

Bobby should be informed of each situation or event that seems to precipitate his tantrums. It is unlikely that he would be aware of why he has tantrums (i.e., because they allow him to control his environment and produce desirable consequences in many instances). The functional value of tantrums in this regard should be reviewed and discussed with Bobby.

Bobby should be informed that in the future, tantrums at school will no longer have a functional value for him and that he will be taught new ways of responding to these situations.

Goal #2—It is very important for Bobby to learn that his tantrums will no longer be an effective means of controlling his environment. The most effective means for achieving this goal is to use a brief timeout each time a tantrum occurs. A ten- to 15-minute timeout is recommended. However, Bobby should not be allowed to return to the classroom until his tantrumming has subsided.

The timeout should be implemented as soon as the tantrumming behavior begins. A good rule to consider for implementation is for Bobby to be sent home if he accumulates more than three timeouts in any school day. Sometimes going into timeout becomes a game wherein a child deliberately engages in behavior that warrants timeout. When this occurs, the child, rather than the teacher, is in control of the situation. A suspension procedure is usually an effective response to this situation provided that the child is not allowed access to such things as play activities or television privileges at home during the remainder of the school day.

The timeout procedure for tantrumming offers a number of advantages. For example, it prevents the tantrum from disrupting the classroom and Bobby from controlling the classroom situation in this way. It also prevents Bobby from obtaining excessive peer and teacher attention via the tantrum. Timeout is usually an aversive consequence for children, and may therefore suppress the frequency of tantrums. The prompt and correct application of timeout for tantrums makes it impossible for the tantrums to have functional value in producing immediate reinforcing consequences from the natural environment. In applying timeout, it is recommended that the guidelines presented in Chapter 5 governing its usage be followed closely.

Goal #3—The timeout procedure described in Goal #2 would probably be effective in controlling Bobby's high frequency of tantrumming. However, it is extremely important that he be taught alternative, adaptive methods for coping with his environment to replace his previous reliance on tantrums. It is likely that his tantrums actually prevent the acquisition of such positive coping methods because the tantrums are usually so effective in producing immediate and desirable (i.e., desirable to Bobby) consequences.

It is recommended that each situation which precipitates Bobby's tantrums be analyzed and a series of alternative, acceptable responses be developed. These should be reviewed with Bobby in a one-to-one teaching session and behaviorally rehearsed if possible. Bobby should then be given feedback, praise, and/or bonus points for handling such situations adaptively and without tantrums. This procedure should be continued until there is clear evidence that Bobby's coping skills in this area are well developed.

— Task Three: Implementation Problems —

List potential implementation problems with the intervention procedures **you** have selected and compare your list with those provided by the author following.

Author's Potential Implementation Problems:

1. Bobby refuses to cooperate and defies the teacher (or counselor) in the initial interview during which his tantrumming is discussed.

2. Bobby sometimes refuses to go into timeout voluntarily, and also occasionally refuses to return to the classroom from timeout.

3. Bobby shows no interest whatsoever in learning alternative adaptive responses to tantrumming.

4. Bobby suppresses his rate of tantrumming. However, he develops more covert, but equally inappropriate, methods of controlling his environment, obtaining peer and teacher attention, and getting his own way.

Any or all of these problems are **possible, not necessarily probable**, in an intervention program of this type. The reader should consider how he/she would respond to them should they be encountered.

_____

Conclusion

This chapter has presented a number of case study applications of the intervention procedures described in Chapters 5 and 6. These applications involve a range of commonly encountered behavior problems in the school setting. It is hoped that the diversity of these case study illustrations will provide the reader with useful clues about the appropriate application of these procedures.

Chapter 9 provides detailed descriptions of two model programs for intervening successfully with students having serious acting-out behavior problems. Both model programs are based upon years of trial testing and successful validation. One is designed primarily for use in regular classroom and playground settings, the other for use primarily in more restrictive settings, such as resource rooms.

Model Interventions for Use With Acting-Out Students in the Classroom Setting

Introduction

With the right supports and access to powerful intervention procedures, it would be possible to maintain a much larger number of acting-out students in regular and resource/special classroom settings than is currently the case. Annually, millions of dollars are invested by families, school districts, health providers, state agencies, and insurance companies in paying the costs of accommodating disturbed/abused children and youth within specialized residential care facilities. Acting-out students, with intractable behavior problems that prove resistant to school-based interventions, make up a significant portion of this residential student population. Such students are referred to these specialized and socially restrictive settings because: (1) their needs are judged to exceed the expertise and services that can be feasibly delivered within community settings, and (2) their behavior problems present challenges to educators that exceed most schools' teachability standards and zones of tolerance.

Instructional and behavioral intervention procedures for effecting substantial improvements in the achievement and social-behavioral adjustment of acting-out students have been available for over 20 years. Yet, these procedures seem to be infrequently applied to the behavioral repertoires of acting-out students in either regular or specialized classroom settings. In fact, school outcomes for this population are abysmal and well below even minimal expectations given their potential for learning and behavior change (see U.S. Office of Special Education and Rehabilitative Services. (1994). *The sixteenth annual report to Congress on the Implementation of the Individuals with Disabilities Education Act*, Washington, DC: OSERS).

The primary focus of school accommodations for acting-out students seems to be on control, containment, exclusion, and punishment. Acting-out students have severe deficits in their academic skills, have below average achievement levels, and need to learn and demonstrate a qualitatively different pattern of school behavior (Maguin & Loeber, in press). They also have an enormous capacity to do so, but they need substantial support and assistance in order to achieve these most important goals. It is in the interest of school systems and society as a whole to invest in achievement of this goal—especially early on in the school careers of acting-out students.

This chapter profiles two model interventions that were designed specifically for remediating the behavioral and academic problems of acting-out students in the primary and beginning intermediate grade ranges. These are: (1) the *CLASS Program for Acting-Out Students* (Hops & Walker, 1988); and (2) the *Engineered Learning Program (ELP) for Acting-Out Students* (Walker & Buckley, 1972, 1974). These model interventions represent best practices with students whose school adjustment and achievement are impaired by long-standing patterns of acting-out behavior. They are complex and powerful interventions that can be implemented, from start to finish, in a period of two to three months by educational personnel who normally work in school settings. They have the potential to teach acting-out students a much more adaptive and productive pattern of relating to others and to better cope with the demands of schooling.

The *CLASS Program (Contingencies for Learning Academic and Social Skills)* is designed for use with acting-out students who are enrolled in regular classroom settings. It can also be extended to other school settings (e.g., the playground, cafeteria) as needed. The *Engineered Learning Program (ELP)* model intervention was designed, developed, and tested for use with acting-out students within a self-contained, demonstration classroom setting. Both interventions have been extensively evaluated, field-tested, and replicated by others (see Hops, Walker, Fleischman, Nagoshi, Omura, Skinrud, & Taylor, 1978; O'Connor, Stuck, & Wyne, 1979; Walker & Buckley, 1972, 1974; Walker, Hops, & Greenwood, 1984).

The *CLASS Program* is a best practice intervention for achieving the following purposes: (1) teaching acting-out children a behavior pattern that matches the ideal student profile preferred by most teachers (see Chapter 10); (2) building peer support and involving acting-out students in class-wide social support systems; and (3) facilitating the transition of acting-out students from specialized to regular classroom settings.

The *ELP* model intervention can be used effectively in resource and self-contained classroom settings. It is also appropriate for use within the classroom components of many residential programs for children and youth having severe impairments. The primary goals and value(s) of the *ELP* model are: (1) to provide a short-term placement for acting-out students whose behavior problems cannot be accommodated in the regular classroom; (2) to provide intensive instruction and intervention to acting-out students in order to improve their achievement and to teach them a new, more adaptive behavior pattern; and (3) as a support setting and base for acting-out students who are reintegrated into least restrictive environment (LRE) settings following placement in a more restrictive setting.

These model interventions share certain common features, as follows:

- They focus on improving academic, study, and social skills and on reducing maladaptive forms of disruptive and aggressive behavior.

- They utilize structured, behavioral intervention procedures that rely on reinforcement (e.g., praise, points, home and school rewards) for teaching appropriate study, social, and academic skills and mild punishment (e.g., loss of points, a brief timeout, suspension) for reducing maladaptive forms of behavior.

- Both interventions use "booster shots" following program completion in order to preserve behavioral and academic gains achieved during intervention. These "booster shots" provide a brief re-exposure to the intervention that helps to maintain gains over the long term.

- Both interventions also provide for the involvement of parents in facilitating the acting-out students' school progress; however, the *CLASS Program* requires more direct parent involvement than the *ELP* model.

The remainder of this chapter profiles these two interventions, provides details of implementation, and presents recommendations to guide best practices in using them. However, before presenting this material, a key question is addressed regarding the cost effectiveness of mounting such interventions.

When to Use Intensive Model Interventions for Acting-Out Students

The *CLASS* and *ELP* model programs are specialized interventions that are somewhat labor intensive even though the implementation period required for each is relatively brief (i.e., two to three months). In the case of *CLASS*, the program should be implemented in the regular classroom context when: (1) less intrusive, behavioral interventions have been tried and failed, and (2) the acting-out student's behavior problems are considered so severe that he cannot be reasonably accommodated in the regular classroom. Acting-out students who are appropriate for the *CLASS Program* generally exhibit levels of rule governed, classroom behavior that are below 50%. Normative levels of appropriate classroom behavior for students in general are typically in the 80-85% range.

Referral to a program such as *ELP* should only be considered when every effort has been made to deal with the acting-out student's problems in the regular classroom, and this effort has been unsuccessful. Failure of the *CLASS Program* to satisfactorily change a student's behavior pattern is an important diagnostic criterion. It means the student has relatively severe behavior problems requiring very intensive intervention(s) for a time; further, it is likely that these interventions must be implemented in a more restrictive setting. Placements of this type should be short-term in nature with a clear target date identified for regular classroom reintegration prior to acceptance into the program. It is an important consideration that students who are exposed to programs such as *CLASS* and *ELP* have behavior problems of such severity that the time and effort required in program implementation are justified.

Profile of the *CLASS Program*

The *CLASS Program* is part of the **SUCCESS** program series, which consists of four behavior management packages designed to address commonly encountered behavior problems in school. Each package targets a different cluster of behavior problems and each is geared for implementation in regular classroom and playground settings. However, the *SUCCESS* series can also be implemented within specialized settings with minor adaptations. The four programs in the series are listed following, along with the target behavior cluster each addresses:

- **CLASS** (*Contingencies for Learning Academic and Social Skills*), a classroom behavior management program for acting-out students

- **PASS** (*Program for Academic Survival Skills*), a class-wide behavior management program for disruptive classrooms

- **RECESS** (*Reprogramming Environmental Contingencies for Effective Social Skills*), a behavior management program for children who exhibit bullying behavior

- **PEERS** (*Procedures for Establishing Effective Relationship Skills*), a behavior management program for children with socially withdrawn behavior

Collectively, these four programs address the most commonly occurring behavior problems and disorders in the beginning and intermediate elementary grades. The development, testing, and validation of these four programs was supported by a continuing federal grant to the author and his colleagues from the U.S. Office of Special Education Programs. These programs were initially developed and tested between 1971 and 1979 (see Walker, Hops, & Greenwood, 1984 for details of the research and development process). (Information about the *SUCCESS* series can be obtained from Educational Achievement Systems, 319 Nickerson Street, Suite 112, Seattle, WA 98109.)

The primary purpose of the *SUCCESS* behavior management series is to assist teachers and other school personnel (e.g., school counselors, school psychologists) in remediating and managing the difficult behavior of students with school adjustment problems. A companion goal is to allow these students to remain within LRE settings by providing behavioral support strategies and appropriate interventions that address their specific deficits and/or behavioral excesses. The key principles upon which the *SUCCESS* intervention approach is based are as follows:

- Behavioral techniques, correctly applied, can be used as a highly effective intervention to change students' inappropriate behavior(s).

- Contracting between the student and teacher is an important intervention procedure.

- Group contingencies and social rewards can be powerful in reducing the inappropriate behavior of target students and building social support from peers.

- Careful monitoring, tracking, and follow-up with the student's family and teacher in rewarding and strengthening appropriate school behavior is key to the long-term success of the program.

- With the assistance of a consultant properly trained in behavioral techniques, a teacher can implement these behavior change programs effectively as part of his/her ongoing management of the classroom.

The *SUCCESS* behavior management series was also included in a resource guide as one of 17 exemplary programs for facilitating the reintegration and mainstreaming of students with disabilities (see Alberg et al., 1994).

Description of the *CLASS Program*

CLASS requires a minimum of 30 school days, from start to finish, for full implementation. Each program day has a specific criterion that must be achieved in order to progress to the next program day. It should be noted, however, that it is rare for an acting-out student to pass every program day on the first try. The program is designed to be set up and coordinated initially by a consultant (e.g., counselor, school psychologist, resource teacher, behavioral specialist, etc.) who can serve the teacher in a consultative role for brief periods each day. The program generally requires about 35-40 hours of the consultant's time spread over a two- to three-month intervention period.

CLASS consists of the following main components: (1) careful monitoring and tracking of the acting-out student's behavior; (2) adult praise from the consultant, teacher, and parents; (3) group activity rewards earned at school that are shared equally with peers; (4) individual home privileges prearranged with the parents; and (5) brief timeouts and therapeutic suspension to address unacceptable forms of student behavior (e.g., tantrumming, fighting, teacher defiance). (Therapeutic suspension refers to a one-day period in which: [1] the target student doesn't come to school, [2] the *CLASS Program* does not operate, and [3] all missed schoolwork must be made up.) There is evidence that all of these components have some influence in changing student behavior; however, when applied in combination with each other, very powerful effects can be achieved.

The *CLASS Program* is divided into three phases: **consultant**, **teacher**, and **maintenance**. The consultant phase lasts five days, the teacher phase lasts 15 days, and the maintenance phase lasts ten days. Brief descriptions of each phase follow.

The first intervention phase of *CLASS* is extremely important to the success of the program and is the responsibility of the consultant, who is also charged with coordinating the overall implementation. In this phase, the consultant monitors the student's progress using a "Green/Red Point Card" (see Figure 9.1). In this system, the green side of the card is shown to the student whenever he/she is behaving appropriately and following rules and the red side is shown when this is not the case. Points are intermittently awarded on the green or red side of the card depending upon whether the student's behavior is appropriate or inappropriate when it is time to monitor his/her behavior. These monitoring sessions are 20-30 minutes in length, and a monitoring session is randomly scheduled both in the morning and the afternoon.

During this first intervention phase, one pont is awarded every 30 seconds on either the green side or the red side of the "Green/Red Point Card." If the student's behavior is appropriate, the point is awarded on the green side of the card; if inappropriate, the point is awarded on the red side of the card. The green points and red points are tallied at the end of the monitoring

Figure 9.1
Green/Red Point Card

Program Day 1

Rules

Removed from class for

1. Hurting or attempting to hurt another person

2. Destroying or stealing property

3. Continual disobedience to a staff member

4. _____

5. _____

6. _____

Points Awarded

Session 1	Session 2
Tally Here:	Tally Here:

Notes:

Red Side

Program Day 1

Student's Name: _____   Date: _____

1. Talk in a moderate voice.

2. Follow the teacher's instructions.

3. Remain in your seat except when schoolwork requires being out of seat.

4. Talk, work, and play at proper times with classmates.

5. Attend to the teacher and your work.

6. _____

Session 1—Time: _____	Session 2—Time: _____
Points possible: 40 Points needed: 32 (80%)	Points possible: 40 Points needed: 32 (80%)
Tally Here:	Tally Here:
Points Awarded:	Points Awarded:

Did/Did Not Earn Points for Home Reward

School Principal: _____

Teacher's Name: _____

Home Privilege: _____

Parent's Name: _____

0:00-0:10	5:20-5:30	10:20-10:30	15:20-15:30
0:40-0:50	5:50-6:00	10:40-10:50	15:50-16:00
1:10-1:20	6:10-6:20	11:10-11:20	16:00-16:10
1:50-2:30	6:50-7:00	11:40-11:50	16:30-16:40
2:20-2:30	7:00-7:10	12:00-12:10	17:20-17:30
2:30-2:40	7:50-8:00	12:30-12:40	17:50-18:00
3:10-3:20	8:10-8:20	13:20-13:30	18:20-18:30
3:40-3:50	8:30-8:40	13:40-13:50	18:30-18:40
4:00-4:10	9:20-9:30	14:00-14:10	19:20-19:30
4:40-4:50	9:30-9:40	14:50-15:00	19:40-19:50

Green Side

session. If 80% or more of the points have been awarded on the green side of the card, a free-time reward is earned.

During the first days of the program, the *CLASS* consultant sits in close proximity to the student while operating the program and gradually moves further away during the five-day period. However, sufficient proximity is maintained so the acting-out student is continuously aware of his behavioral status (i.e., appropriate or inappropriate) during the session. For each session, if 80% or more of the total available points are awarded on the green side of the card, a brief activity reward is scheduled at the end of the session which is shared equally with the whole class. This reward activity should generally take no longer than five to ten minutes, but is highly valued by the acting-out student and his peers. If the reward criterion is met in both daily sessions, then an individual home privilege is earned, which has been previously negotiated with the acting-out student's parents.

Having the *CLASS Program* consultant operate the program in this fashion during the initial phase has a number of advantages. First, most acting-out students who qualify for *CLASS* require careful monitoring and continuous exposure to the intervention in order to produce substantial changes in their behavior. The close proximal relationship of the consultant to the student during this phase accomplishes this goal. Second, most acting-out students test the program to see if it will work as stated; the great majority of this testing occurs within the first five days of the program. Third, the consultant phase is structured so that the teacher can watch the acting-out student's behavior change for the better with no investment in the process. Finally, the program is moved to a point during the five-day consultant phase where the regular teacher can manage the program effectively as a part of the normal teaching and management tasks occurring in any classroom. After the consultant phase, the *CLASS Program* consultant assumes a monitoring and support role for the remainder of the total implementation period.

The length of the session during which the program operates daily is gradually expanded until, by program day ten, it is extended to the full day (or to all those periods during which the student's behavior is considered to be problematic). During the teacher phase, over the next ten program days (i.e., to program day 20) the student is required to work for longer and longer periods to achieve the reward criterion. Simultaneously, the available school and home rewards become less frequent but greater in their magnitude, or perceived value. From program day ten to 20, the acting-out student is required to earn the available rewards by meeting a two-day, three-day, and four-day reward criterion. If the student fails to achieve the reward criterion during any one day within these blocks of time, a "recycling" procedure is

	Duration		Points		Praise Paired With Points		Type of Consequences		Card Should be Shown Each Time Point is Awarded
Days	Length of Session G = Group I – Individual	Child is Ovserved for 10 Seconds for Each	Total Possible	Child Needs 80%	Consultant	Teacher	School	Home	
Day 1	20 Min.-G 20 Min.-I	30 Sec. 30 Sec.	40 40	30 30	9 9	1 1	Group Group	Individual and 3 Social Praises	1:1
Day 2	20 Min.-G 20 Min.-I	1 Min. 1 Min.	20 20	16 16	7 7	2 2	Group Group	Individual and 3 Social Praises	1:1
Day 3	20 Min.-G 20 Min.-I	2 Min. 2 Min.	10 10	8 8	4 4	3 3	Group Group	Individual and 3 Social Praises	1:1
Day 4	20 Min.-G 20 Min.-I	4 Min. 4 Min.	5 5	4 4	1 1	4 4	Group Group	Individual and 3 Social Praises	1:1
Day 5	30 Min.-G 30 Min.-I	6 Min. 6 Min.	5 5	4 4	0 0	5 5	Group Group	Individual and 3 Social Praises	1:1

Table 9.1
Daily Summary Chart Consultant Phase

used in which the student is returned to a previously successful level. Following success at this level, the student returns to the prior reward criterion and tries again.

During the maintenance phase of *CLASS*, the student is working for adult approval and praise; no activity rewards are available during this period. However, the recycling procedure remains in effect during this phase.

Tables 9.1 and 9.2 provide summary overviews of the consultant and teacher phases of *CLASS*, respectively. The program is designed to become more easily manageable as it progresses while simultaneously making greater demands on the acting-out student. Use of the "Green/Red Point Card" is faded out completely after program day 15.

	Duration		Points			Type of Consequences			Card Should be Shown Each Time That Point is Awarded
Table 9.2 Daily Summary Chart Teacher Phase									
Days	Length of Session G = Group I = Individual	Child is Ovserved for 10 Seconds for Each	Total Possible	Child Needs 80%	Teacher	School	Home		
Day 6	30 Min.-G 30 Min.-I	6 Min. 6 Min.	5 5	4 4	1 1	Group Group	Individual and 3 Social Praises		1:1
Day 7	40 Min.-G 40 Min.-I	8 Min. 8 Min.	5 5	4 4		Group Group	Individual and 3 Social Praises		1:1
Day 8	60 Min.-G 60 Min.-I	10 Min. 10 Min.	6 6	5 5		Group Group	Individual and 3 Social Praises		1:1
Day 9	120 Min.-G 120 Min.-I	10 Min. 10 Min.	12 12	10 10		Group Group	Individual and 3 Social Praises		1:2
Day 10	All Day	10 Min.	X		Equal to the Number of Points Child Earns	Group Group	Individual and 3 Social Praises		1:3
Day 11	All Day	10 Min.	X			Larger Magnitude Group (Day 12)	Individual and 3 Social Praises (Day 12)		1:5
Day 12	All Day	10 Min.	X	Calculate as Appropriate					
Day 13 Day 14 Day 15	All Day All Day All Day	10 Min. 10 Min. 10 Min.	X X X			Larger Magnitude Group (Day 15)	Individual and 3 Social Praises (Day 15)		1:10
Day 16 Day 17 Day 18 Day 19 Day 20	All Day All Day All Day All Day All Day	10 Min. 10 Min. 10 Min. 10 Min. 10 Min.	X X X X X			Larger Magnitude Group (Day 20)	Individual and 3 Social Praises (Day 20)		None
Day 21 to Day 30	All Day	All Day	None	None		None	None		None

X = To determine the possible points either: (1) if the time that the child will be in school can be anticipated, then determine the total number of minutes for the day and divide by ten; or (2) if the time cannot be anticipated, count the total number of positive and negative points that the child has received for the entire day. That is the number of possible points.

Evidence of the *CLASS Program*'s Effectiveness

Studies have been conducted of the individual components that comprise the *CLASS Program* as well as implementation of these components in combination within the context of the program's application (see Hops, Walker, Fleischman, Nagoshi, Omura, Skinrud, & Taylor, 1978; Walker, Hops, & Fiegenbaum, 1976). Acting-out students will generally show a 20-30 percentage point gain in appropriate behavior across beginning, during, and final phases of the program.

The long-term durability of the *CLASS Program* has also been investigated. Hops and Walker (1988) reviewed school records for a sample of acting-out students who had and had not been exposed to the program during field testing. Over a three-year follow-up period, acting-out students exposed to *CLASS* consumed significantly fewer special education/related services than control acting-out students who did not receive the intervention.

The *CLASS Program* has been shown to also have cross-cultural applicability. *CLASS* has been translated into Spanish and field tested in Costa Rica using a randomized, experimental-control group design. Experimental students, who received the program, produced significantly greater rates of behavioral gains, as recorded by professionally trained observers, than did control students who did not receive the intervention (see Walker, Fonseca-Retana, & Gersten, 1988).

Finally, an unpublished, systematic training formats study was conducted by the author and his colleagues to evaluate the cost effectiveness of different consultant delivery options for *CLASS*. Three different sites in Oregon, Washington, and Colorado were used in this study. A group of 45 consultants was identified in each participating site and the consultants were randomly assigned to one of three training formats within each. These training formats were as follows: (1) training to mastery criterion on key components of *CLASS* considered to be essential for its effective implementation; (2) a standard *CLASS* training session in which trainees were exposed to all the components of the program and instructed in how to apply them; and (3) a self-training option in which consultants were given all the training materials and asked to train themselves over a two-day period.

Figure 9.2 presents the results of this study. Groups 1, 2, and 3 refer respectively to the mastery, standard, and self-training consultant groups. The data in Figure 9.2 represent the behavior changes of the acting-out students to whom each participating consultant applied the *CLASS Program* procedures. As Figure 9.2 indicates, there were no systematic differences between the consultants who participated in the three training formats with regard to the effectiveness with which they implemented *CLASS*. Overall,

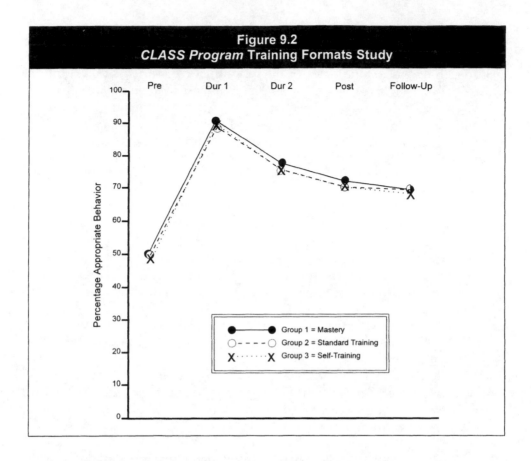

Figure 9.2
CLASS Program Training Formats Study

the *CLASS Program*'s implementation produced very powerful intervention effects. A six-week follow-up indicated that acting-out students maintained a net, residual gain of about 20 percentage points in their appropriate behavior as determined by observations recorded by professionally trained observers. These are very acceptable behavior changes for acting-out students exposed to a consultant-delivered intervention in regular classroom settings.

The *CLASS Program* has been used extensively in the U.S., Canada, and Australia since its original publication. It is a powerful, direct intervention that has substantial value as a vehicle for preserving the access of acting-out students to LRE settings. If an acting-out student fails to respond to the *CLASS Program*, then it is likely an alternative placement will be required for a period of time during which more intensive intervention procedures can be delivered. The failure of powerful interventions such as *CLASS* is often a valid screening device to indicate the need for exposure to an even more comprehensive and powerful intervention.

Implementation Issues and Problems

For students who respond initially to the CLASS Program and then show a deterioration of gains over time, especially in post-program periods, there is often a decay in the teacher's use of praising and scanning. Scanning refers to the systematic monitoring and observing of the classroom by the teacher so as to detect student problems and as a cue to provide praise or approval. This skill is absolutely essential to maintaining the acting-out student's behavioral gains, but it may not be sufficient in and of itself to achieve this goal.

Brief program "booster shots" are often required to sustain the student's improved behavior over the long term. *CLASS* provides four different maintenance options for this purpose, ordered according to their relative cost to the teacher. Consideration of these strategies is strongly recommended since *CLASS*, like all other intervention programs, is not immune to the decay of effects when the original intervention procedures are withdrawn (see DuPaul & Eckert, 1994). Most acting-out students require some continuing exposure to brief variations of the *CLASS Program* over time in order to maintain their appropriate behavior. This kind of follow-up and support should accompany the student **across school years** if truly enduring effects are expected.

The role of parents in the success of *CLASS* is very important. Every effort should be made to: (1) secure the parents' active involvement in the program, and (2) monitor and encourage their support of the acting-out student's progress within the program. Parents must have the program explained to them and give their consent for their child's participation. However, this is sometimes not sufficient to maintain their effective participation in the program. Thus, a key part of the consultant's responsibilities is to work continuously to maximize the parents' role.

Finally, teachers sometimes feel coerced into participating in the *CLASS Program*, especially if other parties are enthusiastic about it and the teacher is not. Some teachers are philosophically opposed to the use of school rewards and/or object to the highly structured nature of the program. In those cases where the regular teacher expresses genuine and continuing opposition on these or other grounds, it is recommended that the program not be implemented.

Some Final Thoughts

The *CLASS Program* contains detailed procedural manuals for the consultant and teacher that describe the role of each in the implementation process. Daily checklists and logs are provided that outline the tasks for each program day, the length of time required, and the materials needed. A program materials packet containing copies of all required forms is also provided. The *CLASS Program* can be used over and over in repeated applications. However, it is recommended that only one student at a time be exposed to the program within a given classroom.

The ease of program implementation and the degree to which the acting-out student is responsive to the *CLASS Program*'s procedures provide an indirect measure of the relative intractability of the student's problems. The more severe the student's behavior problems, the more problematic these factors are likely to be. Acting-out students who fail to respond to the program have an elevated risk for seriously negative developmental outcomes including school failure and eventual dropout.

Profile of the *ELP* Model

Even though approximately 85% of the student population certified eligible as **severely emotionally disturbed** (**SED**) under the aegis of the Individuals with Disabilities Education Act (IDEA) are served in settings other than regular classrooms, the notion of "best practices" in these alternative settings is considered by many to be an oxymoron. Although programming efforts and achieved outcomes for SED students assigned to these settings have been severely criticized by advocates of mainstreaming and full inclusion, these settings do provide the opportunity to achieve rapid gains in social-behavioral and academic areas. Specialized instructional and behavior management procedures can be applied within these settings in an intensive fashion. Because of the generally favorable teacher-student ratios that exist in many alternative settings, instruction can be individualized and fine tuned in a way that is extremely difficult in LRE settings. If properly managed, these advantages can translate into substantial social-behavioral and academic gains for acting-out students.

The *Engineered Learning Program* (*ELP*) model intervention was funded initially by a four-year grant to the author and his colleagues (i.e., Mattson and Buckley) from the U.S. Office of Special Education Programs. A major purpose of this effort was to develop a model intervention for effective use in resource and self-contained settings with acting-out students in the elementary grade range. The remainder of this model profile description section addresses two important topics in this context: (1) rules and guidelines to consider in setting up and operating an *ELP* type model intervention; and (2) behavioral and instructional practices appropriate for interventions delivered in resource and self-contained settings. Before addressing these topics, however, some perspectives on the use of specialized, alternative placements for acting-out and at-risk students are presented briefly.

Perspectives on the Use of Specialized, Alternative Placements for Acting-Out and At-Risk Students

Except in very rare cases, a resource or self-contained placement should not be considered as anything other than a short-term option for remediating the adjustment problems of acting-out students. When assigned to such an alternative setting, the behavioral and academic demands of the regular classroom should be the constantly referenced standard for judging the acting-out student's progress. This placement provides a temporary respite for the referring teacher, the student's peers, and the acting-out student, and simultaneously affords the opportunity to: (1) teach the referred student a more adaptive pattern of behavior; and (2) provide intensive instruction in the basic skill areas that lay an important foundation for academic achievement.

Acting-out students are generally, as a rule, assigned to these settings for too long and well past the point where they can derive additional benefits from them. These too long placements are typically due to the aversive behavioral characteristics of acting-out students, and they tend to isolate them from the normalizing influences of regular classroom routines and peer groups. These practices also run the risk of teaching acting-out students that their disruptive, aggressive behavior will cause them to be placed elsewhere rather than lead to appropriate sanctions. Thus the larger school environment is protected from these students' disruptive presence; but, in the process, the acting-out students are "lost." This loss is not acceptable, especially as the numbers of these students continue to increase.

Educators must strive to reintegrate acting-out students so they will function in a contributing, positive fashion within the regular school environment. The focus should be on teaching them a new, more adaptive behavior pattern, intensively remediating their academic skills, and then reintegrating them back into the referring setting as soon as possible.

There are other compelling reasons for limiting the assignment of acting-out students to these settings. For example, students generally, and acting-out students in particular, are very sensitive to the stigmatizing effects of specialized placements. Regular students will often tease and talk about at-risk and acting-out students during their tenure in these settings. This is especially true with older students (i.e., middle/junior high and high school age). These students do not, as a rule, react well to such taunts, which increases their likelihood of responding negatively to their peers.

More ominously, Dishion and Andrews (1995) reported a study investigating different intervention approaches in preventing the escalation of problem behaviors among high risk adolescents age 11-14 years. These approaches included a parent focus group, a teen focus group, and a combined parent-teen focus group. Results showed that the parent and teen focus interventions were effective in reducing family conflict, in preventing future tobacco use, and in contributing to improved behavior at school. However, when high risk youth were aggregated into separate treatment groups in the teen focus approach, they showed the highest rates of tobacco use and problem behavior at school beginning at the termination of the intervention and persisting into follow-up over a one- year period.

Based on these results, Dishion and Andrews (1995) argue for a careful reconsideration of interventions that aggregate high risk youth into treatment programs. If such students are assigned to these insular programs without parent involvement, are kept in them for long periods, and if the intervention procedures are relatively weak, it may actually make the situation worse in that the students may: (1) bond with each other, (2) model and imitate each other's maladaptive behavior, and (3) support each other's deviance and violation of social norms. Acting-out students need regular contact with other peers, even when assigned to alternative settings, as well as the involvement of their parents to help offset these potential negative effects. It is most important to consider making such accommodations in order to forestall the potential effects observed by Dishion and Andrews.

These issues suggest that there may be threshold effects associated with assignment of acting-out and high risk youth to specialized, alternative settings. That is, a small amount of this intervention may be beneficial, but a larger amount may actually prove harmful. Research on this topic in the context of schooling is urgently needed to determine whether findings like those of Dishion and Andrews (1995) have more generalized effects. At present, the convergence of a number of factors seems to suggest that short-term placements will yield better overall results than long-term placements in specialized settings for acting-out students.

Rules and Guidelines for Setting Up and Operating an *ELP* Type Model Intervention

General guidelines and rules that should be considered in establishing and operating a specialized setting for acting-out students follow:

- There should be a very strong focus on the basic academic skills of reading, math, spelling, and language in a program of this type. The goal should be to help acting-out students progress as far and as rapidly as possible in the basic skill areas during their assignment to the program. The academic losses that students might incur in other subject areas would be more than offset by the importance of the foundational gains achieved in these basic skills.

- The program should be staffed by a teacher who is skilled in direct instruction and academic programming for students with weak academic skills. The teacher should also have excellent behavior management skills and be able to cope with difficult students. The teacher should be supported by a half-time aide, at a minimum.

- No more than ten to 12 acting-out students should be assigned to the setting at any one time. If possible, other students should have regular contact with those assigned to the alternative placement—perhaps through the vehicle of peer tutoring.

- At the beginning of the school year, it is a mistake to admit all appropriate students to the specialized class at once. Students should be staged into the setting in pairs or groups of three and given a chance to adjust to the setting before additional students are admitted. In this way, the teacher (and aide) can effectively socialize the students to the demands and procedures of the setting. The already admitted students can then assist with this process for additional, newly admitted students.

- A dual emphasis should be placed on group versus individual work as part of the intervention in this setting. Acting-out students generally have a great deal of difficulty in participating in group instructional arrangements and they are often unable to work independently for sustained periods. These are both critically important skills in regular classrooms.

- The alternative setting and the model intervention should be highly structured, with maximum feedback provided to students on their academic and social-behavioral progress.

- A point system should be established to provide motivational incentives for the acting-out students which allows for the earning of school and home privileges. Rules for point systems include: (1) making them valuable by pairing them with desired activities; (2) always praising **specific behavior** first before awarding points; (3) refusing to negotiate with students about the value of points or the rate of exchange for back-up rewards; and (4) generally avoiding talking about the points unless the situation specifically calls for this type of exchange.

- A response cost should be used to consequate maladaptive behavior of mild to moderate severity (e.g., talk outs, being out of seat, swearing, and so forth), and timeout or a brief suspension should be used to deal with more severe forms of maladaptive behavior (e.g., aggression, fighting, teacher defiance, and so forth).

- Strategies and tactics of effective teaching that are empirically derived (including cueing, coaching, prompting, debriefing, providing multiple opportunities to correct errors, and maximizing opportunities to respond academically) should be implemented.

Adherence to these general guidelines will contribute greatly to a model intervention that is cost effective and highly efficient.

Behavioral and Instructional Practices Appropriate for Interventions Delivered in Resource/Self-Contained Settings

The following material is based upon procedures implemented within an experimental-demonstration classroom setting operated by the author and his colleagues (i.e., Hops and Greenwood). The procedures described and the outcomes achieved resulted from a four-year investigation with the intention of developing a model intervention for acting-out students suitable for application within alternative school settings such as resource and self- contained classrooms. This research was supported by a four-year grant from the U.S. Office of Special Education Programs. Portions of this material have been previously reported in Walker and Buckley (1972, 1974) and in Walker, Hops, and Fiegenbaum (1976).

This work had three primary goals: (1) the development of screening and assessment methods for identifying children with behavior problems in the regular classroom setting; (2) the development and evaluation of school-based procedures for reducing disruptive classroom behavior and teaching a model student behavioral profile; and (3) the evaluation of techniques and supports designed to facilitate the transfer of social-behavioral and academic gains upon reintegration back into the referral setting.

A point system was established within the demonstration classroom to test a set of intervention procedures that would be both efficient and effective in changing the classroom behavior of acting-out students in desired ways. The classroom setting was very similar to a resource classroom or a special classroom in terms of a reduced teacher-student ratio, an emphasis upon individualized instruction, and in the use of instructional materials designed to remediate academic deficits.

The incentive system within the demonstration classroom included both social and token (i.e., points) reinforcers. The students assigned to the classroom were able to earn points for appropriate social behavior as well as correct academic performance. They were told how they could earn points as soon as they were admitted into the classroom. Points were initially awarded on a form placed on each student's desk; individual students' points were later awarded on a wall-mounted, electronic display board that was especially designed for this purpose.

Items for which points could be exchanged ranged from school supplies to chess and chemistry sets. Points could also be exchanged for free time. Free-time activities included reading, building models, tutoring other children, playing chess, or listening to records. A wide variety of back-up rewards was included to increase the likelihood of having appropriate incentives available that would appeal to each student.

During the four-year period of the study, a total of 67 acting-out students were rotated though this setting, in groups of approximately eight students each, for two to three months of intervention. They were then returned to their original, referring classroom. Four of these students were girls. Behavioral assessment instruments and the *ELP* intervention model were developed during the first two years of the study. The intervention model was replicated with eight successive groups of six children each during the last two years of the study, and a systematic investigation of transition strategies was also undertaken during this period. These strategies were designed to smooth the reintegration process and to enhance the transfer of gains achieved in the demonstration classroom into the referral setting.

In the sections that follow, descriptions are provided of the setting, special equipment, student characteristics, and measures used in the *ELP* model.

— Physical Arrangements —

The classroom facilities were adjoining and affiliated with a public elementary school. The primary area for academic activities contained six double desks (with an approximately 20" x 45" work surface), the teacher's desk, shelves and tables for the display of high interest materials for science and art projects, a carpentry room with a variety of tools and wood, and one-way glass observation facilities. Space was also available for individual testing, tutoring, and remedial instruction. A small isolation room (for timeout) containing a chair and desk adjoined the classroom (see Figure 9.3).

The students used the same playground and lunch facilities as the regularly enrolled students in the school. The acting-out students were in the demonstration classroom daily for approximately three hours and 45 minutes. Of

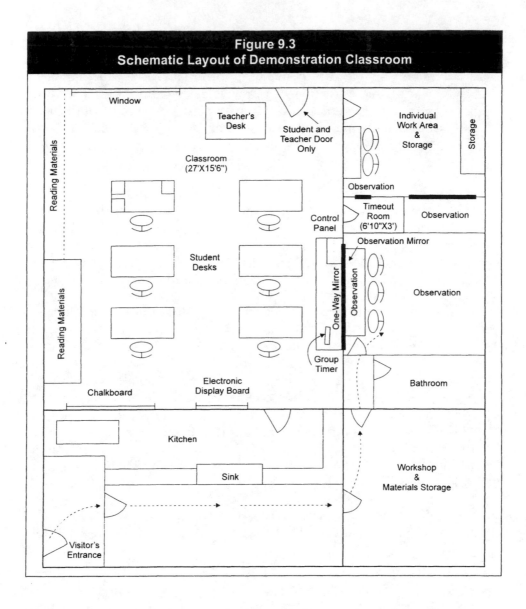

Figure 9.3
Schematic Layout of Demonstration Classroom

that time, approximately two hours and 50 minutes were devoted to academic assignments, 45 minutes to P.E. and recess, and ten minutes were dedicated to the tallying of points and the trading for back-up rewards at the end of the day. The class day ended at 1:45 P.M. and the students were, in most cases, bused back to their respective regular classes for one hour of continued academic work.

Each morning both the teacher and the aide were present in the classroom to manage instruction, answer questions, correct assignments, and to generally monitor student performance. Following the lunch break and for the last 45 minutes of the class day, the teacher operated the classroom by herself.

— Special Equipment —

The special equipment used in the classroom consisted of an electronic display board, individual workboxes, and timers. The equipment was used to: (1) monitor student performance, (2) help the teacher keep track of points earned and facilitate the mechanics of awarding and subtracting points, and (3) provide students with immediate and relatively objective feedback on their behavior. It should be emphasized that such equipment is **not** essential for the successful operation of either a demonstration classroom setting or an *ELP* type model intervention. However, over the four-year period of the study, the study's authors found this equipment to be very useful for research purposes.

ELECTRONIC DISPLAY BOARD

An electronic display board, designed by the author, was used for recording points and for providing students with feedback about their appropriate and inappropriate behavior. The unit was also designed to provide a more systematic presentation and removal of points than could be achieved by the teacher making marks on point cards kept on the students' desks.

The display board (see Figure 9.4) contained a unit for each student with name, stimulus light, a three-digit plus counter, and three-digit minus counter. Points could be either awarded or taken away by operating the plus and minus counters. A similar unit, set below the rest, was used for recording and regulating a group reinforcement procedure. A control panel at the side of the room was used to operate the display board (see Figure 9.3 for detail on placements).

INDIVIDUAL WORKBOXES

The workbox was developed originally by Patterson and his colleagues (Patterson, 1965) for use in regular classrooms. The metal boxes were 3" x 3" x 5" in size and powered by a six-volt battery. The front of each box contained a green light and a red light and matching plus and minus counters. When the green light was on, it signified to the student that he/she was behaving appropriately and was earning points on the plus counter. If the red light came on, it meant that the student was behaving inappropriately and could lose previously earned points. If the red light stayed on for any period of time, the student would begin losing points on the minus counter. The students were told that the red light would come on for such behaviors as looking around the room or daydreaming for extended periods, tantrumming, noncompliance with teacher directives or requests, and so forth.

The teacher, teacher aide, or classroom supervisor operated the box from a hand-held control unit at the end of a 25' cord. The length of the cord allowed the operator to stand in the observation room and manipulate the lights and counters on the box without being visible to the students. The boxes could

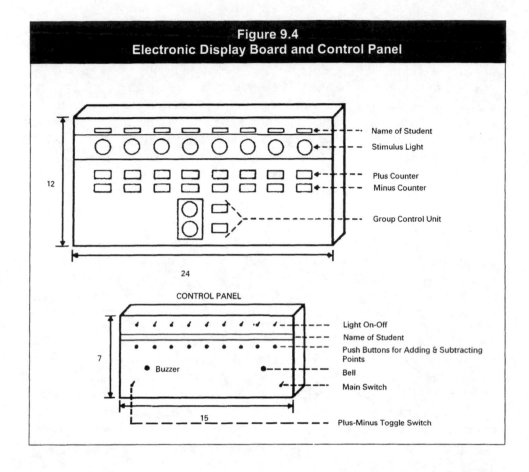

Figure 9.4
Electronic Display Board and Control Panel

also be operated in the demonstration classroom area with the operator visible to the students. The boxes were used for: (1) shaping attending behavior, (2) changing special problem behaviors for individual students, and (3) as part of a follow-up strategy in the regular classroom following reintegration.

TIMERS

Individual, 60-minute kitchen timers, placed on each student's desk, were used in a variety of ways to meet the specific behavioral needs of each student. The timers were particularly effective in reducing high rate distractibility. All the students were monitored with either a timer or a workbox when they were first assigned to the demonstration classroom.

An electric, Gra-Lab Universal Interval Timer was also used in conjunction with the display board to regulate the daily group reinforcement procedure. Dial numbers on this timer's face represented from one to 60 minutes. By setting both the minute and second hands of the timer for predetermined intervals (e.g., six minutes), the task engagement of the group of students could be improved.

The procedure worked as follows. The students were assigned to a group activity task. The Gra-Lab timer was then set for a specific interval and allowed to run. As long as all the students (i.e., the group as a whole) were academically engaged the clock ran and accumulated minutes. But if one or more students stopped being academically engaged during the interval, the timer was reset and the accumulated time lost. At the end of the interval, the number of minutes earned were added to a running cumulative total. Across school days, after a sufficient number of minutes had been accumulated, they were exchanged for a group privilege (e.g., a field trip) shared by all the members of the group.

A small, two-hour pocket timer was used on the playground. The timer could be held easily in the hand, pinned on a shirt, or attached to a student's belt loop. The timer was set for consecutive, five-minute intervals. If all the students cooperated with each other and followed the general playground rules during each five-minute period, they earned an additional five minutes of P.E. or recess time. The timer was then reset accordingly. This procedure was continued until the end of the recess period.

— Students —

Candidates for the demonstration classroom were initially selected and referred by school counselors, regular teachers, and/or principals of local elementary schools. During the study, acting-out students were accepted from 24 of the 32 elementary schools in the local districts. A large number of referrals were evaluated using teacher ratings and behavioral observations recorded by professionally trained observers; as a rule, there were about 20-25 referrals for each group, from which six to eight acting-out students were selected for assignment to the demonstration classroom. Efforts were made to select the most difficult of the referred students.

The vast majority of referrals to the demonstration classroom involved boys. Only four girls were referred to the program during the four-year period, and all easily qualified and were accepted.

In their regular classrooms, the students were enrolled in grades three through six. Selection criteria included average or above average intellectual ability; inadequate academic performance; and disruptive, acting-out behavior occurring within the regular classroom setting. Students referred to the demonstration classroom possessed a number of attributes which made them poor candidates for learning. For example, teacher defiance, short attention spans, hyperactivity, and tantrumming behavior were attributed to the group as a whole. Other behaviors included physical and verbal abuse of peers, stealing, smoking, use of inhalants, negative-aggressive peer interactions, and obscene language. These student behaviors were very annoying to the referring classroom teachers. Although all students scored average or above on standardized intelligence tests, many had educational deficits in math and reading that ranged from one month to as many as four years below grade level.

— Ratings and Observations —

All student candidates for the demonstration classroom were screened using the ***Walker Problem Behavior Identification Checklist*** (Walker, 1983a) and preintervention observations of student behavior recorded for a two-week period in the regular classroom by professionally trained observers. These observers collected ten, six-minute observations, using a structured observation code, on each student in the regular classroom prior to assignment to the demonstration classroom.

Observers coded each student's behavior every 15 seconds for a six-minute period. One or more of the following student behaviors could be coded during each observation interval: being noisy, being aggressive, not attending, peer initiation (peer talks to, gestures toward, or tries to gain the student's attention), initiation to a peer, movement around the room, an inappropriate task, appropriate group behavior, working (on academic assignments), reciting, volunteering, teacher initiation (teacher calls on student, etc.), and initiation to the teacher.

Responses to these student behaviors and the responding agent (i.e., teacher, peer, or observer) were also recorded. There were eight categories for coding responses to the student's behavior. These categories were: no response, attention, praise, compliance, noncompliance, positive physical contact, negative physical contact, and disapproval.

This same observation procedure was used to record student behavior each day during intervention following assignment to the demonstration classroom. Each student was also followed up and observed on a biweekly basis in the regular classroom after reintegration. The observation data were used to evaluate the effects of intervention in the demonstration classroom and to determine how well the achieved intervention effects maintained following the student's return to the regular classroom. These data also provided information on the frequency of the student's interaction with peers, the consistency of the teacher's responses to the student's behaviors, and the frequency with which peers responded positively or negatively to the student's appropriate and inappropriate behavior. This information was also useful in planning individual intervention programs for each student.

The same overall intervention procedures were applied to the behavior of each group of students assigned to the demonstration classroom. However, it was sometimes necessary to design individual programs of a short-term nature to remediate behavior problems unique to a given student.

— Reliability of Observations —

Graduate students in education who were interested in working with students with behavioral disabilities served as observers in the demonstration classroom setting. Before beginning to record observation data, each new observer was given a copy of the observation form and an accompanying manual to read and master. Once the observation categories were memorized to the satisfaction of the observer, he/she was brought into the observation facilities adjoining the demonstration classroom to practice taking observations. The new observer trainee worked with an observer trainer during this trial period. When the new observer felt more comfortable with the coding skills, the trainer collected simultaneous records to check the reliability of the trainee's observations (i.e., inter-observer agreement).

Reliability was calculated by scoring each 15-second interval for agreement. For an agreement to be scored in any one interval, the observers were required to agree on the behavior code as well as the type of agent response that was applied to the student's behavior. The number of agreements was divided by the total number of observation intervals to obtain the percentage of agreement.

The criterion for successful observer training was a minimum of 90% agreement with the trainer over one hour of observations. Generally, the training process required one week of one-hour sessions per day. New observers typically spent two days practicing observations and three days checking reliability with the trainer. Weekly spot checks on reliability were made to maintain inter-observer agreement.

Eight-Week *ELP* Intervention Model

Each group of students was phased into the classroom in pairs during a one-week staging period. Two students each were brought in on Monday, Wednesday, and Friday. Each pair replaced two students from the previous group of students who were being reintegrated into their regular classrooms. This method of staging the entry of new students made it possible for the resident students to orient the incoming students to the demonstration classroom's rules and routines, and to serve as models for appropriate behavior. This procedure also allowed the teacher time to devote her attention more fully to the needs of individual students.

Orientation during each student's first day in the classroom included orientation to the physical aspects of the classroom as well as to the daily classroom procedures. Orientation to the demonstration classroom itself consisted of taking the student on a tour of the facility, including the observation room (discussing the one-way mirror), the timeout room, and the area containing items for which points could be exchanged.

Orientation to the classroom procedures consisted of a teacher-led group discussion of how points were earned and which maladaptive student behaviors resulted in the loss of points, timeout, or suspension. Also discussed were the classroom schedule for activities including recess, P.E., lunch, etc., and functional details concerning the use of daily assignment sheets and other special materials. Use of the display board, timers, and the workboxes was also explained at this time.

Week 1

The initial focus during Week 1 was on reinforcing attending, or on-task, behavior for each student although correctly completed academic work also earned points. Individual timers or workboxes were used to gradually increase each student's attending behavior. Points were given on pink sheets at each student's desk (see Figure 9.5).

Once a student could earn points regularly on a variable ten-minute interval schedule, he/she began to earn points on the electronic display board instead of on the point record form. "Getting on the board" was made an honor. Cost contingencies were kept to a minimum to make the demonstration classroom environment as rewarding as possible. The program for increasing attending behavior could be continued into the second week if necessary. After that each student was placed on the electronic display board, but could only earn half points.

On the electronic display board, the students could earn points for each piece or unit of academic work as it was completed. They earned one point for each page completed, and one additional point if the page was 100% accurate. A maximum of 25 points could be earned each day.

— Procedure for Exchanging Points —

Points could be exchanged at 1:00 P.M. each day for back-up reward items and free-time. There were six levels of point value for these items, ranging

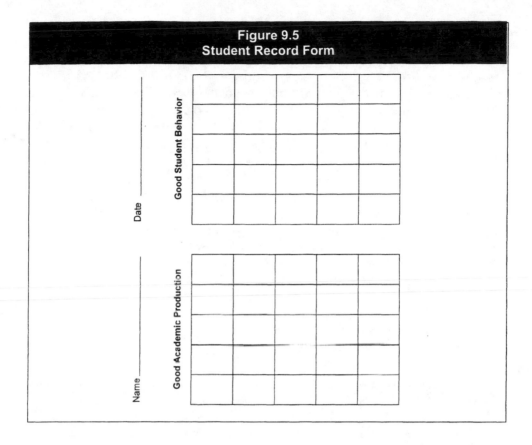

Figure 9.5
Student Record Form

from 25 points to 200 points, with occasional special items for 500 points. The values for these reinforcers were selected to approximate their purchase price (e.g., 25 points would be required for items costing 20¢ to 39¢; 50 points for items costing 40¢ to 65¢; and so forth). The minimum amount of time necessary to earn the least expensive item (i.e., that with the lowest point value) was approximately one day, assuming the students earned most of the available points for that day (i.e., 35 per student).

The students were free to exchange their points for an inexpensive item or privilege or to accumulate them for a more expensive reinforcer. There was rarely evidence of an inability by the students to delay gratification and accumulate points to purchase more expensive items. Academic productivity remained relatively constant regardless of whether the students were receiving an immediate exchange for back-up items or saving points. Points were awarded on the basis of concurrent schedules. That is, a student could receive points on both a variable interval schedule of reinforcement for academic engagement (i.e., attending) and on a fixed ratio schedule for academic production responses.

— Procedure for Increasing Attention —

The attending behavior of each group of students was increased before an intensive academic program was introduced. Attending behavior was defined as looking at the assigned page, working problems, and recording responses. Nonattending behavior was defined as those behaviors which were incompatible with task-oriented (i.e., attending) behavior. The following behaviors were defined as examples of nonattending: (1) looking away from the text/answer sheet by eye movements or head turning; (2) bringing an object into one's field of vision with head and eyes directed toward the text/answer sheet (i.e., other than the pencil, book, and answer sheet necessary for the task); and (3) making marks other than those necessary for the task (i.e., doodling). Using this criterion, most of the *ELP* students had baseline, preintervention attention spans of three minutes or less.

Using either the timers or workboxes, all the students were placed on a variable interval schedule for attending. Variable interval (VI) schedules ranging from three to ten minutes were given to the teacher on 3" x 5" cards in order to facilitate implementation of the variable interval schedule. Table 9.3 illustrates these schedules.

Table 9.3
Variable Interval (VI) Schedules for Levels of Attending in the *ELP* Classroom

VI 3	VI 4	VI 5	VI 6	VI 7	VI 8	VI 9	VI 10
5	7	8	9	7	11	7	11
2	8	9	8	9	12	6	8
1	1	6	6	5	10	8	7
4	6	7	4	6	7	13	10
3	4	5	3	4	5	10	14
6	2	4	7	10	8	11	13
2	3	3	10	11	6	12	9
4	5	2	5	8	9	9	12

In practice, a student's timer (or teacher-controlled, individual workbox) was initially set on an interval which he/she could easily accommodate. As a rule, the students were started on a VI-3 schedule. Some of the students were started on higher intervals. However, none began above a VI-5. Six students could not successfully complete a one-minute attending interval. Consequently, intervals ranging from 20-60 seconds were established for these students at the outset.

Points and social praise were adjusted to ensure that each student would continually try for higher levels of attending. The prestige of "getting on the display board" was also an important factor in shaping attending. As explained following, once on the display board, students were given points for attending on a Vl-10 schedule. For Weeks 3-5, the schedule was raised to Vl-20, and for Weeks 6-8, to Vl-30.

Week 2

During Week 2, most students received points on the display board. Points for academic work were awarded as earned and attending behavior was reinforced intermittently on variable interval schedules. The option to earn group points toward a group activity reward was begun as soon as all the students were on the display board.

Procedure for Operating Display Board —

Each student was required to be seated and ready to begin the assignment before his/her display board light was switched on by the teacher or teacher aide. When the light was on, it signified to the student that access to a schedule of reinforcement for appropriate behavior was being earned. When a student received a point, the display board light flashed (temporarily shorting out), there was an audible click, and the cumulative (+) counter recorded the event. If the student was behaving inappropriately, the stimulus light was turned off. If the inappropriate behavior resulted in a cost contingency or a response cost (i.e., the loss of points), the student was prompted to change his/her behavior. If the student did not change the behavior within a reasonable time period, one point was subtracted for every 60 seconds that the behavior persisted. Each student was made aware of this contingency in advance.

No student's points were ever deducted below zero. If a student failed to change the inappropriate behavior and lost all his/her accumulated points for that day, a brief timeout was used as a back-up consequence. If timeout failed to change the behavior in question, the student was suspended from the demonstration classroom for periods of up to several hours.

At the end of the day, plus and minus points (the total accumulated points) were calculated for each student. The teacher simultaneously transferred the points to a cumulative point sheet. Each day, the students began with zero points on the display board. In this way, each student was able to easily identify his/her daily achievement.

— Group Reinforcement Contingency —

Acting-out, disruptive behavior in the classroom setting is sometimes reinforced by approval and recognition from peers (e.g., by attention, giggles, comments, gestures). A group reinforcement procedure can influence this source of attention by making it more desirable for peers to engage in appropriate than inappropriate behavior.

Once all the students in the demonstration classroom were on the display board, the group reinforcement procedure was implemented on a daily basis. This procedure was in place for two 30-minute periods each day during academic assignments. During these periods, the teacher aide sat at the side of the room and controlled the timer while simultaneously observing the students' behavior. Initially, all the students had to be continuously engaged in study behavior for a five-minute period in order to earn one group point. This interval was increased to ten minutes after all the students were performing well at the five-minute level.

If the entire group was academically engaged (using the same criteria as for individuals) during the time specified, they received a group point and the timer was reset for another interval. If at any time during the interval one or more students were not engaged, the timer hands were turned back to the starting point and not restarted until all the students were reengaged academically. Group points were recorded on the display board as they were earned.

When the criterion number of points was reached, the group was taken on a field trip of their choice. The total number of points required to earn a trip varied among different student groups. The required number of points was adjusted according to the length of time all the students were on the display board. The number of points was determined so that each group had the opportunity to earn at least one trip.

The authors found the group reinforcement procedure to be an effective intervention technique. The procedure was useful for supplementing the individual reinforcement system in addition to providing training in co-operative behavior—a highly valued skill in LRE settings.

Weeks 3 to 5

All the students were generally "on the display board" by this time in the intervention cycle. Points for academic work were awarded as earned, and points for attending were given every 20 minutes if the rate of attending behavior had been at least 80% during that period.

— Recess and P.E. Procedures —

Up to the fifth week, P.E. and recess occurred in isolation from other classes while training in cooperation strategies was undertaken. When a great amount of aggressive behavior occurred in this setting, the group was placed on a timer and had to earn each successive five minutes of P.E./recess by demonstrating appropriate behavior during the previous five minutes. At the fifth week, P.E. and recess were taken with other classes; this allowed for further training in appropriate behavior under conditions more like those in the school settings to which the students would be returning.

Weeks 6 and 7

During the sixth week, in further preparation for the students' return to their regular classrooms, the maximum daily point total was reduced to 20 and points were awarded only three times per day. The students no longer received points for each piece of work completed, but rather received points for completing a whole category of assignments (e.g., math, reading, etc.). Reinforcement for attending behavior was given after variable intervals averaging 30 minutes. Social reinforcement (e.g., teacher praise, approval) continued to be given as frequently as earlier.

Week 8

During the eighth week, the maximum daily point total was reduced to 15 points, while social reinforcement was continued at the previous rate. The points were tabulated and put on the display board only at the end of the day. A checklist was used during the day to keep track of the student's earning of points.

Two students were returned to their regular classes on Monday, two on Wednesday, and two on Friday of the following week. The additional procedures implemented for maintaining the behavioral gains on return to the regular classes are detailed in Chapter 10.

Details of Mild Punishment Procedures

— Timeout —

Timeout was used to reduce such behaviors as talking out, being out-of-seat, throwing objects, and inappropriate verbal behavior (e.g., swearing, name calling). When any one of these forms of behavior occurred, the student spent a brief period of time (usually ten to 15 minutes) in the timeout room which adjoined the main classroom. During this time, the student was unable to receive points, attend to the class, or work on an assignment. The group reinforcement procedure, if operating, was immediately stopped when a student entered timeout and remained suspended until the student reentered the class. When the student had spent the designated time interval in the timeout room, a timer sounded and he/she returned to the classroom.

After the student reentered the classroom and began engaging in appropriate behavior, he/she was reinforced with praise and points by the teacher or teacher aide. This is an important point in ensuring the effectiveness of timeout as a technique. However, initially the demonstration classroom teacher would tend to ignore students for long periods of time following their return from timeout. This would occur even though the students may have been producing appropriate behavior for a long period of time! This practice greatly reduced the effectiveness of timeout in the demonstration classroom. As a result, the classroom supervisor managed the reentry of the students from timeout so as to maximize the chances that they would be reinforced as soon as possible for engaging in appropriate behavior.

The average number of times the timeout room was used per student in each intervention group was seven. This figure represents .88 times per week per student. Overall, timeout was an effective technique in reducing disruptive classroom behavior over the four-year period of the study. However, on the basis of some later work (Walker, Colvin, & Ramsey, 1995), the author would recommend a greater use of a cost contingency, or response cost, and less use of timeout whenever feasible. A cost contingency is easier to manage and appears to suffice in most cases. Timeout could then be reserved for only highly disruptive behavior.

— Suspension —

For highly disruptive behavior such as fighting, leaving the building without permission, foul language and gestures, teacher defiance, creating a disturbance during timeout, or accumulating three timeouts in one day, the student was suspended from school for the remainder of that day or for the following one, depending upon the time of day during which the incident occurred. Readmission to the demonstration classroom was dependent upon the student's successful completion of all regularly assigned academic tasks at home. In addition, all individual points were lost for that period, the group points could not be earned, and the student's parents were asked to limit recreational activities and television viewing while the student was absent from school.

Suspension was normally used one or two times per group during the first few weeks of intervention and then rarely used for the remainder of the intervention period. This technique proved to be quite effective in suppressing disruptive classroom behavior during the study.

Self-Recording of Problem Behaviors

Although a limited amount of self-recording was implemented during academic activities in the demonstration classroom, the procedure was used primarily with social behaviors unique to individual students (e.g., babbling or talking to self during class periods, head tics, compulsive forms of behavior, self-stimulation, and so forth). After trained observers recorded baseline data on each student's target behavior, a self-recording procedure was implemented in which the student counted each occurrence of the target behavior in question. The student also graphed his/her performance each day.

Before implementing the self-recording procedure, the target behavior was defined and a brief discussion was held with the student about the purpose of self-recording. If the behavior being recorded occurred at a high rate, self-recording was implemented for only select periods during the day; if there was a low rate of the behavior, self-recording was usually programmed for the entire day. For some students, the self-recording procedure dramatically reduced the frequency of the behavior, while for others there was only a minimal impact upon the behavior in question. If self-recording did not effectively change the frequency of the target behavior, a formal intervention procedure was designed and implemented. Generally, this involved a point system combined with use of the individual workbox. In the majority of cases, intervention was effective in reducing the behavior in question. Use of the workbox was then gradually faded out over time.

ELP Instructional Program

An individualized instructional program was designed for each student enrolled in the demonstration classroom in the basic skills areas. A combination of specialized and regular class materials was used in developing these programs. Instruction had a heavy remedial focus, and was based upon a diagnostic assessment of each student's academic skills.

Diagnostic Testing

Diagnostic assessment of reading and arithmetic skills was achieved through the administration of two tests: (1) the *Gates-McKillop Reading*

Diagnostic Tests, and (2) the *Stanford Diagnostic Arithmetic Test*. The Gates-McKillop tests were selected because they provide a functional assessment of a wide range of academic skills. They also include standardized indices of functioning in terms of grade level. The *Stanford Diagnostic Arithmetic Test* was selected because it was judged to be appropriate to the varied academic backgrounds of the referred *ELP* students. Level I of the arithmetic test was used most often, primarily because the referred students tended to be functioning well below grade level. To have begun with Level II would not have adequately sampled the students' range of performance. In those cases where Level II was warranted, it was given after Level I and by necessity, on an individual basis.

Alternate test forms were given before and after exposure to the *ELP* model intervention. These standardized indices of functioning made it possible to measure gains in achievement produced by the intervention program.

ELP Instructional Procedures

At the beginning of intervention, each student was assigned academic work that he/she could perform fairly independently, well below frustration level in most subject areas. As study skills were developed and the students became accustomed to the demonstration classroom routines (such as moving from one task to the next without waiting for teacher directives), the content of the instruction became more challenging.

When the students arrived at the demonstration classroom each day, they began following their daily assignment sheets. Each student's assignment sheet was prepared the afternoon of the previous day. Assignments were given on an individual basis according to the quality and kinds of work that had been completed to that point. The current day's work and assignment sheet were used as a reference for filling out the next day's assignment sheet.

The assignment sheet told the students, in a step-by-step fashion, the exact pieces of work they were to complete on that day. All the books and materials needed (except for extra credit options) were likewise placed, in order, on the right-hand corner of their desk, with the assignment sheet on top. As each assignment was completed, the student placed it on the left-hand side of the desk for teacher evaluation/marking and continued to the next piece of work. Papers were marked and returned as promptly as possible. Papers were required to be completed neatly and correctly before points would be given. The students were given feedback on their errors and were required to correct them before progressing to additional assignments.

Figure 9.6 illustrates how the assignment sheet was used in the demonstration classroom. The first major heading on the sheet was math; below that were the subheadings flashcards, worksheets, and math book. The student, upon looking at the sheet, would see that the first task for that day included flashcards (e.g., addition and multiplication). The student would then take the cards, practice them to mastery and place them on the left-hand corner of the desk to signify to the teacher that he/she was ready to be timed. If the teacher was free she would then walk over to the student and time him/her for one-half minute on each set of cards. The results would then be graphed on a bar graph kept on the student's desk. If the teacher was not available,

---

Figure 9.6
Sample Daily Assignment Sheet

Name ____Jack_____ Date __April 23_____

Math	Extra Credit (finish all other work first)
1. Flashcards: addition, multiplication	
2. Worksheets: #1, #2, #3, #4, #5	
3. Math book: p. 69	p. 21, #1-5
p. 308	
Reading	
Hegge, Kirk, & Kirk Drill: #13	1. Library book
	2. S.R.A. (Brown Power Builder)
	3. Following Directions A-B
Palo Alto: #10, pp. 5-10	4. Write a story about your favorite
Sullivan: #11, pp. 35-43	kind of animal
	p. 44
Spelling	
Study words: Write them twice	Put five of your words in sentences
Test	
Language	
Dr. Spello: pp. 29-31 (top)	p. 31 (bottom)
Ditto: #1	#2
Penmanship	
Pages: pp. 2-3	p. 4

---

the student would begin work on the next task until the teacher was available to time him/her.

The five worksheets consisted of four basic fact sheets—one addition, one subtraction, one multiplication, and one division—plus one extra worksheet addressing a special topic, such as place value. The basic fact sheets were used to increase the rate and accuracy of responding. The student was asked to fill in his/her name, date, and starting and ending times. An estimated time for completing the assignment was written in the upper left-hand corner by the teacher. The student's goal was to beat that time. Sometimes the wall clock was used for timing, and sometimes a timer would be set on the student's desk. Originally, a student could earn a bonus point for completion within the allocated time period. As points were gradually reduced over the intervention period, the student had to complete the assignment within the allowed time period in order to earn a completion point. If he/she did not, no point was awarded for the assignment.

When the worksheets were completed, the student usually was given an assignment from a math book, which involved copying and writing both problems and answers. At first, the teacher provided placement cues on the answer sheet, but these were gradually faded out.

After completing math, the student would begin the reading assignments, working through drills, assigned reading tasks, and workbook assignments, writing the answers on a separate piece of paper. The drill and the reader were always read silently first, then orally with the teacher to work on word attack skills and to check for comprehension. The workbook assignments were completed independently and corrected by the teacher. The student was usually given a one- or two-page optional assignment that permitted an extra point to be earned (i.e., extra credit).

Each student was given a new spelling list each day. Sometimes the words were selected from a regular spelling book, and sometimes from teacher-prepared lists. Each student was also tested on the words each day.

In language arts, each student was to complete the specified pages in a *Dr. Spello* book, as well as a teacher-made assignment sheet, perhaps consisting of homonyms, for example. The penmanship assignment was from a for-malized series and was to be completed on special paper which was pro-vided to the students.

Extra credit assignments were available for each student after completion of all regularly assigned academic work. When the student had finished all of the regularly assigned work, then he/she could look at the extra credit column of the daily assignment sheet and choose from the activities available. These options varied by student. If the student did not finish all the regular assignments during the class period, he/she was required to complete the work at home. Admittance to the classroom the following day was dependent upon completion of the assigned work.

Group work was introduced after the students were all attending well individually, usually in the third week of intervention. Group work was introduced primarily because much of the work in a regular classroom involves sitting and listening rather than active responding. This academic work involved teacher-led discussions about the academic work, group problem-solving activities in arithmetic, and participation in oral reading sessions.

The students were taught a standard method for seeking teacher assistance while working on assigned tasks. The student placed a red tag on the left side of the desk whenever assistance was required. With this procedure, even though a student's red tag was out, he/she was expected to keep working until the teacher was free to provide assistance. This meant that if a student was stuck on one assignment or a part of an assignment, he/she was supposed to move on to the next and come back to the trouble spot when the teacher was available with assistance.

The final evaluation of the academic program for each student was based mainly upon post-tests in reading and arithmetic. A fairly extensive final report, complete with academic and behavioral recommendations, was prepared for a final conference with each child's parent(s), regular teacher, and other school personnel from the referring school.

These *ELP* behavioral and academic intervention procedures detailed have very powerful effects in producing positive changes for acting-out students. Results of the *ELP* intervention model, across eight separate groups of acting-out students who were assigned for two to three months each to the demonstration classroom, are presented in the next section of this chapter.

ELP Results and Evaluation

The identical *ELP* model intervention was applied to eight groups of six acting-out students who were assigned to the demonstration classroom setting for two to three months each. Each student group provided an independent replication of the *ELP* model intervention. Four students were lost when their parents moved away while the students were enrolled in the demonstration classroom. This left 44 students in the *ELP* replication studies.

Changes in Appropriate Classroom Behavior

Collectively, the 44 students averaged 44.6% appropriate behavior during pre-intervention (baseline) observations recorded in their respective regular classrooms. During intervention in the demonstration classroom, the average percentage of appropriate behavior for the same students was 90%. Though highly significant, this change could not be attributed with absolute certainty to the *ELP* model intervention because of the absence of a comparable control group of students who did not receive the *ELP* intervention.

Table 9.4 presents the average percentage of appropriate behavior for each of the eight replication groups during baseline (regular classroom) and intervention (demonstration classroom) periods. In baseline, this figure varied from 35.0% to 51.8% across the eight groups. During intervention, this percentage ranged from 85.3% to 95.6% as reflected in the daily behavioral observations that were recorded on the students from behind the one-way glass.

Table 9.4
Percentage of Appropriate Behavior for
Eight Replications of the *ELP* Model Intervention

Replication Group	Mean		Range	
	Baseline (Regular Class)	Intervention (Demonstration Class)	Baseline (Regular Class)	Intervention (Demonstration Class)
1	40.0	86.1	34-43	79-91
2	47.5	87.8	36-66	85-93
3	51.8	89.8	43-67	86-92
4	48.0	93.4	25-75	88-97
5	39.8	85.3	25-66	80-88
6	35.0	95.6	20-61	92-97
7	48.8	92.4	25-65	89-93
8	44.0	93.5	32-54	89-99

Table 9.5 presents the average rate per minute for the 44 students on seven individual behavior categories during baseline and intervention. The seven behavior categories were: noisy, aggressive, nonattending, peer initiation, initiation to peer, movement, and inappropriate task. With the exception of nonattending, these behavior categories had relatively low baseline rates of occurrence. Even so, the *ELP* model intervention was clearly effective in

reducing their frequency. For example, the peer initiation and initiation to peer categories were reduced from rates of approximately five and six occurrences every ten minutes to rates of four occurrences every 1,000 minutes. Although changes in these two target behaviors were the most dramatic, the behavior categories of noisy, aggressive, nonattending, movement, and inappropriate task showed similar decreases in rate of occurrence.

Nonattending had the highest baseline rate of any of the seven inappropriate behaviors. During baseline, the nonattending rate was approximately 1.4 per minute; during intervention, the rate was reduced to approximately one per two minutes.

Table 9.5
Rate of Occurrence Changes in Individual Categories of Behavior Between Baseline and Intervention Periods for 44 Students

Behavior Category	Rate Per Minute	
	Baseline (Regular Class)	Intervention (Demonstration Class)
Noisy	.150	.003
Aggressive	.020	.001
Nonattending	1.390	.490
Peer Initiation	.570	.004
Initiation to Peer	.630	.004
Movement	.790	.060
Inappropriate Task	.130	.010

Two-Month Changes in Achievement

The pre- and post-achievement test measures (*Stanford Diagnostic Arithmetic Test* and *Gates-McKillop Reading Diagnostic Tests*) registered substantial increases in math and reading performance during the intervention period for students in each replication group. For example, the average grade equivalent score for all 44 children in math (see Table 9.6) was 3.4 on pretest and 4.4 on posttest. The range was from 1.5 to 5.2 on pretest and from 1.5 to 6.5 on posttest. The average increase in math achievement was statistically significant well beyond chance levels.

In reading achievement (see Table 9.7), the average increase was from 3.6 on pretest to 4.4 on posttest. Average achievement scores on pretest ranged

Table 9.6 Math Achievement Grade Levels for Eight Replications of the *ELP* Model Intervention					
Replication Group	**Mean**		**Gain**	**Range**	
	Pretest	**Posttest**		**Pretest**	**Posttest**
1	3.40	4.78	1.38	1.6 - 5.2	3.8 - 6.5
2	3.41	4.06	.65	1.9 - 4.5	2.5 - 4.7
3	3.74	4.48	.74	2.2 - 4.7	3.0 - 5.9
4	3.62	4.40	.78	3.1 - 4.3	3.1 - 5.4
5	2.91	3.46	.55	1.5 - 4.8	1.5 - 4.7
6	3.76	5.50	1.74	3.0 - 4.8	4.8 - 6.1
7	3.38	4.94	1.56	2.4 - 4.2	4.0 - 6.2
8	3.26	4.26	1.00	2.0 - 4.6	3.1 - 5.4

Table 9.7 Reading Achievement Grade Levels for Eight Replications of the *ELP* Model Intervention					
Replication Group	**Mean**		**Gain**	**Range**	
	Pretest	**Posttest**		**Pretest**	**Posttest**
1	4.15	5.78	1.63	1.7 - 7.4	2.6 - 7.8
2	4.33	5.76	1.43	1.9 - 7.5	3.4 - 8.6
3	3.46	4.00	.54	2.1 - 5.6	2.0 - 5.8
4	3.98	4.98	1.00	1.8 - 6.3	2.5 - 6.5
5	2.40	3.18	.78	1.6 - 3.3	2.2 - 4.5
6	3.70	4.12	.42	3.0 - 4.6	3.3 - 4.7
7	3.68	3.92	.24	3.0 - 4.3	3.3 - 4.7
8	3.16	3.91	.75	1.6 - 4.4	1.8 - 6.0

from 1.6 to 7.5, and on posttest from 1.8 to 8.6. The average increase in reading achievement was also statistically significant.

The mean gains of a year in math achievement and almost a year in reading achievement seem to far exceed the rate of gain one would expect in the regular classroom setting within a two- to three-month intervention period. However, as with the noted changes in appropriate behavior, these academic gains cannot be conclusively attributed to the *ELP* model intervention because of the absence of a control, comparison group.

Independent Replication of the *ELP* Model

In a well-designed, programmatic study, O'Connor, Stuck, and Wyne (1979) replicated the *ELP* model intervention in two elementary schools in North Carolina. Participating students were groups of second and third graders from a primary (K-3) elementary school serving an affluent area, and sixth graders from an intermediate (4-6) elementary school serving a poor area. The primary level school served mainly Anglo students and the intermediate level school primarily African American students.

A resource room was established in each school that closely resembled the *ELP* demonstration classroom setting. Three separate eight-week intervention phases were conducted in both schools that were close replications of the *ELP* model intervention. A total of eight to ten acting-out students attended the resource room daily from 8:30 A.M. until noon, and then returned to their regular classrooms for the remainder of the day. Each group was exposed to three phases: (1) baseline (regular classroom), (2) intervention (resource room), and (3) follow-up (regular classroom). A matched control group was selected to serve as a no-treatment comparison for each group assigned to the resource room. The control group students remained in their regular classrooms and did not receive the *ELP*-type model intervention. This study made it possible to attribute changes for the resource room group to the model intervention because of the use of control, comparison groups.

Overall, achieved effects in task engagement and academic achievement (in reading and math) were nearly identical for the second/third graders and the sixth graders. For the second/third grade resource room students, their average percentage of **task engagement** was 29%, 93%, 74%, and 76% respectively for baseline, intervention, three to four week follow-up, and seven to eight week follow-up. The percentages for the control, comparison students for baseline and the two follow-up phases were respectively 31%, 43%, and 44%. Nearly identical effects were achieved for the sixth grade students. The resource room students at this grade level averaged 31%, 94%, 79%, and 89% task engagement for these phases while the control, comparison students averaged 42%, 51%, and 50% for baseline and the two follow-up phases.

Similar powerful effects were achieved in **reading** and **math achievement** for the resource room students (see O'Connor et al., 1979). Control, comparison student achievement, as measured by identical standardized achievement tests, showed little to no change during these same periods.

This study powerfully replicated the earlier *ELP* intervention results as reported by the author and his colleagues. Collectively, these two investigations show that short-term exposure to a well-designed model intervention can produce very powerful effects in task engagement and academic achievement. Most acting-out students are capable of making such academic and behavioral changes if given the right supports and exposed to systematic intervention procedures of this type.

Conclusion

Children and youth who bring acting-out, disruptive behavior patterns to the schooling process continue to increase substantially in number. These students are often ill-equipped to meet the behavioral and academic demands that are an inherent part of the teaching-learning process. Such students place enormous burdens upon educators in terms of their needs for accommodation. At the same time, pressures continue to escalate to keep these students in LRE settings and to reintegrate as many as possible from alternative settings. Some observers have noted that these factors are contributing to an increase in the number of students with disruptive behavior disorders who are leaving school early. Such dropouts pose enormous risks and costs to themselves and society (Schorr, 1988).

The public schools, and educators within LRE settings, can and should be expected to provide reasonable accommodation of such students. However, the behavior patterns of many acting-out students are so disruptive, so aversive, and so difficult to manage that they cannot be maintained in regular settings without the investment of extraordinary efforts and resources. Given the increasing numbers of acting-out students, it becomes necessary to maintain a continuum of alternative placement options in which such students can be placed on a short-term basis and provided the intensive services and interventions they need to function effectively.

These placement options have not been known for the quality or impact of the interventions implemented within them. This may be partially a result of the primary goal of such placements, which was removal of acting-out students from regular classroom settings and maintenance within a more restrictive setting where such students are not seen and not heard. In this context, achieving substantial gains in social-behavioral and academic domains may be a relatively weak motivation for many educators.

As the procedures and results presented in this chapter demonstrate, educators have the knowledge and the means to implement **very** powerful interventions for acting-out students in both regular and specialized classroom placements. These procedures have the clear potential to teach acting-out students much more adaptive and socially effective behavior patterns that can contribute greatly to school success. However, educators must find the will and the means to implement these procedures effectively within the myriad competing forces and priorities that increasingly characterize the public schools.

Chapter Ten contains procedures and recommendations for facilitating the transfer of behavioral and academic gains, achieved in a resource room type setting, into a regular classroom setting following reintegration. The author and his colleagues have conducted extensive investigations into strategies for achieving this outcome. The results of this research and guidelines for addresssing this set of complex issues are described.

10

Transenvironmental Programming: Procedures for Reintegrating Acting-Out Students Into the Regular Classroom

Introduction

Students with disruptive behavior disorders are among the very first to be excluded from, or transferred out of, regular classroom settings—and they are among the last to be reintegrated back into such settings (Sarason & Doris, 1978). Historically, these students have been excluded from LRE settings because they present severe management and instructional challenges for their teachers and often disrupt the learning environment for other students. In many cases, the "costs" of maintaining such students in mainstream school settings have proven to be prohibitive in the judgment of teachers, administrators, and some parents. Further, educators are increasingly becoming wary of disruptive students who pose a potential threat to the physical safety of the students, teachers, and other school personnel. One target group who compose the focus of these concerns are those students who have been referred and certified eligible as **severely emotionally disturbed (SED)** under the current federal legislation, the Individuals with Disabilities Education Act (IDEA).

Currently, a significant proportion of students with severe emotional disorders, who are certified as having a disability, are served in specialized educational settings. The U.S. Office of Education (1994) reports that approximately 85% of these students are served primarily in settings other than the regular classroom. The average for all disabilities served in regular classroom settings under the auspices of IDEA is 35%. Further, the *National Transition Study* by Wagner (1989) indicates that approximately 66% of the certified SED student population has disruptive behavior disorders of an acting-out nature. This is likely a major factor in accounting for why so few of these students have primary assignments in regular classrooms.

This denial of access is indeed unfortunate since such students, while often manifesting low achievement levels, do not generally have cognitive limitations that would impair their ability to take full advantage of the curricular offerings and learning opportunities available in mainstream settings. Further, they have the worst educational outcomes (e.g., school dropout, failure to graduate, low grades) of any student disability group. However, their aversive social-behavioral characteristics, combined with the negative to hostile attitudes toward them held by many teachers and peers in LRE settings, provide huge and often intractable barriers to their ability to access LRE settings and to be successful within them.

At present, advocates for the admission of such students into LRE educational settings are conspicuous by their absence. Full inclusionists rarely mention or include acting-out, disruptive, or aggressive students in their advocacy efforts (see Kauffman, 1993; MacMillan, Gresham, & Forness, 1995). The most often heard refrain concerning appropriate placements for this student population involve words (a.k.a. euphemisms) like "alternative schools," "learning centers," or "opportunity schools." These placements are usually nothing more than segregated settings to which disruptive students are referred and placed. It is indeed ironic that the field of special education, in the midst of a furious and ongoing debate about the merits of full inclusion, seeks to reinvent itself, and its past practices, with respect to its treatment of SED students having disruptive behavior disorders.

Nowhere are the pressures to exclude, isolate, and punish such students greater than in the advocacy efforts and rhetoric of national professional organizations representing the interests of educators. Albert Shanker (1995) and the National School Boards Association (1993) have been particularly vocal about this issue. Many school reform efforts across the country have also "dealt disruptive students out of the educational deck" through their actions and policies. The author's spouse, a teacher in a suburban high school, has noted that these students are truly the schools' "homeless street people." They are society's unclaimed children and youth, and social systems such as schools understandably do not welcome or nurture them.

Yet one can make the case that these students have rights of access to an education in the same way that other students do—so long as they do not pose a danger to the physical safety and well-being of other students and their teachers. Further, whenever possible, these students should be afforded the socialization and learning opportunities that exist in the least restrictive of educational settings—the regular classroom. Instead, they are characteristically denied this access, socially stigmatized, and punished in a variety of ways by the school environment. Given these factors, combined with their generally low achievement, negative school histories, and sense of alienation, it is small wonder that so many of these students end up leaving school early. The school is viewed by them as a hostile setting to which they do not belong. Once this perception emerges, school dropout is a very likely outcome.

School dropout, in turn, is associated with a host of correlated, negative outcomes among at-risk student populations. For example, in the city of Los Angeles, it is estimated that nearly 90% of daytime burglaries are committed by truant youth and school dropouts (Bostic, 1994). Thus, while many educators work diligently to exclude these students from school, many are embarking on full-time criminal careers that will prove very damaging to the larger society. In the great majority of cases, competing effectively in the workforce is an unlikely result for school dropouts. Many of these students will be a burden to themselves and others for the remainder of their lives.

So why should educators consider retaining as many of these students as possible and providing them with appropriate access to LRE settings? Because it is in their individual interests, and that of the larger society, to do so. Three of the social toxins that are currently poisoning our society are: **too early parenthood, school failure and dropout**, and **adoption of a delinquent lifestyle** (see Schorr, 1988). These conditions are often interrelated, which tends to exacerbate their individual effects. Staying in school and taking advantage of the skill development and socialization processes it affords is one of the best means available for combating these problems. Further, the school setting provides one of the few opportunities to reach this at-risk population and to provide them with the coordinated supports and services they need in order to turn their lives around. Educators cannot afford to write off this substantial, and growing, segment of the student population. If this occurs, as the current climate suggests will happen, the long-term costs will be astronomical and beyond society's means to absorb.

Having stated this, it is important to reiterate that students with disruptive behavior disorders: (1) should not be excused from assuming ownership and responsibility for their aversive, maladaptive behavior patterns; (2) should expect to receive appropriate sanctions when they choose to engage in such forms of behavior; and (3) should not expect to access LRE educational settings unless they are willing to internalize and abide by the minimal behavioral expectations and social norms existing within them.

However, as Kauffman and Wong (1991) note in their superb review of the attributes needed by teachers of this population, more effective teachers attempt to instruct these students in adaptive behavior patterns rather than simply asserting their authority and control over them. This is an extremely important distinction and one that should be used as a point of departure for guiding educators' efforts in responding to these most challenging of students. That is, educators will be far better off if they invest in these students and attempt to help them learn how to behave appropriately rather than continuing to blame, label, punish, stigmatize, and exclude them from the school setting.

The focus of this chapter is on the use of **transenvironmental programming** as a vehicle for planning and supporting the reintegration of acting-out students into mainstream, regular educational settings. Transenvironmental programming is a set of procedures and guiding principles for preparing individuals to succeed in similar but different environments (Anderson-Inman, 1981; Anderson-Inman, Walker, & Purcell, 1984; Crossen, 1966). It is an especially effective approach for the reintegration of acting-out students into mainstream settings.

In the context of mainstreaming, transenvironmental programming is carefully referenced to the academic and social-behavioral expectations of regular, LRE settings. This approach focuses on identifying and teaching the critical academic skills and social-behavioral competencies that will contribute to adjustment success in these less restrictive educational environments. Transenvironmental programming, as used in the context of mainstreaming, has four major components, as follows:

1. Assessment of target, regular classroom environment(s) to identify the critically important social-behavioral and academic expectations of such settings, and to use this information in selecting a placement setting

2. Instruction and intervention in the more restrictive setting (i.e., self-contained or resource room) to teach the identified skills and competencies required in the target setting

3. Selection and use of transition techniques and support strategies for ensuring the transfer of newly acquired skills and competencies across settings

4. Monitoring and follow-up assistance provided in the target LRE setting to ensure maintenance and durability of effects over time

This approach is ideally suited for the mainstreaming and social integration of acting-out students since they often have weak academic skills and aversive behavior patterns that place them outside the zone of tolerance of many regular classroom teachers. That is, many teachers assign acting-out students very low teachability ratings and are reluctant to invest substantial time or effort for them. Thus, the obstacles that these students face in successfully negotiating a mainstream placement are considerable. Transenvironmental programming procedures are designed to provide acting-out students, and other at-risk students, with the instruction and assistance they need to overcome these obstacles and achieve satisfactory LRE adjustments.

This chapter addresses procedures and guidelines for promoting the transfer of social-behavioral competencies and academic skills of acting-out students who are moved from more to less restrictive settings. These procedures and general guidelines would be applicable for students entering mainstream, regular settings who come from a range of more restrictive placements including resource, self-contained, day treatment, and residential programs. Some best practice models for achieving this goal are briefly reviewed, followed by illustration of specific guidelines and procedures for addressing first social-behavioral and then academic skills and competencies.

Models for Transitioning Acting-Out Students Into LRE Settings

Three similar approaches have been developed for transitioning students from more into less restrictive educational settings. These are: (1) the *SBS (Social Behavioral Survival) Program* developed by Walker and his colleagues (see Anderson-Inman, Walker, & Purcell, 1984; Walker, 1984, 1986); (2) *Choices for Integration* developed by Kauffman and associates (see Wong, Kauffman, & Lloyd, 1991); and (3) *Responsible Reintegration* developed by Fuchs (see Fuchs, 1995; Fuchs, Fuchs, Fernstrom, & Hohn (1991). These three approaches represent best practice models for achieving successful integration into LRE settings, and each is based upon a behavioral-ecological framework in which person-environment fit, or match, is a key guiding principle (see Chapter 7).

Considerable research has been invested in the design and implementation of these three model approaches. The critical features of each approach are addressed in the remainder of this chapter in presenting a recommended generic model for transitioning acting-out students into LRE settings. This information is generally organized around seven essential steps, as identified by Fuchs (1995), that are involved in the transition and reintegration process. These are as follows:

1. **Identification**—Initial selection of the target student

2. **Match Making**—Finding the best class for the student

3. **Information Gathering**—Collecting information about the student and potential placement settings

4. **Planning**—Identifying problem areas for the student

5. **Intervention**—Preparing the student and the receiving classroom setting(s)

6. **Transition**—Making the change

7. **Mainstreaming**—Monitoring the intervention

If these key steps are addressed systematically in the transition and reintegration process, the chances for a successful outcome are greatly enhanced.

Preparing Acting-Out Students to Meet the Social-Behavioral Expectations of Regular Classroom Settings

During the decade of the eighties, the author and his colleagues conducted ten years of research on the task of mainstreaming students, having mild to moderately severe disabling conditions, into regular classroom settings. In addition, from 1966 to 1974, the author and his colleagues maintained an experimental, demonstration classroom setting for elementary age students with conduct disorders (see Walker, Hops, & Greenwood, 1984 and Chapter 9). Students were referred from local elementary schools for two to three months of intensive intervention in this setting and were then reintegrated back into the referring, regular classroom setting. As part of this effort, the author and his colleagues investigated a number of strategies and procedures for facilitating this transition and for promoting the transfer of academic and social-behavioral gains achieved in the experimental, demonstration classroom (see Walker & Buckley, 1972, 1974; Walker, Hops, & Johnson, 1975). Results and findings from this work, and similar work reported in the professional literature on this topic, are summarized following:

- It is extremely important to achieve the best match possible between a target student from the sending setting and the regular teacher in the receiving setting. If the target student deviates too far from the receiving teacher's minimum behavioral standards, or if the teacher feels the student poses an unacceptable instructional-management burden, then another LRE placement should probably be considered. Failing to take into account teacher choice in this matter can lead to deleterious consequences for the student and morale problems for the receiving teacher.

- If the acting-out student is placed in an LRE setting without adequate supports, assistance, and monitoring, he/she will likely not be successful and any academic or social-behavioral gains achieved as a result of prior placement in a more restrictive setting will be quickly lost.

- A carefully designed transition plan must be established that will: (1) prepare the teacher and peers in the receiving setting for the acting-out child's reintegration; (2) prepare the acting-out child to meet the minimal behavioral and academic demands of the receiving setting; and (3) provide for the long-term monitoring of the target student's performance following reintegration.

- Attempts should not be made to mainstream or reintegrate an acting-out student into an LRE settings until: (1) the student can demonstrate, at a minimum level of competence, the adaptive, social-behavioral skills that most teachers in LRE settings say are critically important to a satisfactory classroom adjustment; and (2) the student is within the normal range on the maladaptive, aversive forms of student behavior that most LRE teachers say are unacceptable.

  Table 10.1 provides a listing of the ten adaptive, social-behavioral competencies that most teachers say enhance classroom adjustment and the ten maladaptive forms of behavior that most say disrupt a satisfactory classroom adjustment. These lists were derived from a national survey of over 1,100 teachers as to their judgments regarding the forms of student behavior required for a satisfactory classroom adjustment.

- Teachers in LRE settings should not be expected to invest extraordinary amounts of time and energy in accommodating the acting-out student's skill deficits and behavioral excesses. Regular teachers have a limited amount of time and energy available per student. If the acting-out child makes unusual demands on the teacher, it may create resentment and further reduce the likelihood of successful integration. In addition, without support and assistance provided as the teacher requests it, the reintegration process will be even less likely to succeed.

Table 10.1 High Rated Items on the *SBS Inventory* for Regular Teachers	
Section I - Adaptive	**Section II - Maladaptive**
High Rated Items	
Child complies with teacher commands.	Child steals.
Child follws established classroom rules.	Child is self-abusive (e.g., biting, cutting, or bruising self, head banging, etc.).
Child produces work of acceptable quality given his/her skill level.	Child behaves inappropriately in class when corrected (e.g., shouts back, defies the teacher, etc.).
Child listens carefully to teacher instructions and directions for assignments.	Child is physically aggressive with others (e.g., hits, bites, chokes, holds).
Child expresses anger appropriately (i.e., reacts to situations without being violent or destructive).	Child makes lewd or obscene gestures.
Child can have "normal" conversations with peers without becoming hostile or angry.	Child engages in inappropriate sexual behavior (e.g., masturbates, exposes self, etc.).
Child behaves appropriately (e.g., walks quietly, follows playground rules, etc.) in nonclassroom settings (i.e., bathroom, hallways, lunchroom, playground, etc.)	Child refuses to obey teacher-imposed classroom rules.
Child avoids breaking classroom rule(s) even when encouraged by a peer.	Child damages others' property (e.g., academic materials, personal possessions, etc.).
Child does seatwork assignments as directed.	Child has tantrums.
Child makes his/her assistance needs known in an appropriate manner (e.g., asks to go to the bathroom, raises hand when finished with work, asks for help with work, lets teacher know when sick or hurt).	Child ignores teacher warnings or reprimands.

The body of knowledge that has accumulated from research on mainstreaming and social integration provides clues as to the types of teacher attributes that match up well with the behavioral characteristics and needs of students having atypical patterns of development. Wong, Kauffman, and Lloyd (1991) have reviewed this knowledge base and reported their conclusions as described following.

Table 10.2, from Wong et al. (1991), summarizes the teacher behaviors and attitudes that seem to characterize effective teachers of mainstreamed students. It is noteworthy how closely these attributes overlap with the profile of the generically effective teacher as described in the teacher effectiveness literature (Ysseldyke & Algozzine, 1992). Teachers who meet this profile are more likely to have classrooms that are positive, well-taught, and high achieving.

In addition, Wong et al. have identified five typical practices of teachers who are more likely to be effective with students having emotional and behavioral disorders. These are as follows:

1. High demands for students' academic performance and conduct

2. Careful design of activities to maintain high rates of correct responding and low rates of off-task behavior

3. Frequent praise of appropriate behavior

4. Little use of criticism or punishment

5. Teacher's self-confidence in helping students learn and behave appropriately

Effective teachers of students with emotional and behavior disorders are also able to handle considerable stress, are well-organized, and are able to forge positive relationships with difficult students. It is important to remember that such teachers are more likely to try to directly teach students with behavior disorders a more adaptive behavior pattern rather than merely seeking to establish their control and authority over them. These teachers are also more likely to assume responsibility for student learning rather than to avoid ownership of this outcome.

It is not an easy task to pre-identify teachers who fit this profile and then to persuade them to accept atypical students who are difficult to teach and manage. A procedure is described and illustrated in the next section of this chapter for guiding activities designed to realize these two important goals.

Table 10.2
Behaviors and Attitudes Characterizing Effective Teachers
of Mainstreamed Students*

1. Positive academic performance expectations for students

2. Frequent monitoring and checking of student work

3. Clarity (i.e., clear directions, standards, and expectations)

4. Flexibility/adapts as necessary (e.g., to modifications needed by certain students, schedule changes)

5. Fairness (i.e., a lack of favoritism)

6. Active involvement with students (i.e., remains actively involved with students as they work)

7. Responsiveness (i.e., pays attention to students' responses and comments)

8. Warmth (i.e., has a good relationship with students, is receptive to students' approaches)

9. Patience

10. Humor

11. Structure (i.e., uses highly structured lessons, is predictable)

12. Consistency (i.e., sets and maintains contingencies)

13. Firmness

14. Knowledge of different types of appropriate behavioral interventions

15. Positive attitude toward mainstreaming

16. Knowledge and/or willingness to learn about working with students with emotional/behavioral disorders (EBD), and exceptional children in general

17. Willingness to work with the special education teacher (e.g., sharing information regarding the student's progress, seeking assistance when needed, participating in meetings or conferences involving the student)

18. High perception of self-efficacy (i.e., perceives self as a competent teacher)

19. High sense of involvement (i.e., professional responsibility)

20. High job satisfaction

* Based on research described by Brophy and Good (1986), Englert (1984), and Walker et al. (1985).

Selecting an LRE Placement Setting

In small schools, there may be only one placement option per grade level for reintegrating students. However, in many schools, more than one option will exist. Wong, Kauffman, and Lloyd (1991) note that too often, in mainstreaming efforts, the match between the receiving teacher and the target student is left to chance and is guided by intuition rather than by a systematic, rational decision-making process. Achieving the best possible fit, or match, between the demands of the receiving setting and the characteristics of the target student is of paramount importance in the contexts of reintegration and mainstreaming. In one sense, the ideal reintegration process begins with and rests upon achieving the best possible match between the target student and the LRE teacher. If a good match is achieved at the outset, then the chances of a transition plan working effectively in support of reintegration are greatly enhanced. The **AIMS Assessment System** (Walker, 1986) was designed to facilitate this process, and is described following.

AIMS stands for Assessments for Integration into Mainstream Settings, and is an ecological assessment system for measuring the behavioral demands and expectations of less restrictive settings. *AIMS* is used for three primary purposes: (1) to select potential placement settings in the educational mainstream; (2) to produce information on the minimum behavioral requirements necessary for entry into and satisfactory adjustment within these settings; and (3) to assess the receiving teachers' technical assistance needs in accommodating challenging students integrated into their classes. A total of five instruments comprise the *AIMS Assessment System*; however, the focus herein will be on the **SBS Inventory of Social Behavior Standards and Expectations** by Walker and Rankin (1980).

The *SBS Inventory* is the key instrument used to conduct pre-assessments of potential LRE settings and contains 107 items—56 items describing adaptive forms of student behavior and 51 items describing maladaptive forms of student behavior. The short form of this instrument, containing 40 items total, is included in Appendix F. The *SBS Inventory* is used to pre-assess potential mainstream placement settings in terms of their behavioral demands and expectations in order to select a reintegration classroom and to negotiate the technical assistance necessary following reintegration.

The *SBS Inventory* consists of three sections. In Section I, teachers rate descriptions of **adaptive** student behavior in terms of whether they are **critical, desirable,** or **unimportant** to a successful adjustment in their classroom. In Section II, descriptions of **maladaptive** social behavior are rated along an acceptability dimension of **unacceptable, tolerated,** or **acceptable**. Definitions are provided in the rater's (i.e., teacher's) instructions for each of these three dimensions and points along them. Section III asks the teacher to re-rate the items from Section I marked critical and the items from section II marked unacceptable along a **technical assistance** dimension that indicates whether: (1) a student who is deficient on a critical rated item or is outside the normal range on an unacceptable rated item would have to be at normative levels on them prior to social integration into the receiving teacher's classroom; or (2) the student can be integrated with the deficit or behavioral excess with technical assistance provided following integration to address the deficit or excess; or (3) the student can be integrated with the deficit and/or excess and no technical assistance will be required.

Extensive research has been conducted on the *SBS Inventory*'s psychometric characteristics (see Hersh & Walker, 1983; Walker, 1986; Walker & Rankin, 1983). The *SBS Inventory* is a highly internally consistent instrument and has demonstrated acceptable test-retest stability over time. Teachers who receive higher scores on this instrument (i.e., they rate a larger number of items as critical and unacceptable) tend to fit the profile of the effective teacher (see Gersten, Walker, & Darch, 1988; Walker & Rankin, 1983). High scoring teachers on the *SBS Inventory* are more likely to be structured, demanding of student performance, and to assume responsibility for student learning.

Teachers show a great deal of consistency in terms of the specific forms of student behavior that they prefer and the forms of behavior they find unacceptable (see Table 10.1). However, they show considerable variability in the number of items they rate as critical and unacceptable. Table 10.3 provides a typical scoring profile of 50 regular teachers and 22 special education teachers at the elementary level. The profiles of these teachers are very typical of regular and special education teachers generally. As a rule, about 22% of the adaptive items are rated as critical, 71% are rated as desirable, and 7% or so are rated as unimportant. In contrast, regular teachers usually rate about 55% of the maladaptive items as unacceptable, 44% as tolerated, and 1% as acceptable. These figures apply to the average, or typical, teacher.

However, Table 10.4 shows the scoring profiles of six individual teachers, from the sample of 50 regular teachers, who scored differently from each other on the *SBS Inventory*. These teachers show radically different scoring profiles; their respective scoring patterns are generally found in any group of 25-30 teachers or more. In the author's opinion, regular teachers who receive extreme scores such as these on the *SBS Inventory* should be avoided in mainstream placement settings for at-risk students in general and especially for acting-out students.

Table 10.3
Patterns of Regular and Special Education Teachers'
Scoring on the *SBS Inventory*

SBS Inventory	Regular Elementary (Inservice) N = 50		Special Education Elementary N = 22	
	X̄	S.D.	X̄	S.D.
Section I				
Critical	12.78	13.12	9.13	12.62
Desirable	39.70	12.30	40.63	12.14
Unimportant	3.5	5.80	6.22	8.60
Section II				
Unacceptable	27.96	9.14	25.22	12.76
Tolerated	22.22	8.79	25.00	12.35
Acceptable	0.82	1.73	0.77	1.79

Potential mainstream placement teachers should be asked to complete the short form of the *SBS Inventory* (see Appendix F). The instrument is self-explanatory and is easily self-administered. This short form of the *SBS Inventory* takes

Table 10.4
Divergent Scoring Profiles of Regular Teachers on the *SBS Inventory*

Section I	Critical	Desirable	Unimportant
Teacher 1	0	36	20
Teacher 2	47	9	0
Teacher 3	15	40	1
Section II	**Unacceptable**	**Tolerated**	**Acceptable**
Teacher 4	51	0	0
Teacher 5	8	42	1
Teacher 6	28	22	1

less than 20 minutes to complete per teacher. Teachers should be assured that the information provided by the inventory is confidential and will be used only for purposes of selecting a placement setting and in accommodating the teacher's needs surrounding the reintegration process.

The number of items rated as critical and as unacceptable should be noted and tabulated for each teacher who completes the inventory. A target, mainstream placement setting should then be selected using the teacher scoring profiles in Tables 10.3 and 10.4 as a guide, as well as any available information on the attributes of effective teachers as listed in Table 10.2. Next, negotiations should proceed with the receiving teacher(s) around the conditions and nature of the reintegration process. It is also very important for the teacher to complete section III of the *SBS Inventory* on his/her technical assistance needs, as it provides a partial basis for conducting these negotiations.

Developing a Transition Plan to Support Reintegration

A transition plan, focused on social-behavioral adjustment, that is used to support the reintegration of acting-out students should have four key elements or components. These are: (1) procedures to prepare the receiving setting for the target student's reintegration; (2) procedures to prepare the target student to meet the minimal behavioral demands of the receiving setting; (3) procedures to manage and coordinate the actual transition process as the target student moves from the more to less restrictive setting; and (4) monitoring of the student's progress following reintegration. Each of these elements is described and illustrated following.

However, before considering these factors, the acting-out student and his parent(s) should be consulted regarding the change in placement. These individuals are the ultimate consumers of the reintegration process and they will be the most directly affected by the process. It may be that neither the student nor the student's parent(s) seek such a change in placement. If such is the case, then the issue should probably not be forced unless there are compelling reasons for doing so. For reintegration to have a chance of succeeding, it must have the support of all parties concerned—especially the acting-out student and his parent(s).

Procedures to Prepare the Receiving Setting for the Target Student's Reintegration

An interview should be scheduled with the receiving teacher to discuss and plan for the target student's reintegration. The primary goals of this interview are to: (1) thoroughly apprise the teacher of the target student's behavioral characteristics and what to expect in that regard; (2) to review the teacher's ratings of adaptive behaviors as critical and maladaptive behaviors as unacceptable; and (3) determine the technical assistance required by the teacher in accommodating the student and to negotiate this assistance.

The more information the receiving teacher has about the student's characteristic behavioral tendencies, the fewer the surprises and the better prepared the teacher will be to teach and manage the student. The following areas, at a minimum, should be reviewed as part of this discussion: social skills, impulse control, ability to handle anger and to avoid emotional outbursts, attention span, degree of peer acceptance, and ability to cooperate with others and to work in groups. Though not necessary, one could assign the target student a rating of 1-5 in each of these areas in which 1 is unacceptable, 3 is acceptable, and 5 is outstanding. This rating could best be accomplished by the teacher in the sending setting and/or by the teacher consultant in charge of the transition/reintegration process. These ratings could then be used to guide the discussion about what to expect from the student in each of these areas. It is also important to alert the receiving teacher as to any specific situations the acting-out student has difficulty handling or background factors that negatively influence his response to the demands of schooling.

It is extremely important to pay careful attention to the specific adaptive and maladaptive behaviors that the receiving teacher rates as critical and unacceptable, respectively. If the acting-out student is placed in a mainstream classroom where he deviates too far from the teacher's minimal standards for these behaviors, they are likely to become friction points that can erupt into teacher-student conflict. The student's status on each of these behaviors should be reviewed with the receiving teacher and a joint plan developed to address each one. For critical rated, adaptive behaviors, one could code the student's status as follows: (1) exhibits the behavior consistently; (2) the behavior is improving; or (3) the student lacks the appropriate behavior. Similarly, unacceptable rated maladaptive behaviors could be coded as: (1) does not exhibit the behavior; (2) exhibits the behavior, but is improving; or (3) frequently exhibits the behavior. This is a very useful way of communicating to the receiving teacher where the student is on a continuum, respectively, of skill acquisition versus reduction or elimination of the behavior.

Using the *SBS Inventory* short form previously completed by the receiving teacher, the need and type of technical assistance required for each behavior rated critical and unacceptable should be reviewed. There are three options for the receiving teacher to consider: (1) the target behavior must be satisfactorily dealt with prior to placement; (2) the target behavior can be dealt with after placement, but technical assistance and support will be required; or (3) the target behavior does not have to be dealt with by anyone other than the receiving teacher. Options one and two are most frequently chosen by receiving teachers; however, option three is selected by a surprisingly large number. Technical assistance negotiated and provided in this manner is highly specific and directly responds to the teacher's needs. Assistance and support of this type will be very positively received by most teachers in LRE settings.

Finally, it is a good idea for the mainstreaming consultant/coordinator to interview the receiving teacher about any general classroom rules. Many teachers develop and post a set of rules that communicate their behavioral expectations. Knowledge of these rules can be invaluable to the sending teacher in preparing the student for reintegration. The receiving teacher will also greatly appreciate the pre-teaching of these rules prior to reintegration.

Procedures to Prepare the Target Student to Meet the Minimal Behavioral Demands of the Receiving Setting

There are four key areas that must be addressed in preparing acting-out students to enter and be successful in LRE settings. These are: (1) adherence to the general rules of the receiving setting; (2) achievement of acceptable mastery on the specific critical and unacceptable rated student behaviors that the receiving teacher says must be dealt with prior to placement; (3) learning how to be cooperative with teachers and peers; and (4) development of friendship-making skills. (These four areas are discussed briefly following.)

It is also essential that a reintegration IEP (Individualized Education Plan) be developed in which timelines, specific plans, and expected outcomes are pinpointed (Fuchs et al., 1991). The IEP and its implications should be reviewed and approved by all parties to the transition process (i.e., the student's parent(s), receiving teacher, the student, sending teacher, reintegration consultant, and principal or school-wide assistance team representative, as appropriate). Further, the specific roles that the parents can play in supporting their child during transition and reintegration should be suggested and discussed. These could include providing encouragement, conducting daily debriefings, assisting with homework, and providing praise and home incentives for school performance.

As a first step in the preparation process, the target student, the sending teacher, and/or the reintegration consultant should review and rehearse the rules of the receiving setting. It is extremely important that the student understand both examples and nonexamples of each rule, be able to describe what the rule means, and to behaviorally demonstrate the rule. The target student should be informed that these are the rules that all students in the receiving setting are expected to follow—and that he/she is expected to follow them also.

The critical rated behaviors that must be dealt with prior to placement should be reviewed next. Each one should be defined for the student, role played as necessary, and incorporated into the behavior management plan for the student in the sending setting. This procedure should be repeated for the unacceptable rated behaviors as well. The student should know that the receiving teacher feels strongly about these behaviors and that his/her reception in the LRE setting will depend, in part, upon how well he/she displays and avoids them, respectively.

Acting-out students have a history of being uncooperative with others and generally share a reputation among teachers and peers to this effect. Teaching them cooperation skills is one of the very best things that a sending teacher can do to enhance an acting-out student's adjustment to the regular classroom as well as other school settings. The student should be taught a general definition or rule for being cooperative. Then, incidental teaching procedures, coaching, and/or incentive systems should be used to develop and strengthen the student's cooperation.

Finally, because acting-out students have such aversive behavior patterns, they often find themselves socially isolated from their peers. This leads to bonding with each other, which is not generally in the best interests of the acting-out students. They need to be able to affiliate with students who do not act out, who can provide good models and introduce them to other social networks and activities. Prior to the acting-out student being reintegrated, it is essential that he be systematically taught a set of friendship-making skills.

Table 10.5 contains a distillation of findings from the research literature on peer relations, social competence, and friendship-making skills in the context of mainstreaming (see Hollinger, 1987). Acting-out students, in the context of mainstreaming, would be particularly vulnerable to the actions in this listing that lead to peer rejection and weak in those actions that build friendships. The overall effects of these actions are to socially isolate acting-out students from their peers and deny access to appropriate social support groups. This, in turn, is often associated with rejection, and can contribute to the adoption of a delinquent lifestyle in adolescence. Thus, it is of the utmost importance that acting-out students receive exposure to systematic

---

Table 10.5
Social Skills and Competencies Required for Successful Peer Relations

- Dispensing and receiving positive reinforcements (i.e., praise, affection, compliments) to/from others
- Use of "low risk" tactics for entering ongoing peer group activities
  - Hovering
  - Waiting for invitations
  - Avoiding disagreements, talking about self, stating feelings, or asking informational questions of those involved in the activity
- Use of appropriate social initiations likely to be accepted by peers
  - Initiating during free time as opposed to scheduled work time
  - Being of assistance to others\
  - Volunteering
  - Avoiding demanding or coercive initiating responses
- Displaying high rates of positive social behavior toward peers
  - Providing helpful suggestions
  - Giving attention and approval
  - Being affectionate
  - Being supportive
- Thorough knowledge of how to make friends
- Good communication skills
  - Assuming perspective of interacting partner
- High levels of academic and/or athletic competence
- Specialized or unusual skills/attributes that are valued by peers
  - Making others laugh/having a sense of humor
- Low levels of task-inappropriate behavior
  - Avoiding getting in trouble with the teacher

---

instruction, coaching, and monitoring in friendship-making skills and strategies. Published social skills curricula programs are recommended for this purpose (see Alberg, Petry, & Eller, 1994). Most available social skills programs include a component addressing this topic.

Procedures to Manage and Coordinate the Transition Process

The guiding rule for managing the transition process for reintegration is to provide the acting-out student and receiving teacher with the right amount of assistance and support. This assistance/support should also be provided as nonintrusively as possible. The regimen governing student support should probably follow a daily schedule for the first week or so, and then be gradually reduced as the situation determines. At least weekly contact should be maintained with the receiving teacher, with regularly scheduled debriefing and planning sessions occurring on this weekly basis.

It is a good idea to consider developing a transition "How Did I Do?" card to provide feedback to the acting-out student and to clarify performance expectations between the student, receiving teacher, and other parties, as appropriate. A suggested format for the card is shown in Figure 10.1. Both student and receiving teacher forms of the card can be developed so that the student's self-ratings and those of the teacher can be compared.

This card should be used by the mainstreaming consultant/coordinator to conduct daily debriefings with the student early in the reintegration process. It can also be used as a communication device with the student's parent(s), providing the basis for home privileges for good performance at school.

Figure 10.1
Sample Student Form of "How Did I Do?" Card

How Did I Do?

Student Name_____Date_____Grade_____

1. Followed general classroom rules? Yes ____No ___ ? ___
   Comments:

2. Cooperated with others? Yes ____No ____ ? ___
   Comments:

3. Did his work well and on time? Yes ____No ____ ? ___
   Comments:

4. Tried his best? Yes ____No ____ ? ___
   Comments:

Teacher Signature _____

For acting-out students who experience substantial behavioral adjustment difficulties upon reintegration, one option is to implement the **CLASS Program** (see Chapter 9 for details). The process of implementing this program will provide a vehicle for building peer support and will assist greatly in teaching an acting-out student to meet the teacher's behavioral expectations. *CLASS* is a very powerful intervention program, and is somewhat intrusive in its early stages. It should only be used in a reintegration context if the student's behavior problems are relatively severe. A number of professionals have anecdotally reported using the *CLASS Program* as an effective reintegration tool.

Monitoring of the Student's Progress Following Reintegration

In the social-behavioral domain, it is important to informally monitor the student's progress in the following respects: (1) How does the student think things are going? (2) What are the parents' impressions? and (3) How does the receiving teacher view the student's overall performance and progress? Regular debriefings and contacts can be used to gather this information.

On a more systematic level, it is highly recommended that teacher ratings and inexpensive, structured observation procedures be used to monitor the student's progress. The receiving teacher should be asked to provide regular evaluations of the student's status on the critical rated adaptive behaviors and the unacceptable rated maladaptive behaviors from the short form of the *SBS Inventory*. This can be accomplished by assigning a three-point rating scale to each critical behavior and a similar three-point rating scale to each unacceptable behavior, as shown in Figure 10.2.

Regular teachers are able to make these judgments easily and accurately. Their use provides a sensitive barometer of how well the acting-out student is meeting the receiving teacher's behavioral expectations over time. As part of this evaluation, the receiving teacher should also be asked to indicate

---

Figure 10.2
Response Options for the Receiving Teacher

Format for Critical Rated Behaviors	Format for Unacceptable Rated Behaviors
___ Acceptably skilled	___ Nonexistent
___ Less than acceptably skilled	___ Within normal limits
___ Considerably less than acceptably skilled	___ Outside normal limits

---

problem areas or situations in which the acting-out student is experiencing difficulty and may need assistance.

From time to time (e.g., once weekly), the student's academic engaged time (AET) in the classroom should be monitored with a stopwatch. Stopwatch recordings are simple, easy to administer, and highly accurate. In the classroom, stopwatch recordings of AET should occur during a seatwork period in which independent work is assigned. Each session should be 15-20 minutes in length. When the acting-out student is academically engaged, he is working appropriately on an assigned task and paying attention to this task. The stopwatch should be allowed to run as long as the student is academically engaged and stopped when this is not the case. The stopwatch is turned off and on as appropriate throughout the observation period. When the session is over, the time on the stopwatch is divided by the length of the observation period and multiplied by 100 to obtain the AET percentage. The average level of AET in most regular classrooms is around 75-80%.

A similar procedure can be used to record the acting-out student's social behavior toward peers on the playground. The target behavior which should be observed is negative social behavior toward peers which can be physical, verbal, or gestural in form. That is, the stopwatch runs when the student is being negative and stopped whenever this is not the case. If the acting-out student spends more than 10% of his time on negative social behavior, he is considered to be outside the normal range and intervention may be necessary.

These types of evaluation activities are simple, relatively nonintrusive, and highly sensitive. It is strongly recommended that they be implemented on a regular basis following reintegration.

Preparing Acting-Out Students to Meet the Academic Expectations of Regular Classroom Settings

Research by Lloyd, Kauffman, Landrum, and Roe (1991) indicates that, across the board, regular teachers are much more likely to refer students for academic than social-behavioral reasons. Acting-out students have an added disadvantage in that they manifest a behavior pattern which is highly aversive to teachers and peers. Thus, their referral to more restrictive settings is often compounded by unacceptable performance in both areas.

In the reintegration process, it is extremely important to prepare acting-out students in both these domains before they reenter LRE settings.

The academic goals and instructional programming used in resource and self-contained settings ultimately should be carefully referenced to the task of improving performance in the regular classrooms (Anderson-Inman et al., 1984). However, Fuchs et al. (1991) offer some cogent reasons as to why academic skills often fail to transfer: (1) instruction in resource and self-contained settings is often different in content and format; (2) instructional materials are often unique; (3) student groupings are smaller; and (4) reinforcement frequencies for performance and teacher attention are both richer. As these authors note, while such differences are deliberate in that they are designed to accelerate skill acquisition, they may also account for why the skills fail to generalize.

This section of the chapter: (1) highlights strategies for promoting the transfer of academic skills acquired in resource or self-contained settings; (2) focuses on the need for teaching the acting-out student key study skills; (3) describes some support strategies than can be used to enhance the acting-out student's academic adjustment in the regular classroom; and (4) recommends methods for monitoring the student's academic progress following reintegration.

Strategies for Promoting the Transfer of Academic Gains From More to Less Restrictive Settings

A great deal can be done, prior to reintegration, to facilitate the transfer of academic skills and to prepare the student to function effectively in the regular classroom. A central theme of these efforts should be to match the two settings, as much as possible, in the period leading up to reintegration so that both the acting-out student and the receiving teacher know what to expect of each other.

Both Wong et al. (1991) and Fuchs (1995) have developed forms that can be used to provide an inventory of the academic demands, climate, and style of the receiving teacher. This information can be invaluable to the sending teacher in preparing the student for reintegration. The *Mainstream Classroom Observation Form,* developed by Wong et al. (1991), is divided into five areas that can be completed by the receiving teacher in consultation with the sending teacher or mainstreaming specialist. This form includes questions in the following areas: **use of classroom time; instruction; questioning/feedback/ student involvement; classroom management**; and **classroom climate**. A sample completed copy of this form is shown in Figure 10.3.

Fuchs (1995) has developed a more elaborate form that pre-assesses the instructional environment of the receiving setting as well as the nature and

Figure 10.3
Mainstream Classroom Observation Form

General Classroom Teacher: ___Mrs. Kelsey___   Date of Observation: _9/10_

I. Use of Classroom Time

1. Percentage of time spent on academic learning   _90_ %
2. Percentage of time spent on group work   _75_ %
3. Percentage of time spent on independent work   _25_ %
4. Average amount of time spent in transition from one activity to the next   _2_ (min)/sec
5. Average amount of time unassigned   _5_ (min)/sec
6. Teacher has systematic way of dealing with student wait-time   _✓_ Yes   ___ No

II. Instruction

1. Teacher gives clear and complete directions and instructions   _✓_ Yes ___ No
2. Teacher's lessons are highly structured and clearly presented   _✓_ Yes ___ No
3. Teacher's instruction is responsive to individual needs and the readiness levels of students   _✓_ Yes ___ No

III. Questioning/Feedback/Student Involvement

1. Teacher encourages students to take an active role in learning   _✓_ Yes ___ No
2. Teacher asks primarily low order questions   ___ Yes _✓_ No
3. Students are able to respond correctly to most of the teacher's questions   _✓_ Yes ___ No
4. Teacher gives frequent positive feedback to correct student responses   _✓_ Yes ___ No
5. Teacher gives sustaining feedback to incorrect student responses   ___ Yes _✓_ No
6. Teacher seldom uses criticism in responding to student answers   _✓_ Yes ___ No

IV. Classroom Management

1. Teacher articulates positive expectations for students' academic success   ___ Yes _✓_ No
2. Teacher monitors students' work during independent seatwork   _✓_ Yes ___ No
3. Teacher communicates clear standards and expectations for behavior   _✓_ Yes ___ No
4. Teacher consistently applies consequences for meeting standards and expectations   _✓_ Yes ___ No
5. Teacher keeps students engaged in lessons   _✓_ Yes ___ No
6. Teacher seldom has to intervene in behavioral problems   _✓_ Yes ___ No
7. Teacher seldom uses punitive interventions   _✓_ Yes ___ No
8. Teacher uses supportive interventions   _✓_ Yes ___ No
9. Teacher's interventions appear to be effective   _✓_ Yes ___ No

V. Classroom Climate

Teacher demonstrates the following characteristics (check if yes):

___ Flexibility   _✓_ Consistency   ___ Warmth   _✓_ Active Involvement With Students

_✓_ Fairness   _✓_ Responsiveness   ___ Humor

_✓_ Firmness   _✓_ Patience

content of instruction and the curriculum. This form also provides for direct comparisons between the sending and receiving setting on a host of specific instructional practices (e.g., the number of minutes allocated to different instructional activities, grouping practices, etc.). Figure 10.4 presents the questions and content found in Part I of Fuchs' instructional inventory.

The information obtained through these forms and developed informally through planning interviews with the receiving teacher should be used to help prepare the student to adapt to the instructional demands of the regular classroom. Further, this information can be used to address four performance areas that tend to disrupt or impair the academic adjustment of students who are mainstreamed. These areas are as follows: (1) adapting and placing the student into the receiving teacher's curriculum; (2) adapting the student to the receiving teacher's teaching style; (3) teaching the student formats the receiving teacher uses to elicit academic responses from students; and (4) teaching the student when and how to ask questions. Receiving teachers will **greatly** appreciate these efforts, and they will give acting-out students a far better chance of making a successful academic adjustment.

Teaching Study Skills Required in LRE Settings

Anderson-Inman et al. (1984) distinguish two types of study skills: **academic skills** and **academic support skills**. Academic skills are those that allow or enable progress in the curriculum (e.g., reading and math skills) and academic support skills are those that facilitate academic responses (e.g., seeking assistance, being organized, following directions, and working efficiently). Gleason, Colvin, and Archer (1991) define study skills as . . . "The systematic procedures that students initiate to complete such complex tasks as skimming, determining relevant information, taking notes, and studying material for a test" (p. 137). They note further that study skills can be used for the three major purposes of gaining information, responding to information, and organizing information. There is no more important topic to address in preparing students for success in LRE settings than the systematic teaching of study skills.

Archer and Gleason (1989) conducted a survey of 217 regular teachers regarding their perception of study skills. As part of the survey, they asked participating teachers to indicate how critical each study skill was to classroom success. Table 10.6 presents the ten most highly rated study skills across the 217 teachers. In addition, these teachers were asked to select the three study skills, from the list provided, that students in general were least able to perform. The four most frequently cited skills were as follows: (1) utilizes independent work time in class effectively; (2) listens during lectures/discussions; (3) reads and follows written directions independently; and (4) prepares for tests.

Figure 10.4
Classroom Inventory Part I — Instructional Environment

Teacher Name:_____ School:_____

1. How much student activity or movement do you tolerate? (Circle one number.)

             1   2   3   4   5

     a little   a lot

2. How much student talking do you permit?

             1   2   3   4   5

     a little   a lot

3. What motivational strategies do you use often? (Check one or more.)

   _____ Praise   _____ Posted work   _____ Other (Specify)

   _____ Tokens   _____ Reward system

4. What classroom management techniques do you use often? (Check one or more.)

   _____ Recognize good behavior   _____ Timeout   _____ Reward

   _____ Assign extra work   _____ Ignore   _____ Other (Specify.)

   _____ Verbal reprimand

5. When students experience academic difficulty, how do you provide help? (Check one or more.)

   _____ Individual instruction   _____ Small group instruction

   _____ Use peers   _____ Other (Specify.)

6. How do you typically give directions for assignments? (Check one.)

   _____ Oral   _____ Repeated

   _____ Written   _____ Other (Specify.)

   _____ Oral and written

7. What is your instructional approach in reading? (Check all that apply.)

   _____ Lecture   _____ Workbook activities

   _____ Class discussion   _____ Whole group

   _____ Drill   _____ Small group

8. How often do you require students to respond orally? (Circle one number.)

             1   2   3   4   5

     a little   a lot

9. Where are low functioning or difficult students seated? (Check one.)

   _____ Front of room   _____ Side of room   _____ Nowhere special

   _____ By teacher's desk   _____ Back of room   _____ Other (Specify.)

Table 10.6
Study and School Behaviors Required in Regular Classrooms

Study or School Behavior	Percentage Responding					
	Not Critical			Critical		Combined
	1	2	3	4	5	4 and 5
Asks for help when needed	0	1	5	33	60	93
Listens during lectures/ discussions	0	1	6	25	67	92
Attends class regularly	0	2	7	33	58	91
Comes to class with proper materials	0	2	8	27	63	90
Utilizes independent work time in class effectively	1	2	6	33	57	90
Is ready to work at beginning of class sessions	0	3	9	37	51	88
Turns work in on time	0	4	7	31	57	88
Socializes only at appropriate times	2	2	9	32	54	86
Prepares for tests	3	1	11	27	58	85
Reads and follows written directions independently	0	3	19	36	41	77

These results provide a roadmap for teaching acting-out students the study skills that are most frequently expected by LRE teachers. Each student to be mainstreamed should be assessed on these study skills by the sending teacher. Those on which a student is judged to be deficient should be systematically taught to whatever mastery level is achievable. Following reintegration, the receiving teacher should regularly evaluate the student's performance on these critically important skills. Gleason, Colvin, and Archer (1991) have contributed a set of rules to facilitate the generalization of previously taught study skills to other settings. These rules are:

1. Provide a rationale for use of the strategy.

2. Discuss when and where the strategy can be used.

3. Ensure that students achieve mastery of the new strategy.

4. Teach students effective self-monitoring or self-evaluation procedures.

5. Inform others of the newly taught strategy.

6. Tell students to use the strategy in other settings.

7. Ask students to verbalize their success with the strategy in other settings.

8. Discuss cues in other settings that signal use of the strategy.

9. Use role playing to practice transfer to other settings.

Details associated with these instructional rules are contained in Gleason et al. (1991).

Archer and Gleason (1989) have developed an excellent, and widely used, curricular program for systematically teaching study skills to students in general. This program, *Skills for School Success*, is highly recommended and would be of great benefit to acting-out students who are reintegrated. Ideally, a curriculum of this type should be taught well before reintegration occurs.

Support Strategies for Enhancing the Acting-Out Student's Academic Adjustment in the Regular Classroom

The acting-out student should know that the receiving teacher, sending teacher, the student's parents, and the reintegration specialist will actively support and assist his attempts to meet the academic demands of the regular classroom. The roles of all these individuals should be clarified in supporting the acting-out student's academic adjustment.

Peers are also a major resource in providing academic support to academically unskilled students. Two of the more effective and widely used interventions that involve peers in academic interventions are *Classwide Peer Tutoring* and *Cooperative Learning Strategies* (see Greenwood, Maheady, & Carta, 1991; Johnson, Johnson, Warring, & Maruyama, 1986; Slavin, 1984). Both of these approaches pair less skilled students with more skilled students in a variety of instructional arrangements designed to use the resources of the peer group as an aid in developing the academic competence of students who are at risk or have disabilities. Empirical evidence is strong that these two approaches are effective in realizing this important goal.

These two approaches are especially appropriate for acting-out students in two respects. First, such students often have serious academic deficits and tend to achieve well below their demonstrated ability levels. Second, and equally important, these instructional arrangements systematically expose acting-out students to other classmates within a learning context. This exposure can be very beneficial in laying the foundation for friendship making and the development of social support networks.

Methods for Monitoring the Academic Progress of Acting-Out Students Following Reintegration

Perhaps the two most important dimensions for judging students' academic progress are the quality of the completed work and whether assigned work was completed within the prescribed time limits. The first dimension is most directly assessed by teacher inspection and grading of the products of academic performance (Fuchs et al., 1991). The second dimension can be assessed with great sensitivity and accuracy through the use of curriculum based measurement (CBM) procedures (see Shapiro, 1989; Shinn, 1989 and Chapter 4). It is extremely important that both of these methods be used in monitoring and evaluating the academic performance of acting-out students after reintegration.

Conclusion

At a time when the already narrow tolerance of school systems for accommodating acting-out students grows ever slimmer, this book and this chapter argue that: (1) acting-out students should remain in school as long as possible, and (2) acting-out students should access LRE settings whenever possible. This position can be construed as swimming upstream against a strong current! However, the ever growing number of such students will make excluding them increasingly untenable.

It is likely that the school of the near future will be a site for the coordinated delivery of integrated academic and social services. Such schools will be much more friendly toward and accommodating of the broad range of at-risk students, including those with disruptive or aggressive behavior disorders. The emergence of such schools signals that ownership of the problems that children and youth are bringing to school is finally being shared by other sectors of the society. For too long, America's school systems have been unfairly asked to compensate for the deterioration of society's ability to socialize and nurture its children and youth.

As a society, we must find a way to reach at-risk children early, and to develop strategies for reclaiming those who lapse into a cycle of isolation, alienation, and rejection. We have the means to do so at our disposal.

Analysis of the First 100 Disciplinary Referrals for Fall Semester of the 1992-93 School Year

Referral #	Case	Sex	Office Referral	Action Taken
(1)	#1	F	Insubordination & Leaving class without permission	Saturday school assignment
(2)	Same	"	Fighting/assault	Suspension: 3 days
(3)	Same	"	Hall pass violation	Warning
(4)	#2	M	Off campus during school hours	Warning
(5)	#3	M	Off campus during school hours	Warning
(6)	#4	M	Insubordination & Unsatisfactory behavior	Saturday school assignment
(7)	#5	M	Unsatisfactory behavior	Warning
(8)	Same	"	Study hall violation	Saturday school assignment
(9)	#6	M	Insubordination	Warning
(10)	Same	"	Fighting/assault	Suspension: 3 days
(11)	Same	"	Study hall violation	Saturday school assignment
(12)	Same	"	Vandalism	Other response

Referral #	Case	Sex	Office Referral	Action Taken
(13)	#7	F	Unsatisfactory behavior (trespassing, noncompliance, smoking)	Warning
(14)	Same	"	Hall pass violation	Warning
(15)	Same	"	Off campus during school hours	Saturday school assignment
(16)	Same	"	Off campus during school hours	Saturday school assignment
(17)	#8	M	Insubordination & Unsatisfactory behavior (rudeness, disrespect, noncompliance)	Saturday school assignment
(18)	Same	"	Unsatisfactory behavior (noncompliance, class disruption)	Warning
(19)	#9	M	Insubordination & Unsatisfactory behavior (noncompliance, leaving class without permission)	Saturday school assignment
(20)	#10	M	Safety violation	After school work
(21)	#11	F	Hall pass violation	Saturday school assignment
(22)	Same	"	Off campus during school hours	Saturday school assignment
(23)	Same	"	Off campus during school hours	Saturday school assignment
(24)	Same	"	Off campus during school hours	Warning
(25)	#12	F	Saturday school violation	Suspension: 1 day
(26)	Same	"	Off campus during school hours	Saturday school assignment
(27)	Same	"	Off campus during school hours	Warning
(28)	Same	"	Tobacco use/possession	Warning

Referral #	Case	Sex	Office Referral	Action Taken
(29)	#13	M	Off campus during school hours	Warning
(30)	Same	"	Hazing/harrassment (promoting a fight after school)	Suspension: 2 days
(31)	#14	M	Off campus during school hours	Warning
(32)	Same	"	Hall pass violation	Warning
(33)	#15	M	Vandalism	Other response
(34)	Same	"	Hall pass violation	Warning
(35)	Same	"	Unsatisfactory behavior (insubordination, provocation, disrespect)	Saturday school assignment & Suspension: 1 day
(36)	Same	"	Insubordination (noncompliance, ignoring warning)	Saturday school assignment & Suspension: 1 day
(37)	#16	F	Off campus during school hours	Saturday school assignment & Suspension: 1 day
(38)	#17	F	Profanity/ obscene gesture	Saturday school assignment
(39)	#18	M	Tardy violation	Saturday school assignment
(40)	Same	"	Lying to staff & Off campus during school hours	Suspension: 1 day
(41)	#19	M	Off campus during school hours	Other response
(42)	Same	"	Off campus during school hours	Other response
(43)	Same	"	Off campus during school hours	Other response (credit denial in all classes)

Referral #	Case	Sex	Office Referral	Action Taken
(44)	#20	M	Saturday school violation	Suspension: #1 day
(45)	#21	M	Off campus during school hours	Saturday school assignment & Suspension: 1 day
(46)	Same	"	Off campus during school hours	Saturday school assignment & Suspension: 1 day
(47)	Same	"	Off campus during school hours	Saturday school assignment & Suspension: 1 day
(48)	Same	"	Off campus during school hours	Saturday school assignment & Suspension: 1 day
(49)	Same	"	Lying to staff, Off campus during school hours, & Tobacco use/possession	Saturday school assignment & Suspension: 1 day
(50)	Same	"	Tobacco use/possession	Other response (four sessions with the counselor)
(51)	#22	M	Insubordination & Unsatisfactory behavior (noncompliance, teacher defiance)	Warning
(52)	Same	"	Insubordination & Unsatisfactory behavior (noncompliance, talking out without permission)	Warning
(53)	Same	"	Safety violation (fire alarm)	Suspension: 1 day
(54)	#23	M	Profanity/obscene gesture	Saturday school assignment

Referral #	Case	Sex	Office Referral	Action Taken
(55)	#24	M	Off campus during school hours	Warning
(56)	#25	M	Off campus during school hours	Removal from class
(57)	Same	"	Off campus during school hours	Removal from class
(58)	Same	"	Off campus during school hours	Saturday school assignment
(59)	Same	"	Off campus during school hours	Warning
(60)	#26	F	Off campus during school hours	Warning
(61)	Same	"	Insubordination & Unsatisfactory behavior (rule violation, disruption, talking out)	Warning
(62)	Same	"	Insubordination (rule violation, profanity to staff, unsatisfactory behavior, failure to respond to a correction, escalating interaction)	Suspension: 2 days
(63)	#27	M	Unsatisfactory behavior (not dressing down for P.E.)	Saturday school assignment
(64)	#28	M	Off campus during school hours, Hall pass violation, & Unexcused absenses	Saturday school assignment
(65)	Same	"	Leaving class without permission	Saturday school assignment
(66)	Same	"	Insubordination (disruption in class, teacher defiance)	Other response (failing grade for semester)
(67)	Same	"	Off campus during school hours	Warning
(68)	Same	"	Insubordination	Saturday school assignment

Referral #	Case	Sex	Office Referral	Action Taken
(69)	Same	"	Hall pass violation, Leaving class without permission, Unsatisfactory behavior, & Safety violation	Removal from class
(70)	Same	"	Fighting/assault	Saturday school assignment
(71)	Same	"	Insubordination & Unsatisfactory behavior (loudly arguing)	Saturday school assignment
(72)	Same	"	Insubordination (rudeness)	Detention & Other response (contract)
(73)	Same	"	Vandalism	Other response (fine)
(74)	#27 again	M	Hall pass violation	Warning
(75)	Same	"	Hall pass violation	Warning
(76)	#28 again	M	Hall pass violation	Warning
(77)	#29	M	Safety violation (fire alarm) & Unsatisfactory behavior	Warning
(78)	#30	M	Unsatisfactory behavior (peer conflict, provocation)	Warning
(79)	#31	M	Fighting/assault	Suspension: 3 days
(80)	#32	M	Hall pass violation	Warning
(81)	#33	M	Hall pass violation, Off campus without permission, & Insubordination (radio on campus)	Suspension: 4 days
(82)	Same	"	Off campus during school hours	Suspension: 4 days
(83)	Same	"	Off campus during school hours	Suspension: 4 days
(84)	Same	"	Hall pass violation & Off campus during school hours	Suspension: 4 days

Referral #	Case	Sex	Office Referral	Action Taken
(85)	Same	"	Hall pass violation	Saturday school assignment
(86)	Same	"	Off campus during school hours	Saturday school assignment
(87)	Same	"	Leaving class without permission	Saturday school assignment
(88)	Same	"	Hall pass violation & Off campus during school hours	Saturday school assignment
(89)	Same	"	Hall pass violation	Warning
(90)	Same	"	Off campus during school hours	Saturday school assignment
(91)	Same	"	Off campus during school hours	Saturday school assignment
(92)	Same	"	Off campus during school hours	Warning
(93)	Same	"	Hazing/harassment	Suspension: 2 days
(94)	#34	M	Off campus during school hours	Warning
(95)	#35	F	Off campus during school hours	Warning
(96)	#36	M	Off campus during school hours	Suspension: 3 days
(97)	Same	"	Hall pass violation & Other action	Warning
(98)	Same	"	Off campus during school hours	Suspension: 3 days
(99)	Same	"	Off campus during school hours	Suspension: 3 days
(100)	Same	"	Off campus during school hours & Lying to staff	Suspension: 3 days

Interpreting Classroom Behavior

After the target child's behavior has been systematically observed and recorded, the teacher is faced with the tasks of interpreting the child's behavior and deriving meaning from the behavioral record. Interpretation of child behavior involves evaluating data that is representative of the child's typical performance and making decisions based upon such evaluations. In order to properly inspect child performance data, it should be graphed so that trends and changes in the child's behavior can be detected. The most commonly used graph for recording behavior is the frequency polygon. As a general rule, the behavior being recorded is plotted along the vertical axis of the graph, while observation sessions are plotted along the horizontal axis. Figure B.1 illustrates how a frequency polygon is used to graph out of seat behavior.

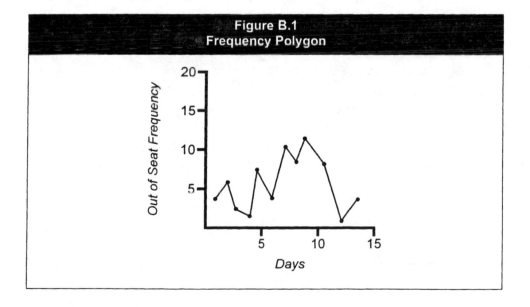

In Figure B.1, 12 days of data on the target behavior (out of seat) are graphed. Close inspection of these data provides considerable information about the child's behavior pattern. For example, during the 12 days in which the child's behavior was observed and recorded, the out of seat frequency ranged from approximately two (on Days 4 and 11) to approximately 12 (on Day 9). The frequency hovered around three or four for the first four days the behavior was observed and recorded. From Days 5 to 10, there was a gradual accelerating (increasing) trend in the out of seat frequency. However, during the last three days (10, 11, and 12), the behavior showed a decreasing trend with the frequency on Day 12 equaling that on Day 1.

More than one behavior or more than one child's performance can be plotted on the same graph to facilitate comparative evaluations. For example, if a teacher records the talk out rate for an acting-out child and his peers, and the teacher wishes to determine whether the acting-out child's rate is below, above, or the same as that of his classmates, then these data would be graphed as shown in Figure B.2.

The data, as shown in Figure B.2, indicate that the acting-out child's talk out rate was consistently higher than that of his peers. There was no overlap among the two rates during the ten-day recording period; that is, at no point was the acting-out child's rate as low as that of the average peer within the same classroom. In this case, the teacher would conclude that the acting-out child's rate of talk outs was clearly excessive and higher than the average rate of his peers. Based on this information, the teacher would probably decide that an intervention program is required to reduce the acting-out child's talk out rate to within normal limits.

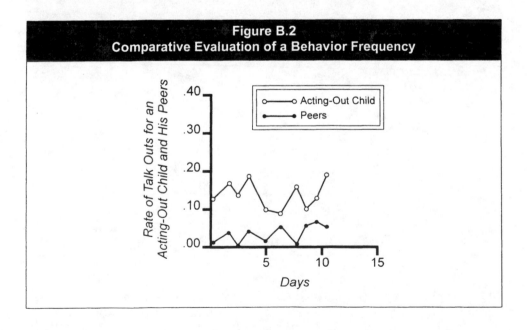

Figure B.2
Comparative Evaluation of a Behavior Frequency

Figure B.3 shows how three inappropriate classroom behaviors can be plotted for the same child on the same graph. Say, for example, the three behaviors in question are "talk outs," "out of seats," and "hits." The teacher observes these three behaviors simultaneously for a 15-minute period each day. The data are plotted in Figure B.3 concurrently for each of the three target behaviors. Figure B.3 yields some interesting information about the frequency of talk outs, out of seats, and hits, respectively, as well as about the relationships among them. For example, the frequency of hits is clearly lower than that of talk outs and out of seats. Hits show a slight and gradual accelerating trend until Day 10, and then do not occur for the last three days of the recording period.

The daily frequency for talk outs and out of seats is approximately the same. If the daily frequencies for these two behaviors were each averaged for the 13 days of recording, the overall means (or averages) would be approximately the same—around five to six per day. Careful inspection of the daily frequencies for talk outs and out of seats indicates that they tend to covary; that is, when one is high, the other is high and when one is low, the other is low. These two behaviors are essentially tied together and may be triggered or enhanced by the same classroom conditions. It is a common occurrence, for example, for acting-out children to also talk out while they are out of their seat. Either or both of these behaviors may be more likely to occur during individual seatwork periods than during teacher-led discussions.

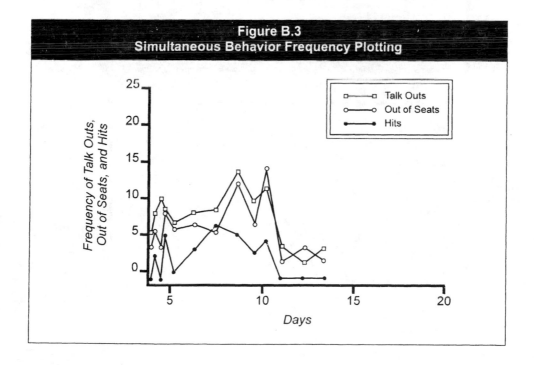

Figure B.3
Simultaneous Behavior Frequency Plotting

Further inspection of Figure B.3 indicates that the frequency of all three target behaviors is dramatically reduced on Days 11, 12, and 13. This could be due to simple random variation in the occurrence of these behaviors, or it could be a result of systematic changes in classroom conditions that control these behaviors' rates of occurrence. Continued simultaneous observation of these target behaviors and the careful noting of any associated changes in classroom conditions could provide clues as to the variables or events that control the rates of occurrence of these three behaviors.

Different behavioral measures (e.g., counts versus duration), can be recorded simultaneously and plotted on the same graph. For example, in observing and recording the social interactive behavior of a shy, withdrawn girl, the teacher may wish to count the number of interactions she has with her peers as well as to time their duration in seconds. These two measures can be plotted so that the relationship between frequency and duration can be inspected on a daily basis. Figure B.4 illustrates how this is done.

Figure B.4 allows one to inspect the relationship or covariation between the frequency and duration of social interactions. The frequency of social interactions is plotted along the left vertical axis while their average duration is plotted along the right vertical axis. The social interaction frequency data indicate that the target student averaged approximately two social interactions daily during the periods in which her behavior was observed and recorded. During these same time periods, her social interactions averaged

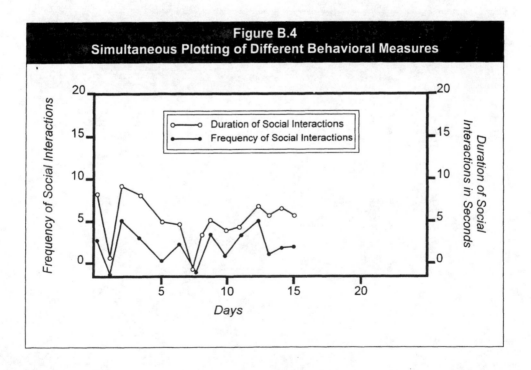

Figure B.4
Simultaneous Plotting of Different Behavioral Measures

approximately nine seconds each. Further inspection of the frequency and duration plots indicates that there was a tendency for the average length of social interactions to increase as the frequency of social interactions increased. In other words, they tended to covary.

Graphing data is also an extremely valuable tool for evaluating intervention programs designed to either accelerate appropriate behavior or to decelerate inappropriate behavior. When plotting data for this purpose, the graph is usually divided into phases. The number of phases used depends in part upon the purpose of the intervention program and upon the amount of energy, time, and resources the teacher is willing to invest in changing the child's behavior.

Most classroom intervention programs consist of two phases (i.e., a baseline, or preintervention phase, and an intervention phase). The baseline phase consists of data recorded on the child's behavior prior to the implementation of any intervention procedures. The intervention phase consists of data recorded on the child's behavior during implementation of the intervention program or procedures. Some classroom intervention efforts also include post-treatment and follow-up phases. The post-treatment phase contains data recorded after the program is over (generally immediately after), and the follow-up phase contains data recorded well after the post-treatment phase. Long-term follow-up is usually considered to be a year or more, while anything sooner than this is referred to as short-term follow-up.

As a rule, an immediate change is expected in behavior after the intervention program is implemented and the intervention phase begins. By plotting and inspecting the data on a daily basis, it is possible to determine to what extent the intervention is effective in changing the child's behavior. If the program is having no effect, then it can be changed or altered to increase its effectiveness. Only by recording data on the child's response to the intervention is the teacher in a position to evaluate precisely its effectiveness and to change it if necessary.

There are a number of criteria that can be used to judge the effectiveness of an intervention. The most commonly used criteria are: (1) changes in the absolute level of the behavior; (2) changes in the trend of the behavior over time (i.e., accelerating or decelerating); and (3) changes in the variability of the behavior. If, after being exposed to the intervention, an inappropriate behavior shows a decrease in level or an appropriate behavior shows an increase in level, the intervention is usually judged to be a success.

Sometimes there is no change in the level of the behavior immediately following introduction of the intervention procedure. However, there may be a gradual accelerating trend in the data which suggests that the effects of the intervention are not immediately apparent. Finally, there may be no change in either behavioral level or trend, but the variability (fluctuations) in the child's behavior may be reduced. In some situations, an intervention producing this effect would be judged a success, albeit a limited one.

Figure B.5 illustrates a change in the absolute level of a child's attending behavior from baseline to intervention. Inspection of these data clearly indicates the presence of a positive intervention effect. Further, this effect was evident as soon as the intervention program was introduced. During baseline, the child was observed engaged in attending behavior an average of 38% of the time (shown with the dotted line). During the intervention phase, this figure was approximately 83%. The was no overlap among the data points for the baseline and intervention phases. Based on these results, the teacher would conclude that: (1) the child's behavior had changed in the desired direction, and (2) the intervention program was a success.

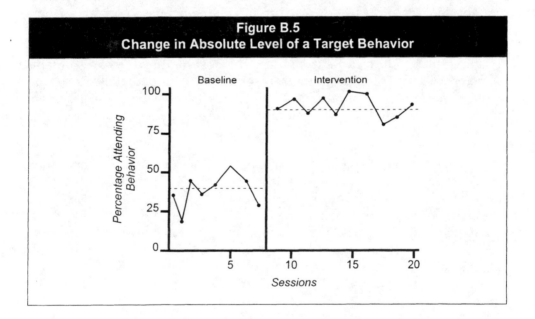

Figure B.5
Change in Absolute Level of a Target Behavior

Figure B.6 demonstrates a gradual accelerating trend in the proportion of time an acting-out child complies with teacher directives. The data points for the first four sessions of the intervention phase do not show an intervention effect. However, the intervention program's effect is very apparent during the next six data points. Gradual accelerating trends of this type are a fairly common occurrence in the educational setting. Because of the accelerating trend in the data, the intervention program in Figure B.6 would be judged a success in spite of the modest increase in the overall level of the behavior.

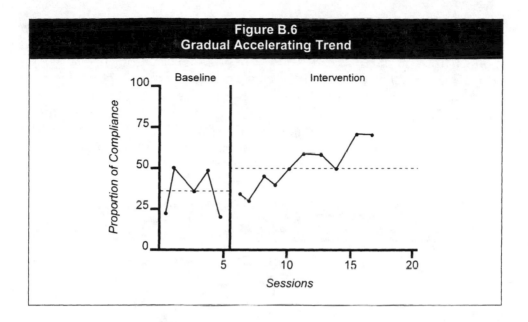

Figure B.6
Gradual Accelerating Trend

Figure B.7 presents data for an intervention program designed to reduce an acting-out child's frequency of asking irrelevant and unnecessary questions. It is obvious from the data plotted in Figure B.7 that the intervention program cannot be judged a success in terms of either an absolute change in behavioral level or in terms of an accelerating trend. However, there did appear to be a slight reduction in the daily variability of the behavior. It is often difficult to make a case for a successful intervention when results such as these are obtained. However, there are occasions when a reduction in variability can make the target behavior easier to manage.

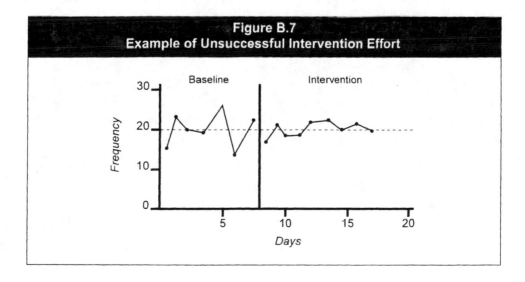

Figure B.7
Example of Unsuccessful Intervention Effort

Figure B.8 presents an acting-out child's rate of completing math facts correctly across four phases: baseline, intervention, post-treatment, and follow-up. The data indicate a low rate of correct math facts completion during the baseline phase. With the introduction of the intervention, there was a substantial increase in the child's correct rate, accompanied by a slight accelerating trend. After the intervention program was terminated (post-treatment), there was a gradual decelerating trend in the data. When the follow-up data were recorded some time later, there was a significant decrease in its level to near baseline levels.

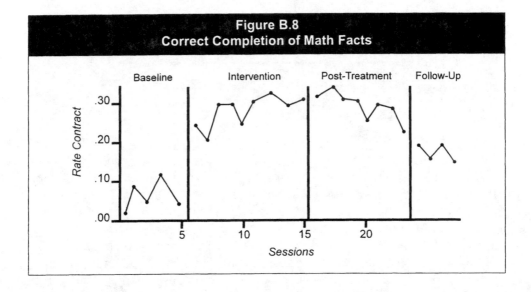

Figure B.8
Correct Completion of Math Facts

When intervention procedures are abruptly withdrawn, there is likely to be a decrease in the level of the behavior. There are cases in which a behavior that is increased with a specific intervention program continues to maintain at a high level following withdrawal of the intervention procedures. However, such a result seems to be the exception rather than the rule. There are a number of techniques that can be used to facilitate the persistence of intervention effects following termination of formal intervention procedures. The reader is urged to consult the professional literature for reference material on this extremely important topic.

The importance of systematically observing and recording child behavior in the classroom cannot be overemphasized. The information produced can be invaluable in the process of instructing and managing the classroom behavior of children in general. This is especially true of acting-out children.

Many teachers observe and record classroom behavior because they have been told that it is an important component of good teaching. However, such data are not always used in reaching decisions about a child's behavior. This is unfortunate, and represents a waste of energy, time, and resources. Unless such data are used in a meaningful way in decision making, it makes little sense to collect the data.

Teacher Rank Ordering Form for Classroom Dimensions

This form can be reproduced without permission and used to rank order students on a number of relevant classroom dimensions, including: academic achievement, at-risk status, popularity with peers, aggression, and so forth. The student who **best** exemplifies the dimension being ranked is assigned the rank of "1"; the student who **least** exemplifies the dimension is assigned the rank of "N" (e.g., 30 in this form). All remaining students are ordered on the dimension in between these two ranks according to how well they exemplify the dimension.

Rank Ordering

Dimension: _____

1. _____	16. _____
2. _____	17. _____
3. _____	18. _____
4. _____	19. _____
5. _____	20. _____
6. _____	21. _____
7. _____	22. _____
8. _____	23. _____
9. _____	24. _____
10. _____	25. _____
11. _____	26. _____
12. _____	27. _____
13. _____	28. _____
14. _____	29. _____
15. _____	30. _____

Sample Praise Statements for Classroom Teachers

1. "Andrew, your math paper was 100% correct."

2. "Your math is improving every day."

3. "It took you less time to finish the assignment today and you did two more problems."

4. "You're exactly right."

5. "Andrew is really paying attention."

6. "Andrew is sitting quietly and doing his work very nicely! Good job!"

7. "That's good thinking, Andrew!"

8. "Wow, look at Andrew study!"

9. "Everyone in here stop and look at Andrew. He's really working hard!"

10. "Good job!"

11. "I can really tell Andrew is thinking by what he just said. Good!"

12. "I really like the way Andrew is working on his spelling book; keep up the good work!"

13. "I really like the way Andrew has listened today. That's very polite, Andrew, thank you."

14. "Fantastic!"

15. "Excellent!"

16. "You're doing just great!"

17. "Far out!"

18. "You look nice today."

19. "Andrew is thoughtful."

20. "I really appreciate the way you sit quietly and listen to me when I'm giving a lesson Andrew."

21. "Thank you for your attention Andrew."

22. "Andrew just earned another point by sitting and listening to me when I was reading. Good job, Andrew!"

23. "Andrew's a hard worker today."

24. "Right on!"

25. "Right!"

26. "Good!"

27. "That's the best job I've seen you do."

28. "Nice!"

29. "It makes me very happy to see you working so hard."

30. "Andrew walked to his seat very quietly. Thank you, Andrew."

31. "When Andrew got up to get his materials, he returned to his desk and started right to work; good job!"

32. "I like the way Andrew raised his hand when he wanted to share something with the class."

33. "The whole class is really being polite in listening to one another."

34. "That was a courteous thing to do for Ann, Andrew."

35. "I'm glad you sharpened your pencil before class; now you're all set to go. Good!"

36. "Andrew has all of his supplies on his desk and is sitting quietly waiting for instructions. Good!"

37. "Andrew and his whole row are sitting with their materials ready."

38. "It's been a long time since I had to take any objects away from the people in this class. You really know how to show that you're responsible people."

39. "Andrew really knows how to follow instructions."

Example Rewards List

I.   SCHOOL REWARDS

   A. Activities

      1. Presenting at "Show and Tell"

      2. Helping the teacher

      3. Being in a play

      4. Playing "teacher"

      5. Singing in class

      6. Reading with a friend

      7. Holding the flag

      8. Being "captain"

      9. Reading a new book

     10. Cleaning the chalkboard

     11. Playing a game with a friend

     12. Drawing on the chalkboard

     13. Teacher "surprise" (teacher-selected reward; can be gender-specific)

     14. Stamping papers for the teacher

     15. Chance to change seat assignment on the bus

     16. Teacher "surprise" for the whole class

     17. Poster to take home

18. Eating in the room with the teacher

19. All boys (or girls) in the class eating in the room with the teacher

20. Whole class eating in the room with the teacher

21. Eating in the room with a friend

22. Five minutes of free time

23. Working the film projector

24. Being the scorekeeper for "Spelling Baseball"

25. Surprise for teacher

26. Playing a game during P.E.

27. Five minutes of extra recess

28. Five minutes early dismissal

29. Special story or an extra story time

30. Special record or film strip

31. Reading froma joke/riddle book

32. Free time for the class

33. Special art activity

34. Use of special equipment during P.E.

35. Access to computer games alone or with a friend

B. Use of Special Materials (Usually for a Prespecified Length of Time)

1. Language Master

2. Book to look at or read

3. Viewmaster

4. Game with a friend

5. Tape recorder

6. Records/tapes and record/tape player

7. Typewriter

8. Art materials

9. Bringing own game or records/tapes

C. Time With a Special Person (Teacher, Aide, Counselor, etc.)

   1. To hear or read a story

   2. To play a game

   3. To talk

D. Time in a Special Place

   1. In the library

   2. In the art room

   3. In the office helping the secretary

E. Special Classroom Duties

   1. Messenger

   2. Team leader

   3. Attendance taker

   4. Scorekeeper

F. Classroom Games

   1. Seven-Up

   2. Musical Chairs

   3. Simon Says

   4. 'Round the World

   5. Hot/Cold

6. Fruitbasket Upset

7. Twenty Questions

8. Eraser Game

9. Black Magic

10. "It is I"

11. Blanket Cover-Up

12. Activity Pantomime

II. OUTSIDE SCHOOL REWARDS

1. Field trip

2. Taking a class pet home

3. Trip to a fair

4. Tutoring younger children

5. Class picnic

6. Swimming trip

7. Trip to a museum

8. Trip to the zoo

III. HOME REWARDS

1. Extra television time

2. Staying up later than usual

3. Extra play time

4. Having a friend sleep over

5. Having a special dish prepared for dinner

6. Family picnic

7. Going to a movie

8. Being excused from daily chores/tasks

9. Increased allowance

10. Earning special toys or equipment

11. Participating in special events with parents (e.g., shopping or going fishing)

Short Form of the *SBS Inventory*

General Instructions

This inventory, reprinted with permission and reproducible, consists of two sets of items descriptive of **pupil behavior** in the classroom setting and a checklist about handicapped pupils' behaviors. The first set of items (Section I) describes pupil social behavior competencies and skills that are considered appropriate to the classroom setting. The second set (Section II) describes pupil behavior that is considered maladaptive, inappropriate, disruptive in the classroom setting. The third section requires you to review the previous items and indicate the ones for which you would want assistance in working with a handicapped pupil. A fourth section asks that you simply check behaviors that would make you resist placement of a handicapped pupil in your classroom. As a classroom teacher, please make **one of three** rating judgments about each item in Sections I and II of the inventory and then complete Sections III and IV.

Section I: Descriptions of Adaptive, Appropriate Pupil Behavior(s)

Instructions

For the items in this section, please indicate whether the behavior described is (a) **critical**, (b) **desirable**, or (c) **unimportant** to a successful adjustment in your classroom by placing a check in the appropriate parentheses. The line to the left of each item will be used later.

Critical—means that possession of the behavior is absolutely essential to successful or satisfactory adjustment in your classroom.

Desirable—means that possession of the behavior is not essential or critical to a satisfactory classroom adjustment but is encouraged.

Unimportant—means that you perceive the behavior as not being necessary or required for a satisfactory adjustment in your classroom.

In the brackets, please mark C for Critical, D for Desirable, or U for Unimportant.

_____ 1. Pupil seeks teacher attention at appropriate times. [C] [D] [U]

_____ 2. Pupil makes her or his assistance needs known in [C] [D] [U]
an appropriate manner, e.g., asks to use the
restroom, raises hand when finished with work,
asks for help with work, lets teacher know when
sick or hurt.

_____ 3. Pupil listens carefully to teacher instructions and [C] [D] [U]
directions for assignments.

_____ 4. Pupil complies with teacher commands. [C] [D] [U]

_____ 5. Pupil improves academic or social behavior in [C] [D] [U]
response to teacher feedback.

_____ 6. Pupil produces work of acceptable quality, given [C] [D] [U]
her or his skill level.

_____ 7. Pupil cooperates with peers in group activities [C] [D] [U]
or situations.

_____ 8. Pupil compliments peers regarding some attributes or behavior. [C] [D] [U]

_____ 9. Pupil has independent study skills, i.e., can work adequately with minimal teacher support, attempts to solve a problem with school work before asking for help. [C] [D] [U]

_____ 10. Pupil copes with failure in an appropriate manner, e.g., doesn't give up on assignments or projects. [C] [D] [U]

_____ 11. Pupil behaves appropriately in nonclassroom settings (restroom, hallway, lunchroom, playground), e.g., walks quietly, follows playground rules, etc. [C] [D] [U]

_____ 12. Pupil resolves peer conflicts or problems adequately on her or his own without requesting teacher assistance. [C] [D] [U]

_____ 13. Pupil can accept not getting his or her own way. [C] [D] [U]

_____ 14. Pupil ignores the distractions or interruptions of other students during academic activities. [C] [D] [U]

_____ 15. Pupil can participate in and contribute to group instructional situations or activities. [C] [D] [U]

_____ 16. Pupil has good work habits, e.g., makes efficient use of class time, is organized, stays on task, etc. [C] [D] [U]

_____ 17. Pupil makes productive use of time while waiting for teacher assistance, e.g., continues to work on problems that do not prove difficult. [C] [D] [U]

_____ 18. Pupil completes tasks within prescribed time limits. [C] [D] [U]

_____ 19. Pupil expresses anger appropriately, e.g., reacts to situations without being violent or destructive. [C] [D] [U]

_____ 20. Pupil does seatwork assignments as directed. [C] [D] [U]

Section II: Descriptions of Maladaptive, Inappropriate Pupil Behavior(s)

Instructions

For the items in this section, please indicate whether the behavior described is (a) **unacceptable**, (b) **tolerated** or (c) **acceptable** in your classroom.

Unacceptable—means that you would not tolerate the behavior occurring in your classroom. Should an instance of the behavior occur, you would initiate active methods to (a) suppress or eliminate it and (b) prevent its future occurrence.

Tolerated—means that while you will "put up" with the behavior in question (at least temporarily) you would prefer to see it reduced in frequency or replaced by an appropriate, incompatible behavior.

Acceptable—means that the behavior presents no problems for you and you would not initiate procedures to decrease or eliminate it.

In the brackets, please mark U for Unacceptable, T for Tolerated, or A for Acceptable.

_____	1. Pupil is easily distracted from the task or activity at hand.	[U]	[T]	[A]
_____	2. Pupil has tantrums.	[U]	[T]	[A]
_____	3. Pupil lies.	[U]	[T]	[A]
_____	4. Pupil ignores teacher warnings or reprimands.	[U]	[T]	[A]
_____	5. Pupil cheats, e.g., copies work from others.	[U]	[T]	[A]
_____	6. Pupil becomes visibly upset or angry when things do not go her or his way.	[U]	[T]	[A]
_____	7. Pupil damages others' property, e.g., academic materials, personal possessions, etc.	[U]	[T]	[A]
_____	8. Pupil asks irrelevant questions, i.e., questions serve no functional purpose and are not task related.	[U]	[T]	[A]
_____	9. Pupil reacts with defiance to instructions or commands.	[U]	[T]	[A]

_____ 10. Pupil steals.   [U]   [T]   [A]

_____ 11. Pupil does not follow specified rules of games or class activities.   [U]   [T]   [A]

_____ 12. Pupil obeys only when threatened with punishment.   [U]   [T]   [A]

_____ 13. Pupil argues and must have the last word in verbal exchanges with peers or teacher.   [U]   [T]   [A]

_____ 14. Pupil appears to be unmotivated, e.g., not interested in school work.   [U]   [T]   [A]

_____ 15. Pupil displays high levels of dependence, e.g., needs excessive amounts of assistance, feedback, or supervision to complete simple tasks.   [U]   [T]   [A]

_____ 16. Pupil does not respond when called upon.   [U]   [T]   [A]

_____ 17. Pupil creates a disturbance during class activities, e.g., is excessively noisy, bothers other students, is out of seat, etc.   [U]   [T]   [A]

_____ 18. Pupil interrupts the teacher when the teacher is engaged in a presentation or activity.   [U]   [T]   [A]

_____ 19. Pupil engages in inappropriate sexual behavior, e.g., masturbates, exposes self, etc..   [U]   [T]   [A]

_____ 20. Pupil does not follow or give in to necessary rules of games and class activities.   [U]   [T]   [A]

                                          Appendix F

Section III: Technical Assistance Needs

Instructions

The purpose of this section of the SBS Inventory is to identify your technical assistance needs in teaching and managing handicapped children who, at some future point, could be integrated into your classroom. These children are likely to be deficient in some of the skills or competencies described in Section I and outside the normal range on some of the maladaptive social behaviors described in Section II.

Please make one of three judgments for each item in Section I that you rated as **critical** and for each item in Section II that you rated as **unacceptable**. On the line to the left of each item you marked as Critical [C] in Section I, write A, B, or C to indicate whether:

(A) You would insist that the pupil have mastered the skill or competency **prior** to entry into your class or,

(B) Following entry, you would accept responsibility for developing the skill or competency, but you would expect technical assistance in the process of doing so, or

(C) Following entry, you would accept responsibility for developing the skill or competency and would **not** require technical assistance.

Similarly, for each item you marked as Unacceptable [U] in Section II, write A, B, or C to indicate whether:

(A) The pupil must be within normal limits on the social behavior in question **prior** to entry into your class, or

(B) Following entry, you would take responsibility for moving the pupil within normal limits on the social behavior, but only with technical assistance provided, or

(C) Following entry, you would take responsibility for moving the pupil within normal limits on the social behavior and would **not** require technical assistance.

When you have reviewed the items in Sections I and II and marked them appropriately, please go on to the last section.

Section IV: Correlates

Instructions

Handicapped students often display many of the characteristics and conditions listed below. Please place a check by any items below which would cause you to resist placement of a handicapped student in your class.

[ ]   1. Pupil drools.

[ ]   2. Pupil is hyperactive.

[ ]   3. Pupil is incontinent, i.e., has inadequate bowel control.

[ ]   4. Pupil is eneuretic, i.e., has inadequate bladder control.

[ ]   5. Pupil has deficient self-help skills, e.g., dressing, feeding, toileting.

[ ]   6. Pupil has mobility problems requiring braces, crutches, or a wheelchair.

[ ]   7. Pupil requires specialized or adapted instructional materials to progress academically.

[ ]   8. Pupil requires large amounts of individualized instruction to progress academically.

[ ]   9. Pupil has severely disfluent speech or impaired language.

[ ]   10. Pupil is at times uncontrollably aggressive.

[ ]   11. Pupil cannot write.

[ ]   12. Pupil requires continuous medical monitoring, e.g., has diabetes, heart problems, hemophilia.

[ ]   13. Pupil derives little benefit from large group instruction.

[ ]   14. Pupil has personal hygiene problems.

[ ]   15. Pupil has a very slow rate of academic progress compared to nonhandicapped students.

[ ]   16. Pupil has nervous tics.

[ ]   17. Pupil attempts to take advantage of handicap by using it to avoid certain tasks or activities.

[ ]   18. Pupil cannot always recognize situations involving danger to herself or himself.

[ ] 19. Pupil can stay engaged in academic tasks for only short periods.

[ ] 20. Pupil cannot follow or has difficulty following time schedules.

[ ] 21. Pupil's school attendance is erratic and unpredictable.

[ ] 22. Pupil cannot follow oral or written instructions without special help.

[ ] 23. Pupil has serious visual impairments.

[ ] 24. Pupil has serious hearing impairments.

Would the provision of technical assistance ranging from a classroom aide to access to a special education consultant cause you to change any responses you may have made to the preceding items? If yes, please indicate which ones by circling those item numbers you would change if you had access to the kinds of resources mentioned here.

References

Achenbach, T. (1985). *Assessment and taxonomy of child and adolescent psycho-pathology*. Beverly Hills, CA: Sage.

Achenbach, T. (1991). *The Child Behavior Checklist: Manual for the teacher's report form*. Burlington, VT: Department of Psychiatry, University of Vermont.

Alberg, J., Petry, C., & Eller, S. (1994). *A social skills planning guide*. Longmont, CO: Sopris West.

Algozzine, R. & Ysseldyke, J. (1992). *Strategies and tactics for effective instruction*. Longmont, CO: Sopris West.

Allport, G. (1966). Traits revisited. *American Psychologist, 21*(1), 1-9.

Allport, G. (1974). Personalistic psychology: A trait approach to personality. In W. S. Sahakian (Ed.), *Psychology of personality: Readings in theory*. Chicago: Rand McNally.

Anderson-Inman, L. (1981). Transenvironmental programming: Promoting success in the regular class by maximizing the effect of resource room assistance. *Journal of Special Education Technology, 4*(4), 3-12.

Anderson-Inman, L., Walker, H.M., & Purcell, J. (1984). Promoting the transfer of skills across settings: Transenvironmental programming for handicapped students in the mainstream. In W. Heward, T. Heron, P. Hill, & J. Trap-Porter (Eds.), *Focus on behavior analysis in education* (pp. 17-37). Columbus, OH: Charles E. Merrill.

Archer, A. & Gleason, M. (1989). *Skills for school success*. North Billerica, MA: Curriculum Associates.

Axelrod, S. (1990). Myths that (mis)guide our profession. In A. Repp & N. Singh (Eds.), *Perspectives on the use of nonaversive interventions for persons with developmental disabilities* (pp. 60-72). Sycamore, IL: Sycamore Publishing.

Ayllon, T., Layman, D., & Kandel, H.J. (1975). A behavioral-educational alternative to drug control of hyperactive children. *Journal of Applied Behavior Analysis, 2,* 137-146.

Azrin, N.H., & Holz, W.C. (1966). Punishment. In W.K. Honig (Ed.), *Operant behavior* (pp. 380-447). New York: Appleton-Century-Crofts.

Bandura, A. (1969). *Principles of behavior modification.* New York: Holt, Rinehart & Winston.

Barker, R. (1968). *Ecological psychology: Concepts and methods for studying the environment of human behavior.* Palo Alto, CA: Stanford University Press.

Barker, R. & Schoggen, P. (1973). *Qualities of community life: Methods of measuring environment and behavior applied to an American and an English town.* San Francisco, CA: Jossey-Bass.

Barkley, R. (1990). *Attention-deficit hyperactive disorder: A manual for diagnosis and treatment.* New York: Guilford.

Bendix, S. (1973). Drug modification of behavior: A form of chemical violence against children? *Journal of Clinical Child Psychology, 2*(3), 17-19.

Block-Pedego, A. E. (1990). Early identification and prediction of students at-risk for dropping out of school using the School Archival Records Search (SARS) (Doctoral dissertation, University of Oregon, 1990). *Dissertation Abstracts International* (Order # 9111092).

Bornstein, P. & Kazdin, A. (Eds.). (1985). *Handbook of clinical behavior therapy with children.* Homewood, IL: Dorsey Press.

Bostic, M. (1994, May). *Juvenile crime prevention strategies: A law enforcement perspective.* Paper presented at the Council of State Governments Conference on School Violence, Westlake Village, CA.

Brophy, J. & Evertson, C. (1981). *Student characteristics and teaching.* New York: Longman.

Brophy, J.E. & Good, T. (1970). Teachers' communication of differential expectations for children's classroom performance: some behavioral data. *Journal of Educational Psychology, 61,* 365-374.

Brophy, J.E. & Good, T. (1974). *Teacher-student relationships: Causes and consequences.* New York: Holt, Rinehart & Winston.

Brophy, J. & Putnam, J. (1979). Classroom management in the early grades. In D. Duke (Ed.), *Classroom management: The 78th yearbook of the National Society for the Study of Education* (Part II). Chicago: University of Chicago Press.

Bullis, M. & Walker, H.M. (in press). Characteristics, causal factors, and school-based interventions for children and adolescents with antisocial behavioral disorders. In L. Meyer (Ed.), *Issues and research in special education* (Vol. 3). New York: Teachers College Press.

Bushell, D., Jr., Wrobel, P.A., & Michaelis, M. (1968). Applying "group" contingencies to the classroom study behavior of preschool children. *Journal of Applied Behavior Analysis, 1,* 55-61.

Cohen, D., Douglas, V., & Morganstern, G. (1971). The effect of methylphenidate on attentive behavior and autonomic activity in hyperactive children. *Psychopharmacologia, 22,* 282.

Colvin, G. & Sugai, G. (1989). *Managing escalating behavior.* Available from Behavior Associates, P.O. Box 5317, Eugene, OR 97405.

Comly, H. (1971). Cerebral stimulants for children with learning disorders? *Journal of Learning Disabilities, 4*(9), 20-26.

Connors, C.K. (1973). What parents need to know about stimulant drugs and special education. *Journal of Learning Disabilities, 6*(6), 349-351.

Conrad, W.C., Dworkin, E.S., Shai, A., & Tobiessen, J.E. (1972). Effects of amphetamine therapy and prescriptive tutoring on the behavior and achievement of lower class hyperactive children. *Journal of Learning Disabilities, 4*(9), 509-517.

Copeland, W.D. (1978). Processes mediating the relationship between cooperating teacher behavior and student teacher classroom performance. *Journal of Educational Psychology, 70,* 95-100.

Cossairt, A., Hall, R.V., & Hopkins, B.L. (1973). The effects of experimenter's instructions, feedback, and praise on teacher's praise and student attending behavior. *Journal of Applied Behavior Analysis, 6,* 89-100.

Council for Children with Behavior Disorders. (1990). Position paper on use of behavior reduction strategies with children with behavioral disorders. *Behavioral Disorders, 15,* 243-260.

Crosson, J. (1966). *The experimental analysis of vocational behavior in severely retarded males.* Doctoral dissertation, University of Oregon.

Denhoff, E., Davids, A., & Hawkins, A.B. (1971). Effects of dextroam-phetamine on hyperkinetic children: A controlled double blind study. *Journal of Learning Disabilities, 4*(9).

Dishion, T. & Andrews, D. (1995). Preventing escalation in problem behaviors with high-risk young adolescents: Immediate and one-year outcomes. *Journal of Consulting and Clinical Psychology, 63*(4), 001-0011.

Dodge, K.A., Price, J.M., Coie, J.D., & Christopoulos, C. (1990). On the development of aggressive dyadic relationships in boys' peer groups. *Human Development, 33*, 260-270.

Doyle, W. (1977, November-December). Learning the classroom environment: an ecological analysis. *Journal of Teacher Education*, 51-55.

Doyle, W. (1979, June). Classroom effects. *Theory into Practice*, 139-144.

Dryfoos, J. (1990). *Adolescents at risk*. New York: Oxford University Press.

DuPaul, G. & Eckert, T. (1994). The effects of social skills curricula: Now you see them, now you don't. *School Psychology Quarterly, 9*(2), 113-132.

Edmonds, R. (1979). Some schools work and more can. *Social Policy, 9*, 28-32.

Engelmann, S.E. & Carnine, D.W. (1982). *Theory of instruction: Principles and applications*. New York: Irvington Press.

Epstein, M., Nelson, M., Polsgrove, L., Coutinho, M., Cumblad, C., & Quinn, K. (1993). A comprehensive community-based approach to serving students with emotional and behavioral disorders. *Journal of Emotional and Behavioral Disorders, 1*(2).

Evertson, C. & Anderson, L. (1979). Beginning school. *Educational Origins, 57*, 164-168.

Ferster, C.B. & Skinner, B. F. (1957). *Schedules of reinforcement*. New York: Appleton-Century-Crofts.

Feshbach, N. (1969). Student teacher references for elementary school pupils varying in personality characteristics. *Journal of Educational Psychology, 60*, 126-132.

Finch, A.J. & Rogers, T.R. (1984). Self-report instruments. In T. H. Ollendick & M. Hersen (Eds.), *Child behavioral assessment: Principles and procedures* (pp. 106-123). New York: Pergamon Press.

Firestone, G. & Brody, N. (1975). Longitudinal investigation of teacher-student interactions and their relationship to academic performance. *Journal of Educational Psychology, 67,* 544-550.

Fish, B. (1971). The "one child, one drug" myth of stimulants in hyperkinesis. *Archives of General Psychiatry, 25,* 193-203.

Forehand, R. (1977). Child compliance to parental requests: Behavioral analysis and treatment. In M. Hersen, R. M. Eisler, & P.M. Miller (Eds.), *Progress in behavior modification* (Vol 5, pp. 111-147). New York: Academic Press.

Forehand, R. & McMahon, R. (1981). *Helping the noncompliant child.* New York: Guilford Press.

Forness, S. (1993, February). Keynote address presented to The Oregon Conference, Eugene, OR.

Fuchs, D. (1995, April). *Transition strategies for socially integrating behavior disordered students.* Paper presented at the Annual Convention of the Council for Exceptional Children, Indianapolis, IN.

Fuchs, D., Fuchs, L.S., Fernstrom, P., & Hohn, M. (1991). Toward a responsible reintegration of behaviorally disordered students. *Behavioral Disorders, 16,* 133-147.

Gerber, M.M. & Semmel, M.I. (1984). Teacher as imperfect test: Reconceptualizing the referral process. *Educational Psychologist, 19*(3), 137-148.

Gersten, R., Walker, H.M., & Darch, C. (1988). Relationships between teachers' effectiveness and their tolerance for handicapped students. *Exceptional Children, 54*(5), 433-438.

Gleason, M.M., Colvin, G.T., & Archer, A. (1991). Interventions for improving study skills. In G. Stoner, M. Shinn, & H. Walker (Eds.), *Interventions for achievement and behavior problems* (pp. 137-160). Silver Spring, MD: National Association for School Psychologists.

Golly, A. (1994). *The use and effects of alpha and beta commands in elementary classroom settings.* Doctoral dissertation, University of Oregon.

Good, T.L. (1981). Teacher expectations and student perceptions: A decade of research. *Educational Leadership, 38,* 413-422.

Good, T.L. & Brophy, J. E. (1978). *Looking in classrooms* (2nd. ed.). New York: Harper & Row.

Green, K. & Forehand, R. (1980). Assessment of children's social skills: A review of methods. *Journal of Behavioral Assessment, 2*, 143-159.

Greenwood, C.R., Hops, H., Delquadri, J., & Guild, J.J. (1974). Group contingencies for group consequences in classroom management: A further analysis. *Journal of Applied Behavior Analysis, 7*, 413-425.

Greenwood, C., Hops, H., & Walker, H. M. (1988). *Program for Academic Survival Skills (PASS)*. Seattle: Educational Achievement Systems.

Greenwood, C.R., Maheady, L., & Carta, J. (1991). Peer tutoring programs in the regular education classroom. In G. Stoner, M. Shinn, & H. Walker (Eds.), *Interventions for achievement and behavior problems* (pp. 179-200). Silver Spring, MD: National Association of School Psychologists.

Greenwood, C.R., Walker, H.M., Todd, N.M., & Hops, H. (1979). Selecting a cost-effective screening measure for the assessment of preschool social withdrawal. *Journal of Applied Behavior Analysis, 12*, 639-652.

Gresham, F. (1986). Conceptual issues in the assessment of social competence in children. In P. S. Strain, M. J. Guralnick, & H. M. Walker (Eds.), *Children's social behavior: Development, assessment, and modification* (pp. 143-179). New York: Academic Press.

Gresham, F. & Elliott, S. (l984). Advances in the assessment of children's social skills. *School Psychology Review, 13*, 292-301.

Gresham, F.M. & Elliott, S. N. (1989, Spring). Social skills assessment technology for LD students. *Learning Disability Quarterly, 12*, 141-152.

Gresham, F.M. & Elliott, S. (1990). *The social skills rating system (SSRS)*. Circle Pines, MN: American Guidance Service.

Harter, S. (1982). The perceived competence scale for children. *Child Development, 53*(1), 87-97.

Harvey, J. & Smith, W. (1977). *Social psychology: An attributional approach*. St. Louis: C. O. Mosby.

Herbert, E.W., Pinkston, E., Hayden, M., Sajwaj, T., Pinkston, S., Cordua, G., & Jackson, C. (1973). Adverse effects of differential parental attention. *Journal of Applied Behavior Analysis, 6*, 15-30.

Hersh, R.H. & Walker, H.M. (1983). Great expectations: Making schools effective for all students. *Policy Studies Review, 2*(Special #1), 147-188.

Hinshaw, S. (1992). Externalizing behavior problems and academic under-achievement in childhood and adolescence: Causal relationships and underlying mechanisms. *Psychological Bulletin, 111*, 127-155.

Hollinger, J. (1987). Social skills for behaviorally disordered children as preparation for mainstreaming: Theory, practice and new directions. *Remedial and Special Education, 8*(4), 17-27.

Homme, L.E., de Baca, D.C., Devine, J.V., Steinhorst, R., & Rickert, E.J. (1963). Use of the Premack principle in controlling the behavior of nursery school children. *Journal of the Experimental Analysis of Behavior, 6*, 544.

Hops, H., Greenwood, C.R., & Guild, J. (1975). *Programming generalization of teacher praising skills: How easy is it?* Paper presented at the Annual Convention of the Association for the Advancement of Behavioral Therapy, San Francisco, CA.

Hops, H. & Walker, H.M. (1988). *CLASS:* Contingencies for Learning Academic and Social Skills. Seattle, WA: Educational Achievement Systems.

Hops, H., Walker, H.M., Fleischman, D., Nagoshi, J., Omura, R., Skinrud, K., & Taylor, J. (1978). CLASS (Contingencies for Learning Academic and Social Skills): A standardized in-class program for acting-out children (Part II): Field test evaluations. *Journal of Educational Psychology, 70*(4), 636-644.

Hops, H., Walker, H.M., & Greenwood, C. R. (1988). PEERS—Procedures for establishing effective relationship skills: A program for elementary students with socially withdrawn behavior. Seattle: Educational Achievement Systems.

Horner, R.H., Dunlap, G., & Koegel, R.L. (Eds.). (1988). *Generalization and maintenance: Lifestyle changes in applied settings.* Baltimore: Brookes.

Horner, R. H., Dunlap, G., Koegel, R. L., Carr, E. G., Sailor, W., Anderson, J., Albin, R.W., & O'Neill, R. E. (1990). Toward a technology of nonaversive behavioral support. *Journal of the Association of the Severely Handicapped, 15*, 125-132.

Horton, G., Walker, H. M., & Rankin, R. (1986). Psychometric characteristics of the SBS student inventory of social behavior standards/expectations and the SBS correlates checklist. In R. Rutherford (Ed.), *Severe behavior disorders of children and youth: Monograph in Behavioral Disorders* (Vol. 8, pp. 36-48). Reston, VA: Council for Children with Behavioral Disorders.

Hundert, J. (1976). The effectiveness of reinforcement, response cost, and mixed programs on classroom behaviors. *Journal of Applied Behavior Analysis, 9,* 107.

Irvin, L.K. & Walker, H.M. (1994). Assessing children's social skills using video-based microcomputer technology. *Exceptional Children* (Special issue), *61,* 182-196.

Irvin, L.K., Walker, H.M., Noell, J., Singer, G.H. S., Irvine, A.B., Marquez, K., & Britz, B. (1992). Measuring children's social skills using microcomputer-based videodisc assessment. *Behavior Modification, 16,* 475-503.

Jackson, P., Silberman, M., & Wolfson, B. (1969). Signs of personal involvement in teachers' descriptions of their students. *Journal of Educational Psychology, 60,* 22-27.

Jenkins, B. (1972). *Teachers' views of particular students and their behavior in the classroom.* Doctoral dissertation, University of Chicago.

Johnson, D.W., Johnson, R.T., Warring, D., & Maruyama, G. (1986). Different cooperative learning procedures and cross-handicap relationships. *Exceptional Children, 53,* 247-252.

Johnson, S.M., Bolstad, D.D., & Lobitz, G.K. (1976). Generalization and contrast phenomena in behavior modification with children. In E. J. Mash, L. A. Hamerlynck, & L. C. Handy (Eds.), *Behavior modification and families.* New York: Brunner/Mazell.

Jones, F.H. & Miller, W.H. (1974). The effective use of negative attention for reducing group disruption in special elementary school classrooms. *Psychological Record, 24,* 435-448.

Kanfer, F. (1970). Self-monitoring: Methodological limitations and clinical applications. *Journal of Consulting and Clinical Psychology, 35*(2), 148-158.

Kauffman, J. (1993). *Characteristics of emotional and behavioral disorders of children and youth.* New York: Macmillan.

Kauffman, J. & Wong, K.L.H. (1991). Effective teachers of students with behavioral disorders: Are generic teaching skills enough? *Behavioral Disorders, 16*(3), 225-237.

Kavale, K. (1982). The efficiency of stimulant drug treatment for hyperactivity. A meta-analysis. *Journal of Learning Disabilities, 15,* 280-289.

Kazdin, A. (1972). Response cost: The removal of conditioned reinforcers for therapeutic change. *Behavior Therapy, 3,* 533-546.

Kazdin, A. E. (Ed.). (1985). *Treatment of antisocial behavior in children and adolescents.* Homewood, IL: Dorsey Press.

Kazdin, A. (1987). *Conduct disorders in childhood and adolescence.* London: Sage.

Kelley, M. (1990). *School-home notes: Promoting children's classroom success.* New York: Guilford Press.

Knights, R. & Hinston, G. (1969). The effects of methylphenidate (Ritalin) on motor skills and behavior of children with learning problems. *Journal of Nervous Mental Disorders, 148,* 643.

Kornblau, B. (1979). *Teachers' perceptions of the characteristics of "idealized teachable pupils."* Doctoral dissertation, University of California, Los Angeles.

Kornblau, B. & Keogh, B. (1980). Teachers' perceptions and educational decisions. *Journal for Teaching and Learning, 1,* 87-101.

Kounin, J. (1970). *Discipline and group management in classrooms.* New York: Holt, Rinehart & Winston.

Kounin, J. & Doyle, P. (1975). Degree of continuity of a lesson's signal system and the task involvement of children. *Journal of Educational Psychology, 67,* 159-164.

Kounin, J. & Gump, P. (1974). Signal systems of lesson settings and the task-related behavior of preschool children. *Journal of Educational Psychology, 66,* 554-562.

Ladd, E.T. (1970, November). Pills for classroom peace? *Saturday Review,* 66-83.

Lloyd, J.W., Kauffman, J.M., Landrum, T.J., & Roe, D.L. (1991). Why do teachers refer pupils for special education? An analysis of referral records. *Exceptionality, 2,* 113-126.

Lloyd, J.W., Landrum, T., & Hallahan, D. (1991). Self-monitoring applications for classroom intervention. In G. Stoner, M. Shinn, & H. Walker (Eds.), *Interventions for achievement and behavior problems* (pp. 201-214). Silver Spring, MD: National Association of School Psychologists.

Loeber, R. & Dishion, T. (1984). Boys who fight at home and school: Family conditions influencing cross setting consistency. *Journal of Consulting and Clinical Psychology, 52,* 759-768.

MacMillan, D., Gresham, F., & Forness, S. (under review, 1995). Full inclusion: An empirical perspective. *Behavioral Disorders.* Available from Donald L. MacMillan, School of Education, University of California at Riverside, Riverside, CA, 92521.

Maddox-McGinty, A. (1972). *Children's nonverbal behavior in the classroom and teachers' perceptions of teachability: An observational study.* Doctoral dissertation, University of California, Los Angeles.

Madsen, C.H., Becker, W.C., & Thomas, D.R. (1968). Rules, praise and ignoring: Elements of elementary classroom control. *Journal of Applied Behavior Analysis, 1,* 139-150.

Madsen, C.H., Becker, W.C., Thomas, D., Koser, L., & Plager, E. (1968). An analysis of the reinforcing function of "sit down" commands. In R. K. Parker (Ed.), *Readings in educational psychology.* Boston: Allyn & Bacon.

Maguin, E. & Loeber, R. (in press). Is poor academic performance a cause of delinquency? *Crime and Justice.*

McConnell, S. & Odom, S. (1986). Sociometrics: Peer-referenced measures and the assessment of social competence. In P. Strain, M. Guralnick, & H. Walker (Eds.), *Children's social behavior: Development, assessment and modification* (pp. 215-275). New York: Academic Press.

McDonald, C. (1972). *The influence of pupil liking of teacher, pupil perceptions of being liked and pupil socio-economic status on classroom behavior.* Doctoral dissertation, University of Texas at Austin.

McGinnis, E. (1984). Teaching social skills to behaviorally disordered youth. In J. Grosenick, E. McGinnis, S. Huntze, & C. Smith (Eds.), *Social/affective interventions in behavioral disorders* (pp. 87-120). Des Moines, IA: State of Iowa, Department of Public Instruction.

Merrell, K.W. (1993). *The school social behavior scales (SSBS).* Brandon, VT: Clinical Psychology Publishing.

Merrell, K.W., Merz, J.M., Johnson, E.R., & Ring, E. (1992). Social competence of students with mild handicaps and low achievement: A comparative study. *School Psychology Review, 21,* 125-137.

Miner, S. (1990). Use of a self-recording procedure to decrease the time taken by behaviorally disordered students to walk to special classes. *Behavioral Disorders, 15*(4), 210-216.

Mischel, W. (1968). *Personality assessment.* New York: Wiley and Sons.

Mischel, W. (1969). Continuity and change in personality. *American Psychologist, 24*(11), 1012-1018.

Morgan, D.P. & Jenson, W.R. (1988). *Teaching behaviorally disordered students: Preferred practices.* Columbus, OH: Merrill Publishing.

Neel, R.S. (1984). Teaching social routines to behaviorally disordered youth. In J. Grosenick, E. McGinnis, S. Huntze, & C. Smith (Eds.), *Social/affective interventions in behavioral disorders* (pp. 151-181). Des Moines, IA: State of Iowa, Department of Public Instruction.

Nelson, R. & Hayes, S. (1981). Theoretical explanations for reactivity in self-monitoring. *Behavior Modification, 5,* 3-14.

Novack, H.S. (1971). An educator's view of medication and classroom behavior. *Journal of Learning Disabilities, 4*(9).

O'Connor, P., Stuck, G., & Wyne, M. (1979). Effects of a short-term intervention resource-room program on task orientation and achievement. *Journal of Special Education, 13*(4), 375-385.

O'Connor, R.D. (1969). Modification of social withdrawal through symbolic modeling. *Journal of Applied Behavior Analysis, 2,* 15-22.

O'Leary, K.D., Becker, W.C., Evans, M.B., & Saudargas, R.A. (1969). A token reinforcement program in a public school: A replication and systematic analysis. *Journal of Applied Behavior Analysis, 2,* 3-13.

O'Leary, K.D. & Drabman, R. (1971). Token reinforcement programs in the classroom: A review. *Psychological Bulletin, 75,* 379-398.

O'Leary, K.D., Kaufman, K., Kass, R.E., & Drabman, R. (1970). The effects of loud and soft reprimands on the behavior of disruptive students. *Exceptional Children, 37,* 145-155.

Ollendick, T.H. & Hersen, M. (Eds.). (1984). *Child behavioral assessment: Principles and procedures.* New York: Pergamon Press.

Olweus, D. (1979). Stability of aggressive reaction pattern in males: A review. *Psychological Bulletin, 86,* 852-875.

O'Neill, R. E., Horner, R. H., Albin, R. W., Storey, K., & Sprague, J. R. (1990). *Functional analysis of problem behavior: A practical assessment guide*. Pacific Grove, CA: Brooks/Cole.

Packard, R.G. (1970). The control of "classroom attention": A group contingency for complex behavior. *Journal of Applied Behavior Analysis, 3*, 13-28.

Parker, J.G. & Asher, S.R. (1987). Peer relations and later personal adjustment: Are low-accepted children at risk? *Psychological Bullentin, 102*(3), 357-389.

Patterson, G.R. (1965). Application of conditioning techniques to the control of a hyperactive child. In L. Ullman & L. Krasner (Eds.), *Case studies in behavior modification* (pp. 370-375). New York: Holt, Rinehart & Winston.

Patterson, G.R. (1974). Intervention for boys with conduct problems: Multiple settings, treatment, and criteria. *Journal of Consulting and Clinical Psychology, 42*, 471-481.

Patterson, G.R. (1983). *Longitudinal investigation of antisocial boys and their families* [Research grant from the National Institute of Mental Health]. Eugene, OR: Oregon Social Learning Center.

Patterson, G.R. & Reid, J. (1970). Reciprocity and coercion: Two facts of social systems. In C. Neuringer & J. L. Michael (Eds.), *Behavior modification in clinical psychology* (pp. 133-177). New York: Appleton-Century-Crofts.

Patterson, G.R., Reid, J.B., & Dishion, T.J. (1992). *Antisocial boys*. Eugene, OR: Castalia Press.

Patterson, G.R. & White, G.P. (1969, February). It's a small world: The application of "timeout from positive reinforcement." *OPA (Oregon Psychological Association)* newsletter.

Pervin, L. (1968). Performance and satisfaction as a function of individual-environment fit. *Psychological Bulletin, 69*, 56-68.

Pfiffner, L. & O'Leary, S. (1987). The efficacy of all-positive management as a function of the prior use of negative consequences. *Journal of Applied Behavior Analysis, 20*(3), 265-271.

Phillips, V. & McCullough, L. (1993). *SST: Student\staff support teams*. Longmont, CO: Sopris West.

Pinkston, E.M., Reese, N.M., Le Blanc, J.M., & Baer, D. (1973). Independent control of a preschool child's aggression and peer interaction by contingent teacher attention. *Journal of Applied Behavior Analysis, 6*, 115-124.

Quay, H. (1986). Conduct disorders. In H. Quay & J. Werry (Eds.), *Psychopathological disorders of childhood*. New York: Wiley and Sons.

Quay, H. & Peterson, D. (1987). The revised behavior problem checklist (RBPC). Available from Herbert Quay, Department of Psychology, University of Miami, Coral Gables, FL 33124.

Rapoport, J.L., Quinn, P.O., Bradbard, G., Riddle, D., & Brooks, E. (1974). Imipramine and methylphenidate treatments of hyperactive boys. *Archives of General Psychiatry, 30*, 789.

Rapport, M.D., Murphy, H.A., & Bailey, J.S. (1982). Ritalin vs. response cost in the control of hyperactive children: A within-subject comparison. *Journal of Applied Behavior Analysis, 15*(2), 205-216.

Repp, A. & Singh, N. (1990). Perspectives on the use of nonaversive interventions for persons with developmental disabilities. Sycamore, IL: Sycamore Publishing.

Rhode, G., Jenson, W., & Reavis, H.K. (1992). *The Tough Kid Book*. Longmont, CO: Sopris West.

Rhode, G., Morgan, D., & Young, R. (1983). Generalization and maintenance of treatment gains of behaviorally handicapped students from resource rooms to regular classrooms using self-evaluation procedures. *Journal of Applied Behavior Analysis, 16*, 171-188.

Rist, R. (1970). Student social class and teacher expectations: The self-fulfilling prophecy in ghetto education. *Harvard Educational Review, 40*, 411-451.

Rosenthal, R. & Jacobson, L. (1968). *Pygmalion in the classroom: Teacher expectation and pupils' intellectual development*. New York: Holt, Rinehart & Winston.

Ross, A. (1980). *Psychological disorders of children: A behavioral approach to theory, research and therapy* (2nd ed.). New York: McGraw-Hill.

Rutter, M., Maughan, B., Mortimore, P., Ouston, J., & Smith, A. (1979). *Fifteen thousand: Secondary schools and their effects on children*. Cambridge, MA: Harvard University Press.

Safer, D.J. (1988). A survey of medication treatment for hyperactive/inattentive students. *Journal of the American Medical Association, 260*, 2256-2258.

Safer, D.J. & Allen, R.P. (1973). Factors influencing the suppressant effects of two stimulant drugs on the growth of hyperactive children. *Pediatrics, 51*, 660.

Sarason, S. & Doris, J. (1978). Mainstreaming: Dilemmas, opposition, opportunities. In M. C. Reynolds (Ed.), *Futures of Education for Exceptional Children: Emerging Structures.* Reston, VA: Council for Exceptional Children.

Schaywitz, B. & Schaywitz, S. (1987). Attention-deficit disorder: Current perspectives. In J. F. Kavanaugh & T. J. Truss (Eds.), *Learning disabilities: Proceedings of the national conference* (pp. 369-523). Parktown, MD: York Press.

Schmidt, G.W. & Ulrich, R.E. (1969). Effects of group contingent events upon classroom noise. *Journal of Applied Behavior Analysis, 2,* 171-179.

Schoen, S. (1983). The status of compliance technology: Implications for programming. *Journal of Special Education, 17*(4), 483-496.

Schoen, S. (1986). Decreasing noncompliance in a severely multihandicapped child. *Psychology in the Schools, 23,* 88-94.

Schorr, L. (1988). *Within our reach: Breaking the cycle of disadvantage.* New York: Doubleday.

Sells, S.B. (1966). *Evaluation of psychological measures used in the health examination survey of children ages 6-11.* Washington, DC: Public Health Service (DHEW), U.S. Government Printing Office.

Shanker, A. (1995). Classrooms held hostage: The disruption of the many by the few. *American Educator, 19*(1), 8, 13, & 47.

Shapiro, E. (1989). *Academic skills problems: Direct assessment and intervention.* New York: Guilford Press.

Shinn, M. (1989). *Curriculum-based measurement: Assessing special children.* New York: Guilford Press.

Shinn, M.R., Ramsey, E., Walker, H.M., Stieber, S., & O'Neill, R.E. (1987). Antisocial behavior in school settings: Initial differences in an at risk and normal population. *The Journal of Special Education, 21*(2), 69-84.

Silberman, M. (1969). Behavioral expression of teachers' attitudes toward elementary school students. *Journal of Educational Psychology, 60,* 402-407.

Skiba, R.J. & Deno, S.L. (1991). Terminology and behavior reduction: The case against "punishment." *Exceptional Children, 57*(4), 298-313.

Skinner, B.F. (1953). *Science and human behavior.* New York: The Macmillan Co.

Slavin, R. (1984). Team assisted individualization, cooperative learning and individualized instruction in mainstream classrooms. *Remedial and Special Education, 5,* 33-42.

Spira, D. (1989). *A cross-situational analysis of antisocial behavior exhibited by boys in three settings.* Doctoral dissertation, University of Oregon, Eugene.

Sprick, R.S. & Howard, L.M. (1995). *The teacher's encyclopedia of behavior management: 100 problems/500 plans.* Longmont, CO: Sopris West.

Stokes, T.F. & Osnes, P.G. (1986). Programming the generalization of children's social behavior. In P. S. Strain, M. Guralnick, & H. Walker (Eds.), *Children's social behavior: Development, assessment and modification* (pp. 407-443). Orlando, FL: Academic Press.

Stoner, G., Shinn, M.R., & Walker, H.M. (Eds.). (1991). *Interventions for achievement and behavioral problems.* Silver Spring, MD: National Association of School Psychologists.

Strain, P., Lambert, D., Kerr, M., Stagg, V., & Lenkner, D. (1983). Naturalistic assessment of children's compliance to teachers' requests and consequences for compliance. *Journal of Applied Behavior Analysis, 16,* 243-249.

Strain, P. & Shores, R. (1977). Social reciprocity: Review of research and educational implications. *Exceptional Children, 43,* 526-531.

Strain, P., Shores, R., & Kerr, M. (1976). Experimental analysis of spillover effects on social interaction of behaviorally handicapped preschool children. *Journal of Applied Behavior Analysis, 9,* 31-40.

Sulzbacher, S.I. & Houser, J.E. (1968). A tactic to eliminate disruptive behaviors in the classroom: Group contingent consequences. *American Journal of Mental Deficiency, 73,* 88-90.

Swanson, J., Cantwell, D., Lerner, M., McBurnett, K., Pfiffner, L., & Kotkin, R. (1992). Treatment of ADHD: Beyond medication. *Beyond Behavior, 4*(1), 13-22.

Thomas, D., Becker, W.C., & Armstrong, M. (1968). Production and elimination of disruptive classroom behavior by systematically varying teacher's behavior. *Journal of Applied Behavior Analysis, 1,* 35-45.

U.S. Office of Special Education and Rehabilitative Services. (1994). *The sixteenth annual report to Congress on implementation of the Individuals with Disabilities Education Act.* Washington, DC: OSERS.

Wagner, M. (1989, April). *The national transition study: Results of a national, longitudinal study of transition from school to work for students with disabilities.* Paper presented at the Council for Exceptional Children's Annual Convention, San Francisco.

Wahler, R.G. (1969). Setting generality: Some specific and general effects of child behavior therapy. *Journal of Applied Behavior Analysis, 2,* 239-246.

Walker, H.M. (1983a). *The Walker problem behavior identification checklist.* Los Angeles: Western Psychological Services.

Walker, H.M. (l983b). Applications of response cost in school settings: Outcomes, issues and recommendations. *Exceptional Education Quarterly, 3*(4), 47-55.

Walker, H.M. (1984). The Social Behavior Survival program (SBS): A systematic approach to the integration of handicapped children into less restrictive settings. *Education and Treatment of Children, 6*(4), 421-441.

Walker, H.M. (1986). The Assessments for Integration into Mainstream Settings (AIMS) assessment system: Rationale, instruments, procedures, and outcomes. *Journal of Clinical Child Psychology, 15*(1), 55-63.

Walker, H.M., Block-Pedego, A., Todis, B., & Severson, H. (1991). *School archival records search (SARS): User's guide and technical manual.* Longmont, CO: Sopris West.

Walker, H.M. & Buckley, N. (1972). Programming generalization and maintenance of treatment effects across time and across settings. *Journal of Applied Behavior Analysis, 5,* 209-224.

Walker, H.M. & Buckley, N.K. (1973). Teacher attention to appropriate and inappropriate classroom behavior: An individual case study. *Focus on Exceptional Children, 5,* 5-11.

Walker, H.M. & Buckley, N. (1974). *Token reinforcement techniques: Classroom applications for the hard to teach child.* Eugene, OR: E-B Press.

Walker, H.M. & Bullis, M. (1991). Behavior disorders and the social context of regular class integration: A conceptual dilemma? In J. Lloyd, N. Singh, & A. Repp (Eds.), *The Regular Education Initiative: Alternative perspectives on concepts, issues and models* (pp. 75-94). Champaign-Urbana IL: Sycamore Press.

Walker, H.M., Colvin, G., & Ramsey, E. (1995). *Antisocial behavior in schools: Strategies and best practices.* Pacific Grove, CA: Brooks/Cole.

Walker, H. M., Fonseca-Retana, G., & Gersten, R. (1988). Replication of the CLASS program in Costa Rica: Implementation procedures and program outcomes. *Behavior Modification, 12*(1), 133-154.

Walker, H.M. & Hops, H. (1973). The use of group and individual reinforcement contingencies in the modification of social withdrawal. In L. A. Hamerlynck, L. C. Handy, & E. J. Mash (Eds.), *Behavior change: Methodology, concepts and practice* (pp. 269-307). Champaign, IL: Research Press.

Walker, H.M. & Hops, H. (1993). *The RECESS Program (Reprogramming Environmental Contingencies for Effective Social Skills).* Seattle, WA: Educational Achievement Systems, Inc.

Walker, H., Hops, H., & Fiegenbaum, E. (1976). Deviant classroom behavior as a function of combinations of social and token reinforcement and cost contingency. *Behavior Therapy, 7,* 76-88.

Walker, H.M., Hops, H., & Greenwood, C.R. (1981). RECESS: Research and development of a behavior management package for remediating social aggression in the school setting. In P. Strain (Ed.), *The utilization of classroom peers as behavior change agents* (pp. 261-303). New York: Plenum.

Walker, H.M., Hops, H., & Greenwood, C.R. (1984). The CORBEH research and development model: Programmatic issues and strategies. In S. Paine, G. T. Bellamy, & B. Wilcox (Eds.), *Human services that work* (pp. 57-78). Baltimore: Paul H. Brookes.

Walker, H.M., Hops, H., Greenwood, C.R., Todd, N., & Garrett, B. (1977). *The comparative effects of teacher praise, token reinforcement, and response cost in reducing negative peer interactions (CORBEH Report #25).* Eugene, OR: Center at Oregon for Research in the Behavioral Education of the Handicapped, Center on Human Development, University of Oregon.

Walker, H.M., Hops, H., & Johnson, S. M. (1975). Generalization and maintenance of classroom treatment effects. *Behavior Therapy, 6,* 188-200.

Walker, H.M., Irvin, L.K., Noell, J., & Singer, G.H.S. (1992). A construct score approach to the assessment of social competence: Rationale, technological considerations, and anticipated outcomes. *Behavior Modification, 16,* 448-474.

Walker, H.M. & McConnell, S.R. (1995). *The Walker-McConnell scale of social competence and school adjustment (SSCSA)*. San Diego, CA: Singular Publishing Group.

Walker, H.M., McConnell, S.R., & Clarke, J.Y. (1985). Social skills training in school settings: A model for the social integration of handicapped children into less restrictive settings. In R. McMahon & R. D. Peters (Eds.), *Childhood disorders: Behavioral-developmental approaches* (pp. 140-168). New York: Brunner/Mazel.

Walker, H.M., McConnell, S., Holmes, D., Todis, B., Walker, J., & Golden, N. (1983). *The Walker social skills curriculum: The ACCEPTS program (a curriculum for children's effective peer and teacher skills)*. Austin, TX: PRO-ED.

Walker, H.M. & Rankin, R. (1980). *The SBS inventory of teacher social behavior standards and expectations*. Available from The Center on Human Development, 1265 University of Oregon, Eugene, OR 97403-1265.

Walker, H. & Rankin, R. (1983). Assessing the behavioral expectations and standards of less restrictive settings. *School Psychology Review, 12*(3), 274-284.

Walker, H.M. & Severson, H.H. (1990). *Systematic screening for behavior disorders (SSBD): User's guide and technical manual*. Longmont, CO: Sopris West.

Walker, H.M., Severson, H.H., & Feil, E.G. (1995). *The Early screening project: A proven child-find process*. Longmont, CO: Sopris West.

Walker, H.M., Severson, H., Stiller, B., Williams, G., Haring, N., Shinn, M., & Todis, B. (1988). Systematic screening of pupils in the elementary age range at risk for behavior disorders: Development and trial testing of a multiple gating model. *Remedial and Special Education, 9*(3), 8-14.

Walker, H.M., Shinn, M.R., O'Neill, R.E., & Ramsey, E. (1987). A longitudinal assessment of the development of antisocial behavior in boys: Rationale, methodology and first year results. *Remedial and Special Education, 8*(4), 7-16, 27.

Walker, H.M. & Walker, J.E. (1991). *Coping with noncompliance in the classroom: A positive approach for teachers*. Austin, TX: PRO-ED.

Walker, S. (1974). Drugging the American child: We're too cavalier about hyperactivity. *Psychology Today, 8*(7), 43-48.

Wasik, B., Senn, K., Welch, R.H., & Cooper, B.R. (1969). Behavior modification with culturally deprived school children: Two case studies. *Journal of Applied Behavior Analysis, 2,* 171-179.

Weber, G. (1971). *Inner city children can be taught to read: Four successful schools.* Washington, DC: Council for Basic Education.

Weiner, H. (1962). Some effects of response cost upon human operant behavior. *Journal of the Experimental Analysis of Behavior, 5,* 210-218.

Weiner, H. (1963). Response cost and the aversive control of human operant behavior. *Journal of the Experimental Analysis of Behavior, 6*(3), 415-421.

Werner, E. (1987). Vulnerability and resiliency in children at risk for delinquency: A longitudinal study from birth to young adulthood. In J. Burchard & S. Burchard (Eds.), *Prevention of delinquent behavior.* Beverly Hills, CA: Sage.

White, M.A. (1975). Natural rates of teacher approval and disapproval in the classroom. *Journal of Applied Behavior Analysis, 8,* 367-372.

Willis, S. & Brophy, J. (1974). Origins of teachers' attitudes toward young children. *Journal of Educational Psychology, 66,* 520-529.

Wong, K.L.H., Kauffman, J.M., & Lloyd, J.W. (1991). Choices for integration: Selecting teachers for mainstreamed students with emotional or behavioral disorders. *Intervention in School and Clinic, 27*(2), 108-115.

Zax, M., Cowen, E.L., Izzo, L.D., & Trost, M.A. (1964). Identifying emotional disturbance in the school setting. *American Journal of Orthopsychiatry, 34,* 447-454.

Other Publications of Interest by the Author

The Early Screening Project; Walker, Severson, & Feil (1995). Sopris West, 1140 Boston Avenue, Longmont, CO 80501, $95.00.

A multiple-gating screening process for the early detection of preschool students having behavior problems.

The Walker-McConnell Scale of Social Competence and School Adjustment; Walker & McConnell (1995), Singular Publishing Group, 4284 41st St., San Diego, CA 92105, $54.95.

A social skills rating battery for classroom teachers. Elementary version (K-6); Adolescent version (7-12). Includes rating profile forms, user's, and technical manuals.

Antisocial Behavior in School: Strategies and Best Practices; Walker, Colvin, & Ramsey (1995), Brooks/Cole Publishing, 511 Forest Lodge Road, Pacific Grove, CA 93950, $35.25.

A comprehensive college text focusing on the remediation of antisocial behavior patterns in school.

Coping with Noncompliance in the Classroom, Walker & Walker (1991), PRO-ED, Inc., 8700 Shoal Creek Blvd., Austin, TX 78758-6897, $9.00.

A brief manual for teachers, with illustrations of procedures for coping with noncompliance from oppositional-defiant students.

The Walker Social Skills Curriculums: The ACCEPTS Program; Walker, McConnell, Holmes, Todis, Walker, & Golden (1983); and *The ACCESS Program*; Walker, Todis, Holmes, & Horton (1988), PRO-ED, Inc., 8700 Shoal Creek Blvd., Austin, TX 78758-6897, $39.00 each.

The ACCEPTS (elementary) and ACCESS (secondary) social skills programs are designed for use in teaching key social skills contributing to school success.